STUDIES IN ECONOMIC HISTORY AND POLICY:
THE UNITED STATES IN THE TWENTIETH CENTURY
EDITED BY LOUIS GALAMBOS AND ROBERT GALLMAN

EUROPE, AMERICA, AND THE WIDER WORLD:
ESSAYS ON THE ECONOMIC HISTORY OF WESTERN CAPITALISM

VOLUME 2
AMERICA AND THE WIDER WORLD

STUDIES IN ECONOMIC HISTORY AND POLICY
THE UNITED STATES IN THE TWENTIETH CENTURY

Edited by
Louis Galambos and Robert Gallman

Other books in the series:

Europe, America, and the Wider World

Essays on the Economic History of Western Capitalism

VOLUME 2

America and the Wider World

WILLIAM N. PARKER

PHILLIP GOLDEN BARTLETT PROFESSOR OF
ECONOMICS AND ECONOMIC HISTORY
YALE UNIVERSITY

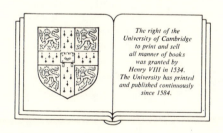

The right of the
University of Cambridge
to print and sell
all manner of books
was granted by
Henry VIII in 1534.
The University has printed
and published continuously
since 1584.

CAMBRIDGE UNIVERSITY PRESS

CAMBRIDGE

NEW YORK   PORT CHESTER   MELBOURNE   SYDNEY

Published by the Press Syndicate of the University of Cambridge
The Pitt Building, Trumpington Street, Cambridge CB2 1RP
40 West 20th Street, New York, NY 10011, USA
10 Stamford Road, Oakleigh, Melbourne 3166, Australia

First published 1991

Printed in the United States of America

Library of Congress Cataloging-in-Publication Data
(Revised for volume 2)
Parker, William Nelson.
Europe, America, and the wider world.
(Studies in economic history and policy)
Includes index.
Bibliography: p.
Contents: v. 1. Europe and the world economy –
v. 2. America and the wider world.
1. Economic history – Collected works.   2. Capitalism
– Collected works.   I. Title.   II. Series.
RC51.P37   1984   330.9181′2   84-3161
ISBN 0-521-25467-1 (hardcover : v. 1)
ISBN 0-521-27480-X (paperback : v. 1)
ISBN 0-521-25466-3 (hardcover : v. 2)
ISBN 0-521-22749-7 (paperback : v. 2)

British Library Cataloguing in Publication Data
Parker, William N. (William Nelson), *1919–*
Europe, America, and the wider world. – (Studies in
economic history and policy: The United States in the
twentieth century)
Vol. 2, America and the wider world.
1. Western world. Capitalism, history
I. Title II. Series
330.122091281
ISBN 0-521-25466-3 hardback
ISBN 0-521-22749-7 paperback

To Doug and Dick and Lance and Nate
    and Bob and Stan and Al and Paul and Peter

> ". . . whom mutual league
> United thoughts and counsels, equal hope
> And hazard in the Glorious Enterprise
> Joynd with me once . . ."
> – J. Milton, *Paradise Lost*, I, 87–89

Contents

Contents

Editors' preface

Volume 1 of this work dealt with Europe and the wider world. Volume 2 is concerned chiefly with America – chiefly, but not entirely. It begins with an account of European influences on American culture and concludes by comparing the American and European experiences of modern economic growth. Between are superb treatments of three major elements of American economic history, to each of which Professor Parker has devoted a substantial part of an extraordinarily productive career. He began his study of the first (contained in Part II) – southern agricultural history – during his years at the University of North Carolina and continued it after he had moved to Yale. It was also at Chapel Hill that he formally began his work on northern agriculture (Part III and Annex A). But he had begun to assemble the resources to deal effectively with this topic many years before. The midwestern resonances of his voice are honestly come by. His understanding of the people of the region was acquired during a childhood in Ohio and associations continued in adult life. Part IV, on northern industrialization, contains the work that has been his principal concern during the past several years.

The volume embodies an exceptionally erudite, thoughtful, comprehensive account of American economic history, placed in the context of the process of modern economic growth. It is the work of an original mind. The editors are grateful for the opportunity to publish it as part of the series Studies in Economic History and Policy.

LOUIS GALAMBOS
Professor of History
The Johns Hopkins University

ROBERT E. GALLMAN
Kenan Professor of Economics and History
The University of North Carolina, Chapel Hill

Preface

This volume is the second of a two-volume work in which are brought together my writings on topics in the economic history of Western Europe and the American South, Northeast, and Middle West. Is there, one may ask, a central meaning and significance of this body of work, sufficient to justify its publication under a single title?

The mind, I fancy, always looks for "structures" in history, for patterns, for explanations, for the intuitively appealing synthesis. I wrote the individual pieces in these volumes with the feeling that they exhibited such syntheses on specific topics, episodes, and aspects of the European and American experience. One essay in Volume 1 (Chapter 12) sketched out the lines of a three-part sequence underlying Western development. I labeled the "stages" Malthusian, Smithian, and Schumpeterian and introduced what I considered a novel element in trying to trace out in some detail how and why the transition from one stage to the next had been accomplished. This was followed by an examination of Europe's chaos between the wars (Chapter 13), which made the link from the economic events to the political, social, and economic structures based on specific sources in human behavior. But economic history, set as it is in a society's political, social, and cultural development, does not admit of simple formulation. Economists' models customarily single out one or a few elements — whether technology, private property, class structures, abundant resources, modes of thought, or relative backwardness — as the ultimate *causa causans* out of which modern development issued.

Human society, moving through history, appears to me to be an immensely complicated system of cultural dynamics, affected at each point in time and space by different circumstances and contingencies. These are not wholly "random" or "stochastic" events (whatever that may mean), for if that were the case, reasoned thought about history would be out of the question. Even the subtlest analogies to physical models — mechanical, electrical, or biological — do not seem to me to get to the essence, which is to model men and women in all their physical and phenomenological complexity as they issue out to create and to be created by society and social organizations. And the problem of including one's self and the background and circumstances of one's own time, place, and personal history and culture in the model follows like a shadow to blur all efforts at wholly abstract and *wertfrei* formulation. This vision of an abstract formulation of "total history," resting not on the "economic man," man the rational maximizer, but on the "whole man" of flesh and blood and passions, has not released its hold on my imagination. It remains the creature of my dreams, and I have worked in the past several years toward giving it concrete, articulated, and communicable form. I never expect fully to succeed. Indeed, one who did so would of course have penetrated the "Mind" of God. Like the substance of every dream, such visions of historical synthesis linger a moment, then vanish as they are embraced. Yet they are what lead a scholar on, and in the effort to specify and formulate, new truth is discovered.

The materials on the American episode of economic expansion presented here were composed over the past several decades by a mind initially innocent of any tempting illusions about 'total' history. They were written each after exposure to a large body of primary and secondary source material, and they represent the unwinding of sequences of thought and recollection on specific, though somewhat compendious and occasionally lofty, topics. They are arranged loosely by region (South and North) and by economic sector (agriculture and industry), with some regard in each section to the chronology of developments. All take their beginning from a problem in *economic* history, that is, the endeavor to contribute to the understanding of the growth of America's material wealth. But in each case they represent a push through tangled networks of prices and markets to roots in social organization and group behavior. The sections on the South and on northern agriculture were published earliest and should be read in the context of the immense outpouring of research of all sorts, both quantitative and socio-psychological, which has appeared from the dozens of able and usually younger historians on those topics, both at the time I wrote and in the past decade.

The longish and very impressionistic essay, "The Industrial Civilization of the Midwest," is rather different from the other studies in origin and scope. I had gone to Paris in 1984–85 as the French–American Foundation's annual nominee to the chair in American Studies at the Ecole des Hautes Etudes en Sciences Sociales. The pay was generous, duties light, students very scarce, and my French colleagues, with one or two exceptions, impenetrably courteous and busy. I had just finished the sketch of New England's early industrialization and, having written on northern agriculture and on the South, was of a mind to round things off by a cycle of research on the Middle West's industrialization. I had no sources at hand and quailed before the prospect of finding much intimate material in Paris libraries. But the Midwest had been my native region. I had much of its small-town and small-city culture bred in my bones. I had absorbed the body of lore about its rural development from original sources, and from work on French Lorraine and the German Ruhr I knew what industrial districts were like. So, armed with rhetoric, intuitions, and basic facts from all these sources, I behaved like a true Midwesterner in an apartment in Paris – as, I fancied, Sinclair Lewis might have done. I sat down each morning for several months and wrote about home. The five-part sketch was essentially completed, except for the section on capital, at that time, and though I have begun to collect library material in the past few years, it has not yet absorbed many research results. It is a sketch, a patchwork of intuitions, a scaffolding on which a historian can stand as he adds to it both strength and detail. Such research will test, alter, and possibly amplify some of the generalizations now so confidently expressed.

Outside these central sections on the economic regions, Parts I and V of this book stray into wider pastures. I offer them in order to expose the link between America and Europe and between America's business culture and a wider world. They were given variously to audiences in Japan, France, and Illinois, where they seemed to have been well received, and perhaps students and that elusive creature, the "general reader," will find them interesting. To compensate strict historians or economists, I have attached two methodological annexes, each designed to follow a formula drawn from economics out to its limits and to point, as from the end of the pier, to history's wide, wide world beyond.

I cannot publish a book on American history, written over thirty years and sent to its publisher in October 1989, without a remark about the bearing of the historical experience of our huge continental nation-state on the astonishing resurgence of democracy, capitalism, nationalism, and supra-nationalism that has engaged Europe, West and East, in the past fifteen months. The essays numbered 14 and 15 here were composed in 1987 and 1988 and were placed at the end of my volume to "round it off" and connect it back, by way of the first essay here, to some of the themes in Parts IV and V of Volume 1, which concerned itself with Europe. These two essays are more speculative than the earlier research studies, and when I first considered including them, I was not sure if they formed a fitting conclusion to a chronicle based on historical scholarship. But it seemed important to me to justify my title – *America and the Wider World* – by reference to some large "lessons" to be drawn from the American experience: the changing meaning of the "nation" in a growing international capitalist society and culture and the possibilities of economic organization under liberal policies in Europe, as in America, on a continental scale.

Preface

Now suddenly in Europe, East and West, these issues so long pondered by intellectuals in the universities have sprung into immediate, pressing, clamorous life. It is not the least consequential of the fall-outs from this dramatic year that its events have given new significance and vitality to the aspects of the U.S. experience featured in the two concluding essays in this volume. Comparing America's multi-ethnic society, and its economy of continental scope, with the history and situation of the other great world areas is no longer simply a scholarly exercise, the fascinating occupation of the seminar table or the lecture platform. It is an intellectual task of the greatest urgency in the renewals of the economic, political, and emotional organization of social life on the planet Earth – and no doubt on any other planet, if there should be one, inhabited by creatures of the passions, brains, and capabilities of humankind.

Acknowledgments

These studies were collected originally at the suggestion of several former students who wished to have a book for class assignments and ready reference. The encouragement of Gavin Wright; George Grantham; Carol Heim; the two editors of the Cambridge University Press series, Robert Gallman and Louis Galambos; a generous but scrupulous reader for the Press (whose identity I suspect); and Frank Smith, the history editor, was especially valuable. For bringing the book to completion not only technically, but as an integrated effort at socio-scientific history, the greatest debt is due to Heather Salome, who combined an enthusiasm and appreciation for the content with a sharp editorial eye, a sensitivity to structure and style, and a firm hand on typists, computer operators, research assistants, and the author himself. The errors, and deficiencies, particularly in the footnoting, are, as always, entirely my own.

Each of the essays also has its own set of acknowledgements for support, research assistance, and typing. Some of these are stated in notes to the essays. The National Science Foundation, the Ford Foundation, the Guggenheim Memorial Foundation, the Gould Foundation, and the Andrew W. Mellon Foundation have all at one time or another had shares in the enterprise. I am particularly grateful to John E. Sawyer, educator and economic historian, and among economists, to James Tobin, Carl Kaysen, and Richard Ruggles, for what I felt to be their sympathy with the intellectual enterprise in which my career has been entangled and for moral support early on and at several crucial points along the way. The debt to wife and family, to students, colleagues, research helpers, librarians, and critics has piled up over thirty years and would bankrupt me many times over if presented for payment.

A word of thanks should be given also, no doubt, to the several reviewers of Volume 1 of this collection, published in 1984. One reviewer scolded me for including some of my own book reviews in the collection. He thought it perhaps vainglorious in me to follow the example of Alex-

Acknowledgments

ander Gerschenkron, in one of the volumes of his collected writings, in this respect. In any case, the review in question discouraged me, both by precept and by its own vivid example, from reprinting any more of mine. I *have* made a stronger effort in this volume to speak out what is in my mind, to make explicit the values, judgments, themes, and inner connections behind the essays, and to shape them in relation to one another in such a way as to bring out what I see as an intellectual unity. I have been fortunate enough to have had quite a number of excellent students, who have given me the feeling that they have taken something of my views and values into their own work. Whether I have been able to communicate these views to professional, and perhaps less educable, colleagues through these written words is not for me to judge.

But book reviewers, like students, can make a dent even in an author's impenetrable ego and cause him, if only very slightly, to mend his ways. They may be likened best to the louse that the poet Burns saw on the lady's hat in church, and they lead one to repeat with grudging gratitude his immortal stanza:

> Oh wad some power the giftie gie us
> To see oursels as others see us!
> It wad frae mony a blunder free us,
>   And foolish notion:
> What airs in dress and gait wad lea'e us,
> And even devotion!
> > "To a Louse: On seeing one on a
> > lady's bonnet in church" (1786),
> > Stanza 8.

A note on notes

These essays, when first written, were, with a few exceptions, subjected to very light footnoting. The sound rule which Joseph Spengler taught his students, that "every statement should have its footnote," was not followed. The effort has been made, however, to establish some credibility, where specific authors or surprising facts are cited, by recovering the original source consulted.

The more general statements, judgments, and theories, however, have not been reinforced by an inventory of my reading in my intellectual antecedents. That would be the job for a separate book and of interest only in allotting property rights in these ideas and interpretations. Occasionally I think myself guilty of some originality in an idea or a perspective, but it may seem so only because my memory is – whether purposely or subconsciously – faulty. In a history so well travelled, claims of originality seem rather absurd. Readers who see in these essays the shadows of Weber, Sombart, Marx, Croce, Beard, Turner, Malin, Phillips, Gray, Taylor, Hofstader, Chandler, and many others may be pleased to be able to make the attributions themselves; others are welcome to take any new thoughts implanted in their minds here for their own. I will be satisfied if any of these studies leads a reader further into the tangled and delightful twin terrains of American history and social theory. This applies particularly to the essay on the American relation to Europe (Chapter 1), the synthetic essays on northern agrarian history (Chapters 7 and 10), and the purely interpretive pieces in Part V. The problem of sources is addressed in the essay on New England (Chapter 11) and that on the diffusion of "folk" practices and materials in agriculture (Chapter 9) by means of some notes and a partial bibliography. Further, more specific documentation can (probably) be supplied upon application to the author.

PART I

America and Europe: a history

I

American civilization: the impulse from Europe

Capitalism, like Christianity, is a pattern of human behavior endemic in Europe and the Americas and showing sufficient uniformities to justify its designation by a single word. In Christianity acceptance of the predominant importance of Jesus Christ – whether as historical figure or as savior and Son of God – forms in the broadest sense the defining characteristic. Capitalism is defined by the lodging of major economic decisions in private individuals or groups rather than in the State, and by the guidance to those decisions provided – whether to so-called owners or to a bureaucracy of managers – through a system of money and prices, by the goal of financial profit.

Capitalism in this sense, like almost all Western ideas, good and bad, came into the civilization of the Mediterranean and thence into that of northern Europe and North America from that peculiar *Gestalt,* that coincidence of geography and human skills, insight, and ambition that appeared in the Greek city-states after the Persian wars. Here a group of governments operating on a moderate scale – midway between family or tribe and empire, with property holders – landowners, slaveowners, and merchants – proved that, at least momentarily, it could hold its own against oriental despotism despite fierce rivalries among its member states. Here a partial separation between wealth and the state first became possible, and property rights could inhere in individual citizens rather than in clans, communes, temples, or the power of the god-king. Capitalism here, on a miniature scale, proved symbiotic with government where state power and wealth ownership were moderately dispersed. States were small and strongly influenced, though not wholly dominated,

Presented originally in slightly amended version to the Sapporo Cool Seminar on American Studies at Hokkaido University, Sapporo, Japan, through the kind invitation of Professor Takamasa Shirai and the Japan-America Foundation, August 20–25, 1981, and published, in Japanese, in the conference proceedings. I am indebted to Jaseem Ahmed for assistance in the preparation of the footnotes.

by numerous wealthy persons, and wealth in the form of money and mercantile stocks could escape the state, moving in a trading network across the eastern Mediterranean, creating colonies and trading posts wherever it touched. Greek capitalism had a form of state government and an inter-state mobility that allowed it to survive and flourish.

The capitalistic city-state bequeathed the concept of private ownership to the Roman Republic, and the Empire did not wholly extinguish it.[1] In essential form, as the British economic theorist J. R. Hicks pointed out in his foray into history, it reappeared in the widespread revival of the Greek spirit, thought, art, and learning in the Italian Renaissance.[2] From this revival the capitalism of the modern world traces directly its origins. The success of Hong Kong and Singapore in the world today shows that the spirit and organizational form of mercantile capitalism are far from dead.[3] The ecology of the world economic order, which shelters the great land monsters of America, Russia, and China yet seems to have a niche for this

[1] "[The] Graeco-Roman World was essentially and precisely one of private ownership, whether of a few acres or of the enormous domains of Roman senators and emperors, a world of private trade, private manufacture." M. I. Finley, *The Ancient Economy* (Berkeley and Los Angeles: University of California Press, 1973), 29. Finley goes on to argue the inappropriateness of a "market-centered" analysis of the ancient world. Having observed earlier that "there were no business cycles in antiquity; no cities whose growth can be ascribed, even by us, to the establishment of a manufacture," (ibid., 23) he makes clear that in his own view the ancient economy was a non-capitalist or pre-capitalist system.

[2] "[The] point comes when it [expansion of trade] no longer absorbs the same energy, art can be pursued for art's sake, and learning for the sake of learning. It was at the end of her period of commercial expansion that Athens became the "mother of arts"; it was after their commercial expansion was completed that Florence and Venice became the homes of the High Renaissance." J. R. Hicks, *A Theory of Economic History* (Oxford University Press, 1969), 58–59. For a view critical of Hicks and his theory of economic history, and in particular the importance Hicks ascribes to the role of the city-states in the development of capitalism, see P. T. Bauer's review article, "Economic History as Theory," *Economica, New Series*, Vol. 38, No. 150 (May 1971), 163–179.

[3] The following table, giving the value of trade in millions of U.S. dollars, indicates in some measure the success of Hong Kong and Singapore:

	1963		1985	
	Exports	Imports	*Exports*	Imports
Hong Kong	874	1,297	29,927	29,592
Singapore	1,135	1,398	22,817	26,286
India	1,626	2,477	8,510	15,092
Republic of Korea	87	560	30,283	31,135
Brazil	1,406	1,487	25,639	13,168

The two cities have outstripped India in value of trade, approaching or exceeding, despite their tiny size, the record of Korea and Brazil. *International Trade Statistical Yearbook*, Vol. 1 (New York: 1986), 194, 485, 506, 576, 868.

smaller form of life, which like a flock of sparrows or a school of minnows, carries on an active, mobile, flexible economy, darting here and there in the quick search for profit. In the Italian city-states not only trade but finance became a source of profit, and from that there began to be effects in the organization of production itself, an intensification of the activities of guilds and craft shops, and some development of specialized industry for sale from manors and peasant households in the countryside.[4]

In Western Europe after the sixteenth century, the organization, financial technology, and legal forms of property and contract were carried over from the city-state proper to a somewhat larger geographical and political unit, the city with an appreciable hinterland, as in Venezia, Tuscany, Catalonia, and most spectacularly the Netherlands. Its half-democratic, half-oligarchic form of government, with commercial freedom at home and extensive connections abroad, flourished along the Baltic and North Sea coasts in the Medieval Hanse, at Antwerp and the Flemish cloth towns, and reached a peak in the Dutch Golden Age of the seventeenth century. And as in differing degrees in Athens, Venice, Genoa, Florence, capitalism in Amsterdam did not confine itself to the home city, but organized production in a rural hinterland; it extended financial and trading connections throughout Europe and established trade and political connection with settlements and trading posts of its own along the fringes of the oceans.[5] The empire of seventeenth century Dutch capitalism stretched from Manhattan to Java. But the fate of mercantile capitalism in the European nation-states indicates the optimal scale on which, under seventeenth and eighteenth century conditions, it could be conducted and the optimal balance of international mobility and domestic productive and military strength necessary for dominance. The military and political techniques which established national kingdoms on the basis of loose feudal hierarchies in the sixteenth and seventeenth centuries allowed for a range in size and scale: Portugal, Spain, France, tiny Denmark with her Norwegian adjunct, the patchwork of German states held in precarious balance by outside force and the fear of mutual destruction (to a degree also, it must be owned, from exhaustion and indolence), the weak and unstable eastern European kingdoms, and the mass of Peter the Great's Russia. Capitalism survived and flourished best where distant trade formed an important part of the national wealth and polity; in their imperial experiences, Portugal, Denmark, Netherlands, England succeeded where Spain floundered and France failed. And

[4]B. Luzzatto, *An Economic History of Italy from the Fall of the Roman Empire to the Beginning of the Sixteenth Century,* translated by Philip Jones (London: Routledge and Kegan Paul, 1961), 102–108.

[5]J. de Vries, *The Dutch Rural Economy in the Golden Age* (New Haven: Yale University Press, 1974).

among the colonial powers, England, it appeared, approximated most closely the ideal combination of size and mobility, a productive rural base and an aggressive and independent urban mercantile enterprise. The development of Western capitalism occurred on the basis of the international rivalry of these enlarged city-states, without the intervention of any notion of the mutual gains from trade or a widening market. What one gained, another lost. The sea power of England opened the world to English commerce and closed it to Spanish, French, and Dutch. It was only after that fact was clearly established that Adam Smith discovered the benefits of a free trade among the nations.

I

In this atmosphere of mercantile capitalism and competing national powers, the North American colonies were established. Their economic and political life before 1700 was experimental, tentative, fragile. Virginia found the path along which she was to travel after a quarter-century of uncertainty and high mortality. Tobacco export drew in planters, indentured servants, and black slaves; a planter class assumed the style of a landed gentry and dominated the politics of a restless society of large- and middle-scale farmers.[6] In her sister colony, Massachusetts, the peculiar religious formation which guided the colony's establishment, as well as the poverty of agricultural resources, left capitalism for six decades under a shadow. Then, with the protection of the Navigation Acts, fishing, shipbuilding, and shipping were found by the early eighteenth century to yield high returns, and mercantile and landed wealth replaced Puritan virtue in the seats of power.[7] The colonies between Massachusetts and Virginia waited for the influx of British and German settlers of the early and middle decades of the eighteenth century to gain a body of population that gave them a characteristic and regionally differentiated economic base.[8] By mid-century, Philadelphia and New York were outstrip-

[6]E. S. Morgan, *American Slavery, American Freedom: The Ordeal of Colonial Virginia* (New York: Norton, 1975), Chs. 4–9. Basic work on this topic has been done by Jacob Price, *France and the Chesapeake: A History of Tobacco*, Vols. 1 and 2 (Ann Arbor: University of Michigan Press, 1973), and in the recent fine study by A. Kulikoff, *Tobacco and Slaves: The Development of Southern Cultures in the Chesapeake, 1680–1800* (Chapel Hill: UNC Press of the Institute for Early American History and Culture, 1986).

[7]B. Bailyn, *The New England Merchants in the Seventeenth Century* (Cambridge, Mass.: Harvard University Press, 1955).

[8]Not very many Englishmen came during these years, though a small continued influx added strength to the original colonial stock. The early Scots were lowlanders, followed by Highlanders after the unsuccessful uprising of 1715. Religious differences at home drove out many of the German groups, such as Moravians,

ping Boston as centers of capitalist mercantile activity, and their back country, as far as the Allegheny Mountains, freed in 1763 of the menace of French and Indian attack, had begun an internal development.

The Revolution of these colonies from England was the first and most decisive expression of a common American attitude toward England and Europe at large. It was the first of the string of colonial revolts that has punctuated world history since 1776, and of them all, it is perhaps the most puzzling. Historians' difficulty probably lies in the fact that they have insisted on treating it seriously, almost solemnly, as a profound social event, to be attributed to profound social disorder. Its rhetoric is misleading, and even more misleading is its proximity to the cataclysmic Revolution in France and the series of continental revolutions from 1780 to 1917 which overthrew the agrarian and mercantilist political and social order. From a social or economic view, it appears to be a superficial revolution to which only superficial political causes need be assigned.[9] As Pitt, Burke, and Fox all knew, it was not hard to conceive of a British policy by which the Revolution might easily have been avoided. Internally there was no feudalism in the colonies to overthrow, and class structures based on wealth, birth, and urbanity, fostered by the colonial development, easily survived the upheaval. The force of back country farmers and urban artisans is seen at points pushing events to a crisis, but the colonial aristocracy – except for the very thin layer of Tory merchants, tax collectors, and crown appointees – remained in the lead and in control.[10] It was in some respects a very English affair; in Massachu-

Inspirationalists, and Mennonites, who arrived in Pennsylvania, Virginia, and Carolina between 1720 and 1740. M. L. Hansen, *The Atlantic Migration, 1607–1860* (New York: Harper & Row, 1961), 48–50.

[9] Crane Brinton's view in his classic *The Anatomy of Revolution* is that "the American Revolution was predominantly a territorial and nationalistic revolution. . . ." Crane Brinton, *The Anatomy of Revolution*, rev. and exp. ed. (New York: Alfred A. Knopf/Prentice-Hall, 1965), 24. Bernard Bailyn writes that the Revolution "was above all else an ideological-constitutional struggle and not primarily a controversy between social groups undertaken to force changes in the organization of society." *Pamphlets of the American Revolution, 1750–1776*, Vols. 1–4 (Cambridge, Mass.: Harvard University Press, 1965), Ch. 8.

[10] "The patriot leaders did not envision a new social order and the governments they created did not attempt to alter existing religious beliefs; the distribution of wealth; or the barriers of sexual, racial, and class status." J. A. Henretta, *The Evolution of American Society, 1700–1815: An Interdisciplinary Analysis* (Lexington, Mass.: D. C. Heath, 1973), 173. According to Henretta, the Revolutionary years did see a substantial reduction in the numbers of men with wealthy backgrounds within the legislative assemblies, due to a change in the basis of apportionment. The deference paid to the traditional leadership of wealthy men enabled these men, the original leaders of the independence movement, to retain control of the state governments (Henretta, 167–9). In a similar vein K. A. Lockridge in his *A New England Town: the First Hundred Years, Dedham,*

setts it had the grim determination that had led the English Puritans to cut off Charles I's head a century earlier; in Virginia it resembled the revolts of turbulent Scottish clansmen and border country earls against Elizabeth. It is best understood not by Marxian models of class struggle, but in the simple model of parent and adolescent child. The colonies had thrived and grown under British protection and support. To the south the Spanish had been swept from the seas. To the west and north, French power had been destroyed. Within the Empire, the northern and middle colonies had grown as individual capitalistic city-states, with trade, money, private property, the common law, and the sort of democracy characteristic of the city-state, that is, the essential control through the assembly of free property holders. The southern colonies had grown up as planter-aristocracies contained in governmental institutions functioning with a day-to-day independence from the mother country, similar in degree though slightly different from their northern counterparts. Unlike the Caribbean planters, many of whose owners lived in England and voted there, none of the mainland North American colonies had even indirect representation of its property interests in Parliament. The doctrine held in the minds of many that the colonies were governed not by Parliament, but directly by the crown, through its royal institutions, the Privy Council and the Lords of (later Board of) Trade.[11] The coincidence, so unfortunate from a British imperial point of view, of a sense of independence and safety after 1763 in the colonies with a pettiness on the part of unusually stupid ministers in Britain was the Revolution's immediate cause. Its

Massachusetts, 1636–1736 (New York: Norton, 1970), 174, concludes that "the process of historical change bringing America toward the present was convoluted and ultimately cautious."

[11]In 1650 Parliament did pass an act declaring that the colonies "ought to be subject to such laws, orders and regulations as are or shall be made by the Parliament of England." C. H. Firth and R. S. Rait, *Acts and Ordinances of the Interregnum*, II, 425–9, as quoted in L. W. Labaree, *Royal Government in America: A Study of the British Colonial System Before 1783* (New York: Frederic Ungar, 1930–58), 4, n. 1. Labaree writes, "But the very fact that it seemed necessary to make such a declaration at a time when the Crown was in abeyance lends emphasis to the general doctrine that the colonies were dependent on the King and not on Parliament."

It was generally agreed that the Royal Colonies were ruled under the Crown's prerogative. The Privy Council and the Board of Trade, as agents of the Crown, did take the view that it was a right of the colonists as Englishmen to share in legislation and taxation and to do this the colonists could set up municipal bodies or legislative assemblies. But they took the view also that Parliament itself might pass laws and tax the colonists as it saw fit. Parliament's powers of taxation were indeed upheld by the attorney general and the solicitor general in a ruling deciding the status of Jamaica for revenue purposes in 1724. It was not, however, until 1763 that Parliament began to act upon this view (Labaree, 174, 175, 269, 270, and Chs. 5, 6, 7).

explanation is in a real sense to be found in British rather than in American history. The colonies had grown as independent capitalistic commonwealths; what makes their history so unique and so fortunate was that they had done so under an enforced *pax Britannica,* without the ruinous civil or internecine wars that had afflicted their counterparts in ancient Greece, North Italy, and the North Sea. The American Revolution was not so much a revolt against England, whose laws, property rights, contractual agreements, language, and religion were all left intact, and many of whose political institutions and practices were ardently imitated. It was a simple assertion of what had in fact long been true: "that these colonies are, and of right ought to be, independent states."[12]

It is remarkable that, as independent states, they did not immediately fall out at war among themselves. The comradeship of revolt against a common parent, the self-conscious differentiation of the Republic from monarchical enemies in Europe and – more important in the upshot, the presence of a common task – the expansion of power over a continent, a task city-states had never before encountered – these held the union of sovereignties together for eighty years, and when it broke, it meant that the rival sovereignties of North and South were city-states no longer, but rather inland empires.

The birth of the American colonies as mercantile city-states thus represented the first difference from the great kingdoms of Europe. In 1776, the colonies represented thirteen separate branches of eighteenth-century England. The squirearchy was in the South, the mercantile aristocracy in the

[12]C. M. Andrews argued that the events leading up to the Revolution were generated by the colonists' assertion of their rights as Englishmen – fundamentally, the right to enact their own legislation in their own assemblies, for which they were quick to claim all the privileges and powers of the House of Commons. The exercise of these rights and their extension inevitably required a diminution in the authority of the parent body of Crown and Parliament, so that, as E. S. Morgan observed, "English Freedom meant, paradoxically, to be free as possible, from interference by England." E. S. Morgan, *American Slavery, American Freedom* (New York: Norton, 1975), 143. Andrews argued that the political background and origins of the American Revolution are to be understood in the context of the growth and development of the powers of the legislative assemblies, on the one hand, and in the opposition offered to this growth by the Crown and its agents, on the other. This opposition resulted from the desire of the Crown and its agents to perpetuate a "system of colonial subordination and dependence in the interest of the trade and commerce of their kingdom," to which "they adhered . . . with a tenacity of purpose which took no account of the growth to manhood of the colonies themselves, and which eventually resulted in the American Revolution and to the disruption of the British Empire." C. M. Andrews, *The Colonial Background of the American Revolution* (New Haven: Yale University Press, 1924, 1971), 66. Bernard Bailyn has argued for greater study and recognition of what he calls the "political culture," both in Britain and the colonies. B. Bailyn, *The Origins of American Politics* (New York: Alfred A. Knopf, 1968), Ch. 1.

coastal cities, and along the rivers and passes and forest trails of the hinter-
lands lay lines of yeoman farmers. The differences were not far to seek:
slavery in the South, the mix of German culture in the rich Pennsylvania
valleys, the strange wild conditions of the backwoods, conditions not
encountered in Europe since the migrations of the neolithic farmers of pre-
history. But the ultimate difference was historical: European capitalism
had evolved out of feudalism, by way of royal absolutism and religious and
dynastic wars and in the presence of a fully settled and functioning
manorial and peasant agriculture. American capitalism was "born free,"
as Americans like to say, which is to say that it was "born dominant."
There were some struggles with an established church in New England,
with remnants of feudal titles along the Hudson and in the proprietary
colonies, but these were fragile barriers, swept away the more readily since
the colonial revolution occurred in the ferment of French rationalistic and
revolutionary thought. The U.S. Constitution was formed to join city-
states and agrarian commonwealths in a federation whose system of
checks and balances would ensure the safety of property and the freedom
of contract and of religious belief against all enemies foreign and domestic.
Foreign enemies seemed numerous, lodged mostly in the envious tyranni-
cal empires and kingdoms of Europe. But there were few domestic enemies
to the expansion into the lands north and west of the Ohio River which the
states had ceded to the Confederation or, within thirty years, to the lands of
the Louisiana Purchase and the Spanish and Mexican cessions.

This birth in freedom represented one of America's fundamental differences from the capitalism of the Old World, but the difference created by
the presence of an unsettled inland empire was at least equally fundamental. The experience of that settlement lies at the heart of all the American
ambivalence toward Europe, of American dependence and independence,
of self-conscious provinciality and equally self-assertive superiority, of the
sense of isolation and the impulse to empire, of American self-deprecation
and American boasting, of American wariness and America's gambler's
luck, of American individualism and American susceptibility to smother-
ing conformity, of American wildness and America's superstitious respect
for law and science, indeed, of most of the neuroses, contradictions,
strengths, and excitement of American individuality. I trust I am not venturing too far beyond my discipline to suggest that all this bursts out of *A
Connecticut Yankee in King Arthur's Court* and shimmers across the still
surface of the central novels of Henry James.

The reason for these contradictory attitudes is not far to seek.
Nineteenth-century America still owed an enormous debt to Europe, a
debt that was not only not being repaid but was increasing as American
development continued. Foreign loans for investment purposes began
with the canals in the 1830s and reached a peak during the railway

boom of the 1880s. The credits piled up in England by the sale of southern cotton and northern bonds went initially to finance purchase of textiles and simple iron wares, as well as the expensive travel and imported bric-a-brac of Mississippi planters, New York tycoons, and western beef barons. But increasingly in the railroad era, they went for English machinery and locomotives and later for German motors and coke ovens. As America's own manufactures, protected by the Republican tariffs, replaced European manufactures, the mix of imports shifted toward truly luxurious consumer goods and producer goods embodying high technology.[13] But the stream continued to flow as, by 1900, the American account began to show an export balance in manufactures, and much new borrowing went to pay interest and amortization on the old.

The financial debt formed only the symbolic surface, the accounting residue of the profound cultural borrowing that continued to go on. Virtually the whole body of the agricultural and mechanical arts as it functioned in northern Europe in 1830 had been transferred by that date to the violently growing young nation – through migration of the farmers and craftsmen, through imitation of the exported products, through apprenticeship and book learning, and through simple theft. The money-

---

[13] The growth of American industry is reflected in the composition of imports, which shows a rising proportion of crude materials and a falling proportion of finished manufactures. The share of the former rose from 10.6 percent in 1830–40 to 30 percent in 1893–1903, whereas that of the latter fell from 49.7 to 26 percent in the same period. The last quarter of the century saw a fall in the share of crude and manufactured foodstuffs in exports. Crude materials fell from 66.1 percent in 1830–40 to 28 percent in 1893–1903, whereas there was a long-term rise in the share of finished and semi-finished manufactures from 5.3 and 9.4 percent at the beginning of the period to 10.7 and 24.3 percent, respectively, in the decade around the end of the century. Between 1845 and 1875 the trade account generally displayed moderate to large deficits. The year 1876 saw the emergence of a large surplus in the balance of trade, which served to finance a large and increasing deficit in invisibles. Deficits on invisibles became the rule from the 1860s; though rising, they were initially offset by the inflow of capital from abroad. Payments on foreign indebtedness were a principal contributor to this deficit. These payments amounted to $4.8 million in 1820, $11.6 million in 1850, $25.1 million in 1860, and $125 million in 1890. Tourist balances began to be significantly negative from the 1850s, and immigrant remittances grew to be significant by the early 1880s. These figures are pieced together from U.S. Bureau of the Census, *Historical Statistics of the U.S. from Colonial Times to 1957*, bicentennial edition, Part 2 (Washington: Bureau of the Census, 1975), Series 187–200, and two articles by D. C. North, "The United States Balance of Payments, 1790–1860," and Matthew Simon, "The United States Balance of Payments, 1861–1900," in National Bureau of Economic Research, Conference on Research in Income and Wealth, *Trends in the American Economy in the Nineteenth Century*, (Princeton: Princeton University Press for the National Bureau of Economic Research, 1960).

using, price-quoting, account-keeping technology of capitalist trade and production was also transfused into the new body and bloodstream of material life, along with legal forms, the partnership, the corporation, the law merchant; English precedent lay behind the decisions and the independence of the courts, and continental codes, deriving ultimately from Rome, helped shape the Constitutional structure. West Point was modeled on St. Cyr,[14] and French military engineers trained many of the Army surveyors and engineers, who measured out the public domain on lines of a rectilinear model derived almost certainly from Rome.[15] An even more critical inheritance was the complex of state and federal policies that formed the American counterpart to the mercantilism of the European states. A coinage, a state debt, tariffs, a state bank, subsidies to manufactures, and the promotional schemes of private entrepreneurs – all these

[14]The emergence of a formal structure of instruction at West Point during the second and third decades of the nineteenth century was due largely to the efforts of Sylvaneus Thayer, who was the ranking officer at West Point from 1817 to 1833. Prior to his appointment to West Point, Thayer and a Lieutenant Colonel William McRee were sent to France expressly to acquire European books on the art of war and to study the operations of the French military schools. Much of the shaping of West Point was based on what Thayer had observed at St. Cyr, some of whose graduates he brought to teach at West Point. S. E. Ambrose, *Duty, Honor, Country: A History of West Point* (Baltimore: The Johns Hopkins University Press, 1966).

[15]As reported on 7 May 1784 by a committee of Congress of which Jefferson was chairman, public lands were to be surveyed by compass and divided into "hundreds," that is, plots of ten geographical miles square, and those again to be sub-divided into "sections" one mile square, numbered within each hundred in rows alternately from west to east and from east to west. T. Donaldson, *The Public Domain: Its History with Statistics* (New York: Johnson Reprint Corporation, 1970), 178, 576. Although the committee report cites no source, the two salient features of the plan – division by the compass and into "hundreds" (centuriation) – appear to have derived from Roman land-surveying methods. The details of the plan were worked out by Hugh Williamson, a Pennsylvanian mathematician, who was also a member of various scientific bodies in Utrecht. O. A. W. Dilke has conjectured that the origins of the Jefferson–Williamson plan can be linked to the Romans through Williamson and his Dutch connections. O. A. W. Dilke, *The Roman Land Surveyors* (Newton Abbot: David and Charles, 1971), Ch. 14. Dilke notes that the Dutch had been familiar with Roman rectangular surveying methods, as evidenced by the seventeenth-century land division in the Beemster polder east of Edam on rectilinear lines. Additionally, William Goess had published an edition of the *Corpus Agrimensorum,* the Roman land-surveying manual, in 1674. Dilke suggests that it is very probable that the Goess edition would be well known to a mathematician interested in astronomy, as Williamson was. "If the origin of the one mile squares is to be sought in a Dutch polder, at least the orientation by the compass points, and perhaps the basic idea, may go back to the *Corpus Agrimensorum*" (Dilke, 204). W. D. Pattison, *The Beginnings of the American Rectangular Land Survey System* (Chicago: 1957) makes the attribution of Williamson as co-author of the plan.

had formed the baggage of European governments functioning within the world of mercantile capitalism in the eighteenth century. All were adopted, along with a substantial share of the economic doctrines that accompanied them, by American politicians.

Yet the period from 1789 to 1865 was not one of high European migration into the United States. Except for the burst of Irish and Germans, following natural and political disasters, respectively, in the 1840s, the stream of migrants had slackened.[16] New Englanders had in fact nearly all come before 1660; natural increase had accounted for nearly all the rest and also for almost all the Yankee migrants that filed into New York State and the Old Northwest. In the South, the original English had been supplemented by Scottish and German settlers, particularly in the uplands, and all these, along with the descendants of the slave imports of the early and mid–eighteenth century, now continued to reproduce their agrarian economy across the Old Southwest, as far as East Texas and as far north as Missouri. Whatever the reasons from the side of Europe – the end of religious and dynastic wars, the course of agricultural improvement, the growth of rural and factory industry – it seemed within America as if migration had taken an eighty-year pause to allow the country to digest what it had taken in, to spread it out, develop and re-form its civilization.

To the third-, fourth-, fifth-generation Americans who formed the bulk of the antebellum population, slave and free alike, what had originally been imported from the Old World had been so domesticated and adapted to the conditions of the New as now to appear indigenous to it. The steam engine, for example, that centerpiece of the English Industrial Revolution, had ceased to be an item of import; there were steam engine makers in the Connecticut and Delaware Valleys – even the Miami Valley in Ohio boasted not only a works, but an improver of the engine for steam navigation of western rivers.[17] In machine tools the process that Rosenberg calls

---

[16]By 1840 Irish immigrants accounted for fully half of the total number of immigrants, and Germans for a third. Following the rot that destroyed the Irish potato crop in 1846, the number of Irish immigrants rose more than fourfold, peaking at 221,000 in 1851. Though large numbers of Germans continued to arrive throughout the 1840s, the period 1851–54 saw their greatest expansion. This followed a decline in emigration from Germany in 1850, ascribed by American consuls there to the difficulty faced by peasants in disposing of their property. Continued uncertainty in German markets and politics appears to have induced peasants to accept lower prices for their land and increased emigration the following year. Hansen, *Atlantic Migration,* 284. Not until 1880 was the 1854 peak figure (for all immigrants) surpassed. Here the source for immigration figures is *Historical Statistics of the United States,* Series C-92, C-95.

[17]L. C. Hunter, *Steamboats on the Western Rivers: An Economic and Technological History* (Cambridge, Mass.: Harvard University Press, 1949), 108–20.

"technological convergence" had split textile machinery off from textile companies and then split off the manufacture of machine tools from machinery making, to form a vigorous specialized industry in these same river valley locations.[18] The Industrial Revolution had indeed come to the American Northeast; the form and features had an English cast, but the clothing was locally spun and the accent in the factories unmistakably Yankee. The differences, well known by now, between American machinery and manufacturing processes and the English – lightness and faster depreciation, the greater use of wood in construction, the variety and ingenuity of labor-saving tricks – reflected American resource abundance.[19] The exactness of that adjustment to cost conditions here testified to the thoroughness with which the society had absorbed the essence of efficient capitalistic enterprise.

That American manufacturing should have glided effortlessly into capitalistic organization is not in fact very surprising. In Europe the guild form of industrial organization, with strict apprenticeship, small workshops, and cartel-like controls over supplies, labor, and markets persisted long after the feudal political relations had disappeared. There modern industry had to break the medieval mold through the activities of merchants who circumvented the urban guilds to link idle rural labor and handicrafts to mobile supplies of wool, iron, and a few other materials in order to serve expanding local and distant markets. Then the factories, when they came, had to break through yet a second encrusted layer of vested interests to establish economic relations. But in America, thanks in part to the British discouragement of colonial manufactures, factory industry, serving sizable markets even before the railroad age, could move in directly on top of the primitive domestic manufactures of the backwoods farm families.[20] The market for American manufactures lay then partly in the substitution for British imports and partly in the release of rural domestic industry for migration West or to town and cities or to the tasks of specialized commercial agriculture. Financing could be supplied by merchants' credit arrangements, and transportation by the canal, turn-

[18]N. Rosenberg, "Technological Innovation in the Machine Tool Industry, 1840–1910," *Journal of Economic History,* Vol. 23, No. 4 (December 1963), 414–443.

[19]N. Rosenberg, *Technology and American Economic Growth* (New York: Harper & Row, 1972), 87–116. Contemporary views are reproduced in N. Rosenberg, ed., *The American System of Manufactures: The Report of the Committee on the Machinery of the United States, 1855* (Edinburgh: The Edinburgh Press, 1969).

[20]G. R. Taylor, *The Transportation Revolution, 1815–1860* (New York: Harper & Row, 1951), 215–220. The domestic system had an importance in boots and shoes, in woolen cloth, and in a few miscellaneous manufactures, such as straw hats. Home cotton spinning had succumbed to the factories by 1830.

pike, and railway projects, operating on an extensive scale thanks to the strong support of local state governments.

It was in agricultural expansion and productivity growth that the surprises lay. In contrast to Europe, the American South had the soils and climate to grow semi-tropical crops, notably tobacco, sugar cane, and cotton. The comparative advantage of the United States in these crops was fully apparent in 1800. But who then could have foreseen that the grain and livestock economy of the Northeast and the Old Northwest would within sixty years come to supply not only the immensely enlarged domestic market, but a significant portion of the markets of northern Europe? And who could have thought that in this most conservative of arts, whose techniques and life processes were the most deeply hidden from science and human ingenuity, a continuous rate of improvement could have been maintained, rivaling in every way that of machine industry? North America achieved a comparative advantage among nations in agriculture even as its great industrial development went forward. This was not due simply to rich, virgin soils or a level and uncluttered terrain. Such advantages in central Europe had supported a complex peasant culture and inefficient and unprogressive manorial enterprises. In agriculture America borrowed from Europe, indeed – the seeds, the stock, the tools, and schedules of planting and harvesting. But the American farmer's own skills, the adaptations to new climates, new natural enemies, new terrain, were not derived from his forefathers, and they were exercised in several important directions.

Here at the very first it was not Europe, but the Indian, who furnished the culture. In Virginia the Jamestown settlers, and at Plymouth the Pilgrims, came ill furnished with the skills, tools, or raw materials of agriculture. Their firearms helped them hunt for wild game (and Indians), but the cultivation of the indigenous crops – corn, beans, tobacco – was learned from the natives.[21] The grains that Europe had derived from Asia Minor in the neolithic dispersion were now spread to the new soils. Before 1830 imported livestock, mostly brought from the North Sea countries to the East Coast and from the Spanish colonies into the Southwest before 1700, did not benefit from the breeding improvements that ran through eighteenth-century European agriculture. Instead, through natural selection, aided by the primitive breeding practices of the farmers, they developed into herds adapted to American forage and market use. The frontier hog was the most famous example. Running wild in the woods, feeding on roots and acorns, it reverted to a wild state, grew lean and long-legged, long-nosed, ferocious, and fleet. Cattle were developed

[21]Lyman H. Carrier, *The Beginnings of Agriculture in America* (New York: Johnson Reprint Corporation, 1923, 1968), 94.

either in very large sizes, as oxen to do heavy labor in fields and woods or as the short-horn, general-purpose cow that could pull a wagon, give milk on schedule, and furnish a not wholly unchewable meat and reasonable hide at the end of its busy life. These adaptations were in the East and South. Walter P. Webb's great study, *The Great Plains*, details the adaptations from the Spanish-derived stock, of longhorns and the wild horses of the Southwest.[22] But as commercial influences made themselves felt in the early decades of the nineteenth century, both in the South and North, animal breeding took on a more directed and self-conscious life. Washington and Jefferson had themselves been notable agricultural improvers, and scores of lesser, though sometimes richer, farmers in western Massachusetts and central New York imported the improved cattle, sheep, hogs, and horses from England, Scotland, the Channel Islands, and the Low Countries. With the stock came also a knowledge of the practices of cross-breeding and inbreeding, which facilitated the adaptation to American diets and climate. The South's great contribution to this effort was the breeding of the mule – a Mediterranean art known to the Romans – into an animal superior for many field purposes to the horse and much sturdier and cheaper to feed.[23] The search for strange new plants and improved seeds of the old plants began to be pursued all over the world by farmers' societies and the consular offices of the national government. In a physical and biological sense, America's debt to Europe constituted the larger part of the natural base of its agricultural industry. But when one puts corn, cotton, sugar, potatoes, the turkey, some of the pulses, and many tropical fruits into the scales, the balance of accounts with the standard peasant agriculture of Europe is altered. And the European heritage had to be adapted not once, but many times to new conditions, with the movement to every new tier of states to the West. It was this ability and readiness to experiment and adapt, an attitude so different from that traditionally associated with a peasantry, that showed in this most ancient of occupations the deep penetration of capitalistic enterprise, markets, and financial and psychological compulsions that created the American farmer of the nineteenth century.

The primitive migration of American settlers on to new soil occurred in the presence not only of growing, capitalistically organized markets, but

[22]W. P. Webb, *The Great Plains* (Boston: Ginn and Company, 1959).
[23]The Romans used mules chiefly to draw the Imperial army's field artillery of catapults and darts, and there are numerous references to them in this connection by, among others, Vegetius in his *Epitoma Rei Militaris* and Flavius Josephus, who writes of an engagement that went badly for the Romans, "so they killed the mules and other creatures, excepting those that carried their darts and machines. . . ." *The Works of Flavius Josephus*, translated by W. Whiston (New York: Worthington, 1887), 624.

also of a proliferating industrial civilization based on machinery. Here was another lucky difference from Europe, a fact which incidentally gives the railroad its superiority as a symbol and an educative force, as well as a transport medium, over the barge canal. Eli Whitney's famous cotton gin was hardly a farmer's invention, but contrivance and inventiveness on farms is reflected in other agricultural machinery. The light, strong, ingenious, adaptable, and readily expendable contrivances achieved European recognition by the 1850s in McCormick's harvester and Deere's plows and cultivators.[24] By the 1880s the neolithic sickle and its late medieval improvement, the scythe, had been wholly replaced by machinery that cut, bound, dried, and threshed wheat and oats in a continuous operation, and the horse-drawn technology had reached its peak. Even in rice the mechanical reaper and thresher could be applied. It failed curiously enough in the major non-European crops, tobacco, cotton, and corn, and here thorough mechanization had to wait until the cheaper and more controllable power of the gasoline engine and the stronger and more delicate machinery of the twentieth century could enter the field.

In agricultural techniques, then, America had borrowed from other cultures, largely but not exclusively from her European parent, but in empty lands and running in the high tide of commercial capitalism, she had applied the borrowings with such effectiveness, with so many transformations, and on so broad a continental base as effectively to outstrip Europe. The same may be said for the institutional structure of European capitalism, as it grew in its American variant. The breaking away from English precedent began even in the colonies, in the two centuries when that precedent itself was transforming the position of crown and Parliament, the legal doctrines governing real property and laws of contract and financial associations, the partnership, and the company in joint stock. In the United States the development was not, as a laissez-faire theorist might suppose, to make property ownership and contractual obligation more absolute. Private property is after all held against the state and against other competitors, and contract creates a bind, an inflexibility, in a system of markets. Consequently the historians of American law – most recently, Hurst, Scheiber, Horowitz, and Hughes – have

[24]American exhibits were highly regarded at the Crystal Palace Exhibition at London in 1851, and pride of place went (along with the Colt Revolver) to the McCormick Reaper, which was awarded both grand prize and a council award. Prizes were also awarded to American ploughs. The McCormick Reaper, it was said, "attracted more visitors than the famed Kohinoor diamond." J. W. Oliver, *History of American Technology* (New York: Ronald, 1956), 254–56. The standard contemporary account of the mechanical developments is R. L. Ardrey, *American Agricultural Implements* (Chicago: The author, 1894). J. T. Schlebecker's survey summarizes these inventions: J. T. Schlebecker, *Whereby We Thrive: A History of American Farming, 1607–1972* (Ames: Iowa University Press, 1975).

observed in the legal development not a simple growth of individual freedom, but a sense of community interest and economic efficiency in the interpretation of these fundamental capitalist relationships.[25] Continental and urban development at so rapid a rate would not have been possible without a ruthless application of the state's ancient right of eminent domain and the vesting of it by the legislatures in transport companies and public utilities. Similarly the enormous concern with monopoly and state regulation – a concern sharper and more persistent in the United States than in any other capitalist nation – has been rooted not in abstract doctrines of equity or individual freedom, but in the concern for the "public interest."

Frontier society, with its problems of defense, communication, public education, religious expression, was an intricate fabric of individual initiative, community cooperation, and legal compulsion. And farmers, once the continent was settled, began to show remarkable ability for group action and the exercise of political pressure. In agricultural research most notably, the European institutions – the university and the state-sponsored experiment station – began the transformation of farming from a folk art to a branch of applied science. Similarly, political action by farmers beginning with the Grange and the Farmers' Alliance after 1870, reached a peak in the Populists' campaign of the 1890s. But the farm community was most effective not in a radicalism which in effect denied the capitalist premises on which its culture had been constructed, but in the power of its lobby within the Republican party and in its firm control of key committees in Democratic Congresses. Farmers were faithful party members – to the Republicans in the North and to the Democrats in the South. The Republicans paid them back by vigorous support of agricultural research and extension and the program of public roads, rural free mail services, and control of public utilities, especially the telephone system, to farmers' benefit. The Democratic party's support of low industrial tariffs was less effective than the support of farm export schemes and the development under the New Deal of the program of farm subsidies and price supports. As farming shrank inevitably as a share in national income and the national life, it was farmers' disproportionate political power which until recently, preserved those who had remained on the farms from the full

[25]J. Willard Hurst, *Law and the Conditions of Freedom in the Nineteenth Century United States* (Madison: University of Wisconsin Press, 1956); Harry N. Scheiber, "The Road to Munn: Eminent Domain and the concept of Public Purpose in the State Courts," *Perspectives in American History*, Vol. 5 (1971); Morton J. Horwitz, *The Transformation of American Law, 1780–1860* (Cambridge, Mass.: Harvard University Press, 1977); J. R. T. Hughes, *The Governmental Habit: Economic Controls from Colonial Times to the Present* (New York: Basic Books, 1977).

working out of the free market. In the forms of a rural organization, a balance between private right and community interest was continuously maintained.

If nineteenth-century American capitalism developed a more intense individualism, a greater tolerance of waste and excess, even perhaps harsher labor relations and a disregard for the losers in the economic race, the reason lies then not in a greater love of freedom, but in the nature of the huge developmental opportunity to which all law, all philosophy, all science, and social organization were bent. If comparison is made with individual European countries in, say, 1860, it is evident that America was on the verge of outstripping any of them, even England, in scale, wealth, and economic and political strength, in the modifications of Western technology and the rules and behavior patterns of European capitalism in ways that could yield rapid economic growth. But America's economic advantages were her scale, her natural resources, and her freedom from earlier pre-capitalistic social forms, groups, and interests. The notable exception to this, Negro slavery, which took so great a toll of the South's energies, capital formation, and industrial potential, was about to disappear as a legal institution, leaving its lasting imprint on the folkways.

The bareness and monotony of the American social landscape were also responsible for the sense of provinciality, of cultural inferiority. This is the more apparent if America is compared, as it should be, not with any individual European state, but with western, central, and southern Europe as a whole. Compared to Europe, America was simple, naive, unstructured, and free. That its culture was thin, with far less variety than the European, was the price it paid for national unity, Anglo-Saxon predominance, and a continental reach. In the mid-nineteenth century, the United States, on the eve of the resumption of high rates of immigration from Europe, had the faults of its virtues. American industrial technology was the child of the mechanical Industrial Revolution, and it excelled in the sorts of adaptations to American tasks and materials that an ingenious workman or a self-trained engineer could invent. In European universities, institutes, and societies, whole bodies of scientific thought, of theory and experiment, had been accumulating since the Renaissance in the study of matter, energy, and life. American scientists and research workers shared in this accumulation, but only from the periphery. The country as a whole was not in the position of Germany and France; her institutions were not organized for the research and intellectual labor of inventing the science of chemistry or physics. Yet it was apparent that a democratic nation on a continental scale would have great resources and an immense stage on which these could be organized and exploited once its full energies were turned to that enterprise. Similarly America's monetary institutions and practices in the mid-century were not well developed. The national price system was in fact linked to the London-centered international gold standard from 1850 on. But gold was so cheap relative to silver that the coinage of silver was suspended effectively from the 1850s on despite furious efforts in the 1870s and early 1890s to restore it. America's resources and size substituted for a sophisticated industrial technology, and gold supplies and the persistent inflationary practices of her unregulated banks compensated to a degree for her dependence on the European money markets. In these, as in her literature, philosophy, art, politics, and law, the borrowing from the Old Country was mingled with the inventions of the new.

By 1860 the United States of America had grown together from the thirteen city-states of the Revolution into two nations. The South depended on Britain for her cotton markets; the North for workmen, skills, some machinery, and some capital. A love–hate – or better, a "respect–suspicion" – relationship between the continent of Europe and the continent of North America persisted, a reflection of America's conscious inferiority to Europe in many ways, combined with a self-assured arrogance about all the ways, even slavery, in which America and Europe differed. But at the eve of the renewal of the great European migration streams, which from 1870 to 1910 occurred in population, capital, and technology, rather than in customs, institutions or commodities, there had developed in the United States two branches of the family of the nations of new settlement and Anglo-Saxon culture, nations that were and (the South felt) of right ought to be free and independent states. Following the Civil War over that sentiment, the growth of modern capitalist structures on a truly national scale altered America internally and in relation to Europe, in fact and in perception.

II

In 1865 the British Isles were still for most Americans, except for the newly freed slaves, the mother country. Even the Africans had been given English names and a language, and some also a version of the Protestant religion. The tasks to which Americans had applied themselves over the preceding fifty years had produced a profound regional, even national, self-consciousness and, stronger than ever, the sense of a different nationality, a spirit and destiny different from that inherited from the parent country. But still there was no other part of Europe or Asia to which the bulk of Americans could feel either a sentimental attachment or a rooted antipathy. The German settlements in Pennsylvania, the Carolinas, the river valleys of the Midwest, or farming areas in Wisconsin and East Texas; the Spanish and Indian cultures of the Southwest; and the mixed

French and Spanish culture of Louisiana provided some islands of a different influence, but among the British-derived Americans these were islands distinctly different and apart. Though not so strong as in Canada, a Celtic element was present, both from the eighteenth-century migrations of the Scots and "Scotch-Irish" into the Appalachian valleys and from the great wave of hungry Irish that famine washed up on the southern New England coast in 1846–50. The French-Canadians, too, had come into New England villages and mill towns. But all these non-English elements lived in clusters, filling specific niches in a society of traders, yeoman farmers, planters, and Yankee craftsmen. The society was English derived and rural, and its native traits and institutions, often modifications of the English, were otherwise derived only from native experience and adaptation.

Between 1865 and 1920 American antebellum society was transformed by several massive and interrelated historical movements. In the relation to Europe, the resumption of heavy immigration was crucial. It occurred this time continuously through the decades and from northern through central, eastern, and southern Europe in wave upon wave.[26] But only the first phase of this *Völkerwanderung* – the Scandinavians, Germans, and Bohemians of the 1860s and 1870s – moved into the Plains to take up land.[27] There they mixed with the continuing stream of Yankee and Scotch-Canadian farmers, fitting easily into the network of rural institutions – schools, improvement organizations, Protestantism, Republican politics, and that special combination of cooperation and self-help that characterized Midwest

[26]After 1860 the first great wave of immigrants came largely from Germany and Britain, followed shortly by the Scandinavian countries. In the early 1880s Germany became the major source. In the late 1880s and the 1890s increasing numbers arrived from Russia, Poland, Italy, and central Europe. In Italy a movement began after a cholera epidemic in 1887. From the East, "Poles and Jews, Hungarians, Bohemians, Slovaks, Ukrainians [came] as agriculture took new forms in the Austrian and Russian Empires." O. Handlin, *The Uprooted* (Boston: Atlantic Monthly Press, 1973), 33. There was a decline in immigration between 1894 and 1898, followed by a surge around the turn of the century. This surge was due to the enormous rise in the numbers of immigrants from central Europe, Russia, and Italy, these three areas accounting in 1910 for 60 percent of the total. It was followed by a rapid decline due primarily to government restrictions and economic difficulties. Source: *Historical Statistics of the United States*. For a convenient tabulation of U.S. immigration by source, see B. W. Paulson and J. Holyfield, Jr., "A Note on European Migration to the United States: A Cross-Spectral Analysis," *Explorations in Economic History*, Vol. 11, No. 3 (Spring 1974), 299–310.

[27]What differentiated these groups from the others was not least that they were relatively prosperous and could buy land, usually on a mortgage. The advertising campaigns of the land-grant railroads and the immigration bureaus of the northwestern states focused their efforts on these groups. M. A. Jones, *American Immigration* (Chicago: University of Chicago Press, 1960), 210.

farming and constituted its great strength. Indeed, in the dairying and mixed farming regions of Iowa, Wisconsin, and Minnesota, they developed, together with their Yankee neighbors, the strongest, most intelligent, stable, and prosperous rural culture in North America. But this movement of Scandinavian peasant families directly across the same climatic belt to carry on their old occupations under new and better conditions was the last of such large-scale rural-to-rural migrations into the United States. After 1890, when Ukrainians and other east Europeans came unstuck and began to move into the stream, only the Canadian prairies with their harsher climate were open to settlement.[28]

Into the United States the Irish migration just mentioned exemplifies the later pattern of movement into the industrial and service jobs in cities and mill towns. Just as the earlier rural migrations had occurred in North America in the presence of a fully formed set of capitalist ownership relations and commercial markets, so the migrations of the surplus population of European peasantries after 1870 occurred into the United States in the presence of a strongly developing native industrialism and growing national markets for the products of mines, factories, and urban capital and skills. One must emphasize, looking back a hundred years later, the vast, almost endless extent of this American industrial opportunity and the crudeness of the structures of physical equipment, and human organization thrown up to accommodate it. It was not an opportunity built on the cunning skills of the technician or the craftsman. Abundant natural resources – coal, iron ore, oil, timber – an immense market on farms and in small towns, driving entrepreneurs, a vast and growing body of labor from farms and overseas, and political institutions flexible enough to bear the weight – these were its sources. On these bases American industrial society had first to link together small-scale production organizations by transport and marketing institutions, then to erect large-scale, semi-command organizations – the large corporations and governmental agencies which modern economic life, at least in the past century, has seemed to require.[29] In the European industrialization, a historical imagi-

---

[28]Ibid., 196.

[29]Alfred D. Chandler, *The Visible Hand: The Managerial Revolution in American Business* (Cambridge, Mass.: The Belknap Press of Harard University Press, 1977). As Chandler notes, an important distinction between the European and American experience of the phenomena of the rise of modern enterprise and that of modern capitalism is the role played by the central government in providing transportation and communications and in setting up administrative procedures. In Europe the government served to finance, locate, and even operate the basic infra-structure. Telegraph and telephone came under government ownership, direction, and operation, and apart from Britain, the European nations were far more heavily involved in developing railroads than was the American government. "In Europe, public enterprise helped to lay the base for the coming of

nation may be able to see the forerunners of factory, city, and corporation in earlier structures of industry and government. The Mediterranean lands from Roman and even Babylonian times had contained cities; Roman-derived Spanish centralism had been transplanted through the Empire into Latin America. Central Germany, northern Italy, and the North Sea coast from the Middle Ages had formed a rich fabric of city-states and urban corporations. In the more thoroughly feudalized kingdoms of France and England, two of the world's greatest cities of the eighteenth century had been created: Paris, through royal power resting on a rich agricultural surplus, and London, through royal power and capitalist world trade. The absolute monarchies in the West had created a state apparatus on a large scale; in the East the vast and disparate regions of the Russian and Austrian empires were riveted together by codes, armies, and bureaucracies. North America had no such large organizations before 1860. Indeed, it had been just such organizations that many in the New World had come to escape. All the ingenuity of the founding fathers in devising the checks and balances to diffuse political authority among states and branches of government had been devoted to frustrating them, to driving them from the Western Hemisphere and ensuring that no native counterparts would cloud the face of American liberty. Even American slavery had been vastly decentralized. The very largest of the plantations, with five hundred or so workers, in no way compared to the thousands of acres and serfs that made up the units of European landholding east of the Elbe, and with emancipation, even these had been broken up, placed on the market, subdivided into thousands of tenant farms. The Civil War was a kind of antitrust movement against the whole planter class, and though it did not eliminate its elements of monopoly and collusion in local labor markets, it brought its market power considerably under the influence of the system of prices and markets. Was not bourgeois liberty the very antithesis of political organization and of economic organization under any form other than that of free exchange?

How then was a republic of British yeomen, transformed by the experience of multiplying small farms across a countryside, even with the drives and institutions of small-scale capitalism, prepared to create railroad and telegraph systems; large coal, shipping, and ore complexes; national purchasing, trading, and selling organizations; a well-articulated banking and credit system linked to European financial markets; and a set of national, state, and local governments equipped to contain and control these continental institutions? And one must add to the scope of the task the flowing in of populations of European peasants and village dwellers

modern mass production and mass distribution. In the United States this base was designed, constructed, and operated almost wholly by private enterprise." Ibid., 204.

of different languages and religion, in numbers equal to nearly one quarter of the population of the industrializing states of the Northeast and Great Lakes shores, where they settled and found jobs.[30] Where was the precedent in American experience for organized institution building and city building at so fast a pace and on so gigantic a scale? It is a difficult question and one to which, I would suggest, American historians have not given enough thought. The question is broached here also in Chapter 12 in the context of the development of the Midwest. The question has been looked at largely in a purely American context, and in such a context the development may appear as a natural human reaction to new opportunity but surely not as a phenomenon flowing naturally out of antebellum American culture.

Yet for every national culture of the nineteenth and twentieth centuries something of the same problem of "modernization" presented itself, and one sees it "solved" in different ways, with the intrusions of the world economy and modern technology. For those societies which had never been immersed in small-scale capitalism and the market economy – the Russian, the Japanese, to a degree the German – the earlier structures of deference and political or familial authority remained to give shape and solidity to the new national enterprise. Within the classic capitalist countries of the European West – England, France, Sweden, the Netherlands – many social institutions and social traits still held firm against the corrosion of markets and formed the basis around which urban complexes, large-scale production organizations, labor unions, cartels, and a quasi-socialism could develop. But the United States had a very weak background of this sort. Its problems of expansion and absorption of new peoples and new production techniques were vast and novel. That it could negotiate the transition to modern economic organization seemed little in doubt to the contemporary observers caught up in the growth of the decades before World War I. But in thoughtful retrospect one wonders how on earth, really, it was managed.

Perhaps the need to absorb the immigrants helped to bring it about. To develop a modern society of large-scale organizations one needs pre-existing elements of hierarchy. Although America was at a disadvantage relative to Europe in this respect, it was not wholly without structure. There were after all generally accepted value scales along which human beings were ranged and rated. A new country of rural neighborhoods and small towns based on commercial enterprise held self-won financial suc-

[30]According to the *Historical Statistics of the United States: Colonial Times to 1957*, Series A96, 98, 103, and 105, in both 1900 and 1910 immigrants represented roughly one fifth of the total population of the north-central and northeastern states. This proportion was obviously much higher in the urban industrializing areas of these states, where immigrants settled.

cess as its primary value, where that success was achieved through labor, skill, or business maneuver that contributed to the greater wealth and faster growth of the community. It is not quite fair to say that nineteenth-century America had Mammon for its God. The sheer wealth of czars and princes or, on a much more modest scale, of old aristocratic families had a faint air of illegitimacy compared to the wealth won by a man through his own efforts. Yet a man's wealth might be taken, in the absence of other evidence, as an outward indication of his virtue, just as in the Calvinist theology a virtuous life might be taken as a sign of election by God's grace though that grace was not to be earned by a man's works.

A hierarchy of respect then could exist based on income, modified by consideration of the means by which income was gained. By the theorems of liberal capitalism, income was earned by applying labor or skill, by risking property or reputation, by applying ingenuity to ends through which society as a whole would benefit. Indeed, it was just here that the respectability of the southern slaveholders had come into question in the North, and it was against this ethic that slaveholders had had to erect such an elaborate and obviously self-serving apologetics. Among northern farmers and shopkeepers it was recognized that income differences could appear through luck; in farming in particular the gambling element was strong.[31] But over a generation economic success and the accretion of wealth would come through foresight, good judgment, quick perceptions, and a steady character. In rural and mercantile society wealthier families acquired a certain air of respectability, solidity, and worth. When the family firm and the corporation began to grow large, through investment of capital in new techniques, new markets, and new resource exploitation, it was quite natural that a scale of jobs and compensations would be

[31]As markets grew and mechanization progressed in agriculture, less and less consideration was given to luck as a factor in determining farming fortunes. According to one farmer in *The Rural New Yorker*, "[I]ndividuals [i.e., farmers] constantly range themselves under one of four classes. Class No. 1 is composed of those who are always poor; Class No. 2 includes those who barely make a living all their lives long; Class No. 3 numbers those who acquire a comfortable and a constantly increasing competence; and Class No. 4 is composed of those who acquire wealth. . . . The individuals of each generation range themselves under one or another of these heads – and I believe that I am correct in saying so, notwithstanding the constant averment [*sic*] of classes Nos. 1 and 2 that their want of success is to be attributed to the circumstances surrounding them. The man himself, and what he is made of, determines to what class he will belong. It is true, surroundings are sometimes favorable and sometimes unfavorable, but the energetic and skillful will dodge the unfavorable obstacles and avail themselves with great dexterity of all that will assist their progress." *Rural New Yorker*, Vol. 13 (1862), as quoted in C. H. Danhof, *Change in Agriculture, The Northern United States, 1820–1870* (Cambridge, Mass.: Harvard University Press, 1969), 282.

devised to reward labor and skill according to the degree necessary to attract it, and the enterprise would expand to the point that this market price represented labor's marginal product to the firm. Wage scales matched to a degree the relative scarcities of skills and aptitudes and the relative costs of preparing workers for various jobs. The structure of both a rural community and the family enterprises within it gave some precedent for a moderate hierarchy in the capitalist enterprise.

Now as we have seen, the United States in 1870 was almost as ethnically homogeneous as the countries of Europe and, outside the South, without the strong traditions of subordination which had made European industrial and state hierarchies easy to operate. The American ideal was the self-made man, and the American promise was that every man could be one. Land and commercial opportunity, and the rather severe and continuing scarcity of labor made that promise seem almost possible of realization. But the needs of a developing industrial and urban structure required a large amount of unskilled and semi-skilled labor, particularly a labor trained socially in a family system of authority, a labor with a sense of job and responsibility, ready to accept minimal training, able to be socialized within a city and within a plant or a construction project and even to participate as second-class citizens, as slow achievers in the American dream. In most of the world's industrializations this labor was furnished within the society itself by workers expelled from the surplus populations of the countryside, through many small and short migratory movements. In France, Sweden, the Low Countries, Russia, Central Europe, Japan, this was almost wholly the case; North Italy drew on South Italy; England on Ireland, West Germany on East Germany and Poland. Linguistic uniformity, a large degree of cultural identity, and a connection still with the disciplined and supportive structures of native villages and extended kin structures in the countryside made such labor docile, intelligent, and ready to form a proletariat to earn its daily bread. In North America labor of this sort was located largely in the South, which for its own special and peculiar reasons did not link with northern labor markets until the First World War. The New England antebellum industrialization drew on French Canada in addition to female labor from its own farms. The critical time for labor supply to northern industries, construction projects, and cities came between 1880 and 1910, which was indeed a period when the northern farm population was still growing at a higher rate than could be easily absorbed. A movement off the farm was occurring, by a chain of short migratory hops, through small rural towns and county seats to medium-sized cities and thence to the large cities of which Dreiser wrote. In the absence of a supplementary pool of manual and craft labor, American industrialization would have used these rural migrants, but only at the point at which conditions in agriculture had become so poor and overcrowded as to have made the movement here, as in Europe, an attractive one. Industrialization would perforce have slowed and yielded a lower growth rate for the American per capita income.

The quantitative importance of the migrations from Europe is thus abundantly clear, though one cannot put the tape measure to it. In particular, one cannot know whether the growth of the native population would have been greater in the absence of the immigrant families, or whether they, as Francis Walker and John R. Commons claimed, simply replaced the native stock.[32] In fact, the immigrants into the Midwest cities appear to have moved into industries, mines, urban construction, and services at a socioeconomic level under the migrants from American farms, the latter utilizing their mechanical skills, elementary education, business acumen, and family connections in skilled labor and white-collar jobs and professions. For them the American dream worked well. Immigrants formed ethnic communities, performed manual or semi-skilled blue-collar laboring jobs, sent their children to public schools to learn English, attended Americanization classes, and aspired to better things. The separation from the Old Country was often a poignant one for the first generation of immigrants since for all of them, some spot in Europe represented home. Perhaps one quarter of the thirty millions returned there, either within a few years, frustrated and disappointed, or comfortably off and ready to retire to the native village.[33] But theirs was the same hope that had drawn the "native" Americans West. So it was not surprising that they could be co-opted into starting at the bottom of the same ladder of ambition and worldly success.

The American civilization of 1870 to 1920 then played the same tunes as the antebellum society, but in a higher key, a faster tempo, and with a stronger and potentially discordant bass. The situation in the North was not generally different from that in the South. In both regions, the native white Anglo-Saxon Protestant class – yeomen, gentry, merchants, small manufacturers – moving upward in its income growth and territorial ex-

---

[32]Francis A. Walker, *Discussions in Economics and Statistics,* 2 vols. (New York: Henry Holt, 1899), Vol. 2, 417–451; John R. Commons, *Races and Immigrants in America* (New York: Macmillan, 1907), Ch. 9, 198–201.

[33]According to *Historical Statistics of the United States,* approximately thirty million immigrants entered the United States between 1860 and 1900. Official figures for emigration begin only in 1908, but using figures given in M. Simon, "The United States Balance of Payments, 1861–1900," in National Bureau of Economic Research report, *Trends in the American Economy in the Nineteenth Century,* Table 23, 690, and making some rough estimates for the period 1900–7, a figure of approximately eight million emigrants can be derived for the period 1860–1920, i.e., roughly one-quarter of the total number of immigrants for the period.

pansion had seen inserted into the lower quarter of its society a new class of free citizens. In the South this class was black and had formerly been securely locked in slavery, and this gave the South's social structure a peculiarly un-American rigidity and severity. Even here emancipation brought ideas of social liberty, of landowning, schooling, and market bargaining. In the North the dominant WASP culture split. For the older rural nativist element on depressed and overextended margins of the new agrarian economy, the American dream had been shattered as free land gave out and farms became inextricably tangled in the commercial web of railroads, grain speculators, mortgages, and banks. The idealism of the Populists was radical and Jeffersonian at its extreme; some thought to supplant capitalism by state ownership or forms of cooperative enterprise. But in the main the Populist ideal was fixated on the antebellum model of the small-scale enterprise operating under a generous currency system in markets where all could receive their just deserts, with a high degree of freedom, homogeneity, and equality among its citizens. Such a movement did not look kindly either on imperialism or on immigrant urban labor. Its idealism was to peter out in the 1920s in the tragicomic farce of isolationism – and Prohibition.

The main force of the WASP society after 1870 was expended not in Populism, but in organizing the agrarian and industrial expansion. This was the high tide of the Republican Party, both "old guard" and "progressive." In the Northeast the ancient seats of Protestant learning were transformed like the ecclesiastical foundations of England into training grounds of an elite leadership. The humanities, science, sports, and the law were all taught to prepare young men to carry forward American democracy. In the cities where immigrants had clustered around Democratic bosses of their own national origin, the Progressive Republican reformers came to the fore on platforms of honesty and professionalism in government. Competition, the life of trade, was, to be sure, to be preserved; it was part of Theodore Roosevelt's ideal of the "strenuous life." But order, reason, and efficiency, too, were to prevail; the difference between the "old guard" Republicans and the Progressives lay in the issue of whether that order should be imposed by eastern bankers like Morgan and midwestern industrialists like Rockefeller or Hanna or by lawyers, judges, and public regulatory commissions. And when this split between Republicans was wide enough to let in a Democratic president, Woodrow Wilson, no essential difference in the ethos could be perceived. Wilson was, if anything, the WASP par excellence, so much so that it is almost amusing for an American to hear J. M. Keynes – naive for once – express his astonishment at discovering this fact. "The President," he wrote, "was like a Nonconformist minister, perhaps a Presbyterian. His thought and his temperament were essentially theological not intellectual, with all the strength and the weakness of that manner of thought, feeling, and expression."[34]

The assimilation of the immigrants occurred because, indeed, white Anglo-Saxon Protestant capitalism was an evangelical secular religion. The Protestant missions in Asia and Africa were a significant part of the world scene. Its missionaries went to Hawaii and brought those islands eventually into the Union. In Japan they founded a Christian sect. Through men like Henry R. Luce the influence of its evangelism shaped American policy toward China far beyond World War II.[35] Within America its doctrines, its virtues, its values were joined to national pride. Its governmental ideal was still that of the city-state, the republic of educated citizens, and to this end it erected the vast edifice of the public school system, open to all, indeed, compulsory for all. Here, first, English would be taught, together with hygiene, American history, and "civics." Homemaking and the manual arts were for those who could not go further; typing and commercial skills for young women of the lower middle class. The "academic" subjects – languages, literature, science – were for those who would go on to college. The great state universities were the crown of the system, along with the colleges of the agricultural and mechanical arts. No formal or artificial barriers of race, ethnic origin, or color were raised in the public school system in the North and the West. The children of immigrants were held back only by income level, their own sense of inadequacy, and social snobbery. These were powerful barriers to full equality, but the theory of the law and much of its practice did not support them.

Thus was the American dream, the dream of the liberal city-state, of the republic of citizens, with inequalities in all respects except the opportunity to overcome inequality, transposed from the early Republic to the industrial society of the twentieth century. Since 1930 the industrial economy has no longer seemed so strong, and since 1960 the absorption of the newest immigrants – blacks from southern agriculture and Caribbean and Asian peoples – has been far from complete. The internal successes of American society between 1940 and 1970, in the expansion of the economy and the integration of the disparate population, gave strength, purpose, and an excessively self-righteous compassion to American policy and attitudes toward Europe and the world. Yet despite expansion, the spacious, self-contained, self-confident world as it was for Americans before 1930 has not returned.

American society, American culture has been built up through the

[34]J. M. Keynes, *The Economic Consequences of the Peace* (New York: Harcourt, Brace, and Howe, 1920), 42.
[35]T. H. White, *A Personal Adventure* (New York: Harper & Row, 1978), 126–8, 205–211.

historical experience of succeeding generations of Europeans transplanted in a new environment, as the technology and capitalist organization unfolded, to exploit its material opportunities. The essays in the
three parts of this book show some of the inter-related episodes in that
national experience. After 1930, and most patently after 1950, American society has been obliged, for the sake of its own existence, to give
back to Europe and to a wider world something of what it had absorbed
and transformed in its century of continental development. The past six
decades in its history have been spectacular, troubled, uneasy, violent,
and confused. In the welter of the present and recent past, one may gain
a new view of the unique features of the more distant past – its strengths
and its shallowness – and from that view in turn, gain some measure of
perspective on what is occurring under one's eyes. The essays in Part V
endeavor in a limited way to begin that effort. It is an effort in which the
reader is invited to join.

PART II

The South in slavery and in freedom

2

The slave plantation in American agriculture

Continental North America has offered a generally hostile environment to the large landed estate. Outside the South, farms of large scale have had to compete with industry and trade for labor and investment funds and with the irrationally cheap labor of the small farmer for land and markets. Rarely in any branch of agriculture have the economies to scale of enterprise been sufficient to tip the advantage. In stock raising during the early settlement of the Corn Belt and in the bonanza wheat farms of the Red River Valley of the North during the 1870s and 1880s, the large holding met with transient success. In both cases its advantage rested on prior access to improved stock or mechanized techniques, which soon spread to the smaller enterprises. Only in the cattle and sheep ranches of the arid regions, beyond the reach of the field crops, and on Western truck farms holding a migratory labor force outside industrial labor markets has the large enterprise employing wage labor persisted. Even where debt and tenancy have interlaced the net of family-sized holdings, they have not – except in the South – involved significant concentrations of control. In this hostile environment the plantations formed before the Revolution could endure and spread across the South in competition with the free family farm only through access to a source of non-wage labor. Slavery built a hothouse for the plantation system that the end of slavery did not wholly shatter. Only in recent decades has mechanization in cotton farming produced the large farm with wage labor in Mississippi and beyond.

I

PLANTATION INVESTMENT

The "original accumulation" for the southern plantations was furnished in part by the first adventurers – by the members of the Virginia Com-

33

pany of London, by the Carolina proprietors. But plantation, in terms of an entire colony (to which the word was first applied), was not a manageable unit of agricultural production. The nuclei of plantations, as farming enterprises, were not the enormous grants, even where, as in the case of Lord Fairfax in the Northern Neck of Virginia and Lord Granville in North Carolina, these grants were held privately up to the Revolution. The efforts of the Carolina proprietors to establish a system of tenancy on their domains, organized according to John Locke's *Grand Model,* were no more successful than the charitable efforts of the Georgia trustees to limit holdings to five hundred acres entailed.[1] The quitrents persisted into the second half of the eighteenth century but only as a troublesome obstruction to the free market in land.

The bulk of plantation investment in Virginia came first from the importers of indentured servants under the headright system. In South Carolina the proprietors furnished supplies, but many of its early plantations were founded by planters from the West Indies. Wertenbaker has shown that for Virginia, the seventeenth-century investment did not result in an extremely concentrated pattern of land ownership.[2] Small farms were implicit in the headright system, for those individuals who paid their own passage and sometimes for the indentured servant upon gaining his freedom. But inequality in landholding and in access to non-family labor was sufficiently great to establish the private plantation as rival to the small farm. Given continued opportunity for profitable farming, the reinvestment of plantation profits in expansion was sufficient to perpetuate the system. Like the early American textile mills, the plantations were the source of capital for their own expansion as, to supply the raw material for those textile mills, they reproduced themselves westward into Georgia, Alabama, and after 1830 into Mississippi and Louisiana.

Unlike mills, the plantations not only financed, but physically produced much of the capital required in expansion. Where, as in Georgia, small farms preceded the plantations, land costs were somewhat higher, but risk was appreciably less than in wholly new lands. The import of labor, whether indentured servants in the seventeenth century or slaves in the eighteenth, cost money, but after the initial imports, the purchase of slaves simply transferred money from one planter to another. Like slaves, most items of farm capital – fences, outbuildings, roads, land improvements, livestock herds, even many implements – were plantation products. It was necessary to allocate labor to these uses, as the plantation

[1] Marshall Harris, *Origin of the Land Tenure System of the United States* (Ames: The Iowa State College Press, 1953), 133–138.
[2] Thomas Wertenbaker, *The Planters of Colonial Virginia* (Princeton: Princeton University Press, 1922), republished in Wertenbaker, *The Shaping of Colonial Virginia* (New York: Russell and Russell, 1958), Chs. 3, 4, 8, and Appendix.

economy expanded, but it was in these uses that the labor was accustomed to work. The "machine tools" for farm capital formation were agricultural laborers, and they continued to create farm capital incidentally to their work in current production.

The distribution of holdings by size, derived both from the initial degree of concentration and from differences in profits arising from different soils, ability, and luck, was thus confirmed and extended by reinvestment. To that unimaginative and ignorant inertia that causes profits to be reinvested in the lines from which they spring even in moderately "rational" environments was added the prestige attached to the ownership of land and slaves in a plantation society. Here the scale of the system as a whole was the determining fact. When the plantation became a social system, a self-reinforcing web of values – in both the economic and the ethical sense of the word – confined both plantation profits and plantation ways of thought.

GROWTH OF THE LABOR FORCE

If, as is suggested below, the plantations had no important economies in organization or in the use of capital-intensive methods sufficient to permit them to stand against the small farmers' cheap family labor, then their extension absolutely required the increase in their unfree labor force. The unsuitability of the Indians for field work and the limited supply of indentured servants (a force that in any case did not naturally replace itself) left Negro slaves as the only important source of supply of plantation labor. But the natural increase of the slave population intruded an independent dynamic element which, like profits, produced in the plantation economy both a pressure and an ability to expand. The natural increase of the Negro population in the South between the first Census and 1860 was about as rapid as that of the white population. The reasons for this remarkable fact, so dissimilar to the behavior of slave populations in most other historical instances, are deeply hidden. The probable existence of a domestic slave trade was implied long ago in Von Halle's examination of relative rates of population growth in the border and cotton states.[3] But fertility and mortality rates, and regional and racial differentials in them, can never be fully uncovered. From general impressions one may suggest several elements favoring increase of slave numbers: the relatively mild conditions of slavery, with its semblance of fam-

---

[3] W. E. H. Von Halle, *Baumwollproduction and Pflanzungwirtschaft in den nordamerikanischen Südstaaten*, vol. 1 (Leipzig: Duncker and Humboldt, 1897). See especially Book 3, Ch. 5, Secs. 4 and 5, 128–155, and Ch. 7, 184–189, where the demographic data by state are examined. The book is Volume 15 in the series, *Staats- und sozialwissenschaftliche Forschungen*, edited by Gustav von Schmoller.

ily life on the tobacco and cotton plantations in the border and Atlantic coastal states and the abundant supplies of homely plantation food, often grown by the slave on an individually tilled patch of ground. The gradual but continuous expansion in the opportunities for farming in new regions must also have encouraged the growth. A lesser opportunity might have dimmed the planters' impersonal zeal for slave procreation. A more immediate opportunity in field crop production might have caused slaves to be overworked, to the neglect of the generation and care of a crop of new labor that matured slowly. But the opportunity for the master of young slaves in the East was not at the home plantation, but in a new and distant location to the West. In this sense, the moderate exhaustion of old soils for cotton and tobacco may have saved slavery by sparing mothers and children from excessive field labor in the eastern and border states.

DEMAND AND THE PRODUCTION FUNCTION

The natural increase in capital and the labor force exercised a "push" on the plantation system to expand, while the availability of fresh land permitted it continuously to shift location. At the same time a pull was exercised by the continuous growth in demand for a commercial crop. Had not tobacco proved marketable from Virginia after 1615, rice from Carolina after 1695 and from Georgia a few decades later, sugar from Louisiana after 1795, and finally cotton from the whole region southwest of Virginia, the plantations would have been wholly limited to growing the staple grains and livestock. Throughout this whole period, the commercial market for staple foods was growing less rapidly than the market for exotic foods and textiles. Peasants everywhere continued to supply their own basic food needs long after they had acquired a taste for sugar and had abandoned growing and spinning their own fibers. And to supply the market for foods to industrial populations would have placed the tropical plantations in competition with peasant producers of more temperate climates. It is not quite correct, perhaps, to say that cotton "saved" the plantation system at the end of the eighteenth century; granted a growth in the slave population and a channeling of reinvested profits, the plantations, like the small farms, might have moved West. But if they had survived, their character would have been quite different. From semi-commercial enterprises, they would have been transformed wholly into examples of the patriarchal (or more likely, matriarchal) *oikos* of the ancient world.

But it was not necessary, as is sometimes claimed, that the plantation's commercial crops be peculiarly suited to large farms or slave labor. Under nineteenth-century techniques, cotton and tobacco were as well suited to family labor as dairying and many food crops. They required steady labor for a large part of the year and the auxiliary labor that women and children could furnish in cultivation and harvesting. The routine character of the work, if well suited to slaves, offered little opportunity for a division of labor possible in a large productive unit. Except for the rice and sugar mills and the cotton gin, nineteenth-century techniques required no single piece of equipment larger than the mule—plow combination of the small farm. And like any other piece of milling machinery, a cotton gin could be operated centrally and shared by several producers. The consolidation of several small farms in one plantation made for some economy in management, but slaves required overseers, and the travel time from quarters to field increased with the size of estate. Not superior physical efficiency, but the power of a larger capital, expanding in fixed channels, and exploiting labor at a lower level of existence, permitted the plantation to take the best land and most of the cotton market from the family-sized farm.

II

Unlike Voltaire's God, the southern plantation, had it not existed, would not have had to be invented. Into the cotton-using world at large, it introduced from Africa a supply of labor that otherwise would have been left in peace. That labor was forced to live at a standard below what would have induced free immigrants to grow cotton on this land. But agricultural labor was largely fed, housed, warmed, partly clothed, and reproduced by agricultural labor; it was of little direct concern to cotton consumers how cotton producers lived among themselves. What was important immediately was the price of cotton and the demand for money, credit, and commodities that sales by the cotton producers would generate. The data are inadequate to compare the alternative effects of plantations and small farms in full complexity, but some speculation on the basis of what is known may indicate the probable result of such a comparison.

DEMAND FOR IMPORTS:
PLANTATIONS VERSUS FREE FARM

Assuming similar efficiency in production, the slave plantations could, indeed, sell cotton more cheaply than free family farms. Like family farms, however, they had the alternative of turning their labor force to other uses – to the tasks of farm capital formation or to replacing purchased commodities by home products. In comparing the effects of the two systems on the world economy, the crucial element is the demand pattern of those who made the choices, for themselves and their labor force, between labor and idleness, between labor for home consumption and labor for the market, and among the alternative uses of the money income earned through market production. In all this, we have only scattered information about what the plantations actually did, and we have yet to explore all that is at our disposal. We know less about what the small farmers did, and we know nothing, of course, of how they would have behaved had they dominated cotton production.

On the question of plantation self-sufficiency in food, investigation of the original returns of the 1850 and 1860 Censuses is able to shed some light. In 1860 some large Louisiana sugar plantations and a few of the Mississippi and Louisiana cotton plantations were so specialized that they neglected corn and hogs; this was probably not true of smaller estates nor of even the largest plantations in Georgia. True, the mania for cotton produced food imports, even from distant sources, when it first broke out on new lands, but outside areas immediately adjacent to the Mississippi River, the importance of these has probably been exaggerated by economists hungry for illustrations of triangular regional trade. For industrial products, our knowledge of plantation activity depends upon the extant sample of plantation records and those other sources that are often courteously termed "literary." Carpentry and repairs could not be easily imported, and the older plantation region as a whole, if not every plantation individually, was furnished with slaves and free craftsmen. But the demand for shoes and cloth was very large, and factories could under-bid even slave labor in these occupations. Plantations dependent upon food purchases were surely dependent upon the purchase of industrial items, and large supplies of these were available only from England or the North.

The imported luxuries of plantation life – furniture, fine fabrics, trips to Paris – stood out sharply against their rude surroundings, but hunger for them hardly determined the rate of expansion of cotton production. The region's own imports of capital equipment – particularly rails and rolling stock in the 1840s and 1850s – had at least a modest significance in the regional balance of payments. More interesting, and perhaps more significant, is the possibility of a demand for cash to move crops and finance land and slave purchases within the South itself. Some of the revenues from cotton may have been saved and retained in the form of gold, currency, or bank balances in New York or London, to provide reserves for southern banks and directly to finance capital transactions and current trade.

Were plantations' demand patterns – for imports of cash and commodities – very different from those of small farms with free family labor? The luxury demand, for what it was worth, was stronger, and the capitalization of the labor force produced a minor element in the

demand for the means of finance. On the other hand, land would probably have turned over more rapidly as it was the more finely divided
among holders. The small farm might have been more nearly self-
sufficient in food and perhaps, as in the southern highlands, in cloth.
The plantation industrial laborers would have been absent from farms;
the independent craftsmen in town might have been more numerous.
These latter in turn might have provided a stronger nucleus for a native
manufacturing industry – but it is idle to speculate further. Within the
range of vision, it is not clear that striking differences in demand patterns for imports would have existed under the small farm system.
Through a similar physical efficiency in production and similar regional
demand patterns, plantation and small farm may be imagined to have
had similar effects on cotton supplies and on the opportunity for expansion in the growing industrial regions of Europe and the northeastern
states.

EFFECTS ON INDUSTRIAL REGIONS

What, then, were those effects? The significance of cheap cotton is obvious. But the significance of the complex demand pattern of the cotton
producers is more obscure. The industrializing regions at this time had
two major needs: sufficiently large markets to permit economies of scale
in transport and urban services, and sufficient saving to permit the use of
resources in building canals, rail lines, cities, plants, and equipment. No
doubt the limits of permissible variation in the proportion of consumption and savings were rather wide; agricultural regions in the nineteenth
century furnished both. The stimulating effect of a rising market can
hardly be missed, but the significance of agricultural saving – not balanced by real investment in agriculture – is more subtle. It permitted an
accumulation of money and credit in agriculture and so, in effect, permitted investment where credit was more expansible. Had cotton planters
and wheat growers demanded back in textiles all that they sold in cotton
and food, the textile industry might have surged ahead even further, but
only at the expense of the capital goods sectors of the developing areas.
These effects can probably never be measured with data at hand, but their
importance and complexity should not for that reason be minimized.

In all this, the role of the plantation regions of the world economy was
not essentially different from that of the grain- and meat-producing regions, which were settled with free labor in family farms. Within the
agricultural regions themselves, the plantation system made an enormous
difference, both in the conditions of life and, it would appear today, in the
prospects for development of indigenous industry. The alliance of a free
labor force and industrial growth, which hangs so much in doubt today,

may indeed have been intimate and necessary under nineteenth-century capitalism. If so, then the plantation system appears even more clearly as a tragic aberration from the main course of Western development.

* * * * *

The earth hath bubbles as the water has,
And these are of them . . .

But the earth's bubbles do not break easily. When they explode, they leave a stain which a hundred years cannot wholly erase. Fifty years after 1860, when the Census first recognized the fact of tenant plantations, it found in the cotton counties of the South 39,073 plantations of five or more contiguous farms apiece. The average was ten tenant farms on a plantation, and about one third of the improved land in the cotton South was thus engrossed.

3

Slavery and southern economic development: an hypothesis and some evidence

Suppose that in 1789 the slaves had been freed, given land warrants for forty acres and credit for a mule or, more likely, an ox. Some might have taken up the land – perhaps in Ohio or Tennessee – and farmed it; others, like many of the Revolutionary soldiers, might have found ways of selling the warrants and have become wage laborers on farms or in the few coastal towns near their point of emancipation. Some perhaps would have taken up a trade or used their small capital to open a store. Such free laborers and minuscule capitalists would have infiltrated the economic streams of their white fellow countrymen. It is possible that their rate of population growth would have been the same as it was under slavery before 1860 since even then it was roughly that of the free population. And no doubt color prejudice would have remained to limit the occupations and social situations among the white population to which black men would have been admitted. No doubt they would have remained largely restricted to manual labor or to a few trades and professions where chance or some special circumstance favored them.

Under such a labor market it is possible to suppose that three effects might have been felt on the course of southern development. First, migration flows would have been different in rate, direction, and composition. Under slavery, Negroes' mobility was that of the master, and it is possible that under freedom they would not have moved into the Southwest as rapidly as they did under slavery. In that case they would have piled up in the Southeast, but surely some migration to the West and even perhaps to the cities of the Northeast might have occurred. Looking beyond 1860, one might even suppose that the migration to northern cities which came in fact sixty years after emancipation might have begun in the 1850s and partially supplanted the migrations of European rural labor after 1880. The ability of southern farmers to hire Negro labor to work in cotton would have

Published in *Agricultural History*, Vol. 44, No. 1 (January 1970): 115–125.

depended on the industrial wage rate. The most likely outcome of the various forces and pressures would have been the development of cotton farms in the Southwest on both sides of the Mississippi on the same scale, with respect to capital investment, labor force, and ownership, as that which prevailed in mixed farming in the Midwest. If the technological bottleneck in cotton picking had not been broken, the crop's greater labor requirement would have made the farms smaller in area than those in the North, and a more varied husbandry might have developed as it did on corn–livestock farms. Greater mobility of labor should have raised the incomes earned per acre and possibly the total income earned from the sale of the cotton crop. But the immense power of the family enterprise to compete in a variety of climatic, technical, and market environments across northern Europe and North America – and to exist in symbiosis with plantations in many tropical environments – makes its extension in the cotton region very likely in the absence of the plantation owner's access to a privileged source of labor that could be exploited even more cheaply than the farmer could exploit the labor of wife and children.

A second effect of freedom, then – or rather of the changed income stream produced by a free labor market – would have been a changed income distribution in southern rural areas. The extent of this change depends on the extent of exploitation of labor, reducing slave workers' incomes below what they would have been for hired rural or industrial laborers or for small farmers on tenant or mortgaged farms. In making a surmise on this question, it is not quite fair to look simply at the picture after the Civil War. By 1865 the immobilities produced by extensive and long-continued slavery left Negroes prey to exploitation by landowners, and the violence with which their nominal freedom had been won had increased the fears and prejudices of the master race. Price trends too were unfavorable to small farmers in the Reconstruction period. Even against such odds, the economic status of Negro farm labor probably improved in the border states and in parts of the Southeast. The most revealing comparison is with income distribution in the developing North-west in the antebellum decades. The hypothesis of this paper simply is that the southern and northern streams of farm income were substantially different in their distribution, the southern stream being sharply divided between providing subsistence for the slaves and high incomes for the planters. This neglects the southern yeoman who, however, remained substantially outside the market economy for reasons which are suggested below. Compared to the northern income distribution from the sale of exportable crops, and so compared to what might have prevailed in the South in the absence of slavery, the actual southern agricultural income distribution was – I suggest – characterized by a great gap at the middle levels.

42

Slavery and southern economic development

A third consequence of free labor, had the southern economy enjoyed its blessings, follows from the altered income distribution that would have arisen. The income distribution actually present combined with the plantation type of economic organization to produce in the South a very peculiar structure of demand. It is not quite to the point to say, as Eugene Genovese has done,[1] that the South suffered from a weak market for manufactures in general. The structure of demand produced in fact a very large mass market for simple items of plantation consumption – notably coarse textiles, shoes, and very simple implements. But in the early nineteenth century, these were either items in which a plantation could be self-sufficient (as in the simpler forms of food processing and carpentry) or items which became subject to factory methods on a large scale quite early in the period. At the other end of the spectrum, the income distribution produced the demand for many consumer goods of high quality which required very high degrees of skill and the prestige of foreign workmanship.

What was missing from the southern market was the demand for manufactures for which the technology permitted production on a modest local scale, in small shops scattered across the countryside. This is just the sort of demand which was present in the North – first in New England and the Middle Colonies, then in the Old Northwest – and the sort of demand that would have been present in the South under a different form of agricultural organization and system of labor. But the lack of demand meant a lack of supply, even had capital, labor, and skills been – as perhaps they would have been – ready to move into southern rural areas. It meant a lack of supply of small skills, whose products could be sold on a commercial basis, in carpentry and ironworking, tailoring, equipment-making, and construction. And it meant a lack of demand for the kinds of tangible and intangible capital that went to equip such trades and to keep a local commerce going: schooling, lawyering, bookkeeping, banking, the making of simple machinery that sprang up so readily in Ohio and Illinois in these decades.

If then we can imagine a different income distribution from the sale of the export crop, and thence a different composition of local demand in the South, and thence a growth of village crafts and local commercial institu-

[1]Eugene D. Genovese, *The Political Economy of Slavery* (New York: Vintage Books/Random House, 1967), 167–173. Genovese emphasizes low incomes arising from a low productivity of slave labor, but comparison of the north-central states even with the old cotton states, much less with the south-central states, does not show this (see Table 1). His rich, detailed, and judicious treatment needs only the economist's specific concern with income *distribution* to yield the argument advanced here. His generous but well-qualified comments on the paper show his recognition of the point. *Agricultural History,* Vol. 44 (January 1970): 143–145.

tions and life, then a path of development begins to form. Such a degree of rural industrialization – one cannot yet call it urbanization – would then react back on agriculture to remove the curse of self-sufficiency from the farms outside the cotton economy itself, to provide local markets for food crops, and to commercialize the other sectors of small-scale agriculture. And it is hard to believe that such a developing industrial society would not have reacted back on the productivity of labor in agricultural operations. It is of course possible that the cotton picker still would not have been developed until it could be powered by a gasoline engine. But some of the contrivances similar to those that lightened the toil on the corn–hog farms of the Midwest would surely have been introduced. Nothing so much helps in the solving of an industrial technological problem as the proximity of craftsmen and inventors to the areas where the problem exists.

Finally, more perfect labor and capital markets across the South could not but have permitted the establishment locally of textile mills as this technology became adapted and elaborated after 1790. There was no locational reason why New England should have supplied southern textile markets except for its proximity to capital, enterprise, and a reasonably adaptable labor force. But in the early nineteenth century, textiles were the lifeblood of industrial development – or at least the most potent indicator of a healthy industrial opportunity. In the presence of the things which made factory textile production possible, the supplying and servicing industries could cluster. This much cannot be said for development after 1870, when coal and iron became important bases of industrial location. The South, in short, could not have rivaled the northeastern Midwest after 1860, but she might easily, by any logic of natural advantage, have rivaled New England before that date, and that would have been enough for any antebellum southerner.

A great deal is hung in this argument on the consequences of slavery,[2] and the assumption is implicit that the absence of slavery would have freed the labor market and so altered the income distribution. An alternative is possible, of course: Once freed, the Negroes could have in effect sold themselves back into slavery – wage slavery or the peonage of tenancy and debt. Had they been contented with slavery, this is no doubt what they would have done. And indeed, since these are all matters of

[2]Stanley Engerman's comments in *Agricultural History*, Vol. 44 (January 1970): 137–142, call for the framing and testing of formal hypotheses and the production of numerous comparative studies. His point that sudden freedom, hypothetically in 1790, or actually in 1865, did not make the slaves into free Midwest yeomen is, of course, unexceptionable. Both Genovese's and Engerman's critiques make many valuable criticisms and should be read in conjunction with the paper as published here.

degree, this is what was done to far too great an extent after 1865. Certainly by then cotton had put so strong a stamp on the southern economic society that a technical alteration in the legal status of a part of the labor force so clearly distinguishable and susceptible to prejudice and pressure had all too small an effect in producing real freedom. Perhaps indeed the labor force was more immobilized in the 1870s and 1880s by ignorance, fear, and indolence than it had been when it had followed a master's orders. But history is not the record of immutable human conditions; it is the record of their growth and change, the record in this case of a rut in which the wheel spun deeper and deeper until it could not be dislodged. Perhaps even by 1789 the pattern was too hard-set, and if so, then our hypothetical history would have to go back, perhaps as far as 1619, to find the crossroads at which history took this tragic turn.

APPENDIX

This appendix consists of three tables, based on published census data and on estimates of income for 1860. Its purpose is not, of course, to "prove" the hypotheses of the paper, but to add to their plausibility by showing that they are not inconsistent with some of the available data.

Tables 1 and 2, taken together, are an effort to show how the income distribution deriving from slavery weakened the middle range of the southern income distribution, i.e., the incomes of free, non-slaveholding farmers scattered over the countryside. Table 1 presents regional per capita income estimates prepared by Stanley Engerman using Easterlin's basic data. As Engerman points out in the paper in which these data are

Table 1. *Per capita income by region, 1840 and 1860 (in 1860 prices)*

	Total population		Percent growth	Free population	
	1840	1860		1840	1860
National Average	$ 96	$128	33%	$109	$144
North:	109	141	29	110	142
Northeast	129	181	40	130	183
North-central	65	89	37	66	90
South:	74	103	39	105	150
South Atlantic	66	84	28	96	124
Eastern south-central	69	89	29	92	124
Western south-central	151	184	22	238	274

Source: Stanley Engerman, "The Effects of Slavery upon the Southern Economy: A Review of the Recent Debate," *Explorations in Entrepreneurial History* (Winter 1967): 87, based on estimates by Richard A. Easterlin.

presented, the growth rate in the South as a whole is markedly higher than that in the North. Broken down by subregion, however, it appears that the southern subregions grow at markedly slower rates than their northern counterparts. The westward movement, so pronounced in the 1850s, occurred from the Southeast into a southwestern region of very high per capita income, while the reverse was true in the movement from the Northeast into the north-central states beyond the Ohio River.

What such figures mean, if anything, about the motives of westward movement in the two sections need not be considered here. The *statistical* result of the higher weighting of the western regions in 1860 is to raise the growth rate of the southern section above that of any of its constituent regions and to depress the northern growth rate similarly. The difference in *level* in the two regions is also worthy of observation. The farming regions east of the Mississippi – in both North and South – have about the same level of income per capita of total population, but by 1840 the South Atlantic region stands at a level only one-half that of the Northeast – a differential that does not narrow until after 1920. Since farm incomes in the Northeast are certainly no higher than in the Midwest, the advantage of the Northeast must be in its manufacture, trade, and commerce. Quite evidently, these figures – if they have any meaning – show that the failure of the Southeast to experience the type of industrialization that New England did caused it to fall behind. Moreover, since the *level* of its farm income per capita appears to be at least as high as that in the North, the deficiency – if from the side of demand – must have lain in the distribution rather than in the average level of that income.

Table 2 provides a first, very rough approximation of the southern income distribution among three classes: slaveholders, slaves, and free non-slaveholders, under the following assumptions:

(1) The same average per capita income is earned in the slaveholding and non-slaveholding sectors of the South.

(2) Of the income estimate for the South, slaves receive \$30 a year, i.e., a generous estimate of their maintenance cost. The remainder of the average per capita income earned by slaves plus one per capita income for the slaveholder (e.g., for the South Atlantic region = $[(84 - 30) \times (39.0/3.6) + 841])$ is allotted to the slaveholders.

(3) Incomes in the north-central region are distributed equally at the regional per capita average.

The last columns of Table 2 show that the South's wide area produces a market geographically somewhat thinner than the north-central region. When, in addition, the slave and slaveholder sectors are removed, the remaining demand is half as dense in the region as in the northern agricultural states. If then the slaves were furnished coarse and uniform goods (clothes and shoes) from New England and English factories, and the

46

Table 2. *Data on income distribution and density in 1860*

	Area 10³sq. miles	Population 10³	Slave owners	Other free	Slaves	Population Density per sq. mile	
						Total population	Free non-slaveholders
South Atlantic	267	4,490	3.6%	57.4%	39.0%	16.2	9.7
East south-central	188	4,021	3.5	62.5	34.0	21.4	13.4
North-central (except Dakota)	408	9,193				22.5	22.5

	Per capita income				Income density per sq. mile	
	Total population	Slave-holders	Slaves	Free non-slaveholders	Total population	Free non-slaveholders
South Atlantic	$84	$674	$30	$84	$1,412	$825
East south-central	88	648	30	88	1,882	1,170
South Atlantic + east south-central	86		30	86	1,608	985
North-central	89			89	2,000	2,000

Source: Area, population, and population distribution from the 1860 Census. Income per capita of total population from Engerman (see Table 1), divided among the three income classes, as described in the text.

slaveowners spent their incomes on goods from urban workshops or on imports, the market for local, small-scale manufactures was markedly reduced by slavery.

The thesis of this paper is that it was just this middle-income market which, under the production conditions then prevailing, could be supplied by local manufacture – a stage removed from the household but not yet, except in a few products, concentrated in large-scale establishments in large urban centers. Such medium-scale manufacture may not have been much more productive than commercial agriculture and certainly had not yet clearly in the north-central states raised incomes up to the northeastern level. It is an open question whether agricultural incomes in the north-central states were slightly lower than in the South while the greater importance of local manufactures raised the average up to the southern level. The importance of such local manufacture lay not in its immediate effects on income, but, it is hypothesized here, on the "learning effects" – the development of skills, tastes, and the net of business

47

Table 3. *Number of firms and value of product per 100,000 population in 1860 for industries, North and South, divided into scale categories*

	Firms per 100,000 population		Annual value of product per 100,000 population	
	North	South	North	South
Small-scale	20.7	53.95	32,580	364,245
Medium-scale	345.1	103.1	3,229,430	494,542
Large-scale	16.55	14.45	848,887	479,465
Total	382.15	171.5	4,110,897	1,338,252

Source: See text.

institutions – a business culture which, when technology changed and incomes rose, could generate inland urban centers and large-scale industry and distribution.

In Table 3, an effort is made to compare the scale and volume of manufacture in the north-central states and in the South. The data used are the statistics of the average size of firm in industries, by state, shown in the published tables of the *1860 Census of Manufactures*. No use is made in this table of the census manuscripts, which lie behind the published census tables and are available for further research. The states chosen were Ohio, Indiana, Michigan, Wisconsin, and Illinois for the North; and Georgia, Alabama, Mississippi, and South Carolina for the South. The measure used is the number of reporting firms and the annual value of product in an industry per 100,000 total population in the region. The industries were divided into small-scale, medium-scale, and large-scale according to the size of employment and capital in their average firm as follows:

Employment
1–2 persons employed = small scale.
3–10 persons employed = medium scale.
More than 10 persons employed = large scale.

Capital
0–$999 capital invested = small scale.
$1,000–$10,000 capital invested = medium scale.
More than $10,000 invested = large scale.

If an industry fell into the small-scale category for both employment and capital, it was regarded as a small-scale industry. Likewise for industries whose employment and capital averages both fell in the middle- or the large-scale range. For those industries where employment and capital fell into different ranges, the industry was listed as being in the smaller of the two ranges.

Not many industries, however, fell in this latter category. Table 3 shows the industries in which the average firm in the North or the South, or in both regions, fell into these size classes, with the number of firms and value of product per 100,000 population in the region. The absolute advantage in population of the northern states is thus eliminated, although the fact that these northern states by 1860 had a larger and denser population than the South as a whole (Table 2) is not without significance.

In some careful and valuable work,[3] Fred Bateman and Thomas Weiss have carried this study below the industry level to the actual distributions of firms through samples drawn from the manuscript census of manufactures for 1860. Such an examination seems to show a much narrower gap between West and South at the middle levels, though the overall inferiority of the South in number of manufacturing firms and capital per capita is confirmed. They point out, however, that an examination of industries shows the western states had a wider variety of industries in which middle-sized firms were comparatively more important.

Thus the "thesis" of this article has been seriously modified by the Bateman–Weiss research in the manuscript census. Their point about the importance of variety in a region's industry composition as affecting its "business culture" is one that I would heartily endorse. It should be pointed out, too, that not only variety but *absolute density*, as well as distribution among small, medium, and large firms, is of major significance. The total number of firms per 100,000 population, by size categories according to an output definition of size, stood as follows:

	Small	Medium	Large	Total
a. East	64.2	331.7	186.8	582.7
b. West	61.0	251.7	68.6	381.3
c. South	45.1	156.6	50.6	252.3

Bateman and Weiss, *Journal of Economic History*, 35 (March 1975): 193.

Averaging the Northeast and Northwest (a and b above) together, the northern density was nearly twice that of the South, and in absolute density, the middle-sized firms, which constituted by far the largest share

[3] Fred Bateman and Thomas Weiss, "Comparative Regional Development in Ante-bellum Manufacturing," *Journal of Economic History*, 35 (1975): 194. These findings are repeated in their book, *A Deplorable Scarcity: The Failure of Industrialization in the Slave Economy* (Chapel Hill: University of North Carolina Press, 1981), Ch. 3.

of business units, were at that same relative level compared to the South. Moreover, it must be remembered that the middle term in any class-ordered distribtion has fixed limits; it cannot include firms stretched far distances out along the tails. While the infinitely small firm is not a meaningful category, the analysis must reckon with the average sizes of the firms within the classes in comparing the two regions. Bateman and Weiss do a bit of this in the article cited above, but in this sort of thing, further research and yet more refined treatment are always possible.

4

Labor productivity in cotton farming: a problem of research

Song made in lieu of many ornaments
With which my love should duly have been dect,
Which, cutting off through hasty accidents,
Ye would not stay your due time to expect.
— Edmund Spenser, *Epithalamion*

To speak of my efforts to estimate labor productivity in cotton farming in the postbellum South as "ongoing research" is to do myself an undeserved courtesy. The basic data on labor times per acre, by operation and region, were collected between 1958 and 1961. They were placed in a standardized tabular form at the same time that a similar effort by myself, Judith Klein, and my students at the University of North Carolina was yielding roughly acceptable results for corn, wheat, dairy products, and the tasks of farm capital formation. The dissertation results of Fred Bateman and Martin Primack were published as articles in the *Journal of Economic History*[1] and my work jointly with Judith Klein was published

Published in *Agricultural History*, Vol. 53 (1979): 228–244. I am much indebted to Judith Klein and to David Sibley for much of the research work this paper reports. Mrs. Klein supervised the data collection by a group of graduate students and prepared the basic tables and the Period 2 (1905–14) estimates of yields. She also wrote a preliminary draft of the results. David Sibley gave a second wind to the effort by reviewing the work of the 1960s and bringing the computer and a more sophisticated econometrics into play. Regrettably, neither of these scholars was able to surmount the data deficiencies and other obstacles to a finished work, as reported here. The Ford Foundation and the National Science Foundation provided financial assistance for this project, along with those on the other major crops, at intervals between 1959 and 1977.

For a fuller discussion of the whole effort of which this was a part, see "Quantification in American Agricultural History: A Reexamination," in *Agricultural History*, Vol. 62 (1988): 113–132, reprinted below as Appendix B to this volume.

[1] Fred Bateman, "Improvement in American Dairy Farming, 1850–1910: A Quantitative Analysis," *Journal of Economic History*, Vol. 28 (June 1968): 255–273; Martin L. Primack, "Land Clearing in the Nineteenth Century," *Journal of*

in 1966 as an NBER conference paper.[2] At that time, the Ford Foundation was still sending its life-giving rays into university research, and hopes were high that a rather complete picture of the uses of labor time in American agriculture at the middle and the end of the nineteenth century might be developed as the climax of the research.

The 1960s, however, in their awkward fashion interposed several separate obstacles to the completion of the project. A change in institutional affiliation on my part produced, I found, a subtle shift in my interests and in the uses of my own labor time. The Ford Foundation suffered a shift, too, from university research and education, where it had had a strong and generally beneficial effect, to the wider world, sometimes called the "real world," where the law of increasing entropy appears to have operated on the diffused results of its energies. About this time, too, the sample of the 1860 manuscript census of cotton counties began to be employed by Robert Gallman and his students,[3] by Gavin Wright,[4] and by Robert Fogel and Stanley Engerman,[5] and the passion for studies of slavery, cliometric and noncliometric, began to shake the profession. The antebellum period engaged our fantasy, and the postbellum period suddenly seemed far away. Still more limiting to my efforts to measure labor productivity were the criticisms of the corn, wheat, and oats indices by Franklin Fisher and Peter Temin[6] and the admitted omission of capital from the calculations. After John Kendrick's work on total factor productivity,[7] mere labor productivity seemed suddenly old-fashioned, and the use of index numbers of man-hours instead of a production function of

Economic History, Vol. 22 (1962): 484–497; and Primack, "Farm Capital Formation as a Use of Farm Labor in the United States: 1850–1910," *Journal of Economic History,* Vol. 26 (1966): 348–362.

[2] William N. Parker and Judith L. V. Klein, "Productivity Growth in Grain Production in the United States, 1840–60 and 1900–10," in National Bureau of Economic Research Studies in Income and Wealth, *Output, Employment, and Productivity in the United States After 1800,* Vol. 30 (New York: Columbia University Press, 1966), 523–582.

[3] Most used in the present study was James Foust's Ph.D. dissertation, "The Yeoman Farmer and the Westward Expansion of Cotton Production" (University of North Carolina, 1967).

[4] Ph.D. dissertation by Gavin Wright, "The Economics of Cotton in the Antebellum South" (Yale University, 1969), Appendix 1, 20–27.

[5] Robert W. Fogel and Stanley Engerman, *Time on the Cross,* Vols. 1 and 2 (Boston: Little, Brown, 1961).

[6] Franklin Fisher and Peter Temin, "Regional Specialization and the Supply of Wheat in the United States, 1867–1914," *Review of Economic Statistics,* Vol. 52 (1970): 134–179. The study was, however, reprinted in Peter Temin, *New Economic History: Selected Readings* (Baltimore: Penguin Books, 1973).

[7] John W. Kendrick and Maude R. Peck, *Productivity Trends in the United States,* National Bureau of Economic Research, General Series 71 (Princeton, N.J.: Princeton University Press, 1961).

convenient, but mysterious, shape and properties seemed laughably archaic. And finally, as will appear below, there was the problem of the cotton data themselves. When assembled, after the expenditure of so much time, money, and eyestrain in collection, they seemed shockingly deficient in two important respects. Yields per acre in cotton were not available on a county basis before the great census of 1880 and for the new alluvial and western regions at the mid-nineteenth century the plantation documents, despite diligent search, were found to be void of usable data on labor costs to the fineness which our statistical tables required.

The body of this paper describes a recent attempt to clamber back up the slippery side of the pit in which two decades of disfavor and neglect had buried this effort and to extract whatever meaningful results may be obtained. One is impelled to do this, I think, by a kind of Yankee thrift in the use of money, data, and human energies. To the economist, sunk costs may indeed be sunk, offering no guide to resource allocation, present or future. But to the historian, sunk costs are the raw materials of a craft. It is his *job* to grub among the wreck of old fixed capital, old machinery, and constructions to make what he can of them. This is no less true when the research is not into the papers and manuscripts of others, but into his own fading research notes. He is obliged, perhaps, to do this even though the task has the slightly unpleasant and obsessively introverted air of an animal sniffing its own trail.

THE PROBLEM OF THE COTTON YIELDS

The U.S. Department of Agriculture in the early 1930s published its revised series on acreage harvested and output by state, 1866–1931, for all the major crops.[8] The cotton series was subjected in this publication to some of the same scrutiny which Holbrook Working had applied to the wheat series; the method of estimation was roughly the same and might be subject to the same margins of error. Starting with the census years from 1880, annual projections were made backward and forward on the basis of available evidence from county crop reports as percentage changes in each year from the previous year. When after 1880 the series came up to the next census year, it was linked to the census figure of that year, and an appropriate percentage adjustment was presumably made in earlier years of that decade to diffuse backward at some diminishing rate the effects of what otherwise would be a cumulative error. I have never seen an exact description of this method or an exact statement of the magnitude or direction of the necessary corrections. The important use of

[8] U.S. Department of Agriculture, Bureau of Agricultural Economics, Crop Reporting Board, "Revised Estimates of United States Cotton Acreage and Yield, 1866–1931" (Washington, 10 May 1933).

the USDA series is to determine whether and how far a census year deviated from normal and to show something of the year-to-year fluctuations between the census dates.

My intention, as in the earlier studies, was to estimate the normal levels of yields, the trend values, as of the 1850s (Period 1) and the decade around the census year 1909 (Period 2) for the major geographical regions.[9] This required determination of the county yields at the census date, the grouping of these into the regions, and the adjustment of the regional yield thus derived for the deviation of the census year from the normal. To do this for the later date (1909), the acreages and outputs of the portions of a region in each state were adjusted by the ratio of the census year to the period 1904–1913 for that state, and these figures for intrastate regions were summed by region across states to give the "normalized" production, acreage, and yield figures for that region. To obtain a "normal" estimate for the 1850s was a more difficult matter, however, because of the lack of acreage data. Two methods were possible: Either 1880 "normalized" regional yields could be applied to the 1850 and 1860 census production figures by county, or the trend of the 1880–1910 normalized regional yields could be projected backward for that purpose. The latter method was tried at the cost of immense labor and endless adding machine tapes for the county census data for the four censuses, and at this point the project went into one of its long hibernations. In the meantime the advance of econometric and computer techniques, as well as the skill of a new generation of graduate students, suggested another way. The antebellum censuses give county figures for total land in all crops combined and the outputs of each crop. It was possible then to regress the total land in crops on the output of each crop using a cross-sectional body of data in each region. The coefficients thus obtained

---

[9]I have not treated in the text the problem of the choice of appropriate regions. Ideally a region is naturally defined by relatively homogeneous conditions of production, and this shows up in a statistical array of data by the clustering of the data around regional means. But the number of soil type regions in the cotton belt, as described by Hilgard in his study in the 1880 census, is too large to be manageable. Our data are not numerous enough to permit such fine groupings or to reveal by themselves the natural regional outlines. I have had recourse therefore, as others have done, to the seven geographical regions defined in the *Cotton Report A-7*, WPA National Research Project (Philadelphia, September, 1938).
The regions include portions of states as follows:

Atlantic Coastal Plain	– Va., N.C., S.C., Ga.
Gulf Coast	– Ala., Miss., La.
Piedmont	– Va., N.C., S.C., Ga., Ala.
Eastern Hilly	– N.C., Ga., Ala., Miss., Tenn.
Western Hilly	– Mo., Ark., Okla., La., Texas
River Bottom	– Miss., La., Ark., Mo., Tenn.
Black Waxy, Gulf Prairie	– La., Texas

Table 1. *Estimated cotton yields, by regions 1850/60–1910*
(lbs. per acre)

Region	Passell Estimate 1850/60	Klein Estimate of "Normal" Yield			
		1879	1889	1899	1909
Atlantic Coastal Plain R1	178.0	119.4	141.1	151.4	161.3
Gulf Coast R2	214.1	167.4	160.2	167.1	117.3
Piedmont R3	126.8	142.1	158.8	177.4	212.7
Eastern Hilly R4	168.5	171.4	156.4	174.7	190.6
Western Hilly R5	280.1	211.4	187.8	184.3	188.6
River Bottom R6	408.7	306.8	270.0	250.2	236.4
Black Waxy and Gulf Coast Prairie R7	252.2	194.2	224.2	187.6	174.0
United States	208.1	171.4	177.2	180.4	183.1

Source: See text.

would, within their limits of probable error, be the reciprocals of the yields per acre of each crop. But county data appeared to be too aggregated, including too many errors of measurement for such an estimation procedure. At this point the so-called Parker–Gallman sample of farms in the cotton regions taken from the census manuscripts of 1860, and supplemented by samples taken by James Foust for 1850, was available.[10] The estimation, made with these farm data grouped by geographical region, yielded the estimates shown in Table 1. These estimates appear quite plausible, both in relation to the postbellum series and when set against contemporary evidence.

Such a relatively successful econometric effort would seem to be publishable; certainly worse econometrics have seen the printed pages of books and journals. However, my own peasant-like skepticism of such methods made me hold back, and the clever student, Peter Passell, who did the work, escaped in the meantime, first to Columbia, then to become an economic editorialist for the *New York Times*.[11] In the six-year interval between his work and my recognition of its value, his manuscript and calculations were lost, and I was left only with the final estimates, without work sheets and – horror of horrors! – without estimates of variance, *t*-statistics, and all the other paraphernalia of a piece of credible econometrics. The whole job must now be done over again simply to establish

[10]See note 3, above.

[11]Some of these results are presented in compressed form in Passell's doctoral dissertation, "Essays in the Economics of Nineteenth-Century American Land Policy" (Ph.D. dissertation, Yale University, 1970), Appendix, 128–36.

its credibility, though it is not likely to yield any substantively improved results.[12]

LABOR TIME, BY REGION AND OPERATION

An estimation of yield per acre requires either aggregative statistics for an area or a very large sample of the massive data base provided by original census returns. The fragmentary sample of yields available in plantation documents and farm accounts would, like most historical data, never pass a statistical test. It may be quite otherwise, however, for data on labor times in the various operations in the field. In the study of the grains, means for a region, computed usually from twenty to forty observations in each period, showed reasonably low standard errors. Also, the conditions of cotton planting and cultivation were more nearly uniform over the whole South, despite differences in terrain, than were those for corn in the country as a whole. In view of the variety of preplanting techniques of soil preparation (clearing, cutting stalks, breaking, bedding, laying-off rows, etc.) there were difficulties in devising a standard set of operations on which averages could be based. For Period 1, Table 2 shows the results of compiling the data from the individual plantation documents for the eight geographic regions.

This table is, of course, the one on which research time was lavished. The printed sources – USDA and state reports and farm journals – were combed, and every considerable collection of documentary material in the South, to the best of my knowledge, was visited. Materials were found in eight of the libraries from the manuscripts of twenty-eight different plantations.[13] Users of southern archives will recognize that this is not a big haul. The reason lay in the extremely exacting nature of the statistical requirement. Rarely did any one document give a complete account of the agricultural work year in cotton for the slave labor force. Sometimes when good account was made of hours in the field, the document cruelly neglected to mention the field's acreage – that presumably being well known. We never found more than thirty figures for any one operation in a region, and our number of cases was usually between five and fifteen. One may or may not give credence to averages based on such small arrays: Their dispersions around the means, not computed in the original draft, do not on inspection appear to be fatally large. But for a study of the entire South, it was necessary also to have figures for the Western Hilly, River Bottom, and Black Waxy regions, which were all in cultiva-

---

[12]They yield total cotton acreage in 1850 of 4.5 million acres to set against DeBow's contemporary estimate of 5.0. See J. B. D. DeBow, *Compendium of the Seventh Census* (Washington, 1850), 176.

[13]Parker and Klein, "Productivity Growth," 523–82.

Table 2. *Labor inputs in cotton, by operation and region: Period 1 (1840–60)*
(man-hours per acre)

Operation	Atlantic Coastal Plain R1		Gulf Coastal Plain R2		Piedmont R3		Eastern Hilly R4		Western Hilly R5		River Bottom R6		Black Waxy R7	
	n	x	n	x	n	x	n	x	n	x	n	x	n	x
1. Clearing land and cutting stalks		(6.3)	3	7.7	1	19.0		(6.8)		(6.8)		(7.0)		(3.2)
2. Breaking	4	10.1	6	10.7	9	11.4		(12.3)		(6.0)		(6.4)		(12.5)
3. Bedding	9	4.6	1	8.3	3	11.5	2	6.4		(8.8)		(5.3)		(2.7)
4. Planting	19	6.2	30	4.9	13	10.1	2	6.9		(6.6)		(5.0)		(5.8)
5. Hoeing	8	56.2	12	30.4	14	43.6	4	23.6		(27.0)		(54.3)		(18.4)
6. Cultivating	9	12.5	12	19.4	14	21.8	3	18.5		(33.3)		(20.2)		(7.8)
Total pre-harvest (1–6)		95.9		81.4		117.4		74.5		(88.5)		(98.2)		(50.4)

Source: Compiled as described in text. Worksheets showing the source and data of each case are available from the author.

Notes: n = number of cases – one case being the record for a given plantation on a given area in one year. x = mean of the distribution of cases. Figures in parentheses are shadow values – see text.

57

tion in 1860. For these no usable records of labor times could be found. Here I was faced once again with the harshness of the statistical method, against which none of the devices of an historian's rhetoric can avail. It demands and devours figures, as the Minotaur devoured maidens. They must be delivered in exact quantity and on time. Without a figure in every box, one could not compile the indices of change between the two periods. The figures in parentheses in Table 2 then were devised, or invented, and dignified by the title of "shadow values," on the basis of the interregional relationships revealed in Period 2, as displayed in Table 3. Assuming that productivity changes affected all the regions similarly, these shadow values were prepared by assuming that the missing regions bore the same relation to the average of the regions for which data were available in Period 1 as they did in Period 2. The data for Period 2, drawn largely from USDA circulars and bulletins, from several state bulletins, and from the great WPA National Research Project study made retrospectively in the 1930s, looked adequate.[14] Indeed, coming to them from the waste desert of the plantation documents, they seemed a land flowing with milk and honey, and having gorged myself on them for a time, I felt ready to prepare the indices.

INDICES OF LABOR PRODUCTIVITY

An economic historian should approach the preparation of an index as a priest in a mass approaches the elevation of the Host. After interminable mumblings and mutterings, after prayers and chants, the locking and unlocking of boxes, the assembly of materials of the most varied sorts, at last the moment comes, a bell is rung, a hush comes over the crowd and the solemn propitiatory rite reaches its climax. Table 4 presents the basic data, produced from Tables 2 and 3, together with the yield data and the shares of the regions in total output at the mid-nineteenth- and early twentieth-century dates. These are the final ingredients from which, by a process of vast multiplication, the index is produced. Some indication of the probable errors of the estimates of labor and yields should accompany the figures, and these are still to be extracted from the original work sheets. The picking time, it will be noted, does not distinguish Period 1 from Period 2, because of an assumption that techniques in the interim had not changed. This too needs to be further checked, and in fact the plantation documents yielded a rather abundant sample of picking times, which remains yet to be tabulated. The two sets of output weights make possible an index for the whole South (R1–R7) and for the three Old South regions for which Period 1 data are actually available. The formula

[14]See Appendix B, below.

Table 3. *Labor inputs in cotton, by operation and region: Period 2 (1900–20)* (man-hours per acre)

Operation	Atlantic Coastal Plain R1		Gulf Coastal Plain R2		Piedmont R3		Eastern Hilly R4		Western Hilly R5		River Bottom R6		Black Waxy R7	
	n	x	n	x	n	x	n	x	n	x	n	x	n	x
1. Clearing land and cutting stalks	11	2.7	3	5.0	7	4.3	3	2.9	6	2.9	3	3.0	3	1.3
2. Breaking	11	5.1	3	3.9	7	4.7	3	5.4	9	2.7	2	2.8	8	5.5
3. Bedding	10	3.6	3	6.9	7	6.6	3	3.9	8	4.9	2	4.0	3	2.0
3a. Harrowing	10	1.2	3	1.6	7	1.6	3	1.6	8	1.1	2	1.1	5.	0.9
3b. Laying-off rows	9	1.2	2	1.0	7	1.3	3	0.9	6	0.5	–	–	4	1.6
4. Planting	13	1.7	4	1.7	8	2.1	5	1.8	13	1.7	4	1.4	12	1.6
5. Hoeing	12	24.7	3	29.8	8	24.6	3	28.5	12	17.4	4	31.6	11	10.7
6. Cultivating	12	21.7	3	22.8	8	24.9	3	22.9	12	14.8	4	21.6	11	8.4
Total pre-harvest (1–6)		64.9		77.4		74.7		72.8		48.4		66.3		32.0

Source: Compiled as described in text. Worksheets showing the source and data of each case are available from the author.

Note: n = number of USDA or state surveys used, each containing 100–300 farms. The figures (x) are means of the surveys, weighted by the number of farms in the sample.

Table 4. *Basic data for productivity indices, by region and period (1, 2)*

Region	Preharvest labor (man-hr/acre)		Picking time (man-hr/lb)	Yield (lb lint cotton/acre)		Output weights (R1–R7)[a]		Output weights (R1–R3)[b]	
	1	2	1–2	1	2	1	2	1	2
Atlantic Coastal Plain R1	95.9	64.9	.203	178.0	161.3	.125	.206	.197	.391
Gulf Coast R2	81.4	77.4	.240	214.1	117.3	.263	.121	.414	.228
Piedmont R3	117.4	74.7	.186	126.8	212.7	.248	.200	.389	.380
Eastern Hilly R4	74.5	72.8	.203	168.5	190.6	.232	.095		
Western Hilly R5	88.5	48.4	.189	280.1	188.6	.037	.157		
River Bottom R6	98.2	66.3	.198	408.7	236.4	.086	.079		
Black Waxy and Gulf Coast Prairie R7	50.4	32.0	.148	252.2	174.0	.009	.140		

Source: Tables 1, 2, 3.

Note: Periods used in labor data are 1840–60 and 1900–20. For yields, 1849–59 manuscript census figures were used for Period 1, and 1909 census data, "normalized" as described in text, for Period 2. Output weights were computed from yield acreage estimates for the same periods.

[a]The first set of output weights shows the region's share in the output of the entire South (R1–R7).

[b]The second set of weights shows the shares of the three southeastern regions in that area's output.

for the index gives labor time per pound of cotton by dividing preharvest labor by yields, and the addition to that of the per-pound fixed estimate of picking time. When this figure computed for each region is multiplied by the region's share of total output, expressed as a decimal, and the results are added, the final figure is the weighted average labor time per pound of cotton, and the reciprocal of this is the cotton output per man hour for the South in Period 1 and Period 2. The Period 2 figure expressed as a percentage of Period 1 figure constitutes the desired index showing the percentage increase in productivity over the period.

When this arithmetic is performed, the following results are obtained:

	Labor input (man-hours per pound)	
	Entire South	Three southeastern regions
Period 1	.742	.897
Period 2	.551	.679
Productivity index: Period 1 × 100 = Period 2	135	132

These indices may be compared with those in the study of grains for the United States as a whole: wheat – 417; oats – 363; corn – 365.

The problem of analysis, however, is not solved by such simple indices, or such simple comparisons. One wishes to find out all that the statistics will tell about why the index moved in this way. As already noted, it is compounded of four elements: (1) pre-harvest labor per acre; (2) yields per acre; (3) picking time per pound; (4) the distribution of the crop among the regions. The changes in pre-harvest labor per acre between the period show the effects of improved implements, particularly the planter and the cultivator, and improvements in draft animals, set against some additional labor costs in land preparation and manure spreading. The changes in yields per acre show the effects of fertilizers and any genetic improvements set against the further depletion of the natural qualities of the soil and the loss, in the river bottom region, of the high yields of the area's virgin years. The changes in regional weights show the effects of the westward movement of the crop, despite the recovery due to fertilizer in the Atlantic Coastal Plain. In the absence of mechanical changes, picking times, by region, may be presumed not to have changed much between the two periods.

To these commonsensical and not very startling conclusions, the data, for what they are worth, carry us. One may be somewhat troubled by the feeling that the data must not have been so bad if they give conclusions which seem so in accord with one's preconceptions. Is this the method of Science? one may ask. In the studies of the northern products, the quality of the data tempted my students and me to go one step – one fatal step – further. Which of the major elements, we asked – technical improvements in handling the soil and the standing crop, biochemical improvements affecting the yields, or westward movement from lower yield and higher cost regions to a new terrain – was the most important in producing the combined outcome shown in the index? Why cannot one vary the three components in the index one at a time, to show what labor productivity *would have been* if labor costs per acre by region had changed but yields and the distribution of the crop among the regions had remained at their 1850 levels? Or if labor costs per acre by region had not changed but yields had changed while the crop remained distributed as before? Or if neither labor costs nor yields had changed but the crop had moved from its 1850 to its 1910 geographical distribution? Or if any two of these had changed while the remaining one had stayed put?

Arithmetically this operation is easy to accomplish. One simply creates new indices for each of these conditions on the 1850 base, as shown in Table 5. What one has done then is to create six hypothetical histories for the cotton industry of the South in these decades. The prospect is appalling, even blood-curdling, to a historian who, though given to statements about the importance of the various factors, insists that history can be told only "as it really happened." Yet some of the hypothetical indices do seem to have an intuitive plausibility. It is possible, for example, to imagine a southern cotton industry moving west without appreciable mechanical or genetic changes, except such as were required to keep labor inputs and yields stable in each region during the process. Then index i_4 tell us that productivity would have gone up by 10.1 percent as against the 34.7 percent by which it actually rose. The reader may amuse himself with delineating the histories that the other indices tell. The fly in the ointment, however, as Temin and Fisher pointed out, is that output was not the same in 1909 as in 1849. In fact, the census figure increased from 2.5 million pounds in 1849 to 5.4 in 1859 to 10.6 in 1909. This fact is less damaging for those indices where westward movement is allowed than where it is not. A growing output was indeed accommodated in large part by the West, and it is conceivable that it would have been produced under the 1850 techniques, though the absolute growth in the Southeast would have still affected yields there. But it is quite impossible to imagine costs in the East under the pressures of the growth of demand if the West had *not* been there or had been confined only to its 1850 share. To follow this hypothetical history would require a vast surmise about *intra*-regional expansion and technical change in the old cotton belt and would lead into lifetimes of research into what never occurred. Even more than usually,

Table 5. *Labor input and productivity indices in cotton production (all-region average) for entire South (R1–R7) and three eastern regions (R1–R3): actual (i_8) and hypothetical ($i_2 - i_6$) figures under alternative historical assumptions*

Period	Value of			Labor input (man-hr/lb)		Productivity index ($i_1/i_n \times 100$)	
	a	Y	V	R1–R7	R1–R3	R1–R7	R1–R3
i_1	1	1	1	.742	.897	100.0	100.0
i_2	1	2	1	.748	.840	99.2	106.8
i_3	2	1	1	.614	.591	120.8	151.8
i_4	1	1	2	.674	.904	110.1	99.2
i_5	2	2	1	.643	.741	115.4	121.1
i_6	2	1	2	.529	.669	140.3	134.1
i_7	1	2	2	.693	.813	107.1	110.3
i_8	2	2	2	.551	.679	134.7	132.1

a = pre-harvest labor, man-hours per acre
Y = yield of lint cotton per acre
V = region's share in output

Source: Produced from data of Table 4, according to the formula:

$$\text{L/O} = \sum_{R_1}^{R_n} \frac{a_{ij}}{Y_{ij}} + b_j \, V_{ij} \qquad \begin{array}{l} i = 1,2 \\ \\ j = 1,2\ldots,7 \end{array}$$

where

L/O	=	average labor input per pound of lint cotton for all regions.
a_{ij}	=	preharvest labor in man hours in period i (1,2) for region j (R1–R7).
Y_{ij}	=	yield (lint cotton in pound) per acre in period i for region j.
V_{ij}	=	output weight in period i for region j.
b_j	=	picking time per pound of lint in region j.

Note: Since picking time is assumed to be the same by region in both periods, it has been omitted in computing the indices. This produces a minor inaccuracy, due to interregional differences in picking times, in indices with Period 1 output weights.

the econometric historian trapped in such a labyrinth would have cause to repeat Whittier's famous lament about the failed romance of Maud Muller and the judge:

> Of all sad words of tongue and pen,
> The saddest are these: it might have been.

Though it was "amid the ruins of the Capitol" that this work was conceived and though it has indeed "amused and exercised nearly twenty years of my life," it would be thought outrageous of me, I am sure, to rise at this point to a Gibbonian leave-taking of the labor. I may, however, perhaps be permitted to repeat Gibbon's apology: "The historian may applaud the importance and variety of his subject; but, while he is conscious of his own imperfections, he must often accuse the deficiency of his materials." Gibbon got six volumes from his imperfect materials, so perhaps I may be permitted one short paper.

APPENDIX: SOURCE BIBLIOGRAPHY

PERIOD I

U.S. Documents
1. Commissioner of Patents, *Reports on Agriculture,* 1845.
2. Commissioner of Agriculture, *Annual Report,* 1867, 1876.
3. Commissioner of Labor, *13th Annual Report,* Washington, 1898.
4. Department of Agriculture, *Division of Statistics,* Bulletin 16, Washington, 1899.
5. Department of Agriculture, Experiment Station Bulletin, No. 33, *The Cotton Plant,* Washington, 1896.
6. Department of Agriculture, Bureau of Agricultural Economics, Crop Reporting Board, *Revised Estimate of Cotton Acreage, Yield and Production,* Crop Years 1866–1928.
7. Census of Agriculture, 1840–1910.
8. Census of Agriculture, 1880, Vols. V and VI, *Cotton.*
9. Department of Agriculture, *Atlas of American Agriculture,* Washington, 1918.
10. Works Progress Administration, National Research Project (NRP), Changes in Technology and Labor Requirements in Crop Production: Cotton Report A-7.

Periodicals
1. *Alabama Agriculturalist*
2. *Skinner's Journal of Agriculture*
3. *Southwestern Historical Quarterly*

Pamphlets
Letter from the Secretary of the U.S. Treasury transmitting Tables and Notes on the Cultivation, Manufacture and Foreign Trade of Cotton, Washington, 1836. (Levi Woodbury's Report on Cotton)

Manuscripts

Library	Title	County and/or state
1. Duke University	Araby Plantation Cotton Book	
2. Department of Archives, Jackson, Miss.	William Archer Papers, "Killona Plantation"	Holmes, Miss.

3. Department of Archives, Jackson, Miss.	Aventine Plantation	Miss.
4. Southern Historical Collection, University of North Carolina, Chapel Hill	Plantation Journal of John D. Ashmore	Anderson and Sumter, S.C.
5. Department of Archives, Louisiana State University, Baton Rouge	Eli J. Capell Plantation Diaries and Record Books	Amite, Miss.
6. University of South Carolina	Caleb Coker's Plantation Book	Darlington, S.C.
7. University of South Carolina	Mrs. H. L. Coker's Plantation Book	Darlington, S.C.
8. University of South Carolina	Capt. Wm. Coker's Plantation Book	Darlington, S.C.
9. Duke University	Cotton Book	
10. University of South Carolina	"The Oaks," L. R. Crosswell, Overseer	South Carolina
11. Department of Archives, Louisiana State University, Baton Rouge	Evans Plantation Diary, "Oakland Plantation"	W. Feliciana Parish, La.
12. South Carolina Library, University of South Carolina, Columbia	Samuel P. Gaillard Plantation Journal	Sumter, S.C.
13. University of South Carolina	E. Spann Hammond Plantation Book	Aiken, S.C.
14. Duke University	Joseph M. Haynes Plantation Account Book	Rankin, Miss.
15. Duke University	Kyline Cotton Books	
16. Southern Historical Collection, University of North Carolina, Chapel Hill	Francis J. Leak Diary	Miss.
17. Department of Archives, Louisiana State University, Baton Rouge	Le Blanc Collection	Louisiana
18. Department of Archives, Louisiana State University, Baton Rouge	Liddell Collection, Plantation Diary, "Llanada Plantation" (Vol. 35)	Louisiana
19. Department of Archives, Louisiana State University, Baton Rouge	The Marston Papers (Henry W. Marston and Family) Plantation Diary	Feliciana Parish, La.
20. Southern Historical Collection, University of North Carolina, Chapel Hill	Farm Journal of Nicholas Massenburg	Franklin, N.C.
21. Department of Archives, Louisiana State University, Baton Rouge	The Mercer Papers "Laurel Hill Plantation"	Adams, Miss.

22. North Carolina Department of Archives and History, Raleigh	Mial Papers – Cotton Book	North Carolina
23. Department of Archives, Louisiana State University, Baton Rouge	Monette Diary	Morehouse Parish, La.
24. Southern Historical Collection, University of North Carolina, Chapel Hill	Stephen A. Norfleet Diaries	Bertie, N.C.
25. Southern Historical Collection, University of North Carolina, Chapel Hill	The Philip H. Pitts Papers	North Carolina
26. Department of Archives, Louisiana State University, Baton Rouge	John Hampden Randolph Plantation Cotton Book	Wilkinson, Miss.
27. Georgia Department of Archives and History, Atlanta	Diary Ledger and Account Book of James Washington Watts	Bartow (Cass), Ga.
28. Tennessee State Library and Archives, Manuscript Section, Nashville	Robert White – Notes for Overseer	Davison, Tenn.

PERIOD 2

U.S. Documents

1. *Department of Agriculture*
    (a) Department Circulars 83, 183.
    (b) Department Bulletins 896, 961, 1181.
    (c) Bureau of Agricultural Economics, Division of Farm Management, *Cost of Producing Cotton in Fifteen Selected Areas*, Washington, 1923.
    (d) Office of Farm Management, *Farm Management Circular* 3, Washington, 1919.
    (e) *Atlas of American Agriculture*, Part V, Washington, 1918, Advance Sheet 4, Cotton.
2. Commissioner of Labor, *13th Annual Report*, Washington, 1898.
3. WPA–NRP Cotton (see Period 1)

State Documents

1. Alabama: Alabama Polytechnic Institute Extension Service, Circular 33, Auburn.
2. Georgia: Georgia State College of Agriculture, Extension Division, Bulletin 273, Athens.
3. North Carolina: Commissioner of Agriculture, *9th Annual Report*.
4. South Carolina: Commissioner of Agriculture, *7th Annual Report*.
5. Texas: Texas A. &. M., AES Bulletin No. 26, College Station.

5

The South in the national economy, 1865–1970

> With countless variations, two great traditions interpret and evaluate historical trends in the relationship between households and markets: the tradition of most economists, descended from Adam Smith, which views the spread of markets and specialized production as a progressive development, an improvement of resource allocation, an encouragement to advancements in knowledge and progress, and an opportunity for higher standards of living on and off the farm; and the tradition of Marxian writers (though in this American application with a strong Jeffersonian flavor as well), which views the market as an invading, intruding force, a maelstrom that lures or sucks households into its orbit, whirling them in historical circles beyond their control, and permitting no escape. Usually these traditions talk past each other, obscuring the extent to which each one contains elements of truth in describing the same historical developments, and failing to ask why it is that some cases fit one version, some the other.
>
> – Gavin Wright, *The Political Economy of the Cotton South*, 182

The antebellum South was no stranger to the forms of market capitalism; the master/slave relationship existed within a world network of prices and markets. This paradox had formed the essential and peculiar feature of the tropical economies of the New World for two hundred years. Were

Presented to the Third Conference of the U.S./USSR Historians at the Academy of Sciences, Moscow, December 1–5, 1978, and published in the *Southern Economic Journal*, Vol. 46, No. 4, (1980), 1019–1098. Preparation was assisted and informed by an extensive survey of the secondary literature, particularly on sharecropping and tenancy systems, by David F. Weiman, then a graduate student in economics at Stanford University. In the original publication of this article, this survey formed the basis of rather voluminous footnotes, prepared largely by Weiman. Since 1978, the postbellum South has replaced slavery as the favorite target for scholarly attention, and it is impracticable to bring these notes up to date. Citations published within the original article still form the basis of the text, which, like everything that has appeared on this subject, still owes most to C. Vann Woodward's original beautiful treatment, *The Origins of the New South, 1877–1913* (Baton Rouge: Louisiana State University Press, 1951). The treatments of aspects of the subject by Roger Ransom and Richard Sutch, *One Kind of Freedom:*

such economies less than fully capitalistic, in that they lacked markets for day-to-day labor? Or were they super-capitalistic, since labor itself was capitalized, bought and sold as a capital good, even raised as an item of commodity production? However such questions are answered, there lay at the heart of the slave system a political, non-wage relationship adequate to control cheap and productive labor for the production of large volumes of the staple crops. With the Civil War, the Emancipation Proclamation, and the 13th and 14th Amendments to the U.S. Constitution, market capitalism began to penetrate to this heart of the South's labor system. The agrarian history of the next seventy-five years may be written as a seesaw between an intruding free labor market and the activity and interference of various resistances to its penetration.

The problem for this history lies in discovering decisive and complete evidence to show just how fast market penetration went and what obstacles it met. But lack of the evidence does not keep scholars from suggesting explanations, particularly on issues as explosive as those of interracial and interregional inequality. Unquestionably the postbellum South was poor relative to the rest of the nation, and within the South, the former slaves along with large numbers of propertyless whites, were poorest. But over the long run, markets should equalize net returns to productive factors regardless of the race or location of their owners. Why did free labor and capital markets fail to produce such an effect in this case? Since 1940, differentials between the South and the rest of the Nation and within the South between black and white have indeed diminished. Why then did capitalism take so long to do its liberating and equalizing work?

To answer these questions, American observers and historians, beginning in the 1880s, developed a chain of explanation intuitively appealing and logically strong, supported by the rather scanty available data. It developed themes of exploitation current in the populist agitation of the 1890s and revived in various forms throughout twentieth-century American history. It had a resemblance to a Marxian analysis but lacked the theoretical rigor and the standardization of categories and classes which a

The Economic Consequences of Emancipation (New York: Cambridge University Press, 1977), and Gerald Jaynes, *Branches Without Roots: Genesis of the Black Working Class, 1862–1882* (New York: Oxford University Press, 1985), rest on the exploitation of new primary sources and add evidence and bring more concrete specification to the conclusions, without, however, altering their main thrust. Robert Higgs, *Competition and Coercion: Blacks in the American Economy, 1865–1914* (Chicago: University of Chicago Press, 1977, 1981), is an interesting study, and Gavin Wright's two books, *The Political Economy of the Cotton South* (New York: Norton, 1978) and his later study, *Old South, New South* (New York: Basic Books, 1986) are both, in my perhaps biased view, masterly pieces of work.

Readers are referred to the original publication cited above for citations and detailed discussions of the literature.

Marxist might employ. To a neoclassical economist, this "populist" explanation implies three types of economic exploitation as that term is defined in neoclassical economic theory. These all derive from an inability of productive factors to move to their use of highest return. The result of such immobility, such entrapment of labor or capital, is the earning of monopoly rent by the scarce factor and earnings below the market return elsewhere by the over-abundant factor. The three points at which exploitation may be alleged to have occurred in the postbellum South are these:

(1) Immediately after the war, an exploitation of landowners by unreliable freedmen, and thereafter, an exploitation of propertyless blacks and poor whites by landowners,

(2) Exploitation of tenants and small landowners by local monopolists: merchants and money-lenders,

(3) Exploitation of planters and southern merchants by northern oligopolists: railroads and sellers of capital, capital goods, and supplies.

The fundamental obstacles to labor's moving out of the South, especially out of southern farming, and to capital's moving within and into the South, lay in underlying social conditions – the destruction of physical capital in the Civil War, the race prejudice of whites in the North and the South, the lack of a strong native commercial and industrial capitalism in southern agrarian society, ignorance and prejudice of the mass of northern capitalists, and the rapaciousness and acuity of a few. The southern economy became fixed – it is argued – in a mold of "underdevelopment" in the decades immediately after the Civil War. The South's relative poverty was then perpetuated through the 1930s by the vicious circles familiar to students of poor countries and regions. Immobility produced poverty which in turn produced low public expenditures on education, health, and agricultural improvement, so that the "human capital" stagnated and even deteriorated, deepening the ignorance and confirming the immobility. With deterioration of human capital came also – it is alleged – deterioration of the land and an unimaginative fixation on cotton farming. This squalid economic scene was in turn set in a political atmosphere of diffused terror and repression through which the propertied whites determinedly regained control of the apparatus of state governments, creating laws and an administration of injustice which confirmed a biracial caste system and accentuated the immobilities already created by poverty. It follows from this analysis that only a massive jolt from outside the system could break the links in the chain that held the South in racism and poverty.

I. LANDLORD MONOPSONY?

The first link in the chain of circumstances which, it is said, bound the South to poverty and its poorer inhabitants to extreme poverty, was forged by the reconstruction of southern agriculture around the staple crops which flourished under slavery – notably cotton. In the seventy-five years following Appomattox, cotton was a peculiarly unlucky crop. The bonanza days of the black belt and the delta and alluvial soils were ending even before the Civil War; extensions of acreage into Texas and upland areas east of the Mississippi were made at higher costs. Only drastic applications of fertilizer kept yields in the older regions at a commercial level. Furthermore, cotton demand, which had boomed in the cotton textile phase of the Industrial Revolution in England, New England, and the Continent, continued to increase enough to encourage planters, but in fact at a decelerating rate. The ancient desperate compulsion to get hold of labor to make fortunes or even a modest living in staples production still existed, and the reconstructed labor system held up through the depressed years of the 1870s and 1890s to permit a strong response to the upsurge of demand between 1900 and 1920. But the contraction of the 1920s and 1930s plunged an even larger industry, with even tighter labor relationships, into even deeper misery, relative to the nation at large.

To add to these market difficulties, the sheer physical tasks of cultivating and picking cotton and tobacco appear to have been resistant to technical improvement. Cultivators were developed to go between rows, and breeds of mules were improved to draw them, but much hoeing was still required. The harvesting operation, unlike that in wheat or rice, required fingers rather than broad motions of an arm, and fingers proved very difficult to imitate mechanically. Federal and state agricultural research agencies made some progress in plant breeding and in weed and insect control, but the boll weevil and pink boll worm were never eliminated; the weevil's advance from the Texas border to Virginia between 1890 and 1925 was probably not even much slowed down. An arsenal of weapons – early maturing varieties, pesticides, insect enemies, hand picking – confined losses to between 10 and 30 percent of the crop through the 1930s, but to the end the weevil's greatest enemy remained, not man, but a cold winter.

Nevertheless, the southern planters and small farmers after 1865 could hardly have taken any other road to agricultural reconstruction. Both planters and ex-slaves knew how to grow cotton; it was the *only* thing that many of them knew how to do. Equipment, implements, field patterns, commercial connections were specialized to the cotton culture. Cotton was the crop on which the South's fortunes had been made, after the labor problem had been solved by slaves and the cotton gin. Whether in desperation or with those high and greedy hopes of the 1830s, landowners turned to the problem of tying down the necessary labor. The former slaves had a problem, too – to get food, shelter, and clothing now that the customary source of these had disappeared with emancipation. Emancipation was the sheerest creation of an army of the unemployed that history had ever seen. The planters were, to be sure, not compensated for their capital loss, but they retained the land, the remaining livestock, and the implements. Efforts to endow the former slaves with a modest complement of capital to enable them to become independent farmers came to naught. The freedmen then needed employment, and preferably at their customary occupations. In an industrial context, capitalism's solution to such a problem was, as Marx noted, the establishment of wage labor. Some plantations operated with wage labor even in the ruinous price falls of the 1870s and 1890s, and their numbers increased with the revival of cotton markets after 1900. But they did not predominate. The planters and their former slaves did not read *Das Kapital* as it appeared and did not realize that it was historically necessary for labor to be totally separated from the means of production.

How extensive was the effort to establish a wage system? Why was a wider effort not made or, when made, so often a failure? From the landowners' side, two considerations were probably governing. For one thing, money – working capital in liquid form – was scarce because of the years of little or no cash income at the end of the war and also because banks and credit institutions had always been deficient in the South's vast agrarian interior. Slavery had meant that all cash or credit transactions stopped at the master, who used his credit with seaboard and distant mercantile houses to import commodities to be doled out directly to slaves. Smaller independent farmers had kept a small cash and credit economy going through local storekeepers, but both plantation and small farm had been very largely self-sufficient, or sufficient within small rural neighborhoods, for most of life's requirements. Still, the technical problem of financing working capital was not the major obstacle; agrarian and frontier communities intent on linking up with commercial and industrial capitalism have always found ways to secure or invent the means of finance to gain access to commodity markets and to create markets for land and other non-wage inputs. It is interesting to observe the variety of devices needed to overcome this institutional *lacuna* in the early growth of southern textile mills, where wages, supplies, and equipment had to be financed. The main obstacle to a wage economy in southern commercial agriculture in the 1860s was the same obstacle that created slavery in the first place and in free societies gave such strength to the peasant holding and the family-sized farm. In simple fact, a free labor force on a farm cannot be readily motivated, supervised, or kept honest, reliable, and dependable by direct controls on a large scale on the model of a factory.

The reasons for this lie in the agricultural production function, particularly in the spread of its tasks over space, which makes supervision difficult, and in the seasonal sequences of the tasks requiring a dependable core of workers over the growing season. Farms of course customarily hire peakload labor and some auxiliary year-round help. But costs of supervision and the risk of loss from unreliable workers rise rapidly as the number of such workers is increased and as the landowner absents himself from the heart of the operation. The capital losses inherent in negligent use of the soil and care of livestock are also likely to be heavy in the absence of an owner-manager system or tenant contracts offering incentives to labor to participate in the benefits of careful husbandry.

No doubt there was something to planters' complaints that the freedmen were unusually unreliable in their first few years of freedom. The intrusion of the Union armies first made for disruption; slaves, even before their formal freedom, often escaped to the protection of the northern troops. Lacking property or fixed employment, often with family members having been sold into other districts, the freedmen engaged in much moving around, once freedom was confirmed. Time horizons were short, and planters who paid wages on a weekly or monthly basis might be left without hands at picking time. Despite the supposed greater efficiency of the large-scale plantation, it could not be reconstructed in the exact image of the slave organization. From the freedmen's point of view, the wage gave, to be sure, maximum freedom. But many former slaves had skills and technical knowledge about farming which a wage system could not well utilize. Some had ambitions to become freeholders themselves, if not by a government grant of land, then by buying land, just as under slavery some hoped to buy their freedom. The slaves in the large plantation areas resisted the restoration of the gang labor system under overseers or drivers, which it was the planters' natural impulse to try to re-establish. Nothing so well demonstrates the fact that the supposed greater efficiency of the large-scale slave plantation was really an efficiency in the coercion of the slave than does the impossibility of re-establishing work routines of such intensity with free labor at any wage which a planter could afford to pay.

The solution to this problem was some form of joint interest of capitalist and laborer in their joint product, possibly even in the management of the operation and the care of the land and stock. So the slave plantations followed the pattern of the slave estates of the late Roman empire as its social organization broke down. The former slaves, or their replacements, were "hutted," placed in separate cabins on the land and given specific acreages on which to expend their labor. If tenants of this sort were to be kept at work, they could not be paid till the crop was in; in the meantime they had to be furnished provisions or the means of provisioning themselves. The relationship had to be a contractual one, under a form which, like the tenures of peasants in a medieval village, had a wide flexibility to cover the different properties, skills, capital holdings, and preferences of the different landlords and laborers. So the southern tenure system developed in share or fixed rent contracts, with payments specified in kind and generally in cotton or in cotton and corn.

The rich variety of these relationships has been the subject of an extensive historical and theoretical literature and of much dispute. Economic theorists have pointed out that the terms of the various types of contract can be, and on competitive markets would be, adjusted so that each pair of landlords and tenants would maximize their joint preferences in the exchange and would be indifferent in further contracts as to the choice among tenant forms. To attain such an optimum would require exceedingly perfect markets and exceedingly good information on both sides as to the terms on which available tenancies were being offered or sought. Thus landlords with capital and managerial skills would seek out tenants lacking these and fix them in contracts giving them small plots, a low share of the crop, and close supervision. One may speak of a basic sharecropper contract as essentially of this sort. In others, terms might be adjusted to give greater scope to tenants' capital or skills. The latter were designated share rent contracts, and a definite legal difference existed between the status of the laborer in the two cases. In the sharecrop contract the laborer received his share of the crop at the end of the season, as a wage from the landlord. In the share rent contract, he paid a share of the crop, as a rent, to the landlord. But all share contracts involved the sharing of the risks of weather and yields between the two parties, as against a fixed rent or wage payment in kind, and the risks of markets and price as well, as against a fixed cash rent or wage. Still, though some theorists make much of the question of risk sharing, it is not clear that the tenant or cropper had much to risk. He was supplied with provisions over the growing season, and whether he ended the season with a cash surplus or a debt depended not only on the size of the crop, but also on the terms on which the provision had been furnished. The sharing of risk then would appear decisively subordinated to the sharing of management and capital, the fixing of plot sizes and choice of crop, and the provision of supervision and control in producing the predominance of share contracts in the southern tenure system.

In the choice between share and fixed rent, the provision of management supervision by the landlord appears to be the major issue. Fixed rent tenants, bearing all the risk and responsibility, would not readily yield to supervision on their hired lands. Such contracts must have been favored most by absentee landlords who accepted the danger of deterioration in their lands to be free of the responsibility of managing them and of policing the terms of a complicated share contract.

Theorists have sought to find a simple explanatory principle out of which the mix of contractual forms would fall, and their analyses have done much to clarify the true nature of share and fixed rent tenancy. It seems unlikely, however, that a comprehensive theory can be developed and tested by the available data. The contracts have many dimensions, and the circumstances of the individual contractors differ rather widely, so that contracts and modes of enforcing them could be highly individualized. But the fault does not wholly lie in the level of abstraction at which theorists approach such problems. Our sample of such contracts is small, and even were it larger, we could never know the correspondence between contract and economic reality. Moreover, the censuses from 1880 through 1900 are extremely confusing in their efforts to describe the extent of each type of tenure.

How much exploitation of one group by another within the South existed in these arrangements? This depends partly upon the knowledge that tenants and landlords had about the alternative contracting possibilities and upon their freedom to change at the termination of a contract. Long-term leases of the European type do not appear to have been much used, and nearly all contracts were open to renegotiation at the end of each season. A landlord then might turn off an unsatisfactory tenant or alter the terms of the contract to his disadvantage; tenants might move on – as they often did – to another landlord and another arrangement. It is at this point, in the absence of decisive evidence, that prejudice, disguised as the historian's intuition, comes into play. Economists, struck by the penetrative power of the market and the robustness of the profit-maximizing assumption in explaining history, tend to emphasize the variety of share contracts and other tenures as indicating how well tailored were the market devices to the matching of individual situations and preferences. They point, too, to evidence of blacks' economic progress in the postbellum South as indicative of the possibility that markets were not the principal vehicle by which racism enforced discrimination. Discrimination in hiring by an individual employer is costly, and planters could not afford to incur unnecessary costs. Others, notably Roger Ransom and Richard Sutch in their study, *One Kind of Freedom*, following the "populist" interpretation, discount the differentiation among contracts. They might, even so, take their variety as evidence of the perfectness of the exploitation, where the landlord acted as a discriminating monopolist. The issue depends, as Robert Higgs points out, on whether landlords may be conceived as acting as a class, in setting the terms of rental, with means of enforcement on profit-maximizing mavericks who would break ranks to their own advantage.[1] That such class action was engaged in overtly and explicitly is hard to credit, but there are those who find it hard to believe that the conditions of social, political, and legal

---

[1]Robert Higgs, *Competition and Coercion: Blacks in the American Economy, 1865–1914* (Chicago: University of Chicago Press, 1977, 1981), 61.

discrimination in the South did not have their economic counterpart. Surely in many cases and regions – in the densely settled and cultivated plantation areas in particular – both tenants' and landlords' freedom of action in going outside certain customary forms of contract was greatly constrained by fear of social pressure and by the threat of illegal social violence. A liberal-minded economic historian is impelled to render a mixed judgment. Almost certainly the dissolution of the master–slave relationship into a variety of para-market relations resulted in an improvement in economic welfare and an enlargement in freedom of choice for the blacks. Evidences of economic advance by blacks and the similarities of black and white sharecrop contracts indicate that racial discrimination was less than total. On the other hand, it is hard to believe that, once they regained political ascendancy following the failure of the radical Republican reconstruction, white landlords were not able to act to a degree as an economic class, catching up black and white labor in a system of laws, debt, ignorance, fear, and crop choice which can hardly be squared with the "rules of the game" under capitalism.

II. MERCANTILE MONOPOLY?

The arrangements between landlords and tenants in the postbellum South fall into a form familiar to landlord societies the world over, a mixture of personal relations and social pressures set within capitalistic markets. To what degree did these personal relations and social pressures both on landlords and tenant-laborers produce differing degrees of factor immobility, enabling one factor to "exploit" the other? As the reverberations of slavery with its fears and loyalties died away, markets should surely have become more nearly perfect, at least for labor and the leasing of land. One difficulty was that, whatever the arrangements between land and labor, a third factor – finance – was needed to buy supplies over the growing season, to carry livestock, equipment, and buildings, and provide funds for land and crop transfers. The provisioning of these items of real and financial capital was a function of the markets for money and credit. In the unsophisticated state of southern financial institutions, these cannot be presumed to have been very perfect. There was room then for exploitation of borrowers by lenders, of those who needed advances by those who had supplies of materials, cash, or lines of credit. The other side of an imperfect market is, of course, the pressure of pools of capital not flowing into their use of highest return. In this sense, to use North/South interest rate differentials to show that southern labor was exploited by capital is tantamount to showing that northern capital was similarly exploited by northern labor.

By the "populist" interpretation of the history, southern agriculture was short of credit for the usual reasons that apply to agricultural areas in a commercial economy – seasonality of crops, remoteness from supply sources, ignorance on the part of lenders and borrowers, inexperience of farmers in business transactions. These applied also to the antebellum southern planter, especially in cotton, because of the traditional modes of financing the cotton crop movement and also because of special problems presented by the need for financial capital for the slave trade. Far more than the northern crops, wheat and livestock products, the southern staples were bound to specific, rather narrow channels of shipment and marketing, and supplies were brought in through those same routes. The financing of the colonial Virginia tobacco trade set to some degree the mold in which the other crops were financed. There the planter typically transferred his crop to an English "factor," who took title at the plantation's dock and managed the shipping services or owned the ship himself. The planter in turn received a credit on the merchant's books, which he could draw on until the next harvest. His supplies came to him by the same route that his shipments went out, and he was bound to that route by ties of personal, customary relationship. If a planter overdrew his account with his factor, he was in effect borrowing on his next year's crop, and many, probably most, planters were thus chronically in debt. Note-issuing banks were not known in the colonies during most of the colonial period, and their introduction, even in small numbers, to some extent freed many planters from the ties of debt to their factors. The financing of the antebellum cotton shipments from the larger planters followed much this same pattern, the principal difference being that factors in Atlantic or Gulf ports played a principal role. At the same time, beginning at least in the 1830s, local banks and, more extensively, local storekeepers and merchants, connected with jobbers and wholesale supply houses in major cities, entered the scene. The latter were important for handling smaller or odd lots of cotton and distributing supplies to the thousands of small free, or one-slave, farms in the upcountry. In plantation areas, the plantation store itself may have served such a function, foreshadowing the mixing of the roles of planter and merchant which became so significant after Reconstruction.

In the financing of larger wealth transfers – slave sales and land transfers – other types of lenders, banks and mortgage institutions, played a role. No doubt, too, much of the long-term credit for these purposes in the South, as in the North and West until well into the twentieth century, came from the sellers themselves or from private rural money lenders. But probably the most serious possibilities of distortion in resource allocation from year to year came from the lack of good markets for commercial credit. Even in the colonial period, and more strongly in the immediate antebellum decades, the complaints could be heard that the involvement of planters with merchants kept them confined to a sure cash crop and restrained the development of a more risky, but more diversified and possibly, in the long run, more productive, agriculture.

The dependence of the antebellum plantations or small farms on merchants had been modified, however, by the degree of self-sufficiency which they had attained. Without sacrificing too much cash income, i.e., through the use of surplus or seasonally idle labor, it had been possible to grow most of the needed food, and even, by training slaves or hiring local laborers, to substitute home manufactures for purchased industrial goods. The cash income from the crop could then be saved or used for less essential items. We know very little about the interregional capital flows, but there is the very live possibility that on balance capital moved out of, rather than into, the South in years of good crops and high revenues in the 1850s. However, the fact that necessities were provided for by non-cash means did not necessarily reduce the planter's greediness for luxury. Debts were surely as often incurred and maintained for extravagant imports, works of art and furnishings, clothing, and the like, as for slaves' clothing or farm equipment. Much farm capital was formed on the farm – livestock, fences and buildings, and the maintenance and repair of structures and equipment, even shoes and clothing. But wherever the large income from cotton ultimately went, very little appears to have gone into holding stocks of money or liquid funds to enable planters to finance their own trade.

These problems of agricultural finance appeared in exaggerated form as the farm tenancy system established itself in the southern plantation and upland areas after 1866. In the immediate postwar Reconstruction decade – the "carpetbagger" era – many of the planter families, because of poverty and the sheer inability to manage, were forced to sell some or all of their holdings. By one (somewhat dubious) estimate, over one-half of the agricultural land in the South changed hands in this period.[2] And for old or new owners to start up production, advances on supplies were frequently required. At this juncture, several new elements which had appeared in the southern landscape before 1860 began to make themselves felt in such a way as to produce, in conjunction, a new system of short-term credit. The small-town merchants at their antebellum locations were reinforced and multiplied by footloose ex-soldiers and northerners looking for a lucrative occupation. A new element of petty capitalism penetrated into the interior of the southern agricultural society. Sharp, narrow, close-fisted, trading on a small capital and on connections to northern manufacturers, jobbers, and mercantile houses, the merchants watched for every opportunity for a profit, whether inland pur-

[2] W. L. Fleming, "The Economic Conditions During Reconstruction," in J. C. E. Ballagh et al., *The South in the Building of the Nation*, Vol. 6 (Richmond: Southern Historical Publication Society, 1909), 3.

chases, storekeeping, money lending, or horse trading. But the group could not have achieved its wide distribution across the South without the continued extension within the South of the railroad. The older factorage system had been built in part on the orientation of farms and plantation to river and ocean shipment. The movement of the railroad into the interior produced a sudden alternative to the southern ports – an alternative, moreover, which was not single but multiple, carrying out the crops and bringing in supplies to and from any point in the network. Together, the railroad and the spread of small-scale merchandising produced a decentralization in the conditions of supply and credit in the southern interior, providing overwhelming competition to the older lines of credit and the seaport mercantile houses. Merchants – men with money and credit derived from mercantile activity – entered the agrarian economy itself, buying up land and entering into close relations with landowners and tenants.

We come then to the two questions at the heart of the traditional explanation of southern agrarian poverty. One question relates to the effects of the tenancy and credit system on the distribution of the income from cotton; the other relates to the long-run development effects which the system may have imposed. If the closer analysis by "new" economic historians fails to exonerate it on both counts, the crop lien–tenancy system, with exploitation of debtors by creditors and with creditor interference in production decisions, may be accounted the principal source of southern rural poverty from year to year – accounting thus for a deterioration of "human capital" – and also the cause of the failure of the region to improve its agriculture or to industrialize.

Proximately, the short-run question relates to the prices set by creditors – the rates of interest expressed directly in contracts and indirectly in differences between cash and credit prices in the stores, as well as in the level of price set at stores and the whole terms on which supplies were furnished and charged. Where payment was made in cotton one can imagine opportunities for petty thievery on both sides. The basic question on which scholars seriously disagree is the extent of competition among such local merchants and moneylenders. The "populist" interpretation would have it that landlords and tenants, and particularly the latter, were bound to their supplier – landlord or merchant (or one who embodied both) – even more tightly than the antebellum planter had been to his factor. Often, it is said, the tenant could not even play landlord and merchant supplier off against one another. Where the landlord directly furnished supplies, he too may have depended on a middleman to furnish them to him. Once the tenant fell in debt to landlord or storekeeper, he lost his freedom of action. The bonds of both on the tenant were fixed formally by the crop lien system, in which supplies both for production and subsistence were advanced against a lien on the season's crop or on its proceeds. In this case, the merchant's lien came to take an increasing prominence alongside the landlord's lien, and even where there were laws to the contrary, the courts in some cases permitted a carryover of the unsatisfied portion of a debt from a lien on one year's crop to the next season. The hold of this system of debt was tightened, it is said, as the South's deficiency of banks and other institutions of general agricultural credit continued. The National Banking Act of 1863 is blamed particularly because of the prohibitive (10 percent) tax it placed on state bank notes and the high capital requirements which made federal chartering difficult. More important, however, is the effect of the contracts and the provisioning system on land use and crop choice. Is it true that it locked tenants and landlords into producing crops that perpetuated their dependence on mercantile suppliers? Was it to the merchants' advantage to require this, and was it to the customer's disadvantage to accede to the requirement?

The effects of the tenure and credit system on welfare and social justice in the South are not irrelevant to the longer-run question of southern economic development. On the one hand, it could be argued that even if the system allocated income unevenly, it may by virtue of that fact have created a labor force more readily available for employment outside of agriculture. Too much agricultural poverty may be bad for industrial development, since it not only dries up the market for industrial goods but also retards the development of a spirited, educated, and mobile population. On the other hand, too much rural wealth may create a contented, relatively self-sufficient peasantry for whom industrial life has no attraction. But it is hard to argue that the south was too rich; the immobility of its labor was more clearly the result of its poverty and ignorance and the social discrimination practiced against one of its principal components. Apart from the quality of the human capital which the southern economic system created, however, the main questions for long-run development center around that system's effect on the choice of crops and techniques. Rather than fixing so strongly on restoring the cotton culture after 1860, would southern agriculture have been in the long run more prosperous if it had developed more diversified cropping patterns, similar to those which have been developing in the Southeast since 1940? And if so, did tenancy, sharecropping, and debt, with the system of merchant credit and crop liens, retard such a development? These questions suggest themselves from both the statistical evidence of the crop pattern and from contemporary comment. The federal censuses of 1850–80 show an increasing cotton–corn ratio in the South. And DeCanio's survey of the contemporary material shows the immense concern with cotton "overproduction."

On this question two "new" economic historians, Gavin Wright and Stephen DeCanio, have done interesting work which, though pointing in rather different directions, is capable of synthesis into a conclusion which is balanced (though not for that reason necessarily correct). DeCanio shows, by comparison of cotton prices with those of other crops, that cotton was the highest-yielding cash crop, hence that the southern farms were well advised to grow it and to buy at least a certain portion of their foodstuffs.[3] This analysis neglects two points: (1) the question of risk, (2) the long-run effects on the soil and on the farmers of monocrop agriculture. Wright points out that small farmers and tenants would be forced into the cash crop, even though its riskiness was at a level beyond what they would have preferred, by a need for cash to extinguish debt. However, as Wright points out, too, the South was not in a geographically favorable position to develop a northern-style diversified agriculture, particularly in competition with the northern producers. Self-sufficiency in food to reduce risk plus reasonable cash earnings, i.e., in the antebellum pattern, may have been all it could hope for. Still, cotton demand was not growing as rapidly as before 1860, and in any case it was in the Southwest, not the older regions where the output expansion occurred. Particularly in the Southeast, the development of some alternatives to the restoration of cotton through heavy and costly application of fertilizer might well have been possible in 1870 under a more imaginative and risk taking agricultural entrepreneurship. Smaller farmers with enough corn for subsistence might have been more risk-taking on their cash crop and experimented more with alternatives. Still that is not clear, since, as wild forage lands became occupied, the hogs now required more corn for feed and the South could hardly have competed with the Midwest as a commercial raiser of corn and hogs at the yields and techniques of this period. Wright's final conclusions on the whole matter carry the ring of truth:[4]

More generally, the case also shows that increasing specialization, division of labor, and exchange – all of which enhanced economic efficiency in conventional terms – had no necessary connection with the emergence of a prosperous, progressive agriculture, the improvement of living standards, or the acceleration of technological progress. This is so, not just because the South was in a position to depress the world's cotton price by expanding production, but because the choice of cash crops was limited, demand for cotton was low, and the region's manufacturing sector was late developing. The opposite conditions held true in the North, and hence it made sense for that region's farmers to welcome the market with open arms.

[3]Stephen J. De Canio, *Agriculture in the Postbellum South: The Economics of Production and Supply* (Cambridge: MIT Press, 1974) 177–80.
[4]Gavin Wright, *The Political Economy of the Cotton South* (New York: Norton, 1978), 183.

III. REAL AND ALTERNATIVE GROWTH PATHS

Wright's judicious conclusion about southern agriculture posits in effect an alternative growth path for the southern economy between 1860 and 1940. Under some other form of economic arrangements, he seems to be saying, might it have been possible for southern agriculture to have spread its risks more widely, developed its resources more productively, and secured a higher and better-distributed per capita income for its people? Might the South have overcome the losses of the war and its social disruption more quickly and more fully and moved up its period of catching up with the rest of the country by, say, fifty years? Instead of being even farther behind the North in 1900 than it had been in 1860, with a rigid economy stuck in cotton and dependent on black labor under reinforced and grotesque laws of discrimination, might the South have stood in 1900 as she did in 1940 – on the verge of an upsurge in productivity, industrialization, and personal and legal freedom?

To ask this is to indulge in an exercise in hypothetical history – an activity not greatly favored by conventional historians. Yet an historian has no choice if he wants to think about history, unless he wishes to accept a fatalistic position of sheer determinism. If men are free in some measure to influence their individual lives and collectively to make the conditions of their social life better or worse, then their actions and decisions are meaningful and consequential, and one may speculate on the consequences of alternative courses of action. When an historian says a certain activity or institution is important, his only standard of comparison is his mental image of how history would have moved in its absence. Quantification, the use of theoretical models, and the exercise of historical imagination to test for causation and effect – these are the three poles on which the "new" economic historians' tent is pitched.

But what posture of the national economy would have allowed the South such a history? First, it seems evident from Wright's and DeCanio's analyses that such an alternative lay beyond the ability of any individual southerner. Cotton was the most profitable crop under the institutional arrangements that prevailed, and it was under those institutional arrangements that the economic actors – planters, laborers, businessmen – lived. From an economist's point of view, the key to the situation appears to have been the relationship to northern capital. Why could it not have entered the South more thoroughly, engrafted itself there, and developed an industrial and manufacturing sector more closely comparable to the Northeast's or the Middle West's? These questions present us with the third type of exploitation listed at the outset of this paper: the exploitation of southern labor and property by northern capitalists. It is necessary, before considering the hypothetical question – what might have been – to deal with the real question of the South's alleged "colonial status."

Within agriculture itself, the hypothesis of colonialism has an ironic twist, for it is hard – though possible – to argue that exploitation occurred at all three levels simultaneously. Landlords who used cheap labor to grow more cotton had their advantage transferred *via* lower cotton prices to the cotton consumers – textile manufacturers and ultimately the buyers of cotton cloth and goods. But to the extent that they paid high interest rates or high prices for provisions, the gains from their preferred position in the labor market were transferred to merchants and money-lenders. These in turn, if they worked on borrowed northern capital, saw their monopoly profits eroded and their gains transferred on up the line of high-priced, semi-monopolized goods and credit. To be sure, good property incomes could be earned by southern owners of wealth and by southern entrepreneurs. Still, three possible sources, or aspects, of southern poverty remained: (1) immobilization of labor in agriculture, (2) shortage of southern capital, derived from the wartime destruction, possibly from inadequate savings (a result of poverty) and even – who knows? – from a continued tendency of southern capital to escape to the North or overseas or to misinvest itself within the South, accompanied by an inadequate native industrial entrepreneurial tradition, (3) simple lack of basic industrial natural resources, an unfavorable terrain, and an unskilled labor force. What was needed for a rapid "catch-up" – it would appear – was an out-migration of unskilled labor, an in-migration of skilled labor and entrepreneurs, plus more, and more mobile and competitive, capital in an industrial and service sector. So long as some fundamental interregional misallocation of material resources remained and renewed itself with every year's growth of the labor force and the capital stock, the movement of the South or its inhabitants, wherever located, to a higher growth path and a better share of American prosperity and wealth was hindered. By the same token, to the degree that northern or southern capital earned higher returns in the South, northern labor could take advantage of the protection it held against the in-migration of southerners, thus exploiting – in the neoclassical sense of the word – northern capital. It is little wonder that European migration entered the North in such abundance after 1880 to make use of this opportunity.

The lines on which capital was allocated in the South after 1880 held promise that with sufficient encouragement more might have been done. In a very short time, indeed, the replacement of a planter-dominated society by a society which, though predominantly agrarian, had elements of the small-town business culture with which the North and Midwest had long been familiar began to leaven the agrarian lump. Something is due no doubt to the self-proclaimed "prophets" of the New South – journalists and writers who noisily turned their backs on the past. One wonders too if the sheer political struggle by the so-called redeemers against black Republicanism did not bring new and more capitalistic-minded leaders to places of influence in state and local governments. It should not be forgotten that there is always an essential antagonism between an agrarian and an industrial interest, since each continually threatens the labor supply of the other. In the deep plantation areas, there was still little chance of loosening the control over the labor force which would allow industrial development to occur. Instead, along its margins and at the edge of the old cotton belt, in uplands near numerous streams, the spinning mills and weaving sheds of a nascent textile industry began to appear. Small (often with a few thousand spindles), many operating with second-hand machinery cast off from New England, financed by suppliers' book credit and by local subscription, the mills multiplied like rabbits. The growth of spindles and looms between 1880 and 1900 in the South attest to this rapid expansion. Between 1880 and 1900, the number of spindles in the South increased from 548,048 to 4,299,988, while the number of looms grew from 11,898 to 110,015.[5] Most interesting was their labor source – excess labor in the villages and, after 1900, the scrub farmers and their families from the hills. A gathering of local capital and an excess labor supply finally met with enough local entrepreneurship to take advantage of an industrial opportunity which had presented itself to the cotton South since the very beginning of large-scale cotton cultivation – the conversion of an abundant local raw material with local water power into a great manufacture. In doing so, the local capital of the South essentially bypassed the whole plantation area and economy, as well as its black labor force. Perhaps some financial resources and energies available in this striking industrial development were among those released by the end of the slave trade. More important was the continued population growth in the hills. There is a minor historical irony here, too, in that the grandparents of many of those worker families now stricken by poverty and overcrowding in hill areas and moving into the factory towns of the southern Piedmont had themselves migrated to these hills and valleys a hundred years before from the Scottish Highlands and Northern Ireland, many of them to escape a similar movement to the mills of the English Industrial Revolution.

In the American Midwest, a similar native small-scale capitalism,

[5]Broadus Mitchell, *The Rise of Cotton Mills in the South* (Baltimore: The Johns Hopkins University Press, 1921, reprinted New York: Da Capo Press, 1968), 245, from U.S. Census of Manufactures, 56–57. In her Yale Ph.D. dissertation, *The Role of the Cotton Industry in the Economic Development of the American Southeast* (New Haven, 1969), using Davison's *Textile Blue Books*, Sister Mary Oates documented the continued growth to 1920; the number of spindles increased over threefold from 1900 to 1920 (pp. 14, 30).

though failing to develop textiles, had flourished in all sorts of light manufactures, including machinery, agricultural supplies and services, and transportation, and it laid the basis for an appreciable urban growth. But before 1940, the South's development in these directions remained restricted; textiles, tobacco and cigarettes, lumber and forest products formed the main foci of the industrial activity financed in whole or in part from native capital. At least three elements present in the midwestern development were missing in the South. One was the absence of a large and varied demand for agricultural supplies, services, and processing. In the North, the livestock and dairy industries gave rise to a complicated set of inputs and auxiliary outputs – fencing, feed storage and shipment, slaughtering, storing and manufacturing and preserving milk, butter, cheese, meat, lard, hides, bone meal, glue, etc., etc. Pickling, curing, canning, refrigeration, meat distribution, and butchering – all gave rise to a large non-farm employment. Feed and grain were no less fertile in their "linkages" to machinery, transportation, and food processing. Southern crops, too, required some industrial inputs – fertilizer in the Southeast, simple gins, sugar and saw mills, implements, bagging, presses, and scales. Much of these were purchased outside the South; the efforts of farm cooperatives to supplant hemp by cotton in bagging are an example of an attempt at import substitution which came to naught. But the whole southern farm sector and particularly cotton – a crop easy to raise, to process, and to store – simply did not require and did not support as extensive and specialized a range of auxiliary industrial activities as the varied agriculture of the Northeast and the eastern Midwest. Closely related to this basic technical fact lies the relative absence of a skilled labor force able to transfer from agriculture or agricultural supply and processing industries to other industrial occupations. Immigrants since the 1780s had avoided the South – except for Chinese and some Germans, who refused to work in the cotton fields, and a few Italians, who did not fit into the system. Portuguese, brought in to undercut the labor market, remained in the sugar fields under conditions and wages even below the blacks'. The more important fact is that industrial learning by the native population had been stunted by slavery, by slave owning, and by reliance on imports. Coupled with these deficiencies, an economic geographer would surely find, too, a lack of the abundant native mineral resources on which the upper Midwest's huge industrial plant was based. The same was true of New England in the eighteenth century, but by 1870 wood and water and even considerable capital and business skill were no substitute for iron and coal, and capital and enterprise were migrating to where those weight-losing raw materials were to be found.

This brings us to the other leg of the South's actual industrial development in the 1890s – the heavy industrial development of the Birmingham coal and iron district. Here the difference from the textile development could not be more pronounced. Where that was a light industry starting up on a shoestring from many small beginnings, the heavy industrial development – though with some antecedent local, small-scale enterprise – grew out of the vision of a group of northern capitalists incorporated in the Tennessee Coal and Iron Company. It sprang full-blown from a union of northern capital and southern resources and after 1907 was readily incorporated by J. P. Morgan and Charles M. Schwab into the United States Steel Corporation. Within the South, the Birmingham development in both its mining and its smelting and steel-working departments, remained an enclave, extracting southern coal and minerals, superficially processing them, and sending them North.

A second count in the charge of northern colonialism is the ownership and operation of the railroads. Southern lines were initially southern-built and financed, sometimes with help from the governments of the states and localities through which they hauled. It remained, however, for northern capital seeking a promising outlet to link the local roads into a southern railroad, underwritten by J. P. Morgan. Where northern exploitation ended and mercantile exploitation began, and where the latter ended and southern landed wealth profited, no one now can say. The growth of populist protest in the South, essentially a small farmer movement which became racist and nativist in its ideology, is generally taken as evidence that here, as in the Midwest, between 1873 and 1896, something was amiss and was felt to be so by a large element in the agrarian population.

Whatever one makes of the economic or psychological roots of populism in America or of an explanation of southern poverty derived from its insights into economics, it is clear in retrospect that the remedy for southern poverty, the alternative growth path that might have been followed after 1866, lay outside the reach of decision by farmers, tenants, and planters, acting either individually or as a group. Fundamentally, the problem did not lie in exploitation, a skewed income distribution, or a drain of agricultural profits to the North. All that, if it occurred at all, was simply what the market produced and permitted, with a reasonably good short-run adjustment of crops to the opportunity offered by markets, distribution channels, physical conditions, factor proportions, and the state of knowledge prevalent among the farm population. No tenant, planter, or independent farmer could, in the Bible's phrase, "by taking thought, add one cubit to his stature" except as some might improve their position by enterprise, hard work, or luck, at the partial expense of the rest. Farmers as a group could have done a bit more, not through attacking the trusts and inflating the currency as populists advocated, though those actions would have been of immediate benefit to their condition, but through restricting cotton and supporting the development of a scientific and mechanized technological base for their industry.

In effect, the South's growth path in 1866, the setting of its social controls so as to give an impoverishing agriculture another seventy-five years of life, could hardly have occurred otherwise except as part of a national economic and social policy which would have redistributed labor and capital within the nation, rather than between the North and Europe in the later nineteenth century, without regard to race, locality, or previous social structure. Such a policy was far beyond the dreams or the capabilities or even the interests of the Republican–southern Democratic alliance in the era of laissez-faire and the growth of the large, private corporation. It was even beyond the scope of social action of the New Deal or its wartime and postwar policy instruments. To bring the South – white and black – into the United States after the Civil War required not only a national policy of the scope of the New Deal, with its often ambivalent and contradictory intents and effects, but also the assistance of massive jolts from physical, technological, and extraneous market and political events.

The boll weevil did a little to push cotton out of its traditional stronghold and move it to the drier, open lands of the Southwest, where mechanization came more easily without the physical complexity and social constraints of the East. The tractor and the cotton-picker did even more to uproot the small tenant or independent farmer. The growth of new opportunities in southern agriculture – soy beans, peanuts, citrus and orchard fruits, finally livestock and poultry – gave southeastern agriculture a new character and new commercial markets. A new, footloose character of industrial location in the 1940s and thereafter, allowing movement away from fuels, ores, water transport, and urban agglomerations, gave the Sun Belt its chance, and the immense wealth of oil and natural gas of Texas, Oklahoma, and Louisiana stimulated industry along the Gulf. In the interior of the South, the stimulus of the TVA was strongly felt, and these new pressures and advantages, coming together within a decade, were supported by the impact of the war economy of the 1940s – its disruption of traditional labor markets, its social displacement of young blacks and poor whites into the armed forces and northern jobs, and the immense federal spending programs at camps and bases, both the old Army bases and the new aerospace installations. What a Civil War, populist agitation, limited progressivist good will, New South industrialists, New York capital, self-help and cooperatives could not do over nearly a century, was accomplished at last. The back of the southern institutional peculiarity was broken and the region's energies, its resources, and its racial tensions were released to be merged with those of the national society.

6

Capitalism: southern style

Ideas are like roses. They grow and bloom in the mind. There is a time when they peak. They must be plucked then and put in the vase of some publication. If left on the stem, they get blown about and close up tight again and finally lose all their petals. Of course, in the vase they also wither and droop and lose their petals. To write them down is to take a picture of them at full bloom. But pictures, too, crack and fade. So ideas are better compared to young people – there is no way to keep them beautiful and young. But what I present here is really but the germ of an idea rather than a fully spelt-out explanation with a well-researched substantiation. That is another thing about ideas: One can communicate the germ of one in a few seconds; sometimes it takes an individual a lifetime, or a society a century, to recover from the disease or the dream that they encapsulate.

I

A hundred or even fifty years ago, American capitalists did exhibit, my idea tells me, somewhat different styles of behavior in the three historic regions east of the Great Plains, Northeast, Midwest, and South. I mean specifically the style of *business* behavior, the behavior having to do with buying and selling, hiring and firing, handling money in the scramble to earn a living or to make a profit – or at least to avoid bankruptcy. I mean not the behavior of random individuals, but the similar behavior of large numbers of businessmen, repeated every day in many places and continuing along much the same paths from one generation to another. American economists of an earlier day called this phenomenon "institutionalized behavior." Capitalism, they said, is made up of a certain pattern of such

Prepared for a conference on Continuity Versus Change in Southern Economic Development, held at The University of the South, Sewanee, Tennessee, April 2–4, 1981.

institutions – a respect for individual and small-group ownership of property, extensive use of money and credit, close calculation permitted by an accounting system, free use of one's own body and labor, and the free right to contract away one's right to his own labor time and property in exchange for payment.

As capitalistic behavior spread within and among the feudal principalities and monarchical states of Western Europe in the fifteenth, sixteenth, and seventeenth centuries, it came to organize the trade with coastal lands of far off (Africa, India, China, the South Seas), as it had long done in intra-European trade, coastal and inland. Finally its forms, its ethics, its calculations, penetrated the guild organization of industrial production and, at length, the agriculture of the manorial estate. It was carried, too, in the minds and nerves of European settlers into the empty lands of North America. But though its basic rules and institutions were everywhere similar enough to define a species of economy, they exhibited marked regional and national differences in detail and even, one might say, in spirit. French capitalism was not quite the same animal as British, and German and Italian were different from either. American capitalism, too, from the first exhibited traits distinct from the European. And today economists are pondering deeply on what it is that is so special about the Japanese.

We are concerned here with regional subspecies of the species *Capitalismus americanus,* though some of what is suggested may apply back to international differences as well. There are three points, my idea suggests, at which a regional style may be manifested:

(a) In relations among businessmen and investors – the capitalists of capitalism, the people with money or with the power to move money around – relationships of interdependence or of rivalry;

(b) In relations between this group and their labor force: salaried and wage-relations of domination, negotiation, or cooperation;

(c) In attitudes toward political authority, both local and distant, attitudes of defiance, acquiescence, co-optation, or corruption.

The hypothesis, or hunch, is that in all three of these respects, there were differences in business behavior among the Northeast, the Midwest, and the South in the United States – differences that have left residuals today. Indeed, regionalism and localism are everywhere in the world today like a grass fire, apparently extinguished but alive at the roots. Whether such an observation about the three nineteenth-century American regions is valid or not, I would like to furnish a plausible explanation for it. I want to give the explanation first, since I feel surer of its internal consistency and plausibility than I am of just what it is that it explains.

Capitalism: southern style

II

The differences in business capitalism between the North and the South, an historian would like to feel, arise from their origins in the different agrarian cultures of the two regions. In the *North*, economic life, agrarian and industrial, grew up almost (though not quite) from the start in the skin of a price system, within markets, contracts, private property, and personal freedom. In the *South*, a commercial economy grew up in a narrow sphere of the plantation crops, linked at critical points to what Marx called "pre-capitalist economic formations." The pre-capitalist form in the North and in the non-plantation areas in the South was the semi—self-sufficient family farm. In New England this took the form of the small local economy of the New England village. In the back country of the Appalachian highlands from the Catskills to the Smokies, it meant the economy of the log cabin. There the settler families lived in the thin network of a frontier neighborhood, drawing together for defense or for some joint labor on roads and construction, going on Sunday to church and on election day to the polls, and assembling on the Fourth of July for political speeches, otherwise leading fairly isolated lives, supported by networks of kin relationships, with little trade and only a few specialized industrial craftsmen in a vicinity.

In the South, thanks to the market for cotton and the presence of slaves, this primitive rural economy, with its potential for an idle and easy life, was displaced in the areas best suited for tobacco and cotton by the slave plantations, and these commercial crops entered strongly into the economy of many small farms. In the antebellum South, the slave owners were capitalists, virtually the only important capitalists except for a few merchants in port towns and some speculators in new areas. The peculiarity of slave agriculture was that it introduced into its areas a labor force that had been capitalized, that is, turned into salable chattels, linked to the employer by a political, not a capitalist economic relation. The slave-holder then stood, operating for a profit or a loss, at the center of two nets of pre-capitalist or non-capitalist relations: the one, his legal and physical authority over his slaves; the other, the ties of kin, debt, prestige, political influence, respect, or fear, which linked him to the poorer whites in his district, who owned few slaves or none and could not be called capitalists at all. He was similarly linked to other slaveholders in bonds of intermarriage of common interest, and of culture and through the over-riding common fear of slave revolt and northern interference. To grow cotton with slaves, on farms that could be otherwise fairly self-sufficient, with a single outside link to a factor or distant merchant, was to engage in a very peculiar form of capitalism indeed, and one certain to give a special cast to attitudes and economic relationships in mercantile and industrial enterprise when opportunities for its development appeared later in the nineteenth century.

Development in the North was wholly different from this. In the southern plantation areas, the pre-capitalist family was moved a little way off from the plantations to areas where it continued to flourish and grow; in the North, some frontiersmen forever moved west, but eventually all were transformed either into commercial farmers or, fading, into drifters or occasional labor. The Ohio River Valley, settled from Kentucky and Virginia, had developed by 1830 a thriving river trade and civilization; after 1830, it found its economic life sharpened and transformed by the canals and railroad and by the growing commercial markets for its surpluses of corn and hogs. Areas on to the Rockies, unsettled before 1830, were settled by 1880 directly in the patterns of a capitalist market agriculture on family scale. The northern half of Ohio, Indiana, and Illinois, and all the land to the north – Michigan, Wisconsin, Minnesota – and on across the Mississippi to the Plains north and east of the Missouri was settled under the system of free labor, by commercially minded family farm enterprises, acting under an intense capitalistic drive to organize resources in profitable patterns and bring products to market.

The North, moreover, was settled in the presence of an industry already developed along the East Coast from Baltimore to Boston and far into the interior along Eastern rivers. This circumstance had two effects on the new areas from the very outset. It meant for one thing that the migration streams contained numbers of craftsmen and mechanics, just as had the colonial migrations from the British Isles. Through their labors, a local craft and shop industry spread over the upper Midwest quite unlike that which Virginia and Kentucky mountaineers had brought to the lower river valleys. Equally important was the pre-existing local and factory industry in the North. Agricultural produce from the new areas near the Great Lakes could be exchanged for a wider array of industrial products than the cotton plantations could tap in their expansion. The difference lay in the different shapes of the markets for industrial products in the two regions. In the Northwest, free labor and family farms could get cash incomes; they offered the first mass market in American history for a variety of industrial products. The South bought very simple and crude products for its mass of slaves and hand-wrought luxury goods or European (or ivy) educations for its planters.

The differences between the Northeast and the Midwest, less sharp than the contrast between the South and North, nevertheless persisted throughout the nineteenth and twentieth centuries. The Northeast developed a mercantile, and partially from that an industrial, capitalism with wage labor and much division of labor among its small- and moderate-scale specialized firms. But the region, particularly New England and New York, was deficient in both the agricultural and the mineral resources that the Midwest, from Pittsburgh westward, contained in profusion. Partly from this fact, influenced perhaps by New England's own Puritan heritage, entrepreneurs of the region moved rather early from mercantile and industrial outlets for their money and energies to another characteristic form, recognizable already in Great Britain, that is, financial capitalism. From the time of Michigan copper and the telegraph to transcontinental railroads and telephone, Boston and New York made money by lending money out (their own and other people's), investing, controlling, manipulating the industrial and transport development of the West. The insurance industry grew up in Hartford, the stock and bond market on Wall Street, finally entertainment and advertising in midtown New York City.

Boys raised on small family farms of the Midwest, or in the back rooms over feed and seed stores, or in blacksmith's shops, or in small-town parsonages – in a culture not without a certain parochialism – acquired the scope of vision, the largeness of view that could spot big chances in organizing great monopolies and large manufacturing plants. But how did this ultimately happen? What motivated Ford and Rockefeller and their hundreds of lesser Midwest counterparts? I think there are at least three answers to the question. First, although Midwest culture was more open, more democratic and liberal than that of either the South or the Northeast, it did preserve the structure of the small town. Except perhaps in the Populist regions of the Plains, at times when everybody was poor, it was far from a Jeffersonian yeoman democracy of small farmers. It was a culture in which wealth and personal accomplishments were marks of distinction, and self-acquired wealth combined both. Men in society are, in their attitudes toward wealth, very sensitive to its social implications. Wealth acquired through robbery and exploitation, with no other compensating social product (like the wealth of the slaveholders, the carpetbaggers, or the New York manipulators), takes a generation or two to become respectable. A man must be a strong individualist or have a great urge to found a family if he would bear the stigma of illicit activities during his lifetime for the sake of later reward. The opportunities in midwestern industry were largely those of real productive achievement, engineering, and developing the organization to serve a mass market. Such wealth was itself a sign not merely of personal success but of public benefit.[1]

Midwest industrialists then could grow rich, even through some doubt-

---

[1]This description is elaborated below in Chapter 12, "The Industrial Civilization of the Midwest."

ful maneuvers, without losing their own or their neighbors' respect. But one still wonders where their imaginations were trained to visions of such scope. Those in New England colleges who sell liberal education today to selected sons and daughters of the wealthy and the very poor lay great emphasis on the stretching of the imagination, the widening of a young person's horizons beyond family, town, job, social group, sex, race, and religion to encompass the whole human family; this, we are told, sometimes as a reproof, is our humanistic religion. But these days not many students in a liberal arts college take economics without at least the mental reservation that it will make them better businesspersons. The histories of Ford and Rockefeller – or indeed of the industrialists of the British nineteenth century – do not tell us that, at least in those distant times, this was true. A liberal education in the nineteenth century, acquired by a portion of the southern gentry, was something that a family acquired after it had grown rich. It was for sons or daughters of wealth and fell into the category of the ornamental rather than the useful arts. It was a sign – we would say now, a signal – of status, but it helped one acquire status only through upward mobility in marriage. The virtues it promoted – tolerance, sympathy, aesthetic sensibility, thought, and reflection – are virtues indeed, not only in the gentlemanly conduct and enjoyment of life and leisure, but in some of the learned professions and, as the Renaissance theorists of humanism knew, in statesmanship. In English society they made a sawbones into a great surgeon, a pettifogger into a Queen's Counsel, a pill pusher into a Harley Street specialist, a finagler and social climber into a diplomat, a clerk into a first secretary. The strong hold of humanism on the universities of the Northeast and of the South derived from similar social impulses and had a similar utility in the American setting.

But the great productive achievements of the nineteenth-century capitalists were accomplished through the cumulation of wealth that comes from persistent attention to a succession of small deals. It was a parlaying of wealth. "The heights that great men made and kept / Were not attained in sudden flight." Habits acquired in a feed store, then, could serve perfectly well in the oil or the automobile business; one must simply want to keep on expanding wealth and fail to be impressed by it, once acquired. The difference between a small deal and a large one is simply the number of zeroes in the calculation. A certain lack of imagination and a hard sense of the needs of the moment were all the higher learning that they required. In the crucial period of industrialization in America, from, say, 1880 to 1930, the patriarchal structures inherent in southern regional society were not conducive to successful large-scale financial operations and industrial organization; those of the competitive, calculating individualists in the Midwest small town were just what was needed.

These decades were, of course, a period of noticeable industrial growth in the South. Compared to the two previous centuries, the growth would be called vigorous. Compared to the South's upsurge since 1950, it was a very modest, though definite, accomplishment. Wage and profit income originating in the South per capita of southern inhabitant grew as rapidly as it did in the other regions of the nation. In terms of its capacity to generate income and wealth, the South in 1940 was no farther behind the rest of the country than it had been at the close of the Civil War. Before 1920 this progress had been built in part on the continued expansion of cotton into the Southwest and its restoration with fertilizers in the Southeast. But after that, cotton had little more to offer, and textiles, aluminum smelting, sulfur mining, tobacco, lumber, oil, iron, and steel maintained the trend.

One must note two "catches" in these statements: (1) They refer to "income originating," and that does not make it clear to whom the incomes were paid; (2) the industries in question were all industries with a high component of unskilled labor and heavily weighted toward the stage of primary extraction or just beyond – smelting and the simple processing of natural mineral and agricultural raw materials. On the first count, one does not know from the regional income data whether the southern region ran a trade deficit with the rest of the economy or suffered an adverse movement in the terms on which that trade took place. If northern capital went into southern extractive industries before 1920, even a favorable southern trade balance and continued capital inflow might have been absorbed in outpayments of dividends, interest, profits, and monopolistic prices for rail services and supplies. No one has produced the statistics which would either confirm or refute the allegation that the South was a "colonial" economy. On the second count, the evidence is episodic but certainly on the face of it, quite clear. Northern and southern capital moved into bauxite, sulfur, oil, iron, and coal "because they were there"; southern businessmen operated the companies and supplied attendant services. Southerners in these extractive industries did not go north to seek capital; the capital came to them, and the incomes generated were not distributed among engineers, mechanics, or laborers of growing skills. The case of New England textiles moving south after 1905 is only slightly different. It went south because of cheap and easily disciplined labor, but it needed some skills, both from the laborers and on the part of the local management. There, in particular, the southern entrepreneurial style was tested and met the test. Only in tobacco was an oligopolistic market structure on the Midwest style achieved with southern enterprise. After 1880, James Buchanan Duke ran the American Tobacco Company out of New York. The arts of advertising and marketing, which permitted the penetration of the cigarette into the lungs and purses of women, sustained the market after they had substituted cigarettes for chewing tobacco and snuff among male addicts. But the cigarette industry itself was the only case where a group of southern entrepreneurs was able to parlay a simple natural raw material into a complicated collection of fictitiously differentiated (and hence, high value-added) products.

III

The whole matter goes back to the collection of entrepreneurial and social traits derived from slavery, or rather from slavemastery, and manifested in the body of southern entrepreneurship as it availed itself of the somewhat limited local opportunities. As just cited, they fell under three heads: (1) relations within the entrepreneurial class, (2) relations of managers to labor, (3) relations and attitudes toward the State.

By the first, I would mean a tendency to mitigate competition and to form cartels. This is an activity endemic to business society. Where the natural thrust to competition appears to be very strong, as it did among small businessmen in the 1870s and 1880s, the cartel may emerge as the only device for saving all concerned. Particularly in industries without strong technical economies of scale – mining and textiles are examples – producers unsuccessful in dominating the market may seek refuge in agreements on specific aspects of their competition – price, market shares, wages, patents, and research. The legal atmosphere appears to make a great deal of difference; in the United States, the Sherman Antitrust Act (1890) may have shaped industrial organization into the mold of the large-scale firm and away from the cartel of small producers. To this extent the law worked to the disadvantage of southern firms, whose agreements might then be forced underground into the sorts of tacit understanding achievable as the by-product of social connections. Among French producers in many industries, this sort of understanding has always seemed to be present, not only among producers but between producers and members of the permanent civil service. Let me emphasize that in all of this, I have no direct evidence. I am only asking the question, What sorts of social class and family connections existed among southern businessmen in these years? Did they exhibit an awareness of their mutual interdependence not only in the market (perhaps not much there), but in relation to unions, banks, government, and "the North"? Was this stronger, or conducted with any more skill or gentility than the ostentatious and not always successful efforts at combination in the Midwest?

In attitudes toward labor, the difference between North and South was frequently observed; indeed, it constituted a major reason for many northern firms to move South. The general level of education and skill of the labor force was not high, but it appeared in plentiful supply with a low reservation price. It was English speaking, and derived from farms so poor that even a low wage looked good. The situation with respect to northern labor was quite different and quite complex. Americanized New England craft labor had become high priced, and it was showing itself able to organize. In the Midwest, the labor from farms moving into towns and cities already possessed mechanical and even commercial skills; it could move into the lower levels of independent enterprise or white-collar work the more readily because the immigration from southern and central Europe was furnishing ample supplies of miners, steelworkers, and construction laborers. Firms looking for supplies of English speaking native workers straight from the farm, like those of one hundred years earlier, would be induced then to look south. And many firms, especially before the 1920s, moved to the southern workers, rather than moving the workers to the North. It was the worker *in the milieu* that was sought. It is perhaps peculiar that the southern white worker should have been looked on as particularly amenable to factory discipline. Here I think it is more the model of the kin—network relation than that of the master—slave relation that set the form. Southern workers could be good factory workers because their stubborn individualism did not lead them to look to one another or readily to organize with one another. They looked, as they always had, to the link upward, not to political authority but to the social authority of the employer. And where this was not enough to keep them docile, there was – as there had been in antebellum times – the everpresent threat of black freedom, the fear that poor whites would be drowned in a black sea if they failed to follow the leadership of the planters, the businessmen, and the politicians of their race. That was the trump card, and it was played over and over again.

Finally, with respect to attitudes toward government, fundamentally perhaps southern and midwestern businessmen were not very different, but there was, I think, a different twist to the behavior. Republicans' laissez-faire and southerners' States' Rights had enough in common to hold Progressivism in both pretty well in check until the New Deal. The southern alliance with Roosevelt in his first term and the parting of the ways thereafter is a long but separate story. Of more importance was the relation of business to state and local governments in these years. Here the difference, it seems to me, was this: The midwestern business community looked on government as another object of economic exploitation, as an entity to do business with, to get contracts from, to corrupt where possible, but not really to dominate. Populism and Progressivism came and went in state capitals; farmers and big-city bosses, with a base in democratic and immigrant labor, had strong political forces. Sometimes a sympathetic governor was useful in breaking a strike, but only under extreme duress did the business class look to the sheriff and the state police to keep the customary social structure intact. So thoroughly had the democratic American ethos penetrated through the public schools, so completely were the mores and pieties of capitalist society accepted, that the state, democratic as it was, was in no danger of overturning society. In the South, the case was quite different. The black reconstruction governments and the early stages of the populist movement, where racial distinctions were blurred, put a permanent scare into the hearts of white southerners – the poor perhaps as much as the wealthy. And in relation to the economy, it was not impossible that this same state and local government that so thoroughly policed the social structure could also be used to keep white labor in its place.

The difference is perhaps exemplified in the differing attitudes toward public schools. In these decades, the public school system was the jewel in the crown of state and local government in the North. Even in the rural districts, the school year was long and attendance nearly universal. The consolidated rural school and the large city high schools were racially integrated within neighborhoods, but without gerrymandering and without overt discrimination. States and municipalities spent huge sums on plant, equipment, and a cadre of teachers who had made education their career. Encouragement was given to all to go on to higher education in technical schools and liberal arts institutions; a naive faith in the earning power that came from "learning" – of any and all kinds – permeated popular attitudes. I have suggested earlier that large fortunes were not made through the application of higher education. But those entrepreneurs had at their disposal a very large, well-trained force of technical and clerical workers, intellectually alive and highly motivated toward achievement through the massive operations of the system of public schools. Despite much progress in some areas, the South's public educational system throughout this period was a pale shadow of this. The area was poor, so expenditures per pupil were low, but they were low even in relation to the South's lesser income and wealth. The area was rural, so schools were more costly, and students more at the call of parents for jobs at planting and picking times. And schools were segregated at great expense as a means of maintaining the segregated society. And why not? Southern industry at this period had no need for skilled and educated labor. Too much education was a positive detriment to the docile acceptance of the social and individual status quo on which the system had to depend if it was to function at all.

In these three respects – a sense of class interest, domination of blacks and white troublemakers, hatred of federal intervention – southern business and southern politicians worked hand in hand. But let me repeat the warning I gave at the outset. What I have said here is inference. If the evidence could be supplied, it might change somewhat the image. But I have the feeling it would not modify it in its essentials.

IV

Now having given my explanation of the peculiarities of southern capital-ism, and having tried to suggest some manifestations that are compatible with it, I still have the problem faced by all historical explanations of a contemporary phenomenon. How did the traits of the slaveholders be-come transmitted to their capitalist successors in southern trade and manufactures? This problem appears wherever discussions of enterprise and national character occur. A typical character, if it exists at all, is a generational matter, and styles change precisely because sons and daugh-ters do *not* follow their parents, but adapt what they have learned to new settings. The problem here is especially acute because the southern planter-capitalists lost out in the war. Many were replaced by men with money from the North or from the southern towns. Legend has it that they were crowded out by hard-driving petty capitalists who would do the dirty jobs that the gentility of the planter had made offensive to his children.

There are many things to say about such a problem. First, contrary to what we earlier imagined, I think, the southern planter class was not everywhere ruined. Michael Wayne's study of the Natchez region shows persistence rates of 50 to 60 percent in landholdings between 1860 and 1890.[2] Second, one wonders if the planters were all that genteel anyhow. Those who set up the original plantations in the Southwest were hard chargers themselves and only one generation away from those who re-mained after the war. Even when a family lost its wealth, it retained standing and respect, and these are in fact what the businessman uses for capital. It needed only one energetic son to restore the family fortunes by converting intangible social capital into land and money. But more impor-tant, new men, even northerners coming down, were absorbed by the environment. Cartel-like behavior could be promoted by church atten-dance and membership in country clubs. Authoritarian attitudes toward labor were entangled in a racism which many northerners shared. Migra-tion was selective of those industries and those industrialists who sought just the sort of entrepreneurial climate the South had to offer.

The matter is more complicated than the transmission of a simple regional character. A phenomenon similar to regional character is found among industries. The point can be made even more clearly for agricul-

[2]Michael Wayne, *The Reshaping of Plantation Society: The Natchez District, 1860–1880* (Baton Rouge: Louisiana State University Press, 1983).

ture than for industry. No one would doubt that the life of an agriculturist is related to certain mental and personal characteristics of a peasantry.
Those who raise stock are different from those who follow the plow;
those who grew up in a commercial environment, with free ownership of
their land, or cash tenancy, are different people from those who grew up
in the heavy shadow of rural systems of obedience and deference. It is
really no use saying, as some economists have contended, that peasants
are all alike, that is, all profit maximizers. If so, then investment in human
capital can hardly be of much importance. For that investment results in
unpeasant-like characteristics: market-mindedness, innovativeness, openness to new possibilities. Modernization means the dissipating of the
patterns of fear, suspicion, bitterness, defeat which a peasantry has had to
develop in order to survive. To be sure, a different personality was always
there *in posse,* just as any of us contains the possibility of bitterness and
negativism in the arsenal of attitudes used to cope with life. Each man, as
Goethe and Whitman alike (with differences of emphasis) both tell us,
contains the universe. But which of those patterned attitudes does history,
training, and surrounding environment elicit? And how long does it take
for the time-encrusted social mass of attitudes in a class to shift to a new
configuration? Three generations, or one, or a single lifetime?

As between peasants and commercial farms, in one industry as distinct
from another, there are modal types. Even academics recognize that an
historian thinks and speaks differently from an economist, a mathematician from a chemist, and all from a professor of English. There is no
reason that this should not hold true also for those who have spent their
lives in oil, steel, machinery, or flour. The picture is complicated by the
fact that there are also functionally differentiated types in each of these
industries. Finance men are a breed wherever they exist, but finance men
in a large trucking company have different behavior from those in a bank.
Moreover, firms themselves, like academic departments, are institutions
and the very large corporations put a stamp on all who pass through
them. It is indeed by these correspondences and codes – personal, familial, corporate, professional, industrial – that business is conducted, that
men come to know and to recognize one another, to trust or mistrust, to
communicate, and to deal.

Through the transmission of these complexes of behavioral traits and
attitudes over a span of a century, much of the southernness might have
faded out of the South. Perhaps if northerners had come into the South in
numbers, as they did to the West, there might not have been much of the
southernness left to the South. If they had brought into the region a
culture as radically different from the American as the Mexican or the
Indian, not much mixing would have been possible and the law of survival would have caused the stronger to prevail. Nonetheless, northerners

coming with money and ideas into the South before 1940 were coming into a society powerfully structured and dedicated to maintaining itself intact. The slippage in attitudes of its political and business elite had not been very great since 1870; those had been transmitted and, indeed, put to service in developing an economy based on cheap labor and racial segregation in the intervening decades. It did not much matter if by 1940 only a third or less of the actual members of those elites were direct lineal descendants of the antebellum planters. Nothing had occurred to dislodge those attitudes toward one's class, one's workers, one's government, and much had occurred to confirm and strengthen them. The result had kept the South at income levels no better than half to two-thirds of those in the North and had given her a major part of the one-third of a nation, "ill-fed, ill-housed, ill-clothed," that Franklin Roosevelt suddenly discovered in 1936. Much of that poverty was rural, but not all the rural poverty was by any means to be blamed on sharecropping and cotton. Much was that of isolated hill farms, and much was the rural low-wage economy of workers in mills, mines, lumbering, and service occupations.

* * * * *

There is a real and appropriate sense in which, for the South as it was, 1940 did mark an end. The geological shift, the earthquake that has occurred in American society in the past five decades is apparent in every one of the statistics: the interregional differentials of income and industrial activity, the productivity of labor in farming, the shift of cotton to the West and mixed farming into the South, the spread of truck transport, and the vast new industries of the Sun Belt. The in-migration of northerners to the South has been immense, and it has not been just old folks to Florida. And most important for the South, the redistribution of the black population from southern farms to southern and northern cities has occurred in the presence of marked federal intervention in education, civil rights, voting, and welfare. It seemed in the Kennedy and early Johnson years that the nation, and the South with it, had had, or was about to feel, truly a new birth of vitality and freedom.

That dream is now dissipated. A long swing to the right which began with Johnson's involvement in Vietnam has not reversed itself. It has continued as troubles have multiplied and we seek deeper into the conservative recesses of the past for formulae that will end them. Germane to the subject at hand is the survival value of the southern style of business, not just for the South, but for the nation at large. The sense among businessmen of their common interests, the intent to use and dominate labor rather than to train and educate it, the rejection of government at the national level and its manipulation locally, the incorporation of free capitalism into a system of social classes and castes – is this a pattern that is appropriate to the American nation in the 1990s? Is a capitalism which brought the Western world out of serfdom, out of the domination of kings, nobles, and priests – brought it through the artificiality and cruelty of slavery, into emancipation in a market economy – is this capitalism foundering now, losing its self-confidence, retreating into a structured, corporate economy? The values of the slave or serf society cast a long shadow: They can be discerned in Europe in advanced industrial areas in the 1930s, in what the Germans called National Socialism, the Russians Stalinist Communism, and the Italians, *Il Fascismo*. History, of course, does not end in 1870 or in 1940 or in 1980 or even in that replay of 1848: the flare-up of democratic revolutions in 1989. It evolves, and the social forms it contains revolve in their kaleidoscopic fashion with it.

> Whatever man has done, may do;
> Whatever thought, may think it too.

That used to be quoted to give schoolboys hope and inspiration. But in fact, it is a sobering thought.

PART III

Capitalist dynamics of the rural North

7

Breakthrough to the Midwest

Up to a point, the history of American economic development may be plausibly organized around sequences of physical "opportunities," continuously refreshed from one natural source after another. But such an interpretation lays yet further obligations on the interpreter. For "opportunity" is an equivocal word, with a decided human and social content. What may appear to one human group as opportunity may appear to another as abomination or, more likely, may lie for centuries wholly unobserved. How then did the American population maintain almost from the beginning so quick a recognition of economic opportunity and so ardent and organized a response to the possibilities offered by the continent as settlement crept, or rushed, across it?

To understand the history of the social response for any group, one must begin at some point with certain antecedent social conditions. Specifically and most importantly for the understanding of modern economic growth, a mercantile community must be located, embryonic in a society or touching it from outside, a community with motivations and techniques at least partially developed, able to recognize a trading opportunity as such and to bring it to life. For that to happen it is necessary that that community be encased in a political apparatus that allows it to flourish. The managers of that apparatus must see some benefits in the wealth that the merchants may acquire and stand ready to protect, encourage, even subsidize their operations. Hence in Europe the importance of the modified state mercantilisms in France and England in the sixteenth and seventeenth centuries.[1] Hence, too, in American history the importance of the colonial Revolution, which removed the controls imposed by a distant sovereignty and a competing mercantile community and replaced them by an effective national state. The evolution of a capitalist animal able to crawl from the high seas of commerce, to agricul-

[1] See Part I, above, where this history is also discussed.

tural enterprise on the land, and finally to ascend into the air of high technology in manufacturers and communications did not issue simply from the establishment of the monopolies known as private property rights or the removal of all other state controls in the brief span of nineteenth-century liberal policies. Private property existed in Greece, in Rome, in the Italian states, in Spain, without leading to the unwinding of the commercial, agricultural, and industrial revolutions in sequence.

The State, with its forms and laws, its myths about sovereignty, its police enforcement and war-making powers, and the controls on its policies embedded in a political structure, is an important feature of the economic development. A czar, a dictator, a bureaucracy, revolutionary intellectuals – any or all of these *may* bring a mass of land and peasants into the stream of modern history. The task, if designed by conscious purpose, requires not only will, cleverness, ruthlessness, the control of coercion, but also ideology, persuasion, and some route to eventual legitimation and routinization. Historically in northwestern Europe and the American North this occurred when the mercantilist state, already centralized by royal or princely power, came under the strong influence, *but not the complete domination,* of that community in which an accounting mentality, the enjoyment of acquisition, and the habit of close calculation with widely varying assessments of risk had become ingrained. The Italian city-states in the fifteenth and sixteenth centuries, then on a larger scale the United Provinces of the Netherlands in the seventeenth, exemplified this up to a point, and an escape from the "Malthusian trap" began to show itself.[2]

Great Britain in the seventeenth century gained the edge on the Netherlands, for many and complex reasons. A pause in population growth from 1650 and 1750 was followed by its resumption within the set of economic, political, and social forms that, by their interaction, were able to articulate and give dynamic stability and continuity to the worldwide expansion of its trade, its political empire, its victories, its dominance within its own sphere over the continental powers in the nineteenth century. This swelling of trade then fused with continued sequences of technical change to permit the population expansion to occur after 1850 in the presence of rising per capita incomes.

[2] My development of the sequences in early modern Europe paralleled in some respects that of Douglass North in the late 1960s. D. C. North and R. P. Thomas, *The Rise of the Western World: a New Economic History* (Cambridge: Cambridge University Press, 1973). My own weighting of these elements of population growth, scale of warfare, geographic discoveries, technological change, and the changes in state power over economic life is suggested in *Europe, America, and the Wider Word*, Vol. 1, especially Chs. 1, 2, and 11. It does not lead to the unqualified emphasis on the establishment of the mini-monopolies of state-protected private property, whose beneficial incentive effects North stresses.

Breakthrough to the Midwest

Now the American colonies lay, even in 1775, barely beyond a coast-line two thousand miles long, where the resources of a continent faced the social organization of the mother country – her sectarian religions, her weakened aristocracy, her common law and developing notions of rights and justice, and above all, the growing role of merchants and financial wealth in her representative assemblies. The English forms of landhold-ing, which combined the large holdings of an enterprising rural gentry with a much larger substratum of free yeomen, had been split apart, through the total absence of feudal law and custom, into the slave planta-tion and gentry-dominated system of the Chesapeake, Virginia, and the Carolinas and the extensive and violently growing networks of a free yeomanry, the latter interspersed among the plantations in the South and wholly dominant (except along the Hudson) in the North and shooting out into the back country of every seaboard colony.

Until 1870 – even, some would say, until 1950 – the development of the American South lay arrested in an essentially "Malthusian" or pre-mercantile formation, joined only at the top to the mercantile or "Smithian" world of expanding trade. There is great irony in this since the South's commercial staple crops – tobacco and then cotton – dominated the region's economy and, according to one interpretation, created its social structure. Tobacco in the eighteenth century and cotton in the nine-teenth accounted continuously for well over half the exports from the thirteen colonies taken as a group and from their federal union. Lively markets existed in these staples, as well as in the main factors of produc-tion, land and slave labor, and strong speculative impulses lay behind the expansion into Alabama, Mississippi, and Texas. But the South's mer-chants, except for a few in New Orleans and Charleston, were largely in England or in Philadelphia and New York, far from the local society or government. Such pockets of rent as could be seized in so competitive a market through the planting of a growing slave population on rich land, exploiting it, and organizing it in a hurry on large scale for greater exploita-tion accrued to landowners who knew of nothing but soil and crops, to slave owners whose security and welfare rested not simply on exchange-able landowning wealth but on political power and domination by coer-cion. Whatever dreams – whether of barbaric splendor, military honor, or idyllic patriarchy – beclouded the minds of those who captured most of the South's rents, any steady, conscious, closely calculated reinvestment of those profits, outside of land and slaves and facilities for cotton, held but a small place in their plans. A few railroads could be built, and a few manufactories, devoted to exploiting obvious resources, were installed. But these never got caught up into developing sequences of reinvestment from which the great agricultural behemoth could be stirred to shift its bulk to make room for banks, commerce, factories, and an industrial working class. And in the great and small social decisions about roads, harbors, public facilities, schools, justice, and war, at least before 1880, the culture and mentality of a planting society, composed of planters, middling farmers, laborers, and slaves or ex-slaves, most of whom were either submerged or stalled on the rungs of the agricultural ladder, discouraged inmigration and, in conjunction with poverty and a skewed income distribution, held commerce and manufacturing on a leash.

New England's culture developed quite differently.[3] A different location along the coast, different soils and climate, and different resources unwound a different succession of "Smithian" opportunities. A decidedly different and peculiar original culture elicited an ardent response even as those original characteristics shifted and were modified by the experience. The ideology of Puritanism showed itself far more vulnerable than the mentality of slave ownership to the organizational devices, the behavior patterns, the values and ambitions of the merchant. There were several points in the system at which the virus of capitalism could enter. The most notable one was the intense individualism of the Protestant ethic, the obsession of the individual with his own soul and his own salvation and the emotional release that came in the sensation of a conversion experience – qualified in the case of Calvinism by the perpetual uncertainty as to whether the experience was genuine, the grace of God or the work of the Devil. Beyond this was the point emphasized by Max Weber, the belief that the life of the righteous man could find justification, if at all, only by being lived *in* the world, not by monastic or pietistic withdrawal from its temptations. A well-focused life of work – strenuous, unremitting, sanctified – was the result.

A less well advertised, but equally fundamental, tendency in Puritanism came from the legalistic character of Calvin's theology. The governance of the world, according to Puritan thought, was carried out not through Divine whim, but through Divine law. Even the belief in predestination, in God's absolute foreknowledge, confirmed rather than contradicted this. The covenant of the Law and the covenant of Grace pulled by the theologians out of Scripture, attested to an order in the human and the physical universe that could be discerned, though never wholly encompassed, by human reason. The Puritan church experienced a stormy and contentious existence through the seventeenth and eighteenth centuries as one troubled generation succeeded another, and worldliness, complacency, and rationalism grew while the Puritan theocracy's hold on the state weakened. But in all its later movements, from the Great Awakening to the rise of Unitarianism, its adherents clung to these two great faiths: a faith in the validity of the individual's internal religious experience and a

---

[3]See the treatment reprinted in Part IV, Chapter 11, below.

faith in the mind's examination of Scripture and of the physical world. These were the only means to know God and to appease, if never wholly to satisfy, one's conscience in serving Him.

Seventeenth-century Puritanism came to America trailing clouds of Catholic (or what could loosely be called medieval) thinking. Theocracy was one such thought: the idea of a state-church, or a church-state. In Calvin's Geneva, John Knox's Edinburgh, and Increase Mather's Boston this formed the central point, the unifying, the enforcing agent of doctrine and of a prescribed personal and community morality. That morality, in turn, was the reverse of libertarian; it was community oriented and functioned to maintain order, peace, and continuity in the social and familial life. Its economic component was not only a work ethic, as it is called today, but also expressed a scorn of "vain show," worldly tastes and lavish expenditure, and its economic policy included the policing of markets to enforce the "just price" and the prohibition of "usury." The Puritan village retained, too, habits of deference and respect but gave, or claimed to give, these not to birth, rank, or wealth as such, but to those who showed the signs of salvation by grace in outward conduct by achievement, learning, and piety, who showed strength and righteousness before men but humility before God. The perpetual uncertainty to which the Calvinist was condemned produced not despair, but perpetual struggle. Pride, complacency, confidence in one's salvation were the greatest enemies of salvation, but God, an inward-dwelling God, a conscience – not man, not a minister, not the community – was the ultimate judge.

From these bases, Puritanism[4] derived its great strength and its eventual weakness. It was a fierce religion, ferocious in the demands put on an individual soul, and so unsparing also in the demands such a soul put on others. Love and charity were not extinguished, but they were not among its conspicuous manifestations. New England retained a village form of settlement, even in the migrations West, but the elements of the village – schools, church, civil government – all were but the necessary

[4]And Presbyterianism, Baptism, and later Methodism. The main differences among these Protestant sects existed on matters of church government, on points of ritual, and on the balance between inward light, biblical revelation, and a formal church structure as the means to grace. As used here, the term *Puritan* denotes an impulse inherent in Protestant Christianity and crystallized in all its aspects in Congregationalism. Presbyterianism shared most of its Calvinistic features, but differed on Church government; the Pentacostal sects shared its emphasis on individual experience, but lacked the elaborate theology that bound it fast within a social, natural, and intellectual world. As the nineteenth century went on, the difference among these sects in doctrine, practices, and emphasis became overlaid by differences in social background, wealth, and "respectability." Each thought the others rather queer, stuffy, overly emotional, or in some sense "foreign." These are very fine-spun and sensitive matters. But my concern here is simply with their efficacy in furnishing the emotional support for lives of economic achievement.

stage setting for the drama of the individual soul. Human society was not a delight to be enjoyed, giving moral support in a common task; it was the necessary testing ground for the individual struggle. It had to be erected wherever the Puritan went, even if only as a theater wherein that struggle could be carried on. Conquest, mastery were deeply set in this ethic; even the acquisition of worldly knowledge was not the mere pleasurable exercise of God-given powers. The Puritan did not study and learn to satisfy curiosity, but to achieve a purpose. Life, social relations, business activities, education – all were means to an end. That the end, knowledge of God and justification before Him, were known never to be totally attainable only increased the intensity of the effort and the intolerance of distraction, diversion, and dissent.

These latter characteristics made in New England for victory over a harsh environment; indeed, the match between physical environment and the intensity of the inner flame makes one wonder which was the opportunity and which the response. Was the environment chosen to provide these tests, or did the tests elicit a particularly fierce and stubborn dogmatism by which they could be survived? Such are the mysteries and indeterminacies of social evolution. This classic capitalist spirit was only held back in the seventeenth century in any case by the earlier ethic – in fact, the traditional ethic of an agrarian community. And at bottom all that was communal, all that was social in that ethic had begun to lose its power as soon as Luther and his fellows had abjured the symbols of an anthropomorphic God and the magic and miracles of a universal church. The fractionating radicalism of the Protestant Reformation was carried furthest in the Pietist and Baptist sects, where the individual emotional content was highest and the social content least. Congregationalism and Presbyterianism yet kept up the form of a united and authoritarian church government but by the eighteenth century they had lost their civic power. But in all these sects reliance on an individual's inner experience ultimately destroyed external moral authority and left the world not a church community, but a civic community, a marketplace, and a battlefield. Capitalism, the appropriation of wealth by individuals through exchange, the characteristic activity of merchants, requires, as we have seen, some positive sympathy and support from the state, that supreme controller of power and force, and it flourishes best in the absence of the moral restraints of justice and charity. Protestantism was better for capitalism than Catholic Church government because, even in its ferocious Puritan manifestation, its public morality had a weaker political power over its communicants. Moral authority in society had been dispersed and displaced to someplace deep inside the individual conscience or far away in the eye of an invisible God. Over these two, society and public morality had no police powers, no thought control. So economic behavior and organization – individualized, restless, intelligent, calculating and self-assured – could move out into a fractionated and competitive world of impersonal markets. On this basis, succeeding generations of Yankees, the individuals and their families, motives, values, civic institutions, underwent continual modification and redirection, but not fundamental alteration, from 1750 on, as at home and in the replantings to the West, the succession of opportunities for enterprise and wealth acquisition opened out with settlement across the continent – to Ohio, Texas, California, and Hawaii.

Ideally, a weak religion is better for capitalism than a strong one. But it does not follow from this that best would be no religion at all. Three psychic forces in concert motivate, control, and guide the histories of human societies: the struggle for material sustenance, which in its exaggerated state is called greed; the struggle for social survival, which in its deformed state is sought through political power, the use of force, and fear; and finally the thirst for that unalloyed pleasure derived from activities done for their own sake alone, self-expression and the expressions of love. The church-state rolled all three of these into a single structure. The modern world, in its specializing way, has broken the mold and scattered the pieces to move and develop in the sun, to find in free markets of trade, ideas, and democratic political opinions their natural balance. The history of that effort, of its disasters, its heroic glories, and its periods of even, smoothly functioning performance is the history – economic, political, and social – of the West. It was an effort that found its most novel and innovative manifestations in the settling of Europe's new continents.

To a twentieth-century eye, the Quakers,[5] who founded Philadelphia and created its commercial culture, seem as righteous, thrifty, exclusive, and godly as the Puritans of Boston, but without the Puritan fire in the belly. The sect, from its origins in England and Germany confronted the world of the Reformation from the pietistic side, cultivating an "inner light" and breathing in the peaceful assurances of God's love from the Gospel according to St. John. It had not so much a worship as a comfortable intimacy – not even an intimacy, but a friendship – with Jesus, and it based the perfect life literally on the Sermon on the Mount. The doctrine, if it can be called such, taught simplicity, plain living, and avoidance of

---

[5]I have located only one extended reference to the "Weberian" source of the Quakers' business ethic, in Frederick B. Tolles, *Meeting House and Counting House* (Chapel Hill: University of North Carolina press, 1948). Tolles emphasizes that Quakerism, for all its differences from Calvinism, was sociologically a part of the English Puritan movement. The range of personalities in a meeting house ran from unbelievably pure and gentle mystics to hard-driving merchants and manufacturers who pursued their pietism as part of an active life "in the world." In both sects incessant activity combined with an initial scorn of luxurious expenditure to pile up profits for reinvestment.

luxury, vain show, and the formal trappings of rank and subordination. It taught distrust of strong displays of emotions or enthusiasm and avoided whatever appeared excessive, immoderate, unreasonable. The Quaker lived neither in the world as if to conquer or defy it, as did the Puritan, nor out of the world to avoid its contaminations. He simply affirmed his inward convictions, strengthened them by meeting silently with like-minded families, and waited for sin, evil, violence in the world and in his neighbors to melt away before God's love and truth and the example of a good life which he set. Inner peace, inner assurance, inner calm came from love and virtue, led to virtuous acts, and must spread to others when they saw and felt it. The Puritan's great fault was intolerance and violence; the Quaker's was complacency and hypocrisy. The Puritan's great strength was self-awareness, self-criticism; the Quaker's was an unwavering stead-fastness. To live by either faith seems to a modern mind and sensibility to have required an immense amount of individual strength and nerve and an unbelievable disregard for the opinions of the world round about.

Self-protection and propagation for both sects came not simply from acts of individiual will, but also from the scale on which the faith and the behavior pattern established itself. Puritanism grew in Massachusetts Bay from a base of perhaps twenty to thirty thousand migrants before 1650. Quakers were planted in smaller, undetermined, numbers by Penn on the banks of the Schuylkill and the Delaware.[6] Both groups were colonies of larger communities in England, with many links on the part of the Puri-tans to other Calvinist groups in Protestant Europe and in the case of the Quakers to German pietist sects. Puritanism, with its theory of the state, maintained, as I have said, some of the legal and moral restrictions on the free exercise of the mercantile mentality, and these yielded to the opportu-nities of wealth and the attractions of a less ferocious, rationalistic view of society and the world only after inner upheavals, struggle, and intermi-nable prayer and preaching. The Quaker set probity, honesty, and faithful-ness high among the virtues, but even less than the Puritan did he learn from his faith that calculating behavior was in essence a sin. Shrewdness in the management of assets hurt no one and so was no sin, and Quaker

[6]Lemon writes, "No reliable population statistics exist for colonial Pennsylva-nia. Estimates list the population at about 500 in 1681, 20,000 in 1700, 50,000 in 1720, 100,000 in 1740, 200,000 in 1760, and 300,000 in 1776. After 1740, each of the major groups – English, German, and Scotch-Irish – constituted about one-third of the totals," (45), and further, that the Quakers formed the majority of the Pennsylvania population for the first forty years of settlement and their numbers reached about thirty thousand by 1790 (18–19). James Lemon, *Best Poor Man's Country* (Baltimore: Johns Hopkins University Press, 1972). One recent standard history of Pennsylvania, S. Klein and Ari Hoogenboom, *A His-tory of Pennsylvania* (University Park: The Pennsylvania State University Press, 1973), essentially concurs in estimates of this magnitude.

families were free to take business advantage of the chains of opportunity presented by trade, markets, and production.

The conduct of trade and business within a group whose members trust one another has, of course, immense advantages in minimizing "moral hazard" and "transactions costs." The wealth of the merchant families, and the ease with which they could function over far-flung connections, was based on this. The example of the Jewish banking families in Europe is but the most prominent case of this obvious social truth.[7] The Quakers' eccentric way of setting themselves apart – the insistence on what seem trivial distinctions, the forms of dress and address, distinctions which seem to ask for ridicule, ostracism, and even persecution – were functional in fact, whatever their motivations, to mark them off from other men, maintaining an inner cohesion by creating hostility in their surroundings.

Then followed what is to my mind the central chain of economic events in colonial American history, a growth far more powerful and significant even than the mushrooming of the slave economy of tobacco on the Chesapeake or the spreading out of New England and New York's merchant fleet over the seas. This Quaker colony, through Penn's luck and shrewdness, was set up astride two principal rivers and acted as a funnel for trade from a vast interior. The commodity at first was furs, as it was in New Amsterdam and Montreal, but the Quakers' tolerance and the quiet efficiency of their government brought settlers. More English and Welsh Quakers and servants on indentures clustered there to start farms and some industrial craft shops. By 1710 Philadelphia had the components of a mercantile city-state and awaited only a bulk staple from the interior to flow across its docks. And at this time the Palatine Germans came, by 1740 at least one hundred thousand of them, the first mass

[7] A novel instance of this phenomenon – the development of business acuity among the members of a minority group excluded from the accepted lines of advancement – was found by Alexander Gerschenkron among the "old Believers" in seventeenth- and eighteenth-century Russia. See A. Gerschenkron, *Europe in a Russian Mirror* (Cambridge: Cambridge University Press, 1970), Ch. 2, especially 37–38. This group of fundamentalist adherents to traditional forms of worship (e.g., the use of two fingers instead of three in making the sign of the cross), in response to savage persecution, became a close-knit intercommunicating fraternity of merchants and early capitalist manufacturers. Gerschenkron uses the example to emphasize that the *minority status*, not the specific content of the dogma, was the determining factor. The problem for the Weber thesis, however, is to explain how and where the capitalist ethic became the *dominant* spirit in Anglo-Saxon societies. That requires attention to the beliefs and values of adherents of the dominant religion. Those who question the relevance of the Weber thesis also point out that a capitalist spirit was exhibited by merchants and bankers in the Italian and Spanish cities and in the Low Countries in the Renaissance. All this is treated at more length in *Europe, America, and the Wider World*, Vol. 1, 23–28.

intercontinental migration of free men to pass through the city and take up lands in a deep ring in the counties just to the west. And the land of those counties just happened to be the deepest, most fertile, best-drained farming lands settlers were ever to encounter short of the deep prairie soils of Illinois and Iowa, far into the interior of the continent one hundred fifty years later. Agricultural surpluses from their thrifty peasant farms could hardly be avoided (certainly more than the 10 or 20 percent of the yield of a family's labor in New England[8]), and a farmer did not have to be a very enlightened or aggressive capitalist to release them at favorable terms into the channels of trade. The markets were the West Indies and to some extent the Carolinas, and here Philadelphia had a decided locational advantage over Boston or even New York. A similar phenomenon appeared on the Connecticut below Hartford in the mid-eighteenth century, but on a much smaller scale. Wherever it appeared, accumulations of mercantile wealth and agricultural prosperity followed.

The surrounding lands in eastern Pennsylvania were superior to New England in stands of hardwood timber and were vastly richer in iron and coal. As in New England, but on a larger scale, in greater variety, and with a deeper foundation in the structure of production, the early beginnings of what was to be a great consolidated industrial district were laid, to flourish after 1800 as water power, machinery, and coal and iron made their appearance. But the story does not stop here. Beyond the merchants and the English and German farmers, back toward the colony's Appalachian spine, lay the West. Fort Pitt had featured as an outpost against the French and Indians in the War of 1756–63. At the same time in Philadelphia, the peaceful Quaker oligarchy, which had faced the threat of Indian raids without flinching, withdrew from the responsibility of government by violent means. The Indians were subdued and scattered. But even well before then, the empty central and western lands had been awaiting settlers.

It must not be thought that the Pennsylvanian lands were given away through the charity and kindness of the Quakers. William Penn was interested in getting a return from his holding, and the later members of his family up to the Revolution were active in selling lands and encouraging immigration. But again in the 1740s[9] the mass migration of Scottish

---

[8]Lemon, *Best Poor Man's Country*, 38–39, 154–160, 208–210, gives a picture of grain yields not much higher than those in New England or in the Old Northwest after sustained cultivation. The advantage lay in the quantity of inframarginal lands, the easier conditions of tillage, and compared to the Midwest, the proximity to water transport.

[9]James M. Swank, *Progressive Pennsylvania* (Philadelphia: Lippincott, 1908), 34–7, estimates the flow of Scotch-Irish on the order of five thousand a year during the several waves after 1710. Many passed through and down the valleys

Highlanders, and especially of the so-called Scotch-Irish (Scotch Presbyterians transplanted to Ulster under Cromwell and now rebellious against the rack rents of their English landlords), was released. They are said to have been hearty, passionate, wild men – as well as Calvinists with an ideal combination of qualities to open a frontier. As we know, they did not stop in central Pennsylvania, but poured down the north–south valleys, behind the Blue Ridge, through Western Virginia and North Carolina, and infiltrated the hilly woodlands of Kentucky and Tennessee. Those who went south were stranded in poor hill farms and hamlets for another hundred fifty years, but those who remained pressed on after 1800 into the Ohio territory.[10]

Here then was a dynamic, expansive, American capitalist civilization in the making. Its components were three: (1) the settled merchants and craftsmen clustered along rivers in the East, (2) the settled farmers, largely self-sufficient in meat and grain and wood but supplying, as German peasants had supplied for centuries, their ample surpluses to be the merchants' stock in trade and receiving back the means to an ever more comfortable and more productive life, and (3) those who felled trees, cleared the land, herded cattle and hogs, and, like a construction crew, prepared to move further west. All were contained in a system of laws and business practices, after 1789 under a federal government and protected by its troops. All were within reach of land agents, surveyors, a money economy, some supplies, however thin, of money and credit, however eccentric their forms. As opportunities were turned up in the course of westward movement (coal as early as the 1780s and strongly after 1820, timber, iron, and, in 1856, oil), the cultural underlay of capitalist organization, institutions, and behavior slid beneath them like a sheet of water to float them down to the centers of commerce and to float in a counterflow of settlers and commercial enterprise to each new area.

Take this process as it went on in Pennsylvania, repeat it over and over again, across the Ohio River, across the Prairies, across the Mississippi, and join to it the similar migrations below and around the Great Lakes into northern Ohio, Michigan, Illinois, and Wisconsin from New England and New York, and you have written the history of the American Midwest. At Pittsburgh, Cincinnati, Cleveland, Chicago, Milwaukee, Detroit,

of Maryland and Virginia to western North Carolina. The numbers in Pennsylvania were at least one hundred thousand in 1775, equal to the numbers of English and of German settlers.

[10]The Philadelphia regional development in the antebellum decades is handled in a very valuable quantitative regional study: Diane Lindstrom, *Economic Development in the Philadelphia Region, 1810–1850* (New York: Columbia University Press, 1978).

and beyond to Omaha and Kansas City – whush! whush! whush! – each within a decade or two, one after another out of the ground the cities sprang, to cap the agrarian wealth of the great American plain. On the corn and wheat fields, the hay farms and cattle ranches, they pressed down the iron grid of a nineteenth-century manufacturing and transport technology and reshaped the culture of an agrarian region to the forms and networks of an urban-industrial civilization. The settlement of California was simply the most western and most spectacular example of all this. San Francisco was in the 1850s the Philadelphia of the Pacific, with gold rather than the Quakers' peaceful government as the magnet.

Where then is the mystery in such an achievement? Once the charm was wound up and began to tick, once the response patterns were planted by migrations and the spread of trade, the opportunities unrolled in one sequence after another. On reflection and analysis each incident of the history seems complicated, requiring the concatenation of many natural features of an environment and characterological traits of a population. The timing of events – of migrations, for example, and of inventions – relative to the appearance of "needs" and "opportunities" seems sometimes crucial in the outcome. But the possibilities for substitutions, for alternative paths, were probably endless, given the generosity of the natural environment, the state of the commerical and industrial arts as the development was going on, the essentially simple, democratic governmental structure, the strong hold of Protestant morality and capitalist mentality in the governing classes, and the strength, good health, vigor, and high morale of the population. Like any natural activity (hitting a baseball, sex, digestion), economic development was an immensely complicated affair if one stopped to think about it. But if done thoughtlessly, there was nothing to it.

From the mid-nineteenth century – pushing through the violence and bloodshed of the War – the American agro-industrial society showed the momentum to carry through the remainder of the continental expansion as, at the same time, with the renewal of immigration streams, it burst through the iron gates of technical change into the land of high-tech opportunities and large-scale organization, which on my mental map I have labeled Schumpeterian.[11] Beneath it, even absorbing the immigrants, the culture at its deepest levels altered more slowly, but as in the mid-eighteenth century, so by the 1920s, old ways, old standards, old character structures were melting and transforming into something new and strange. Then in 1940 American culture and capitalism were suddenly jolted into the tortured international and supra-national history of the twentieth century.

[11]See *Europe, America, and the Wider World*, Vol. 1, Ch. 11.

8

Migration and a political culture

History books tell us that the United States in 1860 was divided into three parts: South, Northeast, and West. The South had in turn three sub-regions: the border states, the southeast, and the "Old Southwest"; the Northeast included New England and what had been the Middle Colonies. The Far West had hardly entered into American economic history, except as a land of mining excitements. A new and arid Southwest lay beyond Texas. A new Northwest on the Pacific was replacing the "old Northwest." The latter had hardly become "old"; its settlement and culture patterns were still vigorously penetrating across into Kansas and Iowa heading into the Great Plains. In each of these three sections – South, Northeast, and Northwest – the population had developed a characteristic social organization and with it a chracteristic culture, which the sub-regions exemplified with minor variations.

At a century's distance, and with the record of the War in retrospect, the South appears indeed as a nation, a monolith whose economy, politics, society and morality were dominated by the class of slave-owning planters. Slave owners with their families made up less than one-third of the South's white population and less than one-fifth of the entire population, including slaves. The "planters" with ten or more slaves, whose holdings accounted for three-quarters of the slaves and at least three-quarters of the cotton grown, numbered only about 100,000 individuals out of a southern population of about four million slaves and 7,200,000 free persons.[1] One hardly knows whether to marvel more at the politics

First published as "From Northwest to Midwest: Social Bases of a Regional History" in D. C. Klingaman and R. K. Vedder, eds., *Essays in Nineteenth Century Economic History: the Old Northwest* (Athens: Ohio University Press, 1975), 3–35.

[1] Census of 1860, *Agriculture*, 247. G. Wright calculates that on the basis of a Census sample the top 20 percent of slaveholders (i.e., about 75,000 individuals)

or at the economics of this vast region. Among other peoples and soils, a small aristocracy had ruled over a large area, restricting its economy along lines compatible with its social dominance. One thinks of the eighteenth-century English aristocracy or, more aptly, of the Prussian Junkers and other East European landed groups. But those noble classes ordinarily possessed a degree of local sovereignty, legal control of local justice, and even force, and they dominated the values of a population committed deeply to the principle of social organization through subordination. The achievement of the southern planters was the more remarkable in that it was carried off in a nineteenth-century nation-state, where democracy and free markets had received their supreme expression. To understand the planters' power, one must no doubt look to a system and traditions of local government founded on seventeenth- and eighteenth-century English landed precedent.[2]

The free North presents no such clear picture of class organization and dominance.[3] Along the eastern seaboard from Baltimore to Boston and on to the shipping towns of Maine, the mercantile activity of colonial times, after its crisis from 1808 to 1818, had restored itself by the 1830s. It drew on the cotton trade, whaling, and the speed of clipper ships, and increasingly on the connections with the interior by the canals and railroad, the growing exchange of western grain and meat against European manufactures, and the growing manufactures in southern New England and around New York and Philadelphia. The location, wealth, working population, and financial institutions of the seaboard cities had gathered to them not only shipping, trans-shipping, warehousing, and packaging of the stream of goods, but also the activities of selling, financing, and promoting trade, and with that the job of modifying through manufac-

held 77.7 percent of the slaves and that the top 20 percent of cotton growers grew 77.4 percent of cotton produced in 1860. These are also certainly nearly wholly overlapping classifications. G. Wright, "The Economics of Cotton in the Antebellum South," unpublished dissertation (Yale University, 1969), 102.

[2]Concerning the "oligarchical principle" and influence of the property qualification on English local government, see Sidney and Beatrice Webb, *The Development of English Local Government 1689–1835* (London: Oxford University Press, 1963), Part I. [First published as Ch. 5 of *English Local Government*, Vol. 4 (London: Oxford University Press, 1922).]

The extensions of these principles in Virginia are alluded to by T. J. Wertenbaker in *Patrician and Plebian in Virginia* (Charlottesville: Michie Co., 1910), 33–34, 39, 57–58.

[3]William B. Weeden, *Economic and Social History of New England 1620–1789*, Vol. 2 (Boston: Houghton, 1891), 786–815, 840–876; and Kenneth Lockridge, "Land, Population and the Evolution of New England Society 1630–1790," *Past and Present*, 39 (April 1968), 62–80. See also Robert E. and B. Katherine Brown, *Virginia 1705–1786: Democracy or Aristocracy?* (East Lansing: Michigan State University Press, 1964).

ture the form and qualities of the goods in transit.[4] Their strength as commercial and mercantile centers had been early supported by the scatter of small crafts and rural industry over the countryside, using skills and idle labor of the farm and village population. Even in the late eighteenth century, the shippers and craft shops of the coastal towns gave an occasional and feeble imitation of their counterparts in northeastern Europe, organizing rural labor in variants of the putting-out system. From the 1820s to the 1850s, they extended the bases of their wealth to include the organization of shipping, the fur trade, the ventures of western development, and the new factories along the fall line of the nearby rivers, utilizing an influx of native rural – and mostly female – labor. By the 1840s, their cities were beginning that immense absorption of European immigrant labor that was to continue to 1914.[5] The factories, located near water power or the points of importation of coal, added another layer to the complex economic life of the seaboard. And around and within the industrial net had collected the industries and trades which made the life of sailors, merchants, railroad men, factory workers possible and endurable – construction workers, tradesmen, domestics, and the purveyors of entertainment, government, and gossip. Like some complex sea organism, the society of the Northeast had grown older and ever more structured, piling up layer upon layer of occupations and social groups, adding function to function through complex and interdependent internal markets and contractual arrangements.[6]

Such a growth, through the utilization of a succession of economic opportunities, required strong and adaptable economic forms and sturdy institutions of local government. The development of these forms, the modification of laws and practices of private ownership, contract, social control, and democratic local government which made room for an urban laboring class, powerful financial interests, the practices and influence of the Catholic Church, the power of political bosses, and much else unimagined by Locke, Bentham, or Jefferson – all this constitutes the

---

[4]G. R. Taylor describes the transition from household to factory organization in manufactures in *The Transportation Revolution 1815–1860* (New York: Rhinehart & Co., 1951), 207–249. See also R. M. Tryon, *Household Manufactures in the United States, 1640–1860* (Chicago: University of Chicago Press, 1917), 242–303.

[5]Oscar Handlin, *Boston's Immigrants: A Study in Acculturation*, revised edition (Cambridge, Mass.: Harvard University Press, Belknap Press, 1959), Chs. 7, 8.

[6]Stuart Bruchey analyzes the nineteenth-century social structure of New England in *The Roots of American Economic Growth 1607–1861: An Essay in Social Causation* (New York: Harper & Row, 1965), 193–207. See also, Blanche Hazard, *The Organization of the Boot and Shoe Industry in Massachusets Before 1875*, Harvard Economic Studies XXIII (Cambridge, Mass.: Harvard University Press, 1921).

institutional history of the eastern seaboard. The manner and order in which this institutional structure utilized the opportunities for increasing income and wealth, the distribution made of the result, the examples of skill and efficiency, the stories of fraud and waste – these constitute its economic history. Both are embedded in the area's social history – the history of homes, families, neighborhoods, and other institutions in which the size and characteristics of the populations were regulated and reproduced.

By 1860, then, the North was like a long animal whose head rested in the eastern urban region; its body, including factories, shops, and commercial farms stretched from fifty to one hundred miles inland, and a little like the Cheshire cat, faded back into the woods, hills, and flat lands of the West, half dissolved and uncertain in outline. Despite home gardens and domestic livestock in the cities, the seaboard's food needs, including hay for workstock, were mainly supplied from a vast farming area which for two decades had begun organizing itself into cropping regions on a continental scale. The rural out-migration from upper New England and central Pennsylvania and New York had been in two directions: toward the coastal cities and to the West. Much of the westward migration was in part the transfer of a commercial farming activity to a more suitable region – the movement of grain and meat producers into the Ohio Valley and thence across to the Mississippi, the spread of New York dairying to Wisconsin.[7] These market-directed movements were guided by the prices for land in various locations and strongly affected by the opening of new land and the availability of credit. The degree of spread of a single commercial economy is indicated by the repercussions of the banking crises of 1819, 1837, 1842, and 1857, producing bursts of bankruptcies and unemployment even in young western towns.[8]

The lands between the Ohio and the Mississippi were connected then in 1860 to the seaboard through the market for their farm products – that "surplus" to which the transport improvements had given vent.[9] In this respect their position did not differ from that of the

[7] Lewis D. Stillwell, "Migration from Vermont (1766–1860)," in *Proceedings of the Vermont Historical Society*, Vol. 2 (1937); 135, 185–196, 214, 215.

[8] Richard C. Wade, *The Urban Frontier. The Rise of Western Cities, 1790–1830* (Cambridge, Mass.: Harvard University Press, 1959), 161–202. See also the extended discussion of western cycles in Thomas S. Berry, *Western Prices before 1861* (Cambridge, Mass.: Harvard University Press, 1943), Chs. 12–16.

[9] This development is recognized by G. S. Callender in his discussion of western settlement in *Selections from the Economic History of the United States 1765–1860* (Boston: Ginn and Co., 1909), 600–601.

For a discussion of the "surplus" concept in the South and West, see Ray A. Billington, *Westward Expansion, A History of the American Frontier* (New York: Macmillan, 1949).

South, except that their product was a bit more varied and their position in foreign markets much less prominent or secure. Like the South, the West received back from the East manufactures – textiles and ironware and a thousand miscellaneous items. Both West and South were collections of local economies, of semi-self-sufficient families or neighborhoods which formed economic and political regions not because of an internal interdependence, but because of a common link to eastern and European markets and suppliers. But the West's connection to the East had grown far closer than the cotton South's in more vital and intimate ways – in the movement of loans for land holding and railroad and minerals development and in the movement of men from the same farms and stock as those from which men had moved into seaboard cities.[10] Westward movement both regions had enjoyed, but the Old Southwest was settled from *its* East, where the procession of planters, slaves, and yeoman farmers moved out to reproduce the same social and economic system on new and more fertile soil. The Old Northwest received free small farmers from the border South and the Northeast, and placed them in a social structure looser than the South's and an economic structure more varied and more complex. In 1860 this broad and populous farming region stood on the eve of an industrial development whose end is even today not yet in sight. From a congeries of local economies, of farm families and small village centers, the native population of the Midwest was to furnish food, fuel, metals, and transport together with the skills, drives, savings, steadfast work, sheer human energy, and much of the manual labor that transformed the area into the rich and sometimes alarming industrial society called – with its eastern, southern, and far western extensions – the United States of America.

II

To make some rough assessment of a regional character type and to link it to the response made in following decades to opportunities for acquisition of wealth in industry and commerce is a notoriously risky enterprise. For one thing, it is necessary to sketch and to evaluate those opportunities. A huge study would be required to sketch their sheer magnitude, derivable from physical production advantage – in agricultural productivity, cheap minerals, and easy transport. A physical advantage so well

[10]Douglass C. North, "Interregional Capital Flows and the Development of the American West," and Douglas F. Dowd, "A Comparative Analysis of Economic Development in the American West and South," both in *Journal of Economic History*, Vol. 16, No. 4 (1956); 493–505, 558–74; and James S. Duesenberry, "Some Aspects of the Theory of Economic Development," *Explorations in Entrepreneurial History*, Vol. 3, No. 2 (December 1950); 97–102.

suited to the techniques and markets of the late nineteenth century could hardly have been missed by any population with reasonable access to a knowledge of those techniques and to the means of finance. Furthermore, a single "history" of the response of a population, without specifying a standard of comparison, is not a mode of explanation acceptable to a skeptical modern mind. One ought at least to find a similar opportunity in this period which a population did *not* utilize. The history of southern industrial development, for example, might provide such a comparison, although there the opportunity, at least in heavy industry, was obviously not as great. But certainly industrialization can occur – and could occur in the late nineteenth century – in a variety of social settings. The examples of the northwestern European industrial belt from Dortmund to Liège, of the Saar–Lorraine areas, of Japan and North Italy after the 1870s come to mind. The experience of England and New England must be examined for an earlier period and under a rather different condition of technology and markets.[11]

At the outset of such an effort, one must face the famous "frontier hypothesis" about the American (i.e., midwestern) character. A mere economic historian cannot well assess Turner's hypothesis, its development and use by his "school," and the controversy and revisions it has survived.[12] Some direct impressions from the materials of agricultural and business history may be more to the point.

The rural society of the old Northwest was peculiarly well adapted, it might be argued, to what a Marxist would call its "historic role" in the mid-nineteenth century. Taken across the whole area from central New York and Pennsylvania to the Plains, conditions were remarkably homogeneous. The land, cut up by the rectangular survey and offered at auction sales, had undergone settlement between 1800 and 1860 under rather steady or regularly recurrent conditions of population growth and

[11]The only scheme for organizing these experiences is that offered by Gerschenkron's "relative backwardness" hypothesis. It suffers from three flaws: (1) It attributes to relative backwardness some phenomena of later nineteenth-century industrialization (e.g., greater importance of heavy industry, the greater role of banks) which may be due to the course of the technological and institutional change in the nineteenth century; (2) its applicability to non-European cases (Japan, U.S.A.) has not been made manifest; (3) it fails to specify the mechanism by which a nation's relative backwardness produces "tensions" within the national society. See Alexander Gerschenkron, *Economic Backwardness in Historial Perspective* (Cambridge, Mass.: Harvard University Press, Belknap Press, 1962), 5–30, 353–364. See a critique in Chapter 15, below.
[12]The most interesting postwar work done on the subjects that absorbed Turner is by Allen G. Bogue. See especially his early article, "Social Theory and the Pioneer," *Agricultural History*, Vol. 24 (January 1960): 21–34, and his synthesis of much of his work in *From Prairie to Corn Belt* (Chicago: University of Chicago Press, 1963), especially Chs. 1, 2.

credit availability. Land auctions, the knowledge of insiders, the pressure of squatters, the homemade banking institutions, the presence of eastern speculators – all of these had caused each tier of counties to be settled in turn in a pattern of free farms, clustering in size between eighty and 160 acres, enough to occupy a family labor force, with some help at harvest, and perhaps some surplus land for speculative sale. Unlike the European or early New England pattern, settlement was not in villages, but in the isolated farmstead, set in the middle of a large, consolidated holding, with no common lands and very little fragmentation. Except for mortgaging, landownership was absolute; speculators, early ranchers, states, and railroads, with large holdings held them to sell, not to farm with tenants. Within this monotonously repetitive pattern of rural settlement supplementing and drawing on the versatility of the settlers, a marked specialization of economic function early appeared. Speculators, ranchers, mixed farmers, dairymen, even frontier bankers on occasion moved westward as the comparative advantage of a county shifted with growing density of settlement. The comparison to the movement of an army is more exact than is often realized, for the body of settlers was divided to a degree into corps – cavalry of ranchers, an infantry of woodsmen, quartermaster, ordnance, and signal corps of suppliers of commercial services and contacts. For this reason settlement proceeded rapidly and with a high degree of efficiency.[13]

The homogeneity of the population and of its fortunes was of course not absolute. In the scramble for settlement, families were sucked in from the South as well as the East – from Kentucky and western Virginia, as well as central Pennsylvania, New York, and the upland counties of New England. The Ohio River, geographical boundary between slavery and freedom, was overlapped by a zone of southern border settlement extending into the southern half of Illinois, far up into Indiana and cutting off the southeastern hill country of Ohio. The outlawry of slavery by the Ordinance of 1787 was an absolutely decisive fact in the social development of this region: It meant that the southern stock of settlers – whatever habits of mind and sympathy they evinced – was formed of the non-slave-owning class, the yeoman farmers of Owsley's history[14] – or the drifters and footloose population of the back country and hills. Their attitude both to the blacks and to their beleaguered homeland in the War was an ambivalent one, as evidenced by the cautious approach to emancipation by the most famous of their number, Abraham Lincoln. Their attitudes to commercial farming may have been

[13]For a treatment of Midwest settlement in a Turnerian mode, see Billington, *Westward Expansion*, 246–267, 290–309.
[14]Frank Lawrence Owsley, *Plain Folk in the Old South* (Baton Rouge: Louisiana State University, 1949), Ch. 2.

less wholehearted than those of their northern neighbors, and their location and terrain less suited to it. These divisions of mind may have made the southern-derived population of the Old Northwest less effective in charting the direction and influencing the tone of the region than their numbers would have justified. They formed – with many exceptions – the laboring and poor-farmer stratum of the population, achieving sometimes a better adaptation to Midwest conditions than the New Englanders, but taking risks and pursuing rationality in money-making less ardently perhaps than the Yankees.

New Englanders came early into the territory from the settlements of Connecticut veterans on the so-called Western Reserve, and a steady stream moved from Massachusetts and Vermont after 1830 as those farming regions shifted cropping patterns under the joint pressure of the pull of labor to the mills and the market competition of Western grain and meat. Spreading across northern Ohio,[15] eastern Michigan, where Boston money had always been involved, and down from the lake into central Illinois, Yankee farmers and villagers settled quickly into all the money-making activities that were to be found – activities which included farming but were by no means limited to it.

Between Southerners and Yankees, the migrants from Pennsylvania and New York shared with the German and later Scandinavian migrants to Wisconsin and beyond, a certain peasant-like competence in the agricultural arts. Their origins did not lie in the uplands of Appalachia but generally in flat and fertile farming areas, where careful tillage and husbandry had long been rewarded by good yields, where stable family and village structures had made for a solid, conservative and dependable style of farming and of living – a style which could take root quickly and flourish abundantly on good soils under good market opportunities.[16]

Any reconstruction of a regional character must be partly imaginary, particularly at a hundred years' distance, and a tracing of its origins must involve a degree of plausible myth. Yet it is hard to feel that the midwestern character as it shows itself in farming, business, and politics after the Civil War does not owe something to this mix of rural backgrounds of the region's native population. The three groups shifted westward initially in rather fixed geographical strata: The Yankees moved into the belt of ultimately greater financial opportunity around and below the lower lakes; settlers from the middle colonies and rural immigrants from Europe moved in above and below them; New Yorkers, Germans, and

[15] A. L. Kohlmeier, *The Old Northwest as the Keystone in the Arch of American Federal Union* (Bloomington, Indiana: Principia Press, 1938), 209–211; and F. P. Weisenburger in Carl Wittke, ed., *History of the State of Ohio*, Vol. 2 (Columbus, Ohio: Ohio State Archaeological Society, 1941), 47.

[16] Weisenburger, op. cit., 48–52.

Swedes into Wisconsin after the 1850s; and Pennsylvanians and Germans across the middle counties of Ohio and down the Miami River. The southern hill people settling at the bottom of the area occupied a great southern belt across to the Mississippi.[17] As transportation improved and markets shifted, these groups mixed and mingled, facing a rather uniform natural environment, similar economic experiences, and enjoying easy mobility within a loose and democratic social structure. As they did so, a midwestern character was formed. Is it too fanciful to see in its upper reaches the drives, acuity, shrewdness, and hardness of the Yankee combined with the animal energy, competence and sturdiness of the German peasant, and among its common people an emotionality, tempered by a sophistication about human suffering, that must have belonged to a people that grew up among the moral and human ambiguities of southern slavery?

These distinctions among the population, nebulous as they are, based on its points of ancestral origin, were accompanied by, and not completely correlated with, distinctions based on wealth. How these arose and were reinforced by economic activity is an interesting matter for speculation. It would indeed have been surprising if, despite the rather considerable uniformity in land distribution – at least among the large share of the population that got land – the distribution of wealth or income had been exactly equal. There were some differences in the resources that settlers brought in with them, and considerable difference in their luck at the land sale and in their access to credit. Whatever their source, differences were to a degree reinforced by early ventures in farming or business. Now the shape of wealth distribution in a rural area has important consequences for that area's later industrial development. A very skewed distribution favors saving and capital accumulation but provides only restricted markets, particularly for factory products; an equal distribution has the reverse effect. Obviously, as in most economic problems, there is a level of spending and accumulation which combines these two contradictory effects to an optimal degree for rapid economic growth. Our concern here, however, is with the relation of wealth distribution to the structure of society. Quite obviously, too, as many observers of American manners have pointed out, in a society so new, so democratic and homogeneous in most respects, such differences in wealth stood out as almost the only mark of individual or familial distinction and prestige. The worship of wealth appeared where so little else existed on which men could exercise the impulse to make distinctions or establish a standard by which to define and imitate success.

Beneath the surface of homogeneity and equality in 1860 in the North-

[17]Ibid., 47.

west lay elements of social differentiation based on family origin and especially on wealth. In social organization, too, one sees a similar blending of opposites: the opposition of a family-centered individualism and a community-centered corporate spirit. The frontiersman, it is said, was an individualist with, at the extreme, an almost psychotic hatred of human society: one who cleared his patch in the wilderness and moved on as soon as he saw the smoke from a neighbor's cabin. Added to this is the stereotype of the nineteenth-century competitive entrepreneur in whose breast all human social bonds had been metamorphosed into the selfish drive for money and through money for control over men. The Midwest was wide and rich enough to sustain and encourage numbers of such entrepreneurs, and it called their achievements success. Mixed with such figures is the figure of the insecure, grasping, land-hungry peasant familiar in European history. And since men cannot survive, procreate, and produce a history utterly alone, they were set in the Northwest in the so-called nuclear family of a long North European lineage. Midwestern individualism, as it showed itself in farming and in business achievement, was rooted in the family organization brought into the region and reinforced by the conditions of rural settlers on isolated farmsteads, growing crops initially only for themselves, then for sale in anonymous competition with neighbors for distant markets. A direct physical sharing of crops – the dominant mode of distribution in tribal and village societies from time immemorial in the world's agriculture, the basis on which Egyptian, Oriental, and medieval lords, dynasties, and ecclesiastical organizations were supported and their populations tied to the soil – was wholly unknown, undreamed of by the original rural population of the Midwest. Some exceptions to this stark, small-family individualism appeared among immigrant groups and among adherents to a sectarian religion like the Mennonites,[18] where settlement in larger family or community groups occurred. But these are notable as exceptions, and their cohesiveness was often short-lived under the corrosive influence of the markets for crops and land and the ready mobility of a second or third generation.

And yet – and yet, that is surely not quite the whole story. If it had been, midwestern society could never have survived. In European villages, the peasant household had been incorporated within a village structure. The European peasant of the nineteenth century may have revealed

[18]For accounts of Mennonite religious and community life in Illinois, see Harry Franklin Weber, *Centennial History of the Mennonites of Illinois 1829–1929* (Goshen, Indiana: Mennonite Historical Society, 1931); in Indiana and Michigan, see John Christian Wenger, *The Mennonites of Indiana and Michigan* (Scottdale, Pennsylvania: Herald Press, 1961); and in Ohio, see William I. Schreiber, *Our Amish Neighbours* (Chicago: University of Chicago Press, 1962).

a narrow selfishness when village and feudal organization was dissolved. Then unrelated households were nakedly exposed in all their anarchy, like worms under a suddenly lifted rock. But the earlier agrarian culture of northern Europe added to its nuclear families a certain organization of public cooperation and responsibility. This was evident particularly in the German and Scandinavian groups, but it existed also among native Americans, whose culture derived from England or Scotland of the seventeenth or early eighteenth century.

To this basis for cooperation were added also the effects of common dangers, common tasks, and common abundance in the early western environment. Perhaps loneliness and the desire to escape it are innate characteristics of the human mind, inextricable elements in the human condition. The premium on news must have been high in the darkness and uncertainties of a frontier, and settlers longed not only for the sound of a voice, but for what a voice might say – about Indians, neighbors, politicians, and other potential intruders on their lives. Together with information gained through social contact, community projects – for defense and later for the creation of public goods – yielded high returns to community self-help. The federal government was remote, and, through constitutional theory and the strength of southerners in Congress, it remained weak. State governments financed and organized canals and railroad projects and established a basic framework of control and law. But they were large, and much of their sovereign powers devolved on the locality – the county, the township, the school district. Taxes, roads, fire, police, and schools were all largely local matters; the division of the land into regular townships with surveys contemplated a close local organization of those who purchased their land at a single land office. The abundance of land in new areas, the prodigality of nature in crude necessities – food and lumber – made it easy to welcome the stranger and to incorporate his strength in community tasks. The rural neighborhood with schools, churches, and politics added then to the family life as an indispensable element of social organization. Midwesterners were individualistic on their farms and in their productive activities, but they were generous to neighbors and combined readily in community projects. Clubs, churches, circles, lodges, societies flourished in the Midwest soil – the more so because their members felt themselves to be free and equal individuals. And certainly there were some who found in such association the means to respect and status that seemed so hard to achieve in a near-egalitarian society, except, as we have noted, through lucky and successful economic activity. Of all the puzzles in the frontier character, the paradox of individualistic neighborliness is the most striking and pregnant with promise of strength for the industrial culture that was to come.

The society of the Old Northwest in 1860 is to be viewed, in short, as a variant of the peasant society of Protestant Europe, from which it derived all those intimate values and ethical norms expressed in religion and family structure, and much even of what was expressed in community life. But the conditions of formation of this society differed from those in Europe in two respects – each obvious when taken by itself, but producing together an interaction that might not have been predicted. On the one hand, these farmers and villagers were placed in an economic framework of pure market capitalism and given the means of maintaining independent fortunes and positions. No titles, no feudal dues, no tenancies, no village obligations existed in law or memory to restrain their utter economic freedom. On the other hand, the settlers were placed, as the colonists had been in the first coastal settlements, in a new, unknown, and often menacing natural environment, whose rich returns would be yielded only to individual effort sustained and helped by considerable community organization. The counterpart of individual freedom was the danger of social isolation – no established church, no landlord, no clustered village, and hardly a state. These could be compensated for by hard work only up to a point; beyond that, the performance of their functions required organization.

To what extent did this transforming experience differ from that of the New Englanders or the Virginians two centuries before? The Puritan, more often a townsman than a peasant, brought to the wilderness a firm corporate spirit and a strict hierarchy; he was to see both dissolve under the corrosive influence of free land, money, markets, and trade. The Virginian brought a venturesome individualism, which was transformed along the seaboard, under the opportunities of profit and power, into a caste system. The westerners in both regions from the eighteenth century on form the prototypes of the midwestern spirit and society. A hundred years of semi-self-sufficiency in farmsteads and rude settlements across the Appalachians was the immediate forerunner of midwestern settlement, mixed after 1830 with movement from the already commercialized farms of southern New England and the middle states. What was truly new to the nineteenth century was the growing commercial opportunity for "western" crops – an opportunity which was apparent with the first shipments on rafts down the Ohio and the Mississippi and the driving of animals through the Cumberland Gap, which built up to the intense demand for internal improvements in the 1820s and 1830s and reached a climax in the opening up of European markets after 1850. It was in response to these opportunities before 1860, and for several decades thereafter, that the western character and rural society were to achieve their fixed and final form.

III

The opportunity settlers faced in the Old Northwest was comprised of both the peasant's opportunity for a home and the gambler's opportunity for a fortune. Between these extremes lay the whole range of economic opportunities for men who felt themselves freed from eastern or European society and able partly to determine their own economic destiny. The mix of risk and security, fluctuating income and steady yields, market orientation and self-sufficiency, mobility and steadfast local residence varied with choice and circumstance. Nor could any objective be pursued by a man in isolation from some of the institutions of settled society, from the shade of their protection and the shadows of their unwanted intrusions.

At first glance, the gambler and the peasant as ideal types appear to have much in common. Both wanted to separate themselves in the Northwest from the common experience of the race – the one by lucky windfalls, reaping where he had not sown, the other by the complete security of his own holding. Each might hold more land than he could use – the gambler in hopes of a "killing" on resale, the peasant as a means of saving with later distribution to his family. Both in the new country depended on the institutions of organized government. Their needs from government and from the region's resources, however, were of quite different sorts. The peasant-minded settler needed the rudimentary services of government – notably, physical protection against the Indian and the legal protection to insure security of tenure. The fly-by-night gatherer of wealth needed some of the apparatus of money and markets, so that his winnings could be put into liquid and transportable form, and he needed above all communication – ideally, private news of opportunities and rapid means of moving to take advantage of them. Corresponding to these types of ambitions would come two contrasting geographical patterns in the opening up of the country. The gambler's strategy was to move out ahead of the herd, taking risks, to penetrate deeply inland, to establish early claims, to find fur or minerals, to produce salable surpluses of transportable crops early. At the extreme opposite was the almost mindless steady expansion of an agricultural population like a glacial sheet – the joining of field to field in contiguous and riskless settlement.

History would be simple if these two "ideal" character types corresponded to the pioneers of specific seaboard regional or European material stock. But, of course, no such identification is possible at so distant a date; no one knows just where the Yankee, the southerner, or the Pennsylvania German modal personalities fell along the spectrum. Perhaps individual differences over the range of human nature were more decisive than background. It is clear that both types existed and complemented one another in the rapid development of the region. It would be simple, too, if the gamut of economic opportunities – as they succeeded one another in the region's development – utilized first the gambler, then moved slowly toward the peasant. To some degree, as Turner averred, this was the case. The opportunities – as sketched below – moved from those demanding physical endurance and prowess to those demanding social skills and from the more to the less risky. So the "waves" of Turner's frontiers – trapper, trader, surveyor, land clearer, rancher, farmer – succeeded one another at each location, though with many exceptions and variations. There were gentle, settled spirits even among the first settlers – among the Ipswich, Massachusetts, families that moved to Marietta to occupy the Ohio Company's claim.[19] New Englanders and Pennsylvanians came early from settled villages to establish their lives and fortunes anew. Nor was the freebooting frontier gambler a phenomenon simply of the early stages of settlement; he was a character-type continually recreated in western society, on hand in copper discoveries in Michigan in the 1840s or iron discoveries in Minnesota in the 1880s or in the episodes of transcontinental railroad building and finance. Within the limits of region and period, the riskiness, speed, and efficiency of settlement in the different states and localities depended very strongly upon the general state of organization of civilization, of technology in the region as a whole, just at the time that a specific locality was settled and connected with society to the East. The pioneers into Indiana and Illinois from Ohio or Kentucky in the 1820s and 1830s brought a different experience with them than those into Ohio from New England or Virginia in the 1800s. They came out of an economy connected with the South and the East, possessing techniques of manufacturing, transport, and even of farming and pioneering not known three decades earlier.

Utilizing this array of character types, opportunities unrolled over time and space in the Old Northwest prior to the Civil War. The ventures of fur trapping and Indian trading, organized formally under the federal system of outposts or factories in 1796, were economic activities indeed, but ones more important for the information they yielded about terrain and Indians than for any direct product. The first important economic activity in or over the area was the land grab for the Ohio country just after the Revolution. It took two forms: (1) speculation in the military

[19]"Seldom have people migrated with less hardship than the New Englanders who moved west with the Ohio Co." Billington, *Westward Expansion*, 218. However, this easy transplant was the exception and not the rule. Even those who migrated under the shelter of one of the companies often found they had gambled more than they reckoned. The French settlers who migrated to the Scioto Company's grant, for example, expected a full-scale city, but found only Gallipolis, Ohio, in a very early stage of construction and not enough land to go around.

warrants, entitlements to land issued to veterans by Virginia and by the Continental Congress, and (2) lobbying by groups of ex-generals and other influential citizens to obtain grants of the lands from Congress for resale under favorable terms.[20] What seems a corrupt and privileged system in retrospect did not in fact seem so to contemporaries. Ample precedent existed in the colonial grants of the crown and in the example of the Holland Land Company, which had acquired the land management and sale of most of western New York. A similar arrangement seemed not amiss in encouraging movement into the Ohio country.

One may observe in the early organization of both the Indian trade and land settlement an effort to work under the dying shadow of eighteenth-century mercantilist policies. The system of posts and regulated trade conformed to British precedent in Canada, without the intermediary of a joint stock company. The Ohio and Scioto companies were indeed joint ventures on the model of the company by which Virginia was first settled, but with a clearer title to land and a more single-minded dedication to its profitable settlement and sale. They assumed no political powers and contemplated holding the land only long enough to make a profit of suitable size. Yet it proved impossible at any point to maintain a large para-governmental organization, except for the army and the federal land offices in the area. Even before the Indian danger abated, the federal factories were ignored, and the peculiarly American organization of the Indian and fur trade, by small capitalists working on individual account, with no accountability to the government or other claimant of ownership or sovereignty, asserted itself. The gamblers and high risk-takers took over and swept across the Midwest to the Missouri country and on into the Rockies, until at last, in the 1830s, when – with knowledge more certain and risks reduced – Astor's American Fur Company could take over and the big capitalist could gobble up the little ones. In land settle-ment, too, large private organizations rapidly proved themselves incompe-tent. The Scioto Company failed rather quickly; the Ohio Company and J. C. Symmes rather rapidly divested themselves of their grants. Settle-ment in the Virginia Military District was small scale, even when the warrants had been bought up in blocks, and the settlement into the Connecticut Reserve came in small groups from various towns in the state. The small party of twenty-five to fifty persons from a New England town was the largest unit, the settlers moving over the border from Pennsylvania, squatters in advance of surveys, and the Kentuckians and Virginians moved individually or in small family groups. By 1800, then, the Act of 1796 was in full operation, with surveys of the ranges of

[20]Payson J. Treat, *The National Land System, 1785–1820* (New York: E. G. Treat & Co., 1910), 15–20, 45–64.

townships, land offices, auction sales, reserved school lands, and state lands. Settlers, ranchers, small-scale speculators, successful and well-located farmers, the developers of a town, a county, or a river valley, were firmly in control of the territorial government and brought Ohio to statehood as early as 1803. In Indiana and Illinois, the same organization or settlement proceeded without the eighteenth-century overhang of land companies.

IV

A huge net of opportunity then unfolded over the Northwest as one tier of counties after another was opened up. But land values could rise with settlement only as farming grew more productive of value; that in turn depended both on the growth of a local economy, with trade and specialized production, and on the possibility of export. Settlement, initially and persistently, was not simply to plant homesteads or villages to reproduce a traditional agrarian society in a colonial setting. Settlement brought value to the land, and it did so by realizing on internal or external markets the value of the land's economic potential; the "economic surplus" was a concept well known to readers of Niles' Register long before it was used with a somewhat different meaning by Marxists. And of these opportunities, it would seem clear that to realize on exports from the region was a faster way to wealth than to wait for a thickening settlement to produce internal markets. For the latter to occur, the development of import-substituting manufactures was required, as well as effective local overland transport. Both of these were to occur along with the growth of exports, and indeed their satisfactory response to the stimulus of the incomes earned in exports is largely responsible for the region's growth; it meant that the "export multiplier" (in old-fashioned Keynesian language) applied to rising exports was high and induced further investment and more internal "acceleration" within the region. But clearly before 1830, the lower and eastern Midwest still looked like an agricultural export region, whose fertile soils and favorable terrain were set too remotely into the American land mass to assure easy access to the markets of the South, the East, and Europe.

The period before 1830 was thus one of a decided southern orientation of the Northwest's economy – toward the Ohio and Mississippi valleys. Exact figures on the trade must be viewed with suspicion, but Kohlmeier's search in state and federal documents showed that nearly all the corn and corn products (hogs and whiskey) and over 70 percent of the wheaten flour exported from the Northwest in 1835 went downriver either for consumption or for trans-shipment from New Orleans, and that nearly half the region's imports, by weight, came up that route.[21] This trade was great enough to create Cincinnati as a city of four thousand by 1814 and six thousand by 1816. It was confirmed and intensified by the steamboat in the 1820s.[22] The canals into the Ohio marked the route even plainer, and as settlement extended to the southern counties of Indiana and Illinois, the advantage of trade over this route was even more marked. Until the 1840s, the lower Northwest settlement was an extension of the upper South, without slaves but with mostly southern and border people, with crop mix and farming patterns characteristic of Kentucky and Tennessee. This was the Democratic Northwest – of Jacksonian persuasion, eager to chase Indians, to grab land, to float produce to New Orleans, yet retaining strong distrust of banks and credit and northern ways of doing business. And on top of this stratum was a small business class, merchants and bankers, the western Whigs, followers of Clay and Harrison, without strong feelings about sectional alliances, as ready to combine with southern Whigs as with the party's New England wing – but eager for Union and the "American System," for tariffs to develop home markets and for internal improvements to link the West to them. Thus far had the population of the Old Northwest stratified itself by the election of 1840.

The weakness in the southern orientation lay in the urge to expand to markets in whatever direction. By improved canals, a canal around the Falls of the Ohio at Louisville, and steamboats on the upriver journey, the link of the Ohio River Valley was made via New Orleans with the world. But the canals ran both ways, and steamboats were indifferent as to what region they traversed. Two sorts of events before 1850 – one immediate and major, the other less prominent at first, but later quite decisive – began to cause the region around the lower edge of the Lakes to grow and to be linked within itself and to the East. They were events that were to be repeated with increasing strength over the nineteenth century.

First, of course, were the transport improvements: the National Road opened in 1818 to Wheeling and by 1833 to Columbus, the Erie and Ohio Canals, the clumsy Pennsylvania canal and road system. These for the first time gave shippers in eastern Ohio the chance to play rival routes off against one another and against the great natural route to the South. The timing of these and their economic effects have been often described, or assumed, but never thoroughly analyzed and measured. We may cite several such effects, some directly observed in the record of settlement and shipment, others coming under the head of effects which economic theory tells us must have taken place. First, there was an undeniable speed-up in the rate of immigration from the Northeast, the more rapid

[21]Kohlmeier, *The Old Northwest*, 20–21.
[22]Wade, *The Urban Frontier*, 54.

because it could move into a region where northerners already predominated. But much of the economic efficiency of a new agricultural region depends on the mass of settlement; even without external trade, a large enough population can generate its own industrial civilization. Second, the existing farm population – in particular the wheat growers who had already entered from Pennsylvania – enjoyed a market advantage, and the development of eastern Ohio in wheat soon followed. Third, the impact of eastern manufactures must have had the same effect as that observed along the Erie Canal itself: the disappearance of home industry and a shift of farm labor to farming tasks, notably dairying, or to village manufactures where the small-scale shop still had a place. Finally, it should be emphasized that the East–West improvements were not confined to northeastern and central Ohio. The whole southern shore of Lake Erie was affected by the canal links at Cleveland and Toledo to western Ohio and Indiana. The Illinois–Michigan canal joined Chicago to the Mississippi; and the Soo Canal, opened in 1855, brought surpluses from northern Illinois and the early farms of eastern Wisconsin in reach of the Great Lakes trade. But already by the late 1840s, the lake trade was a flourishing, mercantile enterprise, developing all the institutions of markets, credit, and competition with which Boston, New York, and Cincinnati had long been familiar.

Apart from the water transportation improvements, a second stimulus to wealth accumulation and commercial enterprise with an eastern orientation appeared in the 1840s: the minerals rush into Michigan copper. The rush, coming in the wake of the geological reports of Houghton in 1843, reached a climax in May 1846, when about one thousand permits for exploration were issued in a single month. By 1847 the bubble had burst, but the beginnings of an orderly exploitation and of continued disorderly exploration into the mineral resources of the upper Lakes had been laid.[23] The form of the episode was followed closely in the rush into Pennsylvania for oil in 1856–60. The impetus both for the rush and for the continued exploitation in these two cases came partly from the surrounding areas – from lower Michigan and from Western Pennsylvania – and partly from New England. In Michigan in particular, Boston financial control of the major mines was established as regular exploitation began in the early 1860s. More important than the ore discovered and the dividends paid out was the stimulus given to further exploration in the upper peninsula of Michigan and to the improvement of navigation of Sault Ste. Marie. The south shore of Lake Superior – the farthest reach of the Great Lakes

[23] W. B. Gates, Jr., *Michigan Copper and Boston Dollars* (Cambridge, Mass.: Harvard University Press, 1951), 12–22.

system – was joined to the developing agricultural and industrial region of northern Ohio. By 1855, the way had been laid for the later movement of Minnesota wheat and Menominee and Mesabi iron.

V

By the late 1840s, the lines of connection of Northwest and Northeast were well laid. Two great forces in that decade and the one following were to rivet the two regions together: the railroad and the struggle over slavery.

It is idle, but intriguing, to speculate on a possible northwest–southeast development path if the railroad had been technically and financially practicable just after the War of 1812. Might it have been used to develop Cincinnati's southern connections to Richmond or Charleston? One recalls Hayne's unsuccessful project for this purpose in Charleston in the 1830s. Lincoln is supposed to have said that had it been carried out, the War might never have occurred. But Calhoun did not favor it and looked instead for the rails to join together the parts of the cotton kingdom. The Cincinnati investors, too, dragged their feet, evidently preferring the greater benefits to be derived from building roads within Ohio and attracting immigration from the East.[24] And in the East, the rails followed rapidly upon the canals. The Baltimore and Ohio stretched toward the West in the 1830s, the rivalry of the three mid-Atlantic ports pushed the whole system West, and by the early 1850s local lines in Ohio could be joined to the East at three points with only small extensions of track.[25] In choice of terrain, in mode of finance, in the assembly of construction gangs, in leading settlement and agriculture along lines into which rail traffic could flow – the canals were a test-run of the railroads along many of the main routes. And the rails, with their wider choice of terrain, their all-year operation, and their speed, and with the technical and engineering skills they used and diffused, were decisive instruments of industrial developments – no matter how arithmeticians may calculate, under restrictive assumptions and with self-corroborating data, their exact contribution to the national product in a given year.

The 1850s saw railroad development in the Midwest at two levels: (1) a penetration from the East of lines joining to the great and new trunk system (the Baltimore and Ohio, the Pennsylvania, the Erie, and the New York Central), and with this (2) a great thickening of the connections in

[24]Kohlmeier, *The Old Northwest*, 22–29.
[25]Billington, *Westward Expansion*, 294; Taylor, *The Transportation Revolution*, 45–48; and the fine study by Harry N. Scheiber, *Ohio Canal Era: A Case Study of Government and the Economy, 1820–1861* (Athens, Ohio: Ohio University Press, 1969).

the interior, especially from North to South. The development of the 1840s had connected only a few obvious points, in such a way as to leave the region's orientation still ambiguous. A rail line across southern Michigan effectively gave access from Lake Michigan to Detroit. Indianapolis was joined to the Ohio River, and the Ohio lines followed the Miami Valley from Cincinnati northward, meeting Lake Erie at Sandusky and at Cleveland. Obviously traffic on such lines could move both ways – to the Ohio-Mississippi valley or to the Great Lakes water system. But the movement of the trunk lines from the East across to Chicago and St. Louis effectively settled the outcome. Then local lines became feeders to the North and East, and the days of the downstream river-oriented economy, even in the southern Midwest, were virtually over. The Illinois Central came too late to tie the state into an economic union with Mississippi and the Southwest. Instead, all that Douglas's efforts could do was to direct the produce of the central Illinois prairies north to Chicago – as Douglas himself realized when he invested in Chicago real estate.[26] Paul Gates gives the following telling quotation about the Illinois Central, from the *New York Evening Post* of September 22, 1858 (as cited in the Sparks edition of the Lincoln–Douglas debates):[27]

Jonesboro is a mile and a half from the railroad. The station is called "Anna" and is as large as the town itself. The station is Republican; the town is democratic. The land sales of the Illinois Central Railroad, by opening the country to the advent of settlers, have introduced the men of the East, who bring certain uncomfortable and antagonistical political maxims and thus the time-honored darkness of Egypt (i.e., southern Illinois) is made to fade away before the approach of middle state and New England ideas. Let these land sales go on and a change will take place in the political physiognomy of southern Illinois. All things suffer a "sea change" and already the alternative influence of these new ideas is insensibly felt in this section.

The second source of the connection with the Northeast – the joint struggle against slavery and for the Union – was a more complex affair. American history of the antebellum decade is inevitably directed toward an understanding of the decade's tragic outcome. An economic historian in particular must contribute an answer to at least two questions: First, to what degree did the economic links among the regions in 1860 condition their alignment in the struggle, and second, to what degree did these regional economic interests require of the struggle so violent a course? The first of these questions may be answered by an economist immediately; the second, being impossible, takes a little longer.

[26]G. M. Capers, *Stephen A. Douglas, Defender of the Union*, ed. by Oscar Handlin (Boston: Little Brown and Co., 1959), 16.
[27]Paul W. Gates, *The Illinois Central Railroad and Its Colonization Work* (Cambridge, Mass.: Harvard University Press, 1934), 244.

If war was inevitable in 1860 – which no historian should admit – and if the Northwest had to choose sides, then economics makes clear where its interests lay. The breakup of a political union is chiefly important for the opportunity it gives the constituent regions to conduct their own economic policies. In the mid-nineteenth century, this meant mainly tariffs. But a tariff between Northeast and Northwest in 1860 was unthinkable; all the economic policies and development of six decades had been directed to stimulating trade, lowering transport costs, increasing interdependence. Industrial growth in neither the Midwest nor the South had been sufficient to make the economies of those two regions complementary. The South, indeed, was itself more closely bound to New York, Philadelphia, and the New England mills than to Ohio or the upper Mississippi Valley.

But why then should not the North – east and west – simply have let the South secede? Such a question draws the economist far, far from home. Certainly the "mind" of the Northwest – if one may permit one's self such a construct – as late as the mid-1850s was still divided. Economically, the southern orientation of the region's lower half was far from extinguished. The boom in the Southwest continued to pull trade down the Mississippi; Kohlmeier's figures, shaky but indispensable, show that the transport watershed for the traditional staples – corn and hogs – still ran straight along the line of the National Road from Wheeling and Columbus on west to the Mississippi.[28] What had happened in the previous decade was that the settlement, farming, and light manufactures in the area north of that line, tributary to the Great Lakes, had sprung into life. Paradoxically, then it was the interest most involved in the southern route that was most intent that New Orleans should not be controlled by a southern power. If southern Ohio, Indiana, and Illinois could not secede with the South, then the South should remain in the Union with them. The American system was a living fact in most minds, and its definitions encompassed the vision of the back country along the whole length of the Mississippi, as well as the East–West connections.[29] Yet the Northeast could probably have taken over the surplus produce of this lower region directly at very slight increase in transport cost. Most of the produce

[28]Kohlmeier, *The Old Northwest*, 202–205.
[29]As late as October 1860, Douglas was defining the role and interests of the Northwest as mediate between Northeast and South. At a speech in Dubuque on October 11, 1860, he said, "Bordering upon the Mississippi and upon the Great Lakes; with commerce floating Southward and Eastward, we have an equal interest in the North and in the South. ("That's so" and applause.) We can never consent to any arrangement that would deprive us of our Eastern trade. Nor can we ever permit a toll gate to be established on the Mississippi River, that would prevent our free navigation to the gulf and upon the ocean." Text from R. Carey, *The First Campaigner: Stephen A. Douglas* (New York: Vantage Press, 1964), 86.

found its way back up the Atlantic coast anyway, and the Mississippi route was clearly heading for obsolescence. So one must move to more intangible fears and passions to explain the war.

Here, no doubt, the mere economic historian should retire gracefully, murmuring a *Nunc Dimittis*. But the question is too intriguing to abandon. Two points may be made. First, it is clear that all the politicians in 1860 – including Lincoln – underestimated the idealism and radicalism of the Republican creed and the popular strength of the power structure that supported it. That creed, echoing and repeating the slogans of the French Revolution and the Declaration of Independence, was implicit in the more cautious and materialistic Whiggery of Webster and Clay. Democracy, as represented by the Democratic Party in 1856, had lost much of its idealism; it had become a loose congeries of interests, dominated by professional compromisers. Freedom, material welfare, and property were the goals that could draw far enough down into the population to command a political predominance. Across the North, in towns and rural neighborhoods a structure of income and wealth, of economic ambition and respectability lay, strong as a net,[30] waiting to be drawn together in a cause. The anti-slavery crusade was not quite such a cause, but when sharpened by the danger of dissolution of the Union, the fusion of the Republican Party could occur. Then a northern unity and anger appeared that moved from the mere defense of freedom where it existed or might be extended into a crusading aggressive action against the slave-owning class itself. That many northwesterners came from slave states made some of them ambivalent but made others the more engaged to free the South from class domination. The Civil War was a radical Republican crusade for the Union. That Union's heart and soul was in the free commercial farmers and small businessmen of the Northwest who most appreciated its value and its glory.

Finally, one must ask whether the Republicans' zeal in the 1860s was activated in any degree by foreknowledge of what would lie ahead for the American economy and policy after a northern victory. Across the Northwest from the start had grown up a substantial stratum of local industry. This is not surprising, yet it is often forgotten in focusing on the area's huge agricultural expansions and the central place of construction and transportation projects. Many industrial skills had come in from the Northeast or middle South with the settlers – iron working, leather working, and a wood working that encompassed carpentry and the making of wooden machinery. Rural neighborhoods had organized themselves readily to produce jobs for specialized craftsmen – a blacksmith, a miller,

[30]See Clarence Danhof, *Change in Agriculture; the Northern United States, 1820–1870* (Cambridge, Mass.: Harvard University Press, 1967).

a harness maker, a teacher – quite soon. The rapid growth of small towns – and of central market cities – with good supply of urban services is testimony to this. The respect for schooling and a real interest in the practical arts is everywhere present in the rather thick layer of middle-class "culture" that lay on top of the canal men, laborers, and rough-necks. Wherever an industrial opportunity appeared, the skills, the enterprise, and institutions needed to utilize it were present. The differences in this respect from the civilization of the middle South are very sharp indeed.

So around Pittsburgh, as early as 1800, around Cincinnati and the Miami and Scioto Valley by the 1830s, along the Lakes, at Cleveland, Chicago, and Detroit after 1840, and in a great grid across the whole area where farmers could get out produce for sale, small-scale commercial manufactures arose. The growth was helped by the very lack of water power, which encouraged not only canal building but the making of steam engines. It utilized native materials – flax, wool, wood – to produce for local or regional markets on a large enough scale to maintain competition against imported goods.

The importance of such a grid, and of the business and political institutions accompanying it, for the industry of the upper Midwest after 1860 is obvious. No doubt in retrospect the South, as part of the federal Union, was not essential either as a market or as a materials source for the industry of the Midwest. But the instinct of the small business civilization of the Northwest in 1860 was profound and passionate. A national union, protecting free labor, the free ownership of property, and the integrity and expansion of its own territorial markets, was an economic ideal for American society under which the Republican class of the North-west could dominate and prosper.[31] The political correctness of the instinct that led the Northwest into the Civil War was even more apparent than its economics: In the great Republican era from Grant to Taft, every elected president of the United States, except one, was to call his native state either Ohio or someplace within one hundred miles of her borders.

[31]An abundant historical literature examines these questions. See, for example, the very interesting treatment by Eric Fonor, *Free Soil, Free Labor, Free Men: The Ideology of the Republican Party Before the Civil War* (New York: Oxford University Press, 1970).

9

Technological knowledge:
reproduction, diffusion, improvement

Nineteenth-century American farmers left a record both in the historical documents and in historical statistics. The statistical record shows a rapid settlement of the land, a growth of output from three- to tenfold in the major crops and animal products between 1840 and 1910, steady or slightly rising crop yields in old and new regions alike, and a marked fall in the labor time required per acre and per output unit in many important farm tasks. It shows also, when spread out over the map of the country, a shifting in the location of various crops and a settling down, toward the end of the century, into the present pattern of regional specialization. Analysis of this statistical record indicates that it was produced through uncounted acts of innovation, ranging from small adaptation of practices and genetic materials in new localities to "revolutionary" inventions in equipment. This paper seeks not to state the events in this record of innovation, but to ask why it was produced by these people in this time and place and how they worked together – manning positions in a bit of social machinery – in producing it. To answer these questions, we must go beyond the statistics to the other kind of historical debris – the record of the artifacts and the writings of the farmers and those associated with them. It is a dark terrain, making demands upon scholarship beyond those that can be filled by an essay of limited length. My purpose here is to convey some impressions, the intellectual residue of an examination of a significant portion of these materials. Part I restates certain well-known features of nineteenth-century American history which suggest the eco-

Parts I, II, and III were presented at the Third International Congress of Economic History, Munich, 1965, in the section devoted to technology, under the direction of Professor R. A. Easterlin. Part IV appeared first as the first portion of an article written jointly with Stephen J. DeCanio of the University of California at Santa Barabara under the title "Two Hidden Sources of Productivity Growth in American Agriculture, 1860–1930," *Agricultural History*, Vol. 56, No. 4 (1982), 648–654.

nomic environment in which these innovations occurred. Part II examines how individuals functioned together to produce the innovations. Part III speculates about the relation of the social process of innovation to the intellectual and economic environment in which it operated. Part IV examines the entrance of organized science into the folk art of agricultural innovation through the institution of the Agricultural Experiment Stations.

I

Agricultural techniques like most other social traits in nineteenth-century America combined the influences of European skills and American geography. The basic techniques and materials of farming had been adapted in the seventeenth and eighteenth centuries from the Indians, from Europe, or from other European colonies. By 1800 the colonial imports – livestock and plant types – had become acclimated in the East and were being carried forward by settlers in the next half-century into the Ohio–Mississippi Valleys and along the Gulf states. In the nineteenth century, European connections were continually refreshed by immigrants. European stock was imported by American breeders, European systems of crop rotation and livestock feed were observed and described by American visitors. European seeds were distributed by seed dealers and by the federal government for trial. European implements, even threshing machines, were sold until they could be imitated. The suitability of European practice and materials to American conditions – both East and West – was the subject of argument and practical tests.

It was into the farming just behind the frontier that this eastern and European inheritance could move. But that frontier had acquired a culture which reproduced itself with variation in the succession of American "Wests." That culture was itself a great social innovation – a phenomenon of business, scientific, military, political and ecclesiastical enterprise and energy. By the early nineteenth century its outlines were well-established. Methods of protection and aggression against the Indian, techniques of land clearing and cabin building, crops for first planting, patterns of cooperation and social organization were known and imitated. Movement into prairie soils and finally into the sub-humid West presented new problems and entailed significant adaptations and innovations in practices, materials, and tools. As the frontier moved forward, it left behind these skills in farm-making and home manufactures, some of which had already been forgotten in the settled regions. It left behind, too, a body of local knowledge about climate and soil, and local adaptations of farm implements which the settled agriculturists could inherit.

The line between frontier and settled agriculture cannot, of course, be sharply drawn. The process by which land moved from the original forest to the commercial farm was a complex one, with specialized roles performed by many individuals. The important fact is that the change in environment for any given individual who moved West was less radical than it may appear at first glance. Pioneers moved on, and behind them the somewhat more settled farmers followed in moves from short distances, a few hundred miles at most, just over the mountains or across the river or into the next county. The effort appears at many points to seek out familiar soils and terrain and to remain within the zone of a familiar climate. From New York, farmers moved across to Wisconsin; from Virginia and the Carolina uplands, subsistence farming with surpluses of livestock and feed moved into Tennessee, Kentucky, and the rolling lands just north of the Ohio River. The plantation owners of the East and their sons re-established themselves in the Gulf states. Some European immigrants showed this tendency, too, to a degree – the Scandinavians in the 1870s and, earlier, to a lesser extent, the Germans, seeking out a familiar climate and terrain.

The West then had a "lure" for settlers, no doubt, and the chance to do new things in a new area was an exciting prospect. But, particularly after western products began to disrupt eastern markets after the 1820s, many moves West must have been made to avoid more drastic innovation in the East. Western movement could be an innovation made to avoid innovation, to remain in accustomed routines of life and work by changing location rather than by changing cropping patterns or occupation. Nevertheless, however small the steps taken by a given individual, continuous innovation was a condition of survival and only ingenuity in small matters ensured survival at any reasonable level of efficiency. When crops came to be planted, small adaptations of practice and tools had a very high return. In corn cultivation, for example, hoeing was gradually abandoned as farmers from the northeastern states became accustomed in the Midwest to a terrain where cultivators, invented or adapted for the purpose, could be used. Though techniques in the West came partly from the East, partly from the moving frontier, on each farm they were adapted to specific new conditions.

That new physical conditions were not solely responsible for innovation is shown by the extent of innovation in the East. The radical transformation of northeastern agriculture between 1830 and 1870 under the combined pressure of urban growth and western competition (a competition for labor as well as for markets) is well known. Especially in the livestock industry, a race was on between western resources and English and eastern breeding skills, and the race continued until the two elements met as improved breeds – domestic and imported – came to be introduced to the feeds of midwestern farms and pastures. In the South, the use of fertilizer on cotton lands after the Civil War was surely a rational choice and a widespread one, with striking results on yields.

The eastern readjustment was only one such adjustment, and once made, it was a permanent one. In the West each county went through a similar adjustment as settlement moved ahead. The frontier crop – wheat – and the range hogs were not replaced by corn-feeder operations and mixed general farming because of a restless urge for novelty. They were replaced because they were driven out of markets by supplies yet further West; innovation came in the shifts made by producers behind the frontier – to the complex economy of Wisconsin dairying, for example, and to the livestock feed systems of the corn belt. The simple extension of settlement kept markets in a continual ferment, and yeast was added by technical changes in industry. Urban growth from the 1830s on began to produce the concentrations of demand from which urban milksheds were derived. The European market continued to grow, in cotton steadily and in wheat and meat by fits and starts – in part because America was a marginal supplier in years when it had an advantage in weather over Europe and in part because of the freakish incidence of European tariffs and "sanitary" restrictions. Nor was the general growth the simple one of a rural population expanding at constant incomes; since income grew with population and class structures changed, the relative position of products shifted uncertainly but with surprising speed. In America, the place of pork and corn in diets declined relative to beef, wheat, and milk. Demand had not yet moved before 1900 from staples to the uncertain world of fruits and vegetables, but improvements in food processing – canning and milling – had some impact. Refrigeration in transport, processing, and storage had an effect not only on the relative position of the perishable products but also on the marketing position of all their supplying regions. Similarly the decline of ocean freight rates affected the whole level of American prices in Europe and within the United States. A region's advantage was revolutionized by a canal or a rail connection, and the validity of its market adjustment hung thereafter on the structure of freight rates and storage and middlemen's charges.

These shifts in demand and factor supply produced an environment favorable to innovation, but a tradition-minded farmer, once settled on new land, might have avoided novelty. Where market opportunity was less strong and lines of communication less direct, in the southern highlands, for example, withdrawal into an unimaginative self-sufficiency in a traditional rural culture occurred. In the main commercial regions, the market opportunities for specialization gave the chance for a money income to be earned, but the reason for the desire for money rather than the homemade pleasures of life was another matter. Where did the economic and psychological pressures originate that gave farmers so strong an urge for money income and for the innovations that helped to produce it?

This question in money economies may be looked at in terms of "the push and the pull," the carrot and the stick. The hard pressure exercised on slaves and their successor tenant farmers is notorious, but we need still to know why the slave owners and the landowners felt so strongly the profit-maximizing itch in their operations. On their farms and in the North, something must be attributed to the overhanging presence of fixed charges, mortgage payments, machinery and livestock loans, and taxes. Quantification in economic history has a long way to go before the limits and force of this pressure under fluctuating price levels can be defined. Part of the load of debt is to be attributed to speculative elements in the land system and the initial costs of farm-making. But much of this was a result of the very striving for higher income, the everlasting betting on price rises in land and crops. Many farmers bought on credit more land than they could farm, in the hope of making speculative profits from its sale. Some invested heavily in livestock when a boom was on, and the excessive purchases of machinery and its overrapid obsolescence was a good omen for the market for automobiles that was to follow. The pressures of debt and taxes were reinforcing symptoms rather than fundamental causes of the desire for money income and a money fortune.

At a deeper level the demand for money was perhaps a reflection of the fact that American rural culture was shallow, farmsteads isolated, communications poor, religion inartistic and hysterical, social life thin and harsh. The rituals of a peasant society had not been established, its crafts and amusements had not been taught. Through bare rural areas, in gawky young towns New England factories peddled an increasingly varied, interesting, and useful array of manufactures at prices within the reach of an ambitious farmer or his wife. But that in turn raises another interesting aspect of the question: the position of the woman in the balance of power within the farm family. The distribution of money expenditure between producers' and consumers' goods is largely the outcome on balance of the war between the sexes; the intensity with which the struggle was waged itself added to the demand for money income for both purposes. The impression should not, of course, be given that the nineteenth-century farm was at the stage of "high mass consumption." Spending decisions were far more fully under male control than they are today. No doubt the desire for money income was largely the farmer's own desire not to enjoy, but to establish and enrich himself – for his own sake, for his reputation, for his children. The pressure of contracted debts and the consumption demands of a wife and family acted as reinforcement to the hard drive of these nineteenth-century petty capitalists. No doubt, the fundamental explanation for the mentality is now out of reach; yet it is a mentality observable among other, much narrower groups in other times and places and constitutes one complex human response to a pattern of economic opportunity. Perhaps peculiarly American values produced a peculiarly American variant of the type, but it was perhaps not the psychology, but the opportunity, that distinguished the American farmer from the traditional peasant – an opportunity that highly rewarded successful innovation and adaptation, and threatened utter ruin in society to those who showed no taste for the game.

II

Given a lively interest in new things – new crop combinations and new techniques – the question arises – how were these new things discovered and made generally known? It would be tedious to trace the course of each innovation, even if it were possible to do so. But the process by which novelty made its appearance and spread among farmers is apparent at many points and presents similar characteristics where it can be observed. It is the same process apparent in technical change generally in the eighteenth and nineteenth centuries and has many features similar to the process of exploration for minerals that was going on at the same time.

The American acts of innovation, insofar as we can observe them, follow the haphazard pattern common to the age before the institutions of organized science. In the history of breed improvement in wheat, corn, and cotton, it is not unusual that a farmer observes a specially fine plant, saves the seed, and inbreeds one or two generations to obtain a new variety. In farm implements, the process is much the same as that described by A. P. Usher for mechanical invention. A need is felt, the opportunity to fill it is offered by a new combination of existing materials and ideas, the "act of insight" occurs in the mind of an inventor, and the model of new equipment or the modification of existing equipment is made. The notable element in agricultural invention is the fineness of the divisions of steps in the improvement process. Heroes are, one may venture to say, fewer than in other lines of invention; much is a modification of what exists. Even the reaper was built up, as Ardrey has shown,[1] in a series of small steps. If this is true of the reaper, how much more true is it of the endless modifications of the plow, the cultivator, and the harrow! In livestock feed, in methods of seed selection, in such practices as hoeing and cultivating and in the timing of operations, innovation is inseparable from the infinite variety of farm practice. In reading the controversies in farm journals over corn cultivation, for example, one has the impression that every farmer did things a little differently from his neighbor and was

[1] Robert L. Ardrey, *American Agricultural Implements* (Chicago: Published by the author, 1894).

sure his own way was best. One must remember that ignorance on many points was profound. Where argument occurred over conscious selection of animals for livestock breeding, for example, there could be no definitive settlement. The relation of the physical points of an animal to its efficiency as a piece of capital equipment was not known, nor, even if the linked physical and economic characteristics had been known, was there good understanding of how such characteristics were transmitted.

This variation – a reflection of the independence of judgments – was the seedbed of novelty. The important problem for the agriculture at large was not to produce new forms; both nature and human nature were doing that in abundance. Rather it was to provide a means of testing the ideas and new materials to ensure, if they were valid, their widespread adoption. Here a very great difference existed among the innovations in the degree of suitability to a national or even a regional market. Some practices, seeds, equipment were suitable only in the localities of their origin; others had widespread use wherever a crop or an operation appeared. But no innovation, except a farmer's own, could be adopted until the estimate of the risk attaching to its use in a given neighborhood was reduced. A risk reduction was essential to the diffusion of any technique across a variety of farms and farmers. Here something could be done by the system of communication, by official reports, advertisement, salesmen's pitches, and exhibits at county fairs. The most powerful persuader was an actual exhibition of use nearby under conditions that a farmer recognized to be similar to his own. But if the farmers were usually "from Missouri," the crust of their skepticism was sometimes surprisingly thin – too thin often for their own good. The susceptibility of the farming public to fads and manias is the reverse side of its eagerness to innovate.

Since local demonstration was important, it was important also that high risk-takers be widely scattered and that their activities should be readily communicated. Here the structure of rural society must have played an important part, far beyond what we are able to trace. The wealthier farmers, though hardly rich landowners by European standards, were the most prominent innovators, partly because any given small innovation involved them in less proportionate risk. But much innovation may have been tried by farmers whose fortunes suffered when it failed. A high degree of venturesomeness was often looked on, in America as elsewhere, as a form of insanity. But there were in the rural areas grouped around the county seats, men whose opinion counted and whose example might be followed. And the motives for talking about one's practices, as the literature reveals them, are interesting to examine. The simple love of talk and of boasting, by hardworking, half-educated men, was an important source of conversations over farming. Occasionally one wonders whether a definitive answer to a moot question would be welcomed, since it would destroy the source of the controversy and so of the entertainment. To introduce a practice and to benefit financially from it was only half the game; the rest was to show one's neighbors that one was right. The purely competitive organization of the industry, it should be noted, put no premium on keeping an invention secret, unless it could be patented and sold to other producers. To talk about a successful innovation added pleasure and prestige to the profit. It is no wonder then that in such an atmosphere patent rights were so little respected. If a farmer could not patent a new feed for cattle, why should he, or the local blacksmith, respect a patented modification on the plow?

The farmers in a county acquired then their various reputations – some as rash and harebrained, some as backward, lazy, and ignorant, and some as sound, progressive, and prudent. We cannot measure these distributions of human types at this late a date. But there is abundant indication of a level of tolerance of innovation that admitted a great deal of experiment and a level of skepticism that exercised an effective control over excess. Around the level set by the interest in innovation and by the pressures for money income, the competitive process itself exercised the most effective control. Given the variation in practices in a region, a process of natural selection was at work among farmers as among plants. Suitable adaptations and practices were rewarded; too many errors would make a farmer sink in the "agricultural ladder" and drive him eventually out of farming. The level of required money payments set the lower limit of tolerance to money losses, but even where these were met, disappointment and discouragement in an atmosphere so full of promise and hope could winnow out the farmers with bad judgment or luck as effectively as bankruptcy. And between ownership and abandonment of the land lay gradations of tenancy in which a "bad" farmer could function with some loss of control over entrepreneurial decisions.

Particularly then in "disembodied technology" – the choice of crops and farm practices – successful innovations established themselves as the process of market selection operated on the variations in farmers' practices. The origins of these variations may be traced in turn to the varied backgrounds and resources farmers brought with them and to many small acts of invention practiced by them in a new and changing, natural and economic environment. For marketable inventions a specialization of the innovative function arose from this activity. The farmer, or planter, with a special interest in seeds or stock might become a breeder. Even sharper was the break from farming when an inventive farmer's new implement formed the basis for a manufacture. Then the innovating acts became conscious, purposeful, and profit directed; patents were applied for, funds raised, and the arts of business enterprise – of production and marketing – were brought into play. The level of interest of farmers in novelty still remained important in such inventions, but their pull on new ideas was now reinforced by a powerful push from the side by the producer of new technology. And it is not correct, of course, to find these origins of the farm implement industry wholly within the farm community. Equally important were the small-town crafts – blacksmithing and wagon-making – whose practitioners, while staying in close touch with farms, already formed a specialized trade.

Not only the profits of "embodied" inventions, but the prestige of good advice, too, became the bases of specialized occupations. Since messages were confined to the printed page or to the new system of telegraphic transmission (and could not swarm in word or picture through the air), their effective range and scope was limited. Advertisements reflected in phrasing and content their origins in the pitch of the barker at the county fair, and the farm journalists were practical evangelists spreading a gospel of productivity. It is not clear in what proportions they included men who had succeeded and men who had failed in farming. Their writing was prolific and their readership large. Though riding an occasional personal hobbyhorse, they served mainly as reporters of new practices, advertisers of machinery, seed, and stock, and moderators in the endless debates among farmers to which their columns were always open. (The points at issue in these debates were innumerable – whether to sow wheat broadcast or with a drill, how far to space rows of corn, whether to boil corn for hog feed, whether to soak seeds in tar to discourage crows, what crop rotations to use, how clean of weeds a cornfield must be. They arose largely, of course, out of unrecognized differences in the disputants' experiences and personal preferences or in the different physical conditions for farming.)

The lay evangelism of nineteenth-century adult education appears at many points in the formation of the local and state agricultural societies. Formed on the initiative of opportunistic local merchants, politicians, or reforming farmers, their membership might also include farmers of less progressive bent, interested in airing their prejudices. Their meetings provided a formal setting for the exchange of experiences – like the confessions at a camp meeting – and for the diffusion of some information from other sources. The county fair was the occasion for the display of crops and animals, the award of prizes, and the inspection of local manufactures – including the prodigies of the wifely food-processing industry. In the state fairs, displays of machinery by regional and national producers were a prominent feature, and blue-ribbon standards of achievement of crops and stock were high. But these famous institutions were only one activity sponsored by the state agricultural societies. With state support, or as part of the state administrative structure, the societies or "boards" of agriculture issued publications, collected statistics, and sometimes sponsored research. With their activities we move from folk institutions to the formal institutions of organized science and education. In 1867, the United States Commissioner (later Department) of Agriculture took over and extended the work of the agricultural section of the Patent Office; the lobbying efforts of the United States Agricultural Society were important in its origins. Its functions from 1862 to the 1920s were largely to organize and distribute information and to initiate research. The agricultural colleges, too, had relations to the state boards or societies of agriculture, and the national system of state experiment stations created in 1888 grew partly out of, and depended on, the colleges. With the Act of 1914 establishing the Extension Service, with agents in every county, the formal structure was complete. The whole public effort depended on other elements besides its folk origins in the conversations of talkative farmers around the stove in the country store. Southern planters who shared Jefferson's enlightened curiosity contributed to it, as did, too, the New England ministers of education and godliness – a social group which was undergoing a nineteenth-century transmutation into professors, government administrators, and reformers. The respect for knowledge and the urge to spread it was strong among such groups – indeed, it was disproportionate to the slender stock of real knowledge that could be usefully spread beyond a locality. Men are usually eager to talk before they have anything to say, and this was especially true when the stirrings of agricultural science gave tantalizing and misleading hints of important general truths in genetics and soil chemistry. But in their efforts at uplift, the teachers of the farm population found a ready and receptive audience; even the skepticism with which "book farming" was often met was based not on a mistrust of novelty, but on a superior trust in the folkways by which local experiments had been carried on, tested, discussed, and put into practice.

III

Given the state of fundamental knowledge in the nineteenth century, it seems likely that the social organization of innovation as we have sketched it was well suited to the problem at hand. Of the branches of technology, the mechanical arts were the most highly advanced, and principles capable of very wide application could be incorporated into machinery. It was a fortunate fact that just such inventions were well suited to the use of a relatively thin labor force spread over a great area of land. Where scientific theory was even more unexplored and variation in physical conditions more important, random experimentation on several million farms was the only way that successful novelty could be produced. The problem of covering America with an agriculture suited to the growing and shifting markets was hardly one susceptible of an immediate planned solution. Indeed, the difference between nineteenth-century conditions and those of today lies in just this: that both the physical environment and the sciences to cope with it were then just being explored. In these circumstances, the processes by which mankind has always groped its way through new and strange conditions were brought into play and served the purpose well. What is remarkable in the American nineteenth century is not the innovative process itself but rather the intensity with which, under the stimulus of market expansion, it was pursued.

And yet, one lingering question remains – one which lies just within the reach of speculation and just outside the possibility of a satisfactory answer.[2] If the opportunities and special problems of westward expansion had not existed, would the development of science and novelty have taken a different turn? If, under much the same circumstances of growth in markets and labor supplies, western land had not exercised its dissolving influence on eastern society, might technological change have been a different animal from the one we know? There is no reason to suppose that the application of mechanical principles to agricultural machinery would not have been accomplished. The difficult mechanical problems in corn harvesting and cotton picking would have continued to resist solution, but mowing and threshing machinery suited to eastern farms was indeed introduced to some extent. The more difficult question is whether the institutions of a scientific agriculture would have developed sooner, and if so, whether their efforts would have been rewarded. Could the colossal energies that went into westward movement have gone into fundamental and applied scientific research? No doubt efforts to improve genetic materials and to raise land yields by fertilizer and scientific cultivation would have been intensified. In such a hotbed of experimentation, pressures for government participation and support might early have appeared. It is hard to tell how fast society could have bought knowledge. Much intellectual capital – in equipment, in statistical techniques, in experimental methods – was not yet developed. Its formation took time and fell along the lines of certain sequences of ideas. Opening scientific frontiers is a different task from opening geographical ones, and one for which nineteenth-century America was perhaps less well equipped.

We cannot, of course, very readily or closely measure the effectiveness of these innovation and diffusion processes as they took effect. They were what they were, and they permitted the levels of efficiency which in fact

[2]See the discussion of this counter-factual in the summary article reprinted as Annex A, below.

obtained. Could they have done their work faster, with less experimentation and fumbling? Delays in adjustment to market conditions arising from ignorance or conservatism must be measured, one would suppose, in terms of a decade or two, but no more. By 1890, despite upsets caused by war, the railroad, market shifts, rainfall fluctuations, and the great deflation, the agricultural map of the United States had assumed roughly its present form. The comparative advantage of the regions had been felt out; seeds, stock, and a powerful array of horse-drawn implements had been developed to suit the wide variations in climate, soil, and terrain. At the same time, links with European science had been maintained, and the native institutions of a scientific agriculture were forming. A great assault on the whole body of folklore and idiosyncrasy that made up farming practice had begun. It was to continue till, with the twentieth-century discoveries in genetics and biochemistry, it assumed the form of an attack on the secret and fundamental principles of life itself.

IV. ORGANIZED SCIENCE

The increase in knowledge and improvement of materials for agricultural production occurred in the United States in the nineteenth century at several levels. Simplest and most immediate were the efforts of farmers themselves, described in Parts I and II, above. Singly or in agricultural societies and clubs, they developed new implements and new varieties adapted to new soils and climate. Economic historians have examined the question whether settlement occurred too rapidly for maximum growth or whether the engrossing of land by speculators made it too long delayed.[3] The efficiency of the settlement process for the acquisition of new knowledge, however, has not been tested, though there can be no doubt that the frontier was a school in which much learning took place. Natural adaptations – for example, of cattle and swine breeds – occurred as animals were turned out to survive in the forests; among cereal grains natural selection continued its beneficent innovative work.[4] Seeds and knowl-

[3]For two references, one by an "old," one by a "new" economic historian, see Paul W. Gates, "The Role of the Land Speculator in Western Development," *Pennsylvania Magazine of History and Biography*, Vol. 66 (July 1942): 314–33, and Peter Passell, "Pre–Civil War Land Policy and the Growth of Manufacturing," in Passell, *Essays in the Economics of Nineteenth Century Land Policy*, Dissertations in Economic History (New York: Arno, 1975).

[4]Carl N. Alsberg, "The Objectives of Wheat Breeding," *Wheat Studies*, Vol.4, No. 7 (1928): 271. Alsberg makes the interesting point that where seed is chosen at random from the harvest of mixed breeds, the more prolific varieties are favored since, relative to what was planted, they are the more heavily represented in the harvested crop. This gives an upward bias toward more prolific (though not necessarily best-quality) varieties in reseeding.

edge were imported continually from the European cultures that continued to release migrants to the Plains as late as the 1880s.[5] The similarity
of midcontinent conditions to those of the eastern European plains made
transfer easy. And though larger farmers, especially in the Northeast,
were responsible for most early recorded experimentation, the existence
of growing numbers of farms of moderate size (forty to three hundred
acres) – two million by 1860 – mean that many small experiments were
occurring simultaneously and their results communicated among rural
neighborhoods.

Government work in the Patent Office and the privately sponsored
U.S. Agricultural Society in the 1850s culminated in 1862 in the establishment of the U.S. Department of Agriculture and provision of federal
grants for a college in each state devoted to the agricultural and mechanical arts (the Morrill Act).[6] In the USDA, research bureaus were
organized and had proliferated by 1900 to most branches of agricultural
science.[7] The state agricultural colleges served as providers of education
for farmers' sons (who may or may not have wanted to remain in
farming) and as sponsors of laboratory research, sometimes of a rather
"pure" and academic character, in agricultural chemistry and biology.
In 1887, there was introduced into this structure an intermediate institution of semi-applied research: the Agricultural Experiment Station. Like
the colleges, the stations were set up, one in each state, with federal
funds and the expectation that state governments would provide physical facilities and supplemental funding. In examining this system of
research and educational institutions, the most difficult question to answer is what performance grade to give to the Agricultural Experiment
Stations in the first half century of their operation.

An an idea and a system, agricultural experiment stations are not an
American institutional invention. German agricultural societies and
states of the mid-nineteenth century are usually given the credit for

---

[5]The case of Turkey wheat, probably brought to Kansas by Mennonite refugees
from southern Russia, is only the most famous of these. See James C. Malin,
*Winter Wheat in the Golden Belt of Kansas: A Study in Adaptation to Subhumid
Geographical Environment* (Lawrence: University of Kansas Press, 1944). See
also K. S. Quisenberry and L. P. Reitz, "Turkey Wheat: The Cornerstone of an
Empire," *Agricultural History*, Vol. 48 (January 1974), and Leo M. Hoover,
Kansas Agriculture After 100 Years, Bulletin 392 (Manhattan: Kansas Agricul-
tural Experiment Station, August 1957).

[6]For the early history of the USDA and the land-grant colleges, see Edward
Wiest, *Agricultural Organization in the United States* (Lexington: University of
Kentucky Press, 1923), and E. D. Eddy, *Colleges of Our Land and Time* (New
York: Harper, 1956).

[7]*Yearbook of the United States Department of Agriculture, 1899* (Washington:
U.S. Government Printing Office, 1900) contains an extensive retrospective review of the department's research organization and activities as of that date.

initiating the research "station."[8] But before them, French and American universities and technical schools did some organized experimental work. The station set up at Mönckern in Saxony in 1852 is no doubt the first to call itself by the name, but professional work antedates it by at least a century.

Despite the prominence given to soils and agricultural chemistry in the formal experimentation of the nineteenth century, the rules of thumb of plant and animal breeders were also refined through tests in field and barn. The effort, largely private and even amateur, was to put a solid base of close and controlled observation behind the practical techniques of farmers and agricultural improvers to develop statistical laws of heredity and to account for variation. The separate German states had their own universities and research centers, which resulted in some duplication of effort, but permitted also variety in work and local adaptation. The French station system was more centralized, and remained a feeble effort, poorly supported. The Russian system may have rivaled the American in scope, but little account of it appears in Western language literature.[9]

The American system, though part of a more general development among nations exposed to Western science, had some peculiar advantages and problems.[10] The variety of natural conditions and problems and the scale of effort required to tackle them all simultaneously are the most obvious of these peculiarities. Here the advantage of a mixed federal–local structure made itself felt. Most agricultural research problems are beyond the resources, time horizons, and abilities of an individ-

[8]One of the Connecticut station's founders, Samuel Johnston, was intensely conscious of the contemporary intellectual and organizational history of the movement. See Connecticut Board of Agriculture, *Annual Report* (1883), 92–96.

[9]Louis N. Grandeau, *L'Agriculture et les institutions agricole du monde au commencement du XXe siècle*, Vols. 1–5 (Paris, 1906): Vol. 1, 660–69; Vol. 3, 34–59; Vol. 4, 96–103. Margaret Rossiter's excellent study, *The Emergence of Agricultural Science* (New Haven: Yale University Press, 1975), shows in admirable detail the transfer of European knowledge, methods, and attitudes to the American university departments and the early experiment stations. Her view is that the system did not get started in the 1850s because of the excessively simple view of the chemistry of the problem held by Liebig and his students. See also the valuable recent survey by George Grantham, "The Shifting Locus of Agricultural Innovation in Nineteenth-Century Europe: The Case of the Agricultural Experiment Stations," in Gary Saxonhouse and Gavin Wright, eds., *Technique, Spirit and Form in the Making of Modern Economies: Essays in Honor of William N. Parker*, in *Research on Economic History*, Suppl. 4 (Greenwich, Conn.: SAI Press, 1984), 191–214.

[10]The discussion of the U.S. system here is based on a preliminary survey of materials, largely station histories and reports, and unpublished studies of four stations, two in Connecticut, one each in Kansas and Georgia, made by Lisa Newman.

ual small farmer. Perhaps none of those attacked in the nineteenth century was beyond the resources of an individual state government. But for fundamental scientific development and for problems common to several states, a single center with wide diffusion of results avoids both duplication and the problem of appropriating the results. The U.S. Department of Agriculture began to undertake such work after 1870, and the proliferation of its offices, committees, and bureaus makes an awesome illustration of the dynamics of scientific bureaucracy. But most immediate problems facing farmers involved a variety of intensely local conditions, and here local work was necessary. Research at the level of the states and state substations was useful, too, making of agricultural science a kind of folk institution, educating farmers in its possibilities, and diffusing its results. So long as communication among stations was good and a sophisticated awareness of the limited transferability of results from one state to another was present, the system of state stations could rest like a centipede on American ground, with many feet and one body, moving as a unit but adapting at each point to local conditions. Its sense of direction and efficiency of effort were reinforced by the exchange of information among scientists and research workers; a degree of professionalism grew up, with all the peer-group characteristics of that phenomenon. A formal coordination was given by the Office of Experiment Stations within the USDA, particularly under a strong director, A. C. True.[11]

But why was it necessary for the state-sponsored research to approach all problems and all branches of agriculture simultaneously almost from the outset? The reason lies, of course, in its sensitivity to popular pressure. The American system was the first major effort of a thoroughly democratic government to engage in scientific research and in doing so to go well beyond the popular will and the popular level of sophistication. The complete insulation of agricultural research from popular pressures and demands was not only not possible, but in fact not desirable. Only an awareness of the practical problems and market possibilities could start research in a useful direction or allow its results to command credence and respect. Nevertheless, the state stations were in a peculiarly exposed position in their early decades. Charles Rosenberg's articles have described some of the problems of establishing genetic research in such a

[11] True's administrative history is the standard source: A. C. True, *A History of Agricultural Experimentation and Research in the United States, 1607–1925*, U.S. Department of Agriculture Miscellaneous Publication No. 251 (Washington: U.S. Government Printing Office, 1937); reprint (New York: Johnson Reprint, 1970). H. C. E. Knoblauch, E. M. Law, and W. P. Meyer, *State Agricultural Experiment Stations: a History of Research Policy and Procedure*, U.S. Department of Agriculture Miscellaneous Publication No. 904 (Washington: U.S. Government Printing Office, 1962), provides an important and insightful interpretation.

setting.[12] The positioning of the stations in conjunction with the state agricultural colleges was a mixed blessing. It gave them some underpinning in agricultural chemistry and put a theoretical basis, at least in statistics, under some of the work. On the other hand, it made for an all-too-plausible division of labor between the scientific and theory-based experiment and applied, trial-and-error research. The stations were used to shield the college staff from contact with farmers, and the station farm was sometimes looked on as a demonstration farm, a teaching device. Farmers even expected it to show a profit in its operations. Equally distracting was the tendency to load the stations with regulatory and policing functions. Of these, the testing of fertilizers was the most widespread. Given the rather simple soil science of the 1880s, the analysis of a farmer's soil, a prescription for supplements, and a testing of the commercial fertilizer used seemed to many farmers to be the sum of agricultural research. But milk testing, seed testing, and even forestry work were added to some stations' duties by state legislatures, often without supplemental appropriations.

By 1920 the natural laws of bureaucratic expansion and division of labor had narrowed and fixed the stations' peculiar position and character. An elite of station professionals and administrators developed and made itself felt through the Association of Land Grant Colleges – more strongly in Congress than in the state legislatures. The Granger and Populist agitation of the 1870s and 1890s made the more enlightened movement for agricultural research appear to progressives as a welcome and intelligent alternative. It fitted well with the politics of Republican progressivism. The strong leadership in the USDA under James Wilson and in the Office of Experiment Stations (OES) under A. C. True was supplemented by pressure on Congress and congressional committees. The Adams Act of 1906 doubled the federal funds available to the stations for research. The Smith–Lever Act of 1914 set up an extension service relieving the stations of much of their educational and public relations responsibilities and furnishing channels both for diffusion of research results and for the backward flow of knowledge about the research needs of farming. At the same time, below the surface of field experiments and statistical observations, the foundations of the modern theory of genetics were beginning to form. It was not until the late 1930s that a real payoff began to come from the heavy investment of

---

[12]Charles E. Rosenberg, "Science, Technology, and Economic Growth: The Case of the Agricultural Experiment Station Scientist, 1875–1914," *Agricultural History*, Vol. 45 (January 1971); Rosenberg, "The Adams Act: Politics and the Cause of Scientific Research," *Agricultural History*, Vol. 38 (January 1964); and Rosenberg, "Rationalization and Reality in the Shaping of American Agricultural Research, 1875–1914," mimeographed, n.d.

funds, scientific manpower, political maneuvering, popular education, and intellectual capital formation that had created the modern institutions of agricultural research.

What, then, shall we say about the Agricultural Experiment Station system itself? Was it, in a sense, born before its time? Possibly so, in the sense that the efficient organization of applied agricultural experimentation required scientific knowledge more fundamental than that available in 1887. Mendel was not rediscovered until the early 1900s, and an understanding of the genetic basis and mechanism of the statistical regularities lay four decades ahead. Much of the research was perhaps a form of busy-work, needed to allay anxiety, to do *something,* but not yielding much product. However, the question is not a very serious one, since not many resources were used and those had not much alternative use. Pending full examination of the stations' programs and results, it is impossible to be sure. But two facts are apparent, even in a preliminary survey.

First, the movement could hardly have been suppressed or avoided. By 1900 at any rate it was a political necessity to do something, not just in Washington but at the state level, where it could be visible. The demand did not come from Populist agitators, who in fact paid little attention to production problems. The experiment station movement was demanded by larger, enlightened farmers, with a strong voice in the Republican Party, aware that science had something to do with farming. One must place the institution of agricultural improvement in the context of a capitalistic rural culture, separating itself from peasant and folk mentality, substituting for a faith in tradition and Providence a faith in the ability of experimentation and theoretical science to unlock the secrets of productivity and profit.

Second, it is a delicate matter to say at what time in a process of social change a given institution "should" emerge, or to pinpoint where and in what respects given institutions or attitudes act as impediments or drags on the forward movement of the economy. Yet the analysis of the efficiency of a given institutional structure and the determination of such moments is implicit in any history that claims to give explanations or to teach lessons to its students. In the American research system, it is possible that the state, yielding to democratic pressure, created institutions whose main value lay not in the experimentation undertaken, but in communicating and spreading a scientific culture to the farm population. The fact that in the early decades the stations combined research, regulatory, and educational functions may have been important in establishing their identity and fixing their position. When the extension service was formed, the link between station and county agent could then be very close. The support and expansion of a trained cadre of agricultural scientists had a similar effect, enlarging the total mass of educated people to leaven the social lump.

The history of agricultural experimentation reveals the interplay between the farmers and their educated and political "elites." It is tempting to look at the creation of practical knowledge and useful technology in an economic model as a production structure, with intellectual capital formed at deeper and more abstract levels, and the product, "technology," coming out as an end result. Several problems exist with such a model. For one thing, work went on at all levels – theoretical, statistical, and practical – simultaneously in the nineteenth century. Practical field results are no more the application of laboratory and library research than are the latter the result of the effort to understand "practical" facts. Furthermore, the motivation of the activity at any level is not entirely "economic," in the sense of a market production process. Curiosity, personal and local pride, professional advancement within a peer group whose values are not wholly those of market producers – these all qualify a view of technological change as a wholly economic process. Both these points mean that the productivity-raising effects of a system of technological and scientific research within the economy depend upon its immersion in a culture which may be called eco-technic.[13] Obviously, learning by farmers, their readiness to accept research results and to diffuse techniques, depends upon their participation to some degree in the scientific enterprise itself. "Capitalistic" motivations and the desire to maximize income are not enough since they cannot dictate the level of risk taking a farmer wishes to assume. High risk taking, gambling, credulity were roads to ruin for many in nineteenth-century farming; a certain informed consciousness of the risk was required. Farmers who were skeptical but interested, intrigued even a little by the effort to undertand agriculture as well as to make a killing from it, were probably the best agents for testing and diffusion of new fertilizers and feeds, breeds, seeds, and improved practices. But the reverse is also true: The link of university science to the farm and market by way of the experiment stations helped direct research and thought even on quite abstract levels in developing the deeper understanding of the chemical and biological mechanisms on which life – and with it, medicine as well as farming – is based. In this contribution a capitalistic and democratic organization of farming clearly had an immense advantage over an aristocratic or centrally planned one, once farmers and scientists were brought close enough together to recognize their mutual interdependence.

[13]William N. Parker, "Industry," *The New Cambridge Modern History*, Vol. 13: Companion Volume, ed. Peter Burke (New York and London: Cambridge University Press, 1979), reprinted as "The Pre-History of the Nineteenth Century" in *Europe, America, and the Wider World*, Vol. 1. (Cambridge: Cambridge University Press, 1984), Ch. 2.

BIBLIOGRAPHICAL NOTE

The voluminous publications of the United States Department of Agriculture are both an original source, reflecting much of the thinking of farm leaders, and the results of scholarly research. In the Yearbooks of the Department and a predecessor series of Agricultural Reports of the U.S. Patent Office, one channel of diffusion of new ideas is revealed. The volumes in 1853, 1872, 1899, and 1936 are especially useful to the historian. As the century goes on, these publications take on the character of reports of scientific investigations which are communicated to officials interested in disseminating the results. In this function, the Yearbooks are replaced after about 1900 by the Bulletins of the Experiment Stations, the Farmers' Bulletins, and other services to the farmer. To assess the scientific value of this literature, containing information and some misinformation on every conceivable subject, requires a mastery of agricultural technology. A. C. True – himself a dominant figure in the history of the experiment stations – did much to bring it to bear on the history of agricultural education and research.[14] For the study of innovation and diffusion in the pre-scientific era, the early station bulletins are of interest in showing the development of research techniques and of proper perspectives on the results of individual experiments.

The earlier USDA publications and the reports of the state and county agricultural societies constitute an original source of access to farmers' thinking in the nineteenth century. Much space is devoted to reports handed down "from above" on crops and practices, but the writers are seldom far removed from the farm. The same is true of the literature of the farm journals; a guide to this tremendous source is given in the book by A. L. Demaree, *The American Agricultural Press.*[15] It constitutes our primary avenue of access to nineteenth-century American rural culture. For the present paper, eight of the most prominent of these journals were examined: *American Farmer, American Agriculturist, Cultivator* (Albany), *Country Gentlemen* (combined with *Cultivator* in 1866), *Ohio Cultivator, Prairie Farmer, Rural New Yorker, Southern Cultivator.* In each of these periodicals at least one volume was covered in every decade from 1830 to 1880 for which the periodical appeared. Extract was made of material on farm practices especially in relation to the use of machinery, on methods of seed selection and improvement, and on breeding practices and techniques.

Beyond these sources one moves into the documents of local history – county records, newspapers, and family archives. Some interesting mate-

[14]True, *A History of Agricultural Experimentation and Research.*
[15]Albert L. Demaree, *The American Agricultural Press* (New York: Columbia University Press, 1941).

rial has been published, for example, in the series of Minnesota Farmers' Diaries edited by R. C. Loehr and in the transactions of state historical societies, but an organized effort on the part of the state societies would be needed to produce a significant sampling of such material. Although its bulk is undoubtedly large, it reflects the activity of only a tiny fraction of the farmers and, like all written records, is biased in the direction of the literate and thoughtful part of the population. The insights of fiction writers – Willa Cather, O. E. Rolvaag, Hamlin Garland, Edward Eggleston – must not be overlooked.

Ideas on the diffusion process itself are richly developed in modern studies of technological change and rural sociology. The work by E. M. Rogers is a useful introduction and contains a good bibliography.[16] Here, as in all historical work, the problem is to apply concepts and models to a body of material which is sparse by current standards and cannot be increased by a survey questionnaire. Theory can rarely be tested by such data, but theory can still help the historian to weave together from such data a story which may appear plausible, at least to his contemporaries.

For references to a few of the excellent studies which try to place farmers' innovative activities in the context of regional agricultural development, see Murray Reed Benedict, *Farm Policies of the United States, 1870–1950: A Study of Their Origins and Development* (New York: Twentieth Century Fund, 1953); Clarence H. Danhof, "Agriculture," in *The Growth of the American Economy,* edited by Harold F. Williamson (Englewood Cliffs, N.J.: Prentice-Hall, 1951), Ch. 8; Zvi Griliches, "Hybrid Corn: An Exploration in the Economies of Technological Change," *Econometrica,* Vol. 25, No. 4 (October 1957).

[16]Everett M. Rogers, *Diffusion of Innovations* (New York: Free Press of Glencoe, 1962).

APPENDIX:
SELECTED BASIC DATA ON YIELDS
AND LABOR PRODUCTIVITY

Table 1. *Acreage and yields in major crops, by region, 1859 and 1909*

	Wheat							
	Northeast		South		Midwest		Plains and West	
	A	O/A	A	O/A	A	O/A	A	O/A
1859	1.7	14.3	5.3	8.4	7.5	12.5	0.6	14.7
1909	1.7	17.5	3.9	12.3	14.0	15.7	26.3	13.1

	Corn									
	Northeast		Middle East		South		Midwest		Plains and West	
	A	A/O	A	A/O	A	A/O	A	A/O	A	A/O
1859	2.0	33.4	7.8	22.1	15.0	12.8	12.3	32.4	0.3	28.6
1909[a]	1.9	36.8	10.1	24.4	27.1	16.1	38.2	35.3	17.8	21.8

	Cotton									
	Border		East		Delta		West		Other	
	A	A/O	A	A/O	A	A/O	A	A/O	A	A/O
1859	0.7	181.6	6.5	139.4	4.7	198.4	0.9	199.2	–	–
1909	0.8	217.4	12.0	209.9	6.5	190.6	12.4	154.0	0.1	286.7

[a]Total U.S. acreage reduced by 3.9 percent to allow for corn growth silage.
A = acreage (millions of acres); O/A = yield (bushels [wheat and corn] or pounds [ginned cotton] per acre).

Source: 1859 based on 1866–75 average yield by State and Census production data. 1909 – 5-year averages based on USDA revised estimates.

Wheat Regions
  Northeast: New England, N.Y., N.J., Pa.
  South: Md., Del., Va., W.Va., Ky., Tenn., N.C., S.C., Ga., Fla., Ala., Miss., La., Ark.
  Midwest: Ohio, Ind., Ill., Mo., Iowa, Mich., Wis., Minn.
  Plains and West: N.Dak., S.Dak., Kans., Nebr., Mont., Wyo., Utah, Colo., Nev., Ariz., N.Mex., Idaho, Oreg., Wash., Calif.

Corn Regions
  Northeast: As for wheat
  Middle East: Md., De., Va., W.Va., Ky., Tenn.,
  South: N.C., S.C., Ga., Fla., Ala., Miss., La., Ark., Tex., Okla.

Midwest:	As for wheat
West:	As for wheat

Cotton Regions

Border:	Va. and Tenn.
East:	N.C., S.C., Ga., Fla., Ala.
Delta:	Miss., La., Ark.
West:	Tex., Okla.
Other:	Mo., Ill., Ky., Tenn.

Table 2. *Typical labor imputs, by crop and region, pre-harvest and harvest operations, 1840–60 (Period 1) and 1900–10 (Period 2) (man-hours per acre)*

| | Pre-harvest | | | | | |
| | Wheat and Oats | | Corn | | Cotton | |
	Period 1	Period 2	Period 1	Period 2	Period 1	Period 2
Northeast	19[a]	12	97	49	–	–
South						
Border	12	10	53	[b]	–	–
Southeast	12	10	82	26	109	73
Delta	12	10	82	26	95	70
Southwest	12	5	49	17	[b]	41
West						
Corn Belt	12[a]	5	49	17	–	–
Plains	12[a]	5	49	17	–	–

| | Harvest | | | | | |
| | Wheat and Oats | | Corn[c] | | Cotton | |
	Period 1	Period 2	Period 1	Period 2	Period 1	Period 2
Northeast	14	3	13	13	–	–
South						
Border	12	3	5	6	–	–
Southeast	12	3	5	5	37	43
Delta	12	3	5	5	37	43
Southwest	14	3	13	7	37	22
West						
Corn Belt	14	3	13	7	–	–
Plains	14	3	13	7	–	–

[a]Wheat only. Estimate for oats is about 25 percent less.
[b]No figure for cultivating.
[c]Grain harvest only, excluding shelling.
Note: These figures are the means of series collected for each crop by the Inter-University Project on American Economic History. Further information on range and variance and on sources is given in the publications of this work, cited in Annex A, below. Regions are:

Northeast	Pa., N.J., N.Y., New England
Border	Md., Del., Va., W.Va., Ky., Tenn.
Southeast	N.C., S.C., Ga., Fla., Ala.
Delta	Ark., La., Miss.
Corn Belt	Ohio, Ind., Ill., Mo., Iowa; including for wheat and for corn–pre-harvest, Mich., Wis., Minn.
Plains	N.Dak., S.Dak., Nebr., Kans.
Southwest	Tex., N.Mex., Ariz., Okla.

IO

The true history of the northern farmer

LINES AND TASKS OF SETTLEMENT

The occasional young American of the 1960s and 1970s who fled urban civilization for the hills and the woods in Maine or Colorado encountered suddenly some of the natural conditions faced in every region by its first settlers. Nor was he much worse suited to the job. French peasants along the St. Lawrence or Dutch patroons along the Hudson in the seventeenth century brought something of an older social structure; later, in New Jersey and Delaware, and much later in Minnesota and Wisconsin, Scandinavians brought some techniques of settlement in forested regions. Germans in Pennsylvania in the eighteenth century with other central European peasant stock in the Middle West and east Texas in the mid-nineteenth century had been farmers in Europe before they became pioneer settlers in the new terrain. But inexperience was acute among the main body of English and Scottish settlers along the coast from Newfoundland to South Carolina in the seventeenth and eighteenth centuries. Many, if not most, of the English had been town or village dwellers, adventurers, fishermen, religious malcontents, sailors, drifters, town craftsmen. The Scotch and Welsh had been herders of sheep and cattle; many bore a traditional aversion to the slow life of plow and sickle. All the Europeans, even where they migrated as small communities, had left regions where the tasks of pioneering were buried deep in a medieval, even a neolithic, past.

In New England the Puritan colonists kept in small bands, building villages around a common, raising stock and shooting game along the

Originally published as "The American Farmer," in Jerome Blum, ed., *Our Forgotten Past* (London and New York: Thames & Hudson, 1982), pp. 181–208. An extended treatment of this topic, with source references and a few appropriate statistics forms Chapter 11 of L. E. Davis, R. A. Easterlin, and W. K. Parker, *American Economic Growth: An Economist's History of the United States* (New York: Harper & Row, 1971).

edges of forests and streams. In the southern colonies, adventurers, farmers, and planters moved out from tidewater settlements to small plantations or isolated farms along the streams. In the Middle Colonies – New York, New Jersey, Pennsylvania – Dutch, Swedes and Germans as well as English settled rather thickly along large rivers and had occupied the richest farming soils by 1740. Then began the penetration into the Appalachian mountain range from New Hampshire to North Carolina in three directions. Movements north from Massachusetts and Connecticut began to plant new villages in northern valleys, while southward from Pennsylvania, settlers and new immigrants – Scottish clansmen, German sectarians – moved into western Virginia, and Carolinas, and eastern Tennessee. The westward movement – the principal fact of American agrarian history – went through passes and gaps in the mountain chain, or along major rivers – down the St. Lawrence, along the Mohawk River in New York. Through the Cumberland Gap the pioneers spread out into Kentucky and Tennessee. By 1760, the site of Pittsburgh had been established and the Ohio River reached; by 1790 the edge of the great central plain – the Midwest – began to be colonized. In the South, yeoman farmers moved into the hill country and performed the first tasks of settlement, even in the rich central areas of the "black belt" from western Georgia across Alabama and eastern Mississippi. The expansion of cotton across the interior began strongly after the final resettlement of the Creek and Cherokee Indians in the 1820s.

Across the entire coastal plain and Appalachian areas, as well as in the areas of French Canada, the labor of clearing a few acres for a family's corn patch or pasture was enormous. The stone walls in New England, running still for miles along roads and ancient property lines, separating fields now overgrown in pine and maple, bear witness to the inhospitality of the soil and the compulsive tidiness of the settlers. Stone removal was something of a New England specialty since in no other region did settlers try to cultivate such rocky ground. Other tasks of pioneer settlement included clearing fields of timber and finally of stumps, cabin construction and fencing – whether stone, hedge, post and rail or the primitive "worm" rail fence, which zig-zagged without posts across a field. They included also eventually road building as an area opened up, and the construction of farmhouse, shed, barn, and the community buildings – meeting house and school. These tasks were common to all regions, though pursued with slightly different styles in the South, the Middle Colonies, and the West.

Land clearing was the heaviest of the tasks. The Scandinavians and Germans along the Delaware River whose background was closest to pioneering in new heavily forested areas may have diffused techniques and tools for land clearing and the construction of wooden buildings, in particular the omnipresent log cabin. In the southern colonies standing trees were killed by girdling (stripping off a circle of the bark) – a method not unknown to the beaver. They could then be dismantled over some years while crops were sown in the open spaces under and around the dead branches. In the North, trees were felled by the axe and cleared off by controlled burning. So long as land was plentiful, the arduous task of stump removal might be delayed. Altogether it took a man as many as twenty to thirty-five days to make an acre of land reasonably free of its original cover and ready for first cultivation. A team of oxen was required to do the job well, but the very first pioneers came, like the Indians, on foot, and logs, once felled could only be collected together by rolling. Pioneers moving in by foot or horseback spent their first weeks in a tent; those who came by wagon lived in the wagon while the first trees were felled and the cabin constructed. Log cabin construction itself was an art, requiring the axe and a trimming tool – the adze – to notch the logs at each end and in some constructions to square them off for a tighter fit. These tools and materials, with some clay or mud to daub in the chinks and stone and clay to line the chimney, were all that two men needed to throw up a cabin within two or three days. Not even nails, glass, or screening were used at first; windows might be cut later, and the whole covered with sawn boards or replaced by a frame house of wood siding when sawmills and industrial manufactures came to the region.

Initially, the choice of crops and farming techniques was governed by a family's needs and the knowledge of what the soil could produce and how to produce it. The Indians' crops – maize and beans – were universal; wild game and hogs, penned or running wild in the woods, were the staple source of fat and animal protein. With the hog the seventeenth century settlers also brought cattle; very large and heavy oxen became common. Even more common was a smaller short-horn cow that might even pull a plow as well as give milk and (eventually) meat. As wood was the universal structural material, the maize, or "corn," plant was the universal food; the grain, cracked and ground in a wooden mortar, was cooked in endless puddings, meals, breads, and mush; it was eaten directly from the ear in season, or dried and then soaked, or fed to hogs. Cooked, fermented, and distilled, it was the source of the royal American whiskey, bourbon. The plant itself was animal fodder. The husks, dried, were used to stuff mattresses, and the dried cobs, light and absorbent, were not replaced in some rural outhouses by waste paper until the early twentieth century. Although corn was the universal food and feed grain in all sections of early United States, the mode of harvesting the corn plant early revealed peculiarities of regional character and economic position. In the Northeast and South, the top of the plant and the leaves below the ear were cut off (a practice known as "topping"), tied in bundles, and stored for winter feed. In the eastern Midwest, the whole plant was cut down and stacked in large shocks to dry while the field was made ready for the next planting. In the South, this laborious practice was never adopted; instead, the plant was left standing, topped perhaps for feed where livestock required it, with the ear picked at any time in the fall. When the Midwest became the principal corn- and hog-producing region after 1830, neither shocking nor topping was adopted; in Illinois and Iowa the stock were often turned into the field to harvest the plant for themselves.

Once land had been cleared, the agricultural tasks of pioneer settlement in the absence of commercial markets became less onerous. Wild game and fish were abundant and neither domestic animals nor children required much care. Corn yields on new lands were very high, an acre could yield first thirty to fifty bushels or more of corn, maintaining a steady yield of twenty to thirty bushels (1,000 to 1,800 pounds) after a few years, with occasional rotation with vegetables, wheat, or fallow pasturage, and with little or no fertilizer. An acre or two could support a family the first year, and five acres gave an unmanageable surplus. Unlike the European cereals, corn could be sown in hills, Indian style, arranged in a checkerboard pattern in the field, the soil prepared and cultivated with a hoe. The labor required varied, like a housekeeper's labor, with a settler's standard for a "clean" corn patch, but again unlike the other close-sown cereals, weeds did not mix into the harvested crop, and weeding could be neglected without appreciable loss in yield. Even without a draft animal and without wild game supplement, the labor of growing food for a family on a diet of rude abundance in corn meal, hog meat, vegetables, and poultry could not have occupied more than thirty work days a year for a frontier family. The rest of the time was spent in the tasks of farm formation, in hunting and fishing for the man, and food preparation and preservation for the frontier wife.

The self-sufficiency of log cabin life, however, had one serious drawback. It meant that more time was spent in industrial activities than on farming itself. Hog slaughtering in the late fall was followed by several weeks in which the carcasses were dressed, hides scraped, lard rendered, and hams, bacon slabs, and sides salted and smoked. Apple trees meant a cider mill, and maple trees in the Northeast gave their sap for syrup-making over endless fires fed by cord wood. Nearly every cabin had a spinning wheel; flax and wool were the fibers, and the labor of flax preparation was particularly long and tedious. Soap-making with lye made from wood ashes was almost as widely practiced as the distilling of whiskey.

When settlement reached the grassy prairies in the 1850s in the tier of states from Illinois and Iowa to east Texas, a new learning experience was at hand. Wooded areas were still available as far west as Iowa and eastern Kansas, and settlers first moved along streams and into those areas despite much higher initial clearing costs. To begin plowing in grasslands took only a fraction – no more than 5 to 10 percent – of the initial cost of removing a forest cover. A plow and team were needed, and the settler once encamped on the prairie found a self-sufficient life impossible to sustain. The forest, after all, though an impediment, was also a resource. The pioneers after 1870 on the Nebraska and Dakota plains had only the sod as structural material and buffalo chips as fuel. In the forested areas, even on the most independent homesteads, *some* purchases were required – ironwares, plowshares, salt, spices, the services of a sawmill and a flour mill. Yet a forest environment also offered variety in vegetation, soils, and terrain, along with the resources of field, fish, game, streams, and water power. A rural culture developed east of the Prairies in rural neighborhoods; the ample idle time could be used in rural crafts, and exchanges made by barter in the absence of banks and money. On the Prairies and Plains, farming was the creature of railroads and the commercial market; without them, life above the level of the nomadic Indians could not be sustained. It was 1870, when the Civil War had settled the political structure of the western territories, the railroads had crossed to the Pacific, and the European markets had opened wide to North American wheat and beef, rather than the official date of 1890, that marked the end of the life of the forested frontier.

THE OMNIPRESENT MARKET

Had it not been for its setting in a modern world of intense capitalist commerce, the movement of European and native farmers across North America would have been a primitive affair. But the period of frontier boldness, crudity, and independence was brief, passing over the North American landscape like the shadow of a speeding cloud. In a commercial setting, European villagers and peasants re-establishing themselves in new lands emerged from the experience of settlement as individualistic American farmers. A village agrarian culture of the Old World was broken apart and reshaped, becoming shallower, harsher, more resourceful, more aggressive, mobile, and profitable.

Throughout the late eighteenth and nineteenth centuries, the shadow of the frontier moved ever faster over the landscape. One hundred years were required for a penetration from the coastal settlements two hundred to three hundred miles into the Appalachian uplands; in the next century, i.e., from 1750 to 1850, the frontier moved another five hundred miles just beyond the Mississippi. After that, the surge of settlers across the Prairies and Plains and the back movement east from the minerals rushes in California had covered the thousand miles from Chicago to Denver and another four hundred miles from the Pacific to the western slopes of the Rockies with the skin of settlement and the nerve system of the railroad and telegraph by 1900. The frontier experience lasted two or three generations in the eighteenth-century East. It took less than the span of a single life on the prairies and the Plains. This speed-up was not caused by a mounting pressure of populations. The swarming in the countryside across nineteenth-century Europe contributed to it, but the American rural birth rates steadily declined as population density grew. Nor were there striking changes in the techniques of pioneering – only difficult adaptations to lands that were flat, bare, and dry. Canals, steamship, railroad, and telegraph were essential for it, but such techniques are effective only in the presence of pressures to sell, to move, to communicate between the two ends of their lines. Rather, it was cumulative pressures of productivity change in the northern European and northeastern industrial sector and the thrust of commercial enterprise pushing settlement ahead at an increasing pace that transformed the narrow but leisurely life of a log cabin into the long days of driving labor and tense commercial energies of a profit-seeking agriculture. Only in the deep valleys and secluded nooks of the uplands – the Green Mountains, the Adirondacks, the Smoky Mountains, the Ozarks, the hills and poor soils of eastern Kentucky and western Virginia – did backwoods living, domestic crafts, and a high degree of self-sufficiency persist, independent of the commercial economy and impoverished by that independence.

It is a supreme irony of American history that these pressures and commercial inducements were felt first in that region where their ultimate extension was least pervasive: the semi-tropical South. Sugar and tobacco in the seventeenth century, rice and indigo in the eighteenth, and at last cotton in the nineteenth were colonial products *par excellence*. Like spices, tea, rubber, cacao, and all the rest, they offered a complement rather than a competition to the productions of European peasant farms and manorial estates. Much has been written about the intellectual history of African slavery, its morality, its legality, its ideology, its compatibility or incompatibility with church law and rationalistic Protestant conscience. But southern planters were simply northern farmers in a different economic environment. While northern farmers were performing self-imposed tasks of settlement, growing corn, wheat, and flax for trade with neighbors or coastal towns, seeking an escape from the primitive poverty of self-sufficiency and finding none except by moves deeper into the forest, their southern counterparts were taking up lands in a climate in which, in effect, hard money could be grown through the application of labor to limitless land. In the colonial and early federal South, markets, land, techniques and enterprise all combined to offer the chance to create wealth – a chance so tangible it could be almost smelt and tasted. Only command over labor power was lacking, and human greed ensured that that could be supplied by cruelty and force. No such opportunity existed for the North until world grain and meat markets opened up in the mid-nineteenth century. By that time the mechanical revolution had replaced slavery as the means to the accumulation of capital, and the ideology of freedom was firmly established in American law and American myth – a freedom that was bourgeois, perhaps, and certainly individualistic, Christian, and permissive of exploitation only through the workings of free markets.

By 1860 small, free northern farmers who provided the blood and will to support Lincoln had long since turned necessity into virtue. It was the expansion of their culture, linked with the manufactures of the Northeast, that precipitated the Civil War and predetermined its outcome. That war – the central and peculiar crisis of American nationhood – was a war of competing variants of capitalistic agrarian enterprise. By the standards of European serfdom, the cotton plantations were pitifully small-scale enterprises. Although the slaves were worked almost all in holdings of ten to fifty individuals and a few estates on rich lands along the Missisippi held a hundred and more, the bulk of the *slaveholders* held from one to ten slaves, as an extension of a family enterprise and even on very small farms of family labor. But the slave power and its competing black labor force had been banished by Ordinance from what became the antebellum corn, hog, wheat, and cattle kingdom between the Ohio and the Mississippi Rivers even as early as 1787. The farmers and other small businessmen who had penetrated those rich lands and purchased the soil by the expenditure of their money, labor, and political rhetoric were the fanatics of a free federal Union, extending its free lands and labor to the Pacific. As such, in the 1850s they found political voice with their northeastern counterparts to form the Republican Party, under whose dominance the vast agrarian and industrial growth of the next seventy-five years was carried out.

What, then, were the bases of this agro-business civilization which spread like a flood over most of the continent – in Canada as well as the American Midwest – which destroyed the slave power with an outpouring of blood and righteous enthusiasm, leaving blacks and southern whites in a backwater for nearly a century? At its basis ultimately was, of course, a psychology and a mode of social organization which the settlers brought with them and which both expressed itself and sharpened as families emerged from the experiences of frontier settlement to face the opportunities of commercial agriculture. These patterns of social behavior were made tangible and symbolic in a legal system which blended English common law and continental Roman law through the structures of federal and state constitutions, the powerful decisions of courts, and the enactments of legislatures. In addition, an element of purely native, frontier law was present, a customary law affecting the behavior of lawmakers and judges and emanating from the necessities of social life in a hostile wilderness. As it impinged first on the lives of farmers, the law appeared in the system by which the land itself was distributed.

The American land system was initially a form of tenure characteristic of the late feudal period, in which land was held by grants from the king of England, made to companies, bands of settlers, projectors, and various noble persons. The initial grants were very large and the boundaries exceedingly vague; the companies or proprietors receiving them then regranted them to subtenants and ultimately to individual settlers, usually for a price or in exchange for a nominal quitrent. By 1789, the new federal government in the United States had become both proprietor and sovereign to all the unallocated lands outside the boundaries of the thirteen original colonies, in particular to all the lands west of the Allegheny Mountains, north of the Ohio River, and south of Tennessee. This federal domain extended to the Mississippi River at that time; between 1800 and 1868 the vast acquisitions from France (the Louisiana Purchase), Mexico (Texas, the Southwest, and California), Great Britain (the Northwest), and Russia (Alaska), were added to fulfill the Republic's self-proclaimed "manifest destiny."

The colonial and federal land distribution system formed an important element in the environment facing the first farmers, and their effects are to be seen in American field patterns and the American landscape today. Anyone flying over the eastern United States cannot fail to note how the patchwork of irregular fields east of the mountains changes dramatically into the huge squares and rectangles, often of uniform size, with perfectly straight boundaries extending sometimes for hundreds of miles across the flatlands between the Alleghenies and the Rockies. The surveying and subdivision of the federal domain across the land area of the United States is an artifact directly out of French eighteenth-century rationalism as filtered through the mind of Thomas Jefferson. His basic plan, no doubt on a Roman model, caused the land to be surveyed in great squares, six miles on a side, called townships. Within each township the square miles (called "sections") were numbered, and sold usually in units of a quarter-section (160 acres) or multiples thereof. Underlying, then, the wayward movement of pioneer settlers, the families, and wagon trains, lay a perfectly regular and orderly arrangement of the soil that would have delighted the heart of Jeremy Bentham. The Canadian provinces followed various methods of land distribution, but in the extensive Dominion lands in the Prairies and West, a rectangular survey along the lines of the

American system laid out the plots for disposal through a system of fees and homestead settlement.

After a decade of trial in the federal republic, the seventeenth-century practice of making huge grants or sales to individuals or to trading or land companies was abandoned in response to popular pressure for direct access to the domain. By the Act of 1796, supplemented by numerous adjustments in the terms of sale over the following half-century, federal land offices were established, and the land, once surveyed and subdivided, was placed on auction, a few townships at a time. The land, the age-old basis of sovereignty and social order in Europe, was thus made into a commodity like any other and sold to the highest bidder. Between that date and 1863, the lands to the Mississippi River and just beyond it, north and south, were released to private ownership by thousands of small farmers and small-town land speculators and investors. After 1863, so-called homesteaders could acquire a quarter section of public land simply by claiming it and settling on it. At the same time the system of large grants was revived in order to subsidize railroad construction, particularly across the plains and arid regions, but the railroad companies essentially imitated the federal system of sales to settlers.

There are many other points at which the pioneer experience, combined with the commercial excitement offered to small farmers by abundant market opportunity, altered the legal forms and structures inherited from Europe and made of the law the instrument for a rapid development of small-scale business enterprise. They occur in the law of contract, of eminent domain, of negotiable instruments. A small-town business civilization grew up around land offices, merchants, lawyers, and transport and banking agencies in the farming area as the land was put under the plow. The farmer was apart from this – slightly, but only slightly. He worked with his hands and muscles, he employed animal power and the labor of a wife and children. He commanded the mysterious technology of soil, seed, and rainfall and held to familial patterns of sympathy and sociability. But he largely shared the speculator's ambition to grow wealthy. He would create a physical infra-structure of canals, roads, and towns, and an organizational infra-structure of politics, markets, prices, money, and even those necessary evils, banks and middlemen, in order to do it.

What, then, was this opportunity for wealth seen by the American farmer on his way from frontiersman or peasant to the role of little businessman? It is no part of agrarian history to detail how or where it arose. Put briefly, the opportunity was twofold. First, and most prominently, was the opportunity for large speculative gains both from appreciation in the value of land and from the chance that high yields in early years would be realized in a rising market. Second, and more steadily, the opportunity existed to realize very large physical surpluses of basic food crops above a family's own subsistence. Of course, speculative gains of the first sort were dependent on the prospects of a steady realization of gains of the latter sort. Land speculation – in which every landowner to a degree was involved – was a risky game where the productive capacity of a piece of land and the location of future towns, roads, and railroads were not yet known. In land sales, many gains were made by a bidder's special access to information about the land or its prospects. But the steady growth in land values depended on growing knowledge of the land, growing density of prosperous settlement, and improving markets for the crops. These required the growth in a region of a solid body of steady farmers whose annual surpluses would make the development of transport and business services worthwhile. From the side of supply, then, it can be seen how critical was that surplus above the pioneer's consumption, as mentioned above. In upstate New York and Pennsylvania, and most of all in the new lands beyond the Ohio River, all the talk in the 1820s and 1830s was of "internal improvements" to "realize the surplus." This meant a struggle by any economic, legal, or political means for settlers to use their family's labor to exploit their entire holdings – ten to twenty times the effort needed by a log cabin pioneer – and to deliver these vast quantities of produce to commercial markets. Only in such a way could land rents be generated and land values rise.

The other side of this picture was the market growth in the manufacturing and urban centers in the Northeast from Boston to Baltimore. The southern cotton plantations, like the sugar islands of the eighteenth century, may have taken substantial quantities of produce at certain points, but mostly from nearby farms or from the upper South. But the northern cities and towns were as eager to find markets in the countryside as the farmers were to supply them with cheap food. In a society so hungry for wealth, so obviously able to obtain it on a wide scale, and so responsive to popular pressure and sentiment, the erection of a network of transport and business services was as lightning-like, as inevitable, as the leaping of a spark between two oppositely charged poles. The opportunity for the northern farmer was not simply to produce large physical surpluses and get them hauled away, but to be able to use the income from these sales and the wealth from the rise in land values to buy a mounting array of manufactures both to beautify and facilitate daily life and to increase the family farm's productive capacity. To plug into this profitable circuit of exchanges, the northern farmer was ready to work himself and his family long hours in the field and barn, to borrow in order to hold more land or purchase better tools, to seek continually the best-yielding crop choice for his farm, and to exercise care to select the best seeds and stock. As under similar economic circumstances among the landowners and tenants in eighteenth-century England, there was a "rage for improvement." The peasant suspicion of innovation which had protected agriculturists for centuries from foolish risks was lost in the zeal to "keep up with the times."

Here then was that same tangible, almost tastable, chance that the southern planter had faced earlier in tobacco and faced contemporaneously in cotton – the chance of a lifetime to make a "killing" in farming and landholding – if only the obstacle of labor scarcity could be removed. Slavery was out of the question – though the fear that slaveholders might bring their slaves onto the plains and prairies lay near the surface of political thinking in the 1850s. So long as labor was free and land was cheap, hired labor or even tenant farmers were nearly impossible to find. A family's own labor stretched to the utmost could be supplemented by animal power, but animal power required grain and hay, and before 1840 animals could not lighten the peak labor requirement in the agricultural year, that of harvesting. But the nineteenth century American agrarian settlement was occurring in the presence of an Industrial Revolution in its mechanical phase. Is it surprising then that, given the level of mechanical skills, Patent Office records begin to exhibit a bewildering array of mechanical inventions for use on the farm – and that the most successful of these mechanized the grain and hay harvest?

Outside of German Pennyslvania and French Canada, the North American farmer before 1860 was not a peasant, indeed probably did not derive predominantly from peasant stock. In the South he had become a slavemaster or, failing that, had remained a poor, isolated, half-idle independent mountaineer. In the North he made a good frontiersman exactly because he was not steeped in the traditional lore of peasantry. Particularly in his New England Yankee variant he made quick adjustment to continually changing economic circumstance, to the opening of new areas, to steady and almost continuous shifts in crop combinations, to new techniques and genetic stock. He searched continually to find ways to make his labor go farther, over more land, to produce an ever larger marketable surplus. And he could maintain sanity in conditions so novel, so changeable and unstable, so risky and dangerous, because beneath the improvisation, the innovations, the strangeness of daily life, there lay burning a strong hard drive toward wealth and abundance. The American farmer had a fixed star that kept him on course; it had the glitter in it of silver and gold. But it lay in a firmament across which ran the straight, rationally devised lines of a rectangular system of land survey, and the axioms of private property rights, inviolable except in the interest of a greater wealth for the community. And beneath his feet lay the solid earth of nineteenth-century society, the emotional support and indulgence of family, church, neighborhood, and school.

THE PRODUCTIVE ACHIEVEMENT

Before considering the American farmer as a full social being, it is necessary to trace out the story of his economic success and its attendant ironies over the century since the Civil War. The story is not of society and psychology, but of agricultural technology and the operation of commercial markets. These form a stratum which must be penetrated and whose operation and mediation must be understood before we can reach the human roots out of which the whole social, technical, and economic vegetation grew.

By 1870 it was evident that in improving, expanding, marrying itself to industrial society, the agrarian community in North America had burned its bridges behind it. Settlement on the plains and prairies, the shift into dairying around the Great Lakes, and the introduction after 1900 of specialized and perishable fruit and vegetable crops in Florida and the Pacific coastal states put farmers into commercial agriculture on a continental, indeed, a worldwide scale. In the new areas of the West and the Southwest, even the limited degree of self-sufficiency that midwestern farmers had enjoyed as late as the 1880s was physically not possible except to a very sparse population. More important, the capital structure of farming itself had become fixed to produce large surpluses of specialized crops while also releasing labor to move off the farms to industrial and small-town employment. Like a tree in an ornamental orchard, American agriculture had been shaped, pruned, and set, as it grew, in a design – the design of an industrial world economy.

Geographically, the design may be sketched out on the map showing the distribution of crops in the North American continent at, say, 1910. It is evident that, with one exception, the major farming regions had already assumed their present-day extent. It was, roughly, the design first observed in Europe and rationalized by the German theorist of spatial economics, von Thünen. From the cities and ports of the Atlantic and Great Lakes, perishable and labor-using crops – fruits and vegetables and dairy products – came to be produced on specialized farms devoted very largely to these activities. In a great ring beyond them, from Tennessee through the Old Midwest as far as Iowa and Wisconsin and into south-central Canada, dairying was mixed with meat production and the production of feed grains, especially corn for hogs and farm cattle. Hay for city horses was produced near cities, since it was bulky to haul, but much hay was produced in all areas to feed draft animals. Beyond the area of mixed farming lay the belt of wheat lands – from three hundred to six hundred miles wide, beyond that an even wider belt of the cattle ranges, and beyond them, in the mountains, sheep. On the western side of the Rockies, something of this same succession of patterns appeared in progression from the young port cities of the coast. Across the South through central Texas, it was cotton rather than wheat that spread out across a thousand miles from east to west. This pattern, not dissimilar to that which arranged itself in North European farming around London as a market center in these decades, and whose logic controlled production as far away as Australia, New Zealand, and Argentina, was the reflection on the soil of an efficient transport system, of spatially concentrated markets for food and fiber, and of a natural, space-using agricultural technology. It was the creation of a responsive agricultural population required to serve demand at lowest cost through the operation of competitive markets for produce, for land, and for farm credit. It vastly cheapened farm products; indeed, no other spatial arrangement could have begun to feed the populations that grew up in Europe and North America in the nineteenth century. Between 1890 and 1950 it changed little; its logic remained intact. In North America, cotton spread with irrigation to the Southwest, and partially abandoned its former home in the old slave states, and cheap shipment of perishables sent most of the vegetable industry to California and Florida. Otherwise the main supports of the spatial pattern remained in place.

That no such pattern is proof against a changing technology is shown by another characteristic of the farm capital structure before 1920: the power technology. From the antebellum developments of threshing and reaping machines, operations in all the crops pushed toward mechanization. The goal was attained with varying lags and varying degrees of success. Harvesting of the row crops, corn and cotton, tobacco and vegetables, resisted mechanization until well into the twentieth century. This meant the retention of much labor working (and overworking) during the harvest season. Family labor of sharecroppers and independent farmers was strained, and in the West hired migratory labor filled the need. Particularly awkward was the failure of the steam engine to adapt to widespread farm use. But the important substitute where mechanical power could not be applied was the farm animal – horse, ox, or mule. At the peak of the draft animal population on United States farms, a quarter of the cultivated acreage was devoted to their feed. This was in 1920; by 1950, this whole arrangement had been made obsolete by the tractor. The substitution of petroleum for hay and pasture grasses as an energy source for farm power released to the food crops or other uses about one-quarter of the land under cultivation – about ninety million acres, an area roughly equal to the entire arable area of northwestern Europe.

The growth of specialized farming regions and the ready adoption of mechanical techniques are but two examples of the responsiveness of American farmers to the pressures and incentives of world and continental markets. Specialized regions were the geographical response to urban growth and transport improvement. "Tractorization" was but the most spectacular demonstration of the power of the industrial revolution to affect farming operations. The incessant striving for mechanical improvement, characteristic of northern farming before the Civil War, continued on a vaster scale by thoroughly professional techniques of research and development. Where farmers themselves showed such readiness to make money, one may be sure that a farm equipment and farm service industry lost no time in producing and marketing things to sell to farmers. But modern farm productivity depends less on geography and machinery than on amazing new fertilizers, genetic materials, and field and feeding techniques. These have not derived from the mere play of markets or the simple extension of industrial patents to replace human feet, arms, and fingers in farm tasks. Between 1840 and 1940, agricultural science, which had received its impetus in the technical schools and landed estates of western Europe, was received into American agriculture. The European institutions were recreated, the experiments continued, the research equipment improved, the statistical techniques extended, the genetic and chemical theories modified. Most effective of all, these improvements, coming out of the commercial impulses of a democratic state, were shared and spread. The lag between discovery and application grew shorter, restricted not by communications obstacles or fixed prejudice about technology, but only by the occurrence of the right set of market conditions to make new techniques profitable.

To understand this ultimate, self-extinguishing achievement of the American farmer, it is necessary to look beyond a mere responsiveness to commercial markets, abundant land, or a ready involvement in a scientific and technical development originating in industrial capitalism. Its sociology and ideology are more complex than that and may be made only a bit clear when directly considered in our concluding section of this essay. But the assessment of the whole achievement and its costs to American rural culture cannot at this point be postponed. Geographical specialization and mechanization together by 1940 had in effect solved the labor problem in American agriculture. Output per man since 1840 had increased two- or threefold in cotton and corn; four- to sixfold in wheat and the grasses; in dairying and meat production, similar productivity gains were registered; yields per acre, reflecting improvements in seed and fertilizer as well as the geographical arrangement of production, had increased relatively little, but had maintained their levels in the face of the vastly increased output and shifts to new and drier areas.

It was between 1940 and 1980 that a payoff came to the applications of science and power-driven machinery in American agriculture. Labor requirements in corn, wheat, and cotton had been cut by 1980 to between one-fifth and one-twentieth of their 1940 levels, and yields of land had doubled or trebled. From 65 percent of the American labor force in 1850, farm labor fell to 17 percent in 1940 and 3 percent in 1980. The farm population, which formed just over 50 percent of the U.S. population in 1850, accounted for about 3 percent in the Census of 1980. In Canada after 1920, agricultural productivity showed similar gains. This growth in the productivity of the soil and of the human and capital resources working it may prove indeed to be North America's lasting and peculiar achievement in an industrializing world. But it meant – or at least was accompanied by – the disappearance, indeed, the destruction in America as in western Europe, of the society based economically, socially, and politically on farming and rural ways of life.

The story of the decline in the farm community, its independence, its social values, and its weight in the national culture is not a happy one. It did not occur suddenly through brainwashing or doctrinaire violence such as a planned economy based on Marxian notions of class struggle might have exhibited. It occurred rather through the gradual and fluctuating attrition of market relationships as they acted on the hopes of succeeding generations of new farmers. From 1870 on, through decades of its greatest expansion of output and its greatest technical changes, American farming was afflicted by the disease of relative economic decline. There is no point in simple or static comparisons of farm and non-farm incomes. They show a growth in farm family income roughly equivalent to that in other sectors of the economy. But this growth occurred in the presence of a marked slowdown in the growth of the farm population, a migration of young people from the farms at least as great as the great immigrations from Europe between 1870 and 1920. As a major sector of economy and society, American farming died a lingering death – a fact attributable to its responsiveness to market processes in this great and inevitable transition in the national life.

Hard times on the farms were perceived to occur in two great waves, the earlier of which was a period of great growth in farm output. In the period 1870–96, the so-called Great Depression in world price levels was felt to bear heavily on the American farmer. The specialized literature on these decades of the farmers' discontent is vast, and inconclusive. Perhaps real incomes did not fall; perhaps the terms of trade did not shift strongly against farm products; certainly railroads and machinery companies did produce notable falls in transport and equipment prices. The record of the farm press and farm politicians of the period is nonetheless a litany of complaint directed at the urban-industrial society on which farming had become dependent. The complaints focused on two points: the "unfair" pricing practices of "monopolies" – railroads, communications services, marketing middlemen, equipment suppliers, and banks – and the loss of sons and daughters to the towns and cities. The prairies and plains became the seat of an agrarian radicalism – a revolt against a commercial system which had offered, then snatched away, a dream of prosperity, independence, and continuous expansion. The locus of the radicalism in the United States and, somewhat later, in Canada, is symptomatic of its source. It played little part in the history of groups with the lowest incomes – sharecroppers, black and white, in the cotton areas; hill farmers, still in large part self-subsistent; hired farm laborers; scrub farmers on poor soils in the Canadian Maritime Provinces, New England, or cut-over regions in New York and around Lake Superior. Nor did it make deep inroads on comfortably settled dairy and mixed corn and hog farmers east of the Mississippi. American agricultural expansion had been based partly on the successful provision of suitable commercial produce to regular markets, but much more on the dream of rising land values, farming bonanzas, high risks, and overcommitment on the frontier. It was this opportunity which closed down on the American farmer in the 1870s and 1890s in the Plains and Prairies even as torrents of wheat and meat were pouring out from the new lands. And here the Populist discontent was focused.

The economic ceiling lifted again between 1896 and 1920, and again an investment boom in Midwest farming areas got under way. When finally the slow, dull ache in wheat and cotton markets in the 1920s extended after 1929 to the entire farming industry, even eastern farmers and the most hidebound Midwest Republican individualists sought relief in group action, export bounty schemes, and at last crop limitation and government price supports. For farmers of middling condition, government programs simply eased the transition to extinction. Sharecroppers, laborers and tenants were helped little, if at all. Only the continuous off-farm movement after 1940 reduced what was perceived as poverty in agriculture. Wealth in agriculture then began to reappear in the 1960s and 1970s through the management of large acreages, a heavy capital investment, and the deft use of government support and the tax laws. And much of this prosperity was checked and broke down after 1980.

FARM FAMILIES AND RURAL NEIGHBORHOODS

The development of a successful commercial agriculture in North America did not come directly, then, out of the experience of the frontier or the pioneer settlement. As I have indicated above, that could have led as easily to the formation of a traditional agricultural society. Even without markets, simultaneous industrial growth, and transport improvements, the colonial populations would have continued to reproduce and to spread westward. A view of how that non-commercial American agrarian society might have developed is offered by the experience of the Appalachian uplands, where yeoman farmers, families, and clans spread across a thousand miles of hilly terrain, poor soils, and isolated valleys. The link with the commercial economy was feeble, intermittent, suspect, tentative. Here, out of pioneer stock and primitive conditions, a "hillbilly" culture developed, clannish, fertile, unschooled, independent, religious. People had large families and migrated to form a "southern" and mountain underlay in the lower Ohio and Missouri Valleys, where some transformation occurred. But enough remained on the scrub farms at home like a bubbling spring to continue the culture's contribution to the national life. It was not along this path that American agriculture moved to its feats of commercial, capitalistic, scientific activity.

Instead of a native development from the frontier, one must postulate, I think, an agro-business culture, almost (though perhaps not quite) from the start. Some prerequisites of the development – the land system and the price system working through money, banks, salesmen, and lawyers – rode in the wagons with the settlers. The very term "farm" or "farmer" in Anglo-American usage is indicative. A "farm" means a holding from which revenue is derived. In the American case, the owner, the "farmer," and the tiller of the soil were combined in one person who held his tenure not of a king or a nobleman, but of the price system itself. He was always in danger of losing it, if not to a bank or a mortgage holder, then simply by yielding to the temptation to sell out to someone who could "farm" it at higher return to himself and to society as a whole. Frontier democracy added to the individualism of this capitalist culture, and at the same time, by way of the democratic state, it shaped policies without regard even for private property rights, in the interests of the rapid economic development for the whole community. A small-town business culture set the standard, the values, the measures of worth and success for the rural areas.

Yet the rural culture was rural, after all. Had it been merely individualistic, profit-minded, competitive, shallowly commercial, and unable to act at a social level beyond the individual family, its development could not have been quite so rapid or its achievement so solid. Among the social forms in rural areas, the farm family was fundamental, yet we know very little about its internal structure and tensions, the features that distinguish these from any other set of farm families in western culture. Its nucleus was perhaps closer-knit since farmsteads were scattered across the countryside instead of being grouped in villages; perhaps it was less authoritarian since each member contributed something to the joint labor. In that the farm was a joint enterprise of man and woman, very likely the role and position of women was higher than in peasant families in northern Europe. This may show in the declining birth rates, which begin to fall in the East even in the late eighteenth century and fell from original high levels steadily in every region as settlement proceeded. It may show also in the division of the stream of farm expenditure, which – though accounting for much land purchase and purchased farm capital – left enough for spending in the farm household to create enormous mass markets for work-lightening or life-enhancing consumer goods. The family was also the principal locus of the transmittal of farming techniques to the succeeding generation until schools, colleges, and extension services usurped its function. The obsessive question is whether this family, and the ethical culture of which it was a part, was "puritanical"; that is, did it transmit a sense of sin that led to a life of endless self-justifying labor? What gave rural families the driving zeal that they showed in joining the American pursuit of wealth? Perhaps these values were absorbed from the surrounding commercial milieu; surely no traditional rural society existed to counteract their force.

The next level of social control in Europe above the family, i.e., the village, was missing from the North American scene. Instead, the agrarian culture substituted a communications network stretching for a few tens of miles around a farmhouse: the rural neighborhood. Neighbors met in those pioneering tasks that required joint labor – log rolling, roof raising, fence building – and during the crop year at harvesting. The sharing of teams and equipment occurred, though evidently not on a very formal basis. Threshing, corn husking, and corn shelling especially were tasks where the superior productivity of a work group was apparent. As the surplus produce of a region began to gain in value, labor, too, became worth something; exchanges might be made, and finally a money wage paid. An incomplete drift from primitive gift giving between families to barter and then to hourly or daily hire occurred, but loans of labor still retained a social quality.

Similarly the centers of group activity and communication in a rural area served both an economic and a social function. A small Protestant church met every Sunday – and usually on Wednesday evening as well – and furnished an outlet to individual souls to express and exorcise the fears and terrors of everyday life. But as in a family, around this basic emotional experience, social communication, education, sport, courtship, and the exchange of information and opinion about crops and techniques took their place. Much the same body of concerns and functions are manifest wherever the rural people met – at the schoolhouse, at lodges, clubs, and social circles; at the county seat on business, legal or commercial; or at the county agricultural fair. It must be remembered that the competition among rural people, for land, good yields, high prices, was not really a rivalry such as might occur between two business firms in a restricted market. At most it was a friendly rivalry which spurred each farmer on to greater achievement but rewarded rather than penalized him for sharing his secrets. The market was so wide, the individual participants so small, that gains were not made at the expense of one another. Northern farmers were a reasonably homogeneous people – the Germans a bit apart and a bit clannish among themselves. Their sociability, exaggerated as it was by the relative isolation of a family's daily life, was easily released, permitting a society to form with a certain structure of prestige, based partly on wealth, but also on a general respect for a variety of natural qualities – strength, intelligence, saintliness, eloquence. Ministers, lawyers, schoolmasters, and any with a gift and ambition for political life were respected and listened to. Indeed, of all rural activities, perhaps politics was the most enjoyed, and election day was the center of the warmest rivalry and sentiment.

American northern rural culture, then, was a culture with an internal strength based on strong, relatively isolated families, whose homogeneity of origin and aims permitted fairly easy communication. At the same time, it was a culture that looked outward – to the state for land and local improvements; to the law for the protection of property and the advancement of development schemes; to speculators, bankers, lawyers, and schoolteachers as a literate elite who could advance it in wealth; ultimately to science and industry to organize its research and to the federal government to solve its economic problems and to continue to advance its economic status. It is easy to see how such a society expanded geographically, adopting new techniques and arranging itself in economically rational patterns as part of a developing capitalistic world economy. Among communications techniques the railroad was followed by the telephone and the automobile, and like so many other industrial gadgets, these found in American rural areas a wide and enthusiastic market. Electrification, when it came in the 1930s, completed the transformation of the farm household. Such a culture had no defense against industrialization; it shared an incurable American optimism that what is new, is better. The dark side of modern industrial progress was not wholly missed. The farm community of the 1890s and the 1920s and 1930s suffered a serious loss of morale – so great as to make farmers in the 1930s desert temporarily the Republican faith, to revive populism and ally themselves in the United States to a degree with the foreign mass of urban labor. But by that time farmers were no longer a decisive voice in the national polity or even in the political and developmental decisions that were made at state capitals.

It cannot be said, of course, that the American South shared in this culture to a full extent. Its existence and persistence almost makes one feel that God is a social scientist, intent on furnishing North America with a control group against which to test explanations of northern achievement by comparative study. The answer to the question of the South's relative retardation lies partly in the disaster of the Civil War and partly in the peculiar shape of the international market for farm products. But at bottom, one feels one must seek an answer in social structure. The problem would require a chapter of its own and indeed has furnished the topic for a vast literature by political and economic historians. But the outlines of an answer suggest themselves and seem to fall out of what has already been said. To my mind, the most satisfactory way to look at the South is to consider the southern planter as a counterpart of the northern commercial farmer, appearing as markets appeared, two hundred years before the markets for northern products, and able at that time to avail himself of slave labor. Given that initial development, the southern planter class grew, as a capitalist class, maintaining good connections among its members, each of whom was set at the center of two nets of non-capitalist economic relationships. Around the planter on his land were the slaves, on whose exploitation his wealth depended. But in the surrounding area a net of semi-self-sufficient white farmers, those with one or no slaves, were also allied to him by kinship, debt, and a client-like dependence. The strength of this social formation, which resembles that in much of the rural world in countries of old as well as of recent settlement, is demonstrated by the combination of forces that was required ultimately to shatter it. By 1960, southern planters and northern farmers had both become small-scale industrialists, commanding significant blocks of capital. Pockets of rural poverty, exploitation, ignorant self-sufficiency persisted, but North American agrarian society had transferred most of its population, its culture, its value system, and its social problems to a town or an urban environment and so had ceased to exist as a peculiar social entity.

PART IV

The North: dynamics of an industrial culture

II

New England: the Puritan progenitor

Grau, teurer Freund, ist aller Theorie
Und grün ist des Lebens goldner Baum. . . .
— Goethe, *Faust*, Part I

THREE INTRODUCTORY DIAGRAMS

Omnis est America in partes tres divisa. At least since Henry Adams detected three "intellects" in the three regions,[1] the trifurcation of the North American colonies into New England, the Middle Colonies, and the South has been standard historical practice. But an economic historian cannot begin with "intellect," however willing he may be to slip it in later as an "independent factor," "overdetermining," as Althusserians say, an "economic and social formation." Even under the implausible assumption of uniformity in the social psychology of the original colonists, a simple diagram relating potential income to hours of labor time can show the basis for a threefold division.

Figure 1 is such a diagram. With respect to productive factors and markets, it is based on the following assumptions: (1) that for relevant ranges of population growth, the supplies of land at constant marginal

Published as "New England's Early Industrialization: A Sketch," in Peter Kilby ed., *Quantity and Quiddity: Essays in U.S. Economic History in Honor of Stanley Lebergott* (Middletown, Conn.: Wesleyan University Press, 1985), Ch. 2.

The author is indebted to discussants at the Wesleyan Symposium, at the American History Seminar at the University of Cambridge under Professor Charlotte Erickson, and in the Yale Economic History Workshop. He thanks especially Jeremy Atack for valuable written comments, Ann Kibbey for guidance into the literature on Puritanism, the Yale Program in the History of Science, and particularly, Carolyn Cooper for references on technology and Laura Owen for research assistance. Financial assistance from the Yale Department of Economics (AMAX fund) is also gratefully acknowledged.

[1] Henry Adams, *History of the United States During the First Administration of Thomas Jefferson* (New York: Scribner's, 1889), Chs. 3, 4, 5, reprinted as *The United States in 1800* (Ithaca: Cornell University Press, 1955). Today, Adams's good English word *intellect* would be replaced by the Franglais *mentalités*.

Figure 1. *Potential uses of farm family labor in three colonial regions in agricultural crops (subsistence and surplus production), with differences in resources and external markets and with peak labor constraints, but no land constraint.*

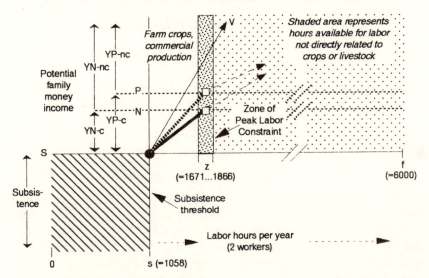

s = Labor hours to produce subsistence.
z = Zone of Peak Labor Constraint in food crops; precise number of hours depends on crop mix.
f = Full adult male family employment: 2 workers × 10 hours per day per worker × 300 hours per year = 6,000 hours per year.
$YN\text{-}c$ = Potential money income from marketable surplus of food crops in New England.
$YP\text{-}c$ = Potential money income from marketable surplus of food crops in Pennsylvania.
$YN\text{-}nc$ = Potential money income from labor not directly related to crops or livestock in New England.
$YP\text{-}nc$ = Potential money income from labor not directly related to crops or livestock in Pennsylvania.
N = Limit to potential crop production, New England.
P = Limit to potential crop production, Pennsylvania.
V = No Peak Labor Constraint shown for Virginia, where tobacco substitutes for food crops.
OS = Subsistence (not assigned market value).

Note: Hours for s and z (in parenthesis) are derived from data for New England.
Source: see Appendix.

Figure 1 represents only a very primitive stage in growth. Beyond the subsistence level OS, various paths to money income emerge, viz.:

(1) Employ off-peak and family labor on specialty crops and industrial craft goods for local trade.
(2) Replace subsistence farming by specialized local producers in farm and industrial products, improving terms of local trade for surpluses of subsistence food crops.
(3) Specialize in export specialty crop, possibly importing even some subsistence products.
(4) Hire, at rates at or below value of marginal product, or impress by force additional labor especially at peak planting or harvesting times.

184

physical productivity are unlimited; (2) that production is organized in family units, and that these units are joined to a limited degree in rural neighborhoods, allowing for local trade in some specialized artisan industrial products and in some agricultural products as well; (3) that external markets for agricultural and resource products differ sharply among the regions; (4) that productivity differences – due to soil, climate, and terrain – in crops grown for home consumption are small and so have little significance for the economic outcome, compared to differences in export opportunities.

The diagram, then, defines the usual impressions of the three regions' differing abilities to provide subsistence and, beyond that, to provide higher standards of physical comfort from farming, traditional crafts, local trade, exports of resource products and argicultural staples. The unit in which income is earned is considered to be not the isolated individual, but a collection of family units within the rural neighborhood. Within such a neighborhood, a moderate degree of division of labor occurs. Some special craftsmen – millers, smiths, weavers – and professionals – a teacher, public official, a minister – subsist through limited local trade or barter of their services and products with the farm households roundabout. The unit of labor is an individual farm plus one family member. Conceptually, this work is considered to consist not only of livestock care throughout the year and work in the subsistence crops, but also of the maintenance of farm capital. It would include the heavy and constant labor of farm wives in food preparation, homemaking, and domestic industry.

Figure 2 shows a rough estimate of the labor hours required, in minimal operations in field and barn, to grow a family's subsistence in New England in the mid-nineteenth century. In this work, New England's conditions do not differ drastically from those there or in the other colonies in the eighteenth century. Two important conclusions derive from such an examination: (1) large amounts of time remain even in

---

Figure 1 *(cont.)*

(5) Develop non-agricultural exports, particularly in a specialized non-farm sector in towns and villages trading with the local farm sector for surplus subsistence goods.
(6) Improve labor productivity in farming, especially in peak load operations.

In developing rural neighborhoods, all three colonial regions used methods (1) and (2) in varying degrees as opportunity offered. The regions are differentiated as determined by agricultural export opportunities, viz.:

Virginia/Maryland, Carolinas, Georgia – (3) in conjunction with (4).
Pennsylvania, New York, New Jersey – intensive local development – (1) and (2), plus some hired, indentured, or extended family labor – (4).
New England – (1), (2), (5).

None of the regions appears to have experienced much technological improvement in farming – (6) – before the early nineteenth century.

Figure 2. *Direct labor requirements for each of two workers in subsistence agriculture (livestock care and field operations) over the agricultural year, pre-1840 (based on 1840–60 data for New England)*

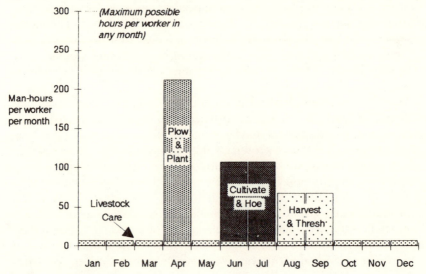

Source: see Appendix.

summer, and particularly in the winter months, for farm capital formation and for growing crops for the market, if a market is present; (2) as a result of (1), productivity differences in the subsistence activities are not very important from one region to another in determining relative income levels. The crucial question is the marketability of the surplus within the local community and in external markets.

With these elemental principles in mind, we may now make the comparison among the three regions: the South, the Middle Colonies, and New England. Line *OS* in Figure 1 shows the similar position of all the regions with respect to the minimum hours of labor and acreage required for a family's subsistence, allowing for traditional exchanges of produce for industrial goods within the rural area. Line *SV* shows the superior value of the uses of labor time beyond subsistence in the South (Virginia), once the tobacco culture was established. Even at the low price at which tobacco settled, farm and planter families could still have imported enough commodities to move well beyond any assumed "satiety" level of a peasant standard of living. Line *SP* shows the "satisficing" life of the Middle Colonial (Pennsylvania) family, made possible to a degree by good land, but even more by the possibility of export shipments of food crops to the West Indies and by trade with the growing seacoast cities. Line *SN* shows the plight of New England families who, without rich resources or an exportable agricultural crop were unable by traditional means to get beyond a moderate margin over subsistence. Their inferior position depended not on harsh winters, thin soils, or a growing season possibly twenty days shorter than that in the lower states. Even if New Englanders were only seeking to perpetuate a peasant economy not much above subsistence, their problem was a market for their surplus labor time.

It is obviously not very significant whether a "satisficing" level of living sometimes credited to pre-industrial societies existed in the mentality of villagers in the colonial economies. In New England, even "satisficing villagers" would have needed to strive and to innovate. In Virginia, despite supplies of family labor, the most strenuous efforts were made to obtain an auxiliary labor force so as to increase the number of acres from which a landowner could obtain a surplus income. At this level, Virginia–Maryland tobacco farming appears as a capitalistic operation from the outset. In Pennsylvania, where perhaps the best case for a peasant-like ideal of "limited good" could be made, the surplus, even in the early eighteenth century, was beginning to be reinvested in urban construction, industrial plant and tools, and mercantile trade.

Arnold Toynbee, in his *Study of History,* cities New England in a list of such classic adverse environments as Central America, the "parched plains of Ceylon," the North Arabian Desert, Easter Island, and the Roman compagna, whose "challenge" produced the response of an aggressive civilization.[2] New Englanders found an economy in their region which, by traditional agricultural or industrial techniques adapted to New World soils and climate, was able to yield a surplus above subsistence. This surplus was adequate to give some room for trade and maneuver, but without the product markets enjoyed by the Middle and southern Colonies, the unrealized surplus forced New Englanders into novel endeavors outside the villages and farms, in trade and industrial occupations. It is at this point that the infamous "Puritan mentality" may have come into play, even as the economic portion of the social experience in the New World was changing the Puritan into a Yankee. This aspect of the matter is touched on only timidly and sketchily in the discussion below.

The historical analysis is developed here on a framework shown in skeletal form in Figure 3. If economic history is to be thought of as walking the line where nature – soils, climate, terrain, resources – meets society – techniques, organizational forms, and human individuals – then that line was formed in the seventeenth century by the western coastline of the Atlantic Ocean. To the white man, the Indians were a part of the

[2]Arnold J. Toynbee, *A Study of History,* abridged by D. C. Somerwell, Vols. 1–2 (New York and London: Oxford University Press, 1947). See Vol. 1, Ch. 7 (1) "The Stimulus of Hard Countries," especially 96–99.

Figure 3. *Interrelation of environment, culture, and economy in New England's industrialization, 1630–1840*

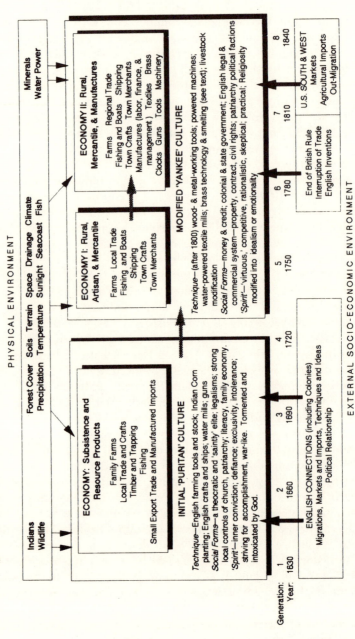

PHYSICAL ENVIRONMENT

Indians   Wildlife

Forest Cover   Soils   Terrain   Space   Drainage   Climate
Precipitation   Temperature   Sunlight   Seacoast   Fish

Minerals
Water Power

ECONOMY: Subsistence and
Resource Products

Family Farms
Local Trade and Crafts
Timber and Trapping
Fishing
Small Export Trade and Manufactured Imports

INITIAL 'PURITAN' CULTURE

Technique—English farming tools and stock; Indian Corn planting; English crafts and ships; water mills; guns
Social Forms—a theocratic and 'saintly' elite; legalisms; strong local controls of church, patriarchy; literacy; family economy.
Spirit—inner conviction; defiance; exclusivity, intolerance; striving for accomplishment, war-like. Tormented and intoxicated by God.

ECONOMY I: Rural,
Artisan, & Mercantile

Farms   Local Trade
Fishing   and Boats
Shipping
Town Crafts
Town Merchants

ECONOMY II: Rural,
Mercantile, & Manufactures

Farms   Regional Trade
Fishing and Boats   Shipping
Town Crafts   Town Merchants
Manufactures (labor, finance, &
management)   Textiles   Brass
Clocks   Guns   Tools   Machinery

MODIFIED 'YANKEE' CULTURE

Technique—(after 1800) wood- & metal-working tools; powered machines; water-powered textile mills; brass technology & smelting (see text); livestock modification
Social Forms—money & credit; colonial & state government; English legal & commercial system—property, contract, civil rights; patriarchy political factions
Spirit—'virtuous,' competitive, rationalistic, skeptical; practical; Religiosity modified into idealism or emotionality

ENGLISH CONNECTIONS (including Colonies)
Migrations, Markets and Imports, Techniques and Ideas
Political Relationship

End of British Rule
Interruption of Trade
English Inventions

U.S. SOUTH & WEST
Markets
Agricultural Imports
Out-Migration

Generation: 1   2   3   4   5   6   7   8
Year: 1630   1660   1690   1720   1750   1780   1810   1840

EXTERNAL SOCIO-ECONOMIC ENVIRONMENT

188

natural environment, and the settlers brought into this setting the skills, knowledge, values, and social relationships that had been acquired in England. This constituted for the young colonial societies an original endowment, made clearer and more unequivocal in New England's case by the fact that the thirty thousand or so "Puritans" came in boatloads within twenty years. After 1660, or even 1650, the society they created did not open itself readily to new arrivals. At least 90 percent of the 1790 population of nearly one million must have been descendants of the original stock. Locked in this box, the Puritans created their farms, seaports, and domestic and artisan industries. The relations, first with England, and the other colonies, then after 1810 with the American South and West, form the third side of the box in which the successive economies of New England grew and in which the cultural transition from Puritan to Yankee was achieved. Within this space (the central boxes in Figure 3), New England's economic activities – farming, fishing, trade, and the industrial arts – had room to develop. With the Revolution, the interruption of foreign trade, and the freeing of industrial life from colonial restrictions, that environment changed and drew an ardent response from a population already trained to market commerce and industry and eagerly seeking outlets in ways that form the subject of the next section of the sketch. The history leads thus into comparison – not made here – with the other colonial areas, especially with Pennsylvania and New York, as their economies developed. It then leads further into a history of how the northern streams of westward migration, with some upper South admixture, blended to form the gigantic mix of light and heavy industries of the American Midwest after 1850.

A PREPARATION FOR THE FACTORIES[3]

The repeated action of the seventeenth-century Puritan settlers over the harsh New England terrain, like water running over rock, created a landscape.[4] Their actions toward one another created a society. At Plymouth, Salem, and Massachusetts Bay, around the inlets along the southern shore, and up the Connecticut River, families formed and reproduced abundantly; towns were founded and lands subdivided; property was defined and crimes against persons, property, and public morality were invented and punished. Town meetings were held; selectmen, deputies, and local officers were elected. A few taxes were collected; money was

[3]A selected bibliography on the industrial history is attached at the end of this chapter, giving some of the principal sources utilized.

[4]The interaction of Indians and settlers with New England's physical environment is examined in an interesting study by William Cronon, *Changes in the Land* (New York: Hill and Wang, 1983).

printed; British regulations of trade and industry were received and sometimes obeyed. The Puritan churches maintained a privileged status; heresies appears in Massachusetts Bay and were put down, to re-establish elsewhere in the region. Puritan morality, Puritan energy, Puritan intellectuality moved ceaselessly in new directions, and the ministry engaged in its tortured and vehement effort to reconcile the doctrines of Calvin to a world that was growing more optimistic, more materialistic, more rational and pragmatic, more American.

It is hardly fair to call such a stage of society – so little traditionalistic, so dynamic, and of so short a life – pre-industrial. It was agricultural, with a significant mercantile enclave, and it engaged perforce in extensive fabrication of industrial items for domestic or local consumption. It contained relatively little manufacture for commercial purposes, and none, except boats, for distant trade. Yet it was a society that stood in 1775 on the edge of industrialization. In retrospect one can see that the prerequisites for an industrial revolution, part native, part an echo of England's, were in place. They appear in the three sectors – agriculture, trade, and artisan industry – and in three respects: (1) the physical flows of supplies and markets; (2) the skilled and motivated population, stable families, literate and competent craftsmen, and some spirited and original entrepreneurs; and (3) the "institutional" structure encased in political constitutions, in laws and law courts, and in the practiced behavior of merchants, farmers, workers, wives, and businessmen.

From farms, grazing meadows, and woodland pastures came that modest surplus of grain, meat, cider, and milk which, processed in the farmhouse or locally, could be exchanged at small trading points for a few imports – notably molasses, salt, tea, and rum – or for the services of local craftsmen and professionals. From woodlots and forested hillsides came firewood and the logs which, processed in a local sawmill, became the materials of construction for furniture and clapboard houses and, along the coast and the banks of the Connecticut, for fishing boats and merchant ships. Farms also harbored supplies of labor, seasonally idled by the weather and the agricultural calendar – the labor of adult males, of young men and women, of children beyond their few seasons of schooling, even on occasion, the labor of overworked wives. All this found outlets in farm capital formation – clearing, stone fencing, construction, and farm industrial tasks, such as woodworking, spinning, leather working, even work at a forge. Farming and much of the domestic industry also required the services of specialized workers and equipment: plows, harrows, and scythes required iron tips and edges, grain quickly encouraged the development of local mills, and water-powered sawmills succeeded the sawyer's pit. Even fishing had its linkages backward to boats, ships, nets, sails, ropes, hooks, and harpoons, to barrels and salt; forward to a growing commerce in which, as with lumber, a New England resource could enter as a principal staple. Boat building, stimulated by the fisheries, readily became an important industrial occupation in its own right, and merchant voyagers could depend not only on boats built in Maine or local shipyards, but also on a cadre of fishermen-sailors ready to go out on the high seas.

But linkages and spillover effects demonstrable in physical flows on an input—output table were perhaps the least important of those interconnections among resource industries, trade, and artisan industry that led into the factories of the nineteenth century. The agricultural calendar, although slack in the winter, did put stress on time at peak seasons. A New England farmer often had to hurry to finish plowing, to get in the wheat, to prepare firewood for winter. The changeability of the weather was a continuous threat, and good days had to be utilized. Work outside in winter was done rapidly, both to keep the body warm and to reduce the time of exposure. The briskness of the Yankee, even the short speech, tight vowels, and nasalizations have been related – half in jest – to the cold air.

Clearer was the effect of the rather complex land system, with its classes of membership in the community – first, the proprietors of a town's original grant, the church members, then the freeholders who were grantees or purchasers, and finally, the inhabitants. A legalistic quality appeared early in New England Puritanism: The arrangement with God – though intensely emotional, even mystical in the personal experience of conversion – was contained in a law-like covenant with God, and that ruler, like the English king, was bound by his promises and previous acts, inscrutable but ultimately legal and righteous. Quarrels over boundaries, rights, and contracts are endemic in peasant villages, but New England towns were notably litigious, and if fee-simple ownership and partible inheritance made for a cleaner definition of rights in real property than had obtained under feudal law, it also made the disputes so much the more bitter and significant. Moreover, in a poor agriculture, the capitalization of the land, with the hopes and dreams it compounds, appears as the only escape from the prison of a narrow income margin; with the accession of some urban landed and mercantile wealth, property had become, even by 1650, a notable object of speculation. A class of wealthier landholders, speculators, and merchants had arisen by the early eighteenth century, and the yeoman farmer himself, often with more land than he could farm, surely had an eye out for sharp deals by which a neighbor or a foreigner could be skinned.

In mercantile trade, among industrial New England's original activities, these intangible preparations for the later industrialization most patently occurred. The story is the familiar one that appears over and over again in the history of the trading world. A few of the merchants whose enterprise gave the colonial Atlantic ports one of the world's largest merchant marines by 1775 had been attracted there from England a century after the first settlement. The urban atmosphere, even of Boston, developed a strong Anglican and royalist component. Yet new English families, too, became acculturated to the not-so-very-different provincial society, and the native impulse to trade had appeared at the very first. Over the countryside, trade occurred among farmers, and between them and villagers, perhaps to the maximum extent that resources permitted. Fishing and flourishing shipyards, utilizing the abundant timber, gave their stimulus. By 1750, most of the organizational devices of mercantile capitalism were in place – partnerships, contracts, bills and notes, accounts, wages to clerks and sailors, intangible forms of property, commercial law and lawyers, bonds and notaries. And intertwined with the commercial activities came information – the knowledge of prices, markets, sea lanes and of distant people, customs, and technologies. From an information industry of colleges, churches, newspapers, and pamphleteers arose the intellectual currents that so disturbed the ministers of Calvinism, penetrating so far into the countryside as to produce in reaction perhaps the witchcraft episode and surely the "Great Awakening." On the back of trade, all the modernizing ideas of the eighteenth century were borne in on the isolated religious society. More tangibly, the wealth of towns attracted artisans from England, as well as from the farms, and created a class with skills and equipment able to rival those of European craft producers, a body of high craftsmanship without which the industry of the nineteenth century, had it derived only from the simple crafts of rural industry, could hardly have so readily reproduced the English industrial revolution.

In New England in the decades from 1790 to 1840, influences from the Puritan countryside mixed with the mercantile culture of the somewhat more worldly towns. From the conjunction derived a powerful and complex stream of factory industry in the first four decades of the nineteenth century. But peasant arts have existed in many cultures, and high mercantile capitalism with craft shops had flourished in Greece, in Rome, in late medieval Europe, and in Italy, Spain, France, and Holland of the seventeenth and eighteenth centuries. Far from stimulating further industrialization, an excess of mercantile activity in those cases tended to stifle it. Why did industry blossom in Massachusetts Bay and in the remote valleys of the Naugatuck and Connecticut Rivers, 150 years after settlement, just as on the European continent the Rhine, the Meuse, and the Rhone Valleys were coming into modern industrial life? An historian must answer such deep questions not at first with general speculation, but with an examination of the specific episodes in question. Industrialization came into New England in two clusters: (1) the textile mills in Rhode Island and eastern Massachusetts and their smaller copies along all the tributary streams where water power could be captured; (2) the metals-smelting and metal-working industry, unfolding in a series of steps to make the Connecticut and Naugatuck Valleys a pair of long machinery workshops. The two histories are quite different and distinct in their origins, in their forms of organization, in their markets, and in their implications for later industrial development.

THE TEXTILE DEVELOPMENT

In textile history, the putting-out system that preceded the textile factories is a notorious part of England's and Europe's industrialization, but it has only a slight echo in the tale of the North American colonies. Here the market was not concentrated; the population was too dispersed; British restrictions, especially on wool, were firm; and British imports could undersell anything except the products of home spinning for domestic use. When the opportunity for putting out came in the 1790s, that phase in spinning had been eliminated by the new factories, and this mode of merchant-organized industry was left to a few products – cut nails, straw hats, and longest and most notably, boots and shoes. On summary view, the familiar history of the New England textile mills presents instead several distinct features – circumstances whose existence seems to have been indispensable for the development as it occurred.

First, there were the English inventions held in the mind of the migratory Samuel Slater,[5] and the other information that Francis Cabot Lowell got on his spying trips to England. The level of craftsmanship was good in Providence and Boston – good enough to construct the machinery that the Browns had set up at Pawtucket and that Slater found inadequate. But the denser net of artisans, the larger scale of effort present in the English Midlands was needed to invent machinery. Without this initial borrowing (or theft) in the textile industry, as later in the brass industry, New England's "revolution" would probably have been long delayed. Moreover, stolen machinery was not patented, and once stolen, its diffusion could be rapid. Only a small start, a small lift over a threshold of knowledge, was required.

A second striking element was the availability in a new country of enough craft workers in construction, in woodworking, in metal fabrication, and in stone masonry to make the machinery and design the buildings, dams, and structures to bring the mills into quick operation. The

[5]Slater's story is told somewhat dramatically in Massena Goodrich, *Historical Sketch of the Town of Pawtucket* (Pawtucket: 1876).

carpenter whom Slater hired to work, in a barn with shades down, to construct the machinery as Slater remembered it, was indispensable, but his equals were to be found at a hundred locations inland and along the coast. And as the mills were built, the machine shops came into being and began their semi-independent history. Machinists trained in textile shops were an important component of machine-tool manufacture when that spectacular development climaxed New England's industrial achievement.

Once the plants were erected, the availability of a domestic labor force, of women and children and some adult males, testifies to the existence of a "labor surplus" and to the real but slight margin of income on which the farms subsisted. But although partially skilled and trained on the spinning wheel, and in need of some training, this labor force's cardinal feature was its diligence and, in the large mills, its emancipation, even if only temporarily, from home and family, its willing independence – in short, its inculcated Puritan values. Later, it was succeeded by a labor force of very different ethnic origin and culture – French Canadians and Irish, who worked equally well. But the presence of the "ladies of the loom" in the first mills solved the problem for the manufacturers that in many peasant societies would have posed a difficult if not insurmountable obstacle.

Nor must one, in an effort to avoid the "great man" interpretation, downplay the boldness, cleverness, and entrepreneurial energies and ingenuity of the Browns, the Lowells, the Cabots, and all the rest. At heart, they were not manufacturers, and their factories were truly an extension of mercantile capitalistic enterprise and its mentality. The raw material was imported, the product largely carried off in trade, as in Hong Kong or Taiwan today. The textile enclave in New England was simply a processing point between remote materials and remote markets, a collection of labor, power-driven machines, and cunning capitalists. It was really not textiles but machinery that the native industry made and with which it transformed imported raw material. And there is evidence indeed that the textile extrepreneurs looked at matters in just that way – and considered their fixed assets as a collection of values to be formed, manipulated, increased, transformed, and sold as the market might dictate. There was perhaps as little feudalism, as little patriarchy in New England textile firms as has ever been exhibited in the early stages of a manufacturing operation. The Boston merchants confined their philanthropies to the distribution of their wealth after – not before – they had made up their accounts.[6]

[6]Some of the points are made in a recent re-examination of the records of the Boston Associates by Jeffrey Oxley in work still, I trust, in progress on his doctoral dissertation, Stanford University, "The Textile Manufacturing Corporation and Boston Capital, the Era of the Lowell System, 1813–1860."

As an extension of such considerations, one cannot help but observe the thoroughness with which textile opportunity was pursued up New England's streams away from the shore. In upstate Massachusetts into the Berkshire hills, in west-central Connecticut, in southern Vermont and New Hampshire, one may say with only slight exaggeration that no possible site for a waterwheel was left untouched. When sheep moved into Vermont, woolen mills followed them; in north-central Connecticut, even a silk mill was opened in mid-century, with Jacquard looms and initially using local mulberry trees and caterpillars.[7] Mills in Holyoke and Chicopee rivaled those on the Merrimack. Unlike the mills of the early southern Piedmont industry that proliferated later in the nineteenth century, many of these establishments were not collections of a few hundred spindles, but substantial operations. This development forms an effective antidote to excessive emphasis on the industry's great men. Enterprise and enough small capital lay ready across the area to come to life at the first demonstrated reduction of risk; the opportunity was hunted up the streams as trappers had hunted beaver two hundred years earlier, with the grim fanaticism of a Javert stalking his criminal prey. Is it too fanciful to call this thoroughness, this almost vengeful obsessiveness in the hunt for profit, a Puritan trait?

METALS AND MACHINERY

The story of the Connecticut Valley's industrialization does not start with Eli Whitney or even with guns and machinery. Almost wholly neglected because wholly obscure are the eighteenth-century activities connected with smelting the few and rather poor deposits of copper, zinc, and iron in the region and with the forging, beating, and casting of the so-called hollow-wares – pots, pans, kettles – and small metal objects – nails, ax heads, buttons, buckles, harness fixtures, pewter tableware, and kitchen utensils. In New Haven and Hartford, these craft objects showed some of the skill and ingenuity common in the more elegant work of the sophisticated shops of Boston and Philadelphia. In smaller villages, from dozens of small shops, came a clattering stream of such wares in the late eighteenth century.[8] Distribution was probably not so much downriver,

[7] H. H. Manchester, *The Story of Silk and Cheney Silks,* (Manchester, Conn.: privately printed, 1916). Manchester does not gives sources, but since he is listed as Managing Editor, "The library of Original Sources," it may be presumed that he had some. I am indebted to Y. V. Pulley for some preliminary research in this area.

[8] The legends of the Connecticut Yankee pots, pans, and peddlers seem to be derived mostly from travelers' reports (de Chastellux, Dwight, Kendall), and from Lathrop's 1909 Yale dissertation, "The Brass Industry in Connecticut."

where competition would come from the seacoast urban artisans, but by peddlers overland – first, on foot into the Hudson Valley, and soon by pack horse, fanning out by 1820 into Pennsylvania, lower Canada, and the upper South. Very little but legend is known of this unique commerce, but certainly it, and not the more prosperous river trade in agricultural products, represents the mercantile phase of the Connecticut Valley's industrialization.

As the nineteenth century's markets opened up, the obsession with alloying, gilding, and plating continued. The unalloyed metals – iron, copper, zinc, tin – were imported in bars. In the Waterbury area brass, fused by a newly invented English technique, became the leading metal, and rolling was added to molding and forging as a technique to form semi-finished or final products. Hardware, buttons, hooks, German silver, and finally, plated silverware became important forms of industry, each in a special town. The climax of this tinkering with the chemistry of molten materials came at last in the vulcanization of rubber by Charles Goodyear, a native of Hamden, after incredible trials and false starts as he moved between Philadelphia and Boston in the years 1835–45.[9] To the proliferating brass works, silverware makers, and hardware shops of the Naugatuck Valley, parallel to the Connecticut, a significant industry in rubber wares was added by 1850. Both industries depended on imported materials out of which inventiveness, craft skill, and ingenious marketing techniques had created a complex group of Yankee manufactures.

Mechanical advancement in the story begins not with the metalwares, but with wooden clocks.[10] Already by 1790, clocks with wooden works were something of an archaism, dating back to fifteenth-century Germany. Clockwares of Paris, London, Boston, and Philadelphia were making works of brass, expensive and finely crafted. Wooden clocks were a country product among German farmers in Pennsylvania, and they exer-

[9]On Goodyear, see Ralph F. Wolf, *India Rubber Man: The Story of Charles Goodyear* (Cadwell, Idaho: Caucton Printers, 1939). Wolf draws on Goodyear's own account, which he published on rubber pages in a rubber binding. See also the account, with references, in *The Dictionary of American Biography.*

[10]J. J. Murphy, "Entrepreneurship and the Establishment of the American Clock Industry," *Journal of Economic History*, Vol. 26 (June 1966): 169–186. In the mid-1980s, a doctoral student at the New School for Social Research, Scott Molan, working under Professor Ross Thompson, a major historian of mechanical technology, went over the ground originally worked over by Murphy and carried the investigation further. Special mention should be made of the early reminiscences of the New Haven entrepreneur Chauncey Jerome, *History of the American Clock Business for the Past Sixty Years, and Life of Chauncey Jerome Written by Himself, Including Barnum's Connection with the Clock Business.* This has been reissued by C. H. Bailey, the managing director of the American Clock and Watch Museum at Bristol, Connecticut (1983). I am indebted to Mr. Bailey for a useful discussion and his interesting exhibition in the museum.

cised the whittling skills and materials of some Yankee farmers. The works were adapted to the peddler system of distribution; they could ride on a peddler's back or in his saddle bag. Crude and sturdy, they could hold up with little or no adjustment and could be relied on to tick when unloaded after a long, bumpy journey and fitted into a locally made case. And here the market called out the clock industry's counterpart to Whitney, Eli Terry, a skilled craftsman himself (more so than Whitney) who trained many more clockmakers in his shop. This entrepreneur-craftsman appears, no less than Whitney, to have conceived the idea of batch production of the parts of mechanisms for later assembly.[11]

Terry, in a shop in Plymouth, Connecticut, with a few assistants, announced in 1807 his intention of producing three thousand clocks in a year. He not only carried out his intention, but even more surprising to his fellow craftsmen, he found no trouble in disposing of his products, at prices much lower than for custom-made clocks, in shops as far south as New Haven and through peddlers into the South and West. Almost nothing is known of Terry's actual methods or machinery, but hand-, foot-, and water-powered lathes were part of the clock shop's equipment by the 1820s. It was in the set-up and repetition of operations on such machine tools, producing large batches of individual parts for later assembly, that most cost saving could occur. Terry's quality as a man is shown in his openness and generosity; many clockmakers – Seth Thomas, Chauncey Jerome – were trained in his shop. And when his fortune was made by the 1830s, he retired from the competition to spend his last years in his shop making clocks for the sheer pleasure of the craft, by the old craftsmen's methods. It is interesting that in the Connecticut Valley the art of woodworking – which in other rural cultures was expressed in statues of saints or ornamentation of doors, thrones, and bedsteads – found its highest expression in the production in scale of moving wheels and balances for the useful purpose of rendering a count of the passing hours.

[11]It is important to emphasize the difference between these methods and those that later produced truly "interchangeable parts." In both early guns and clocks, parts could not be made by hand tools or even by primitive machines with inexact measuring instruments so as to be indiscriminately interchangeable. Once made in batches, they needed shaving or filing to be made to fit. In wooden clocks, the fit could be much looser than in a gun, since the pressures to which the mechanism was subjected were in no way comparable. Moreover, clocks were stationary, while guns had to stand up to very rough treatment. Terry's and Whitney's invention, and that of other gun makers before 1830, was to make parts in batches to save set-up costs on tools or such machinery as was used. By and large, the parts still needed some planing, grinding, or filing to fit an assembly. Hounshell's recent, remarkable book, *From the American System to Mass Production, 1800–1932* (Baltimore: Johns Hopkins University Press, 1984), goes a long way in bringing the story together.

And this art itself, developing from custom handiwork to machined batch production and assembly, fell victim at last to the logic of the market. The panic of 1837 is said to have bankrupted dozens of the overstocked and overextended shops, and recovery found the brass clock, by virtue of improvements in the rolling and stamping of brass wheels, taking over the market; well-designed brass shelf clocks could sell for a few dollars, as against the twelve to eighteen dollars required to cover the cost of a wooden grandfather's clock. By 1840 the metal clock and watch industry in Waterbury and nearby towns had begun its long and profitable career.

Brass and other hardware, rubber wares, clocks – all were important parts of the Connecticut Valley's development. They came early in the region and stayed late. But firearms hold a central place in the history in several respects. As the industry began to develop, the private demand proved to be vast. A gun was part of nearly every farmhouse's equipment on the frontier to protect from Indians, and there and within the frontier to hunt game and keep down rodents. But repeatedly, in the 1790s and again at the times of the Mexican and Civil wars, it was the large block orders from the federal government and the state militias that pushed the craftsmen into machinery and the machinery into mass production. The two armories created by the Act of 1795 followed European mercantilist precedent, but the ease with which personnel, orders, and techniques passed between the Springfield Armory and the private manufacturers – Whitney, North, and Colt – showed how little the distinction between public and private meant for the final result. More striking is the difference in efficiency and progressiveness between the Yankee armory and that at Harper's Ferry, Virginia. Merritt Roe Smith's splendid study of the latter shows the two cultures in sharp contrast.[12] Springfield, especially under Roswell Lee, was a highly organized, efficient body of skilled workmen, not only building guns but also creating gun-making techniques, instruments, and machinery. The shops of Whitney, in Hamden, and North, in Middletown, stimulated by large federal contracts, worked not competitively but in considerable harmony with the armory. In the Virginia establishment, the only efficient portion, devoted obsessively to the ideal of interchangeability and large-scale production, was the rifle works under the mad Maine Yankee, John Hall. Hall maintained his pursuit of exact calibration, by means of a huge array of fixtures and gauges at every step of rifle production, with the obsessive determination of Captain Ahab chasing Moby Dick. His survival in the antagonistic, highly political local culture of the armory – a culture of influence and family connections that extended from Harper's

---

[12]Merritt R. Smith, *Harper's Ferry Armory and the New Technology* (Ithaca: Cornell University Press, 1977).

Ferry to Congress and the White House – has the sound of a morality play of shining Puritan virtue and Virginian vice.

Following Whitney, North, Lee, and Hall, Samuel Colt – a man of many talents – carried the industry into mid-century. Notable in both the clockmakers and the gun makers is a curious combination of skill, ingenuity, and showmanship. Whitney, North, Terry, and Hall were craftsmen of high purpose and enlightened devotion to a technological and engineering ideal that formed a basic part of the Yankee culture. But Whitney and Jerome in clocks, and in guns Colt above all, reminds us that P. T. Barnum was also a Yankee.

FROM MACHINERY TO MACHINE TOOLS

Production of machine-made textiles requires machinery, and the machine shop was an important feature of a textile mill – the principal feature, one might say, of some of the large ones. This aspect of New England's industrialization – the trail from textiles to textile machinery to the machine and power tools to build textile machinery, thence to generalized machine tools for a variety of basic operations on metal – has been chronicled in a well-known article by Nathan Rosenberg.[13] He has dubbed the phenomenon "technological convergence": the simultaneous demand for standard lathes, milling machines, shapers, drills, and the like, needed to make machinery of the most varied and specific sorts and so to turn out the stupendous array of final goods in an industrial economy. Obviously a large market for machinery itself was required to offer the scale economies in the serial production of standardized machine tools. But textile machines could offer only a small part of a market of requisite scale.

Important, and somewhat unobserved, is the nature of the Connecticut Valley manufactures – clocks and guns, which were themselves machines. They had to be made by craftsmen who, if they began to employ batch production and powered tools, became machinists. Unlike the skills in textile manufacture, the skills used to make a gun or a clock were readily transferable to making a machine that would replace hand operations as surely as a chisel would replace a stone axe, or a gun, a bow and arrow.

The New England machine tool industry grew, then, from the two machinery centers: the area west and south of Lowell, from Worcester to Providence, and the Connecticut Valley from Middletown as far up as Windsor, Vermont.[14] Of the two areas, the latter became more central,

[13] Nathan Rosenberg, "Technological Change in the Machine Tool Industry, 1840–1910," *Journal of Economic History*, Vol. 22, No. 4 (December 1963).
[14] Carolyn Cooper's recently completed Yale dissertation, "The Role of Thomas Blanchard's Woodworking Invention in 19th-Century American Industrial Tech-

but in both areas, intensified industrialization shaped cost and market conditions for machine tools and production line in manufacture, and in both areas that intensification corresponded to two phases of especially intense pressure from New England's external environment.

The first was the hothouse effect of the break with England. British restrictions and British competition disappeared from 1776 to 1783, and competition fell away again in the Napoleonic Wars and the War of 1812 and was finally limited by a protective tariff – moderate by later standards, but significant in that it was established, against the initial resistance of the merchants, as a part of the American tax structure and foreign economic policy.[15] Trade with the British Caribbean had been temporarily interrupted, but the breakup of Spain's mercantilist empire in South America gave new outlets. More important, the southern plantations, having completed a cycle of growth based on tobacco, were in 1800 just entering their violent and brilliant history based on slaves and cotton, creating both vast supplies of the raw material and a rapidly growing population, black and white, to be clothed and shod. The antebellum period had its boom decades, particularly the 1830 and 1850s, which gave an unevenness to the movement of demand for purchased farm capital items, and which affected the finanical conditions of the manufacturing firms. But so long as the agricultural population continued its strong and steady increase, and new lands continued to be both abundant and rich, the continued growth of the textile and shoe industries was assured.

The second phase – rather different and more complex than the South's effect on New England's industrialization – derived from the influence of the Old Northwest. In this case the first effect was not by way of markets, but by way of migration. Just as the Connecticut lands had pulled families from Massachusetts in the seventeenth century, so central New York pulled settlers from Connecticut and Vermont in the early nineteenth. The opening of the Ohio country produced several waves of migration; beginning even before 1820, the Connecticut Western Reserve in northern Ohio began to fill up. The effect of the westward movement

nology" (Yale University, Department of History of Science, 1985), studies the role of one Yankee inventor-machinist-entrepreneur Thomas Blanchard – in this development. Blanchard invented a lathe for copying gunstocks, shoe lasts, and other complex patterns; a machine for bending wood; and a number of other devices. The dissertation studies not only the technical but also the legal and social aspects of Blanchard's efforts and career.

[15] F. W. Taussig, *The Tariff History of the United States* (New York: G. P. Putnam, 1892), especially 8–36, 68–108. The costs and benefits of protection are reconsidered with sophisticated measurement in Paul A. David, *Technical Change, Innovation and Economic Growth* (London and New York: Cambridge University Press, 1975), Chs. 2, 3.

on the various New England farming and industrial areas was not uniform. A movement north was going on at the same time as the first movement west, so the period of Vermont and New Hampshire's agricultural decline was delayed by a few decades. Already the mill towns in eastern and central Massachusetts had begun to reach as far away as Quebec and Ireland to attract farm labor into industrial employment. Connecticut was the hardest hit. From 1800 to 1840 the state's population increased only about 5 percent per decade, compared to 35 percent in the United States as a whole. Migrants in numbers equal to the whole of the natural increase, that is, to at least the size of the state's population in 1800, had gone west by 1840.[16]

We have at this point little data, only much theory to guide the story, but the migration must have had a triple-edged effect on Connecticut's young metals and machinery industries, influencing the market, labor supplies, and technology. The migrants, with their companions from other states, must have been mostly farmers moving to where, on new lands, they could farm much the same array of crops and livestock products as they had done, but more productively. Almost from first settlement on, the "East" was to a large degree fed, particularly in meat, from successive "Wests" – from central Massachusetts, from central New York, from central Ohio, and finally from Illinois and, after 1860, Texas and the Plains. The return shipment of the western surpluses, after construction of the canals of the 1820s and the trunk lines of the 1840s, caused the abandonment of farms and basic shifts in the crop mix. The shift from grains reduced labor requirements in northeastern farming, although dairying and hay production to some degree balanced this off. But the sale of those surpluses enlarged the market among farms, small towns, and growing cities in the Old Northwest for just the kinds of consumer durable goods that the manfacturers had begun to turn out. At the same time, with cheaper food and growing markets as a lure, the migrations surely caused Connecticut some loss in its artisan and skilled work force. The occupational composition of the migration stream is not known, but even if it was composed mostly of farmers, the supplies of artisan labor in Connecticut clearly did not increase. The occupational lists of the Midwest towns show a good complement of smiths, mechanics, millers, and the like. Surely many of these had been among the migrants.

Some economic historians, with a fascination for economic theory, have averred that under the market tension in which they existed, and

---

[16]Clarence H. Danhof, *Change in Agriculture: the Northern United States, 1830–1870* (Cambridge, Mass.: Harvard University Press, 1969). Chapter 1 has a good account of the Midwest/Northeast interaction, from the viewpoint of the areas receiving the immigrants.

relative to the obviously not very ample supplies of something called capital, American farming and industry nevertheless suffered a chronic shortage of labor, particularly of unskilled labor.[17] The textile industries met this challenge by adopting the machinery that, with some use of a mechanic's labor and working capital, greatly increased the productivity of unskilled or semi-skilled, formerly domestic labor. Women and children and unskilled farm labor from French Canada and ultimately from Ireland could be used on the machines. In western farming, too, the story is of the labor-augmenting inventions, with modest capital requirements and farm-fed horsepower, that could keep a farmer fairly busy over wide enough acreage to yield a large commercial surplus. The sewing machine, shoe machinery, later even the typewriter – all had the effect of substituting an item of manufactured "capital" for only moderately skilled craft and household labor, stretching the labor force to handle a larger volume of resources or semi-finished materials. Overall, this is no doubt the way American industrialization worked, and this circumstance may have given a peculiarly strong "labor-saving bias" to the inventive effort and to practice in shop and field. Interchangeable parts, the systematization of work, the ever-finer division of labor, then, may be seen as having been adopted not to utilize idle supplies of unskilled labor, but to economize on labor so as to use abundant raw materials by furnishing processes and machines for the tasks to be done – even de-skilling artisan labor through the abandonent of hand processes, with a substitution of system and machinery for skill.

The situation of the Connecticut clock and gun manufacturers fits this model, but with a difference. Here it was not relatively unskilled seamstresses, but relatively skilled machinists whose labor needed "augmentation," and the products by and large were themselves machines for the final market. The same workers who could produce these machines could with a little retraining, devise and work out machines to produce these machines, that is, machine tools. Wages and the array of skills were presumably much the same at both levels of production. No doubt, at some absurdly high rate of interest it would have been too expensive to

[17]Two recent contributions to this topic are the papers by Alexander Field, "Land Abundance, Interest/Profit Rates, and Nineteenth-Century American and British Technology," *Journal of Economic History*, Vol. 43, No. 2 (June 1983), and by John James and Jonathan Skinner, "Labor Scarcity in Nineteenth Century Manufacturing," University of Virginia Seminar Papers (Charlottesville 1983). The topic has been complicated by the need to take England as a standard of comparison, although until Field's paper, it was never clear whether the ratio of capital costs to wages was higher or lower there, since America seemed to be both "labor-scarce" *and* "capital-scarce," relative to land. The problem appears to be full of internally created puzzles, and will probably drift out of sight before a "solution" that conforms both to logic and to the facts can be achieved.

withdraw workers from current production to form this capital. But it would not have taken much for the value of machine tools to rise enough to swamp the additional interest charges. And once the production structure was thus lengthened, with the maintenance of active competition among producers, not only the cost of consumers' capital, but the cost of producers' machinery and of machine tools themselves would fall. This process cheapened real capital, and so stretched the stock of savings for financial capital, thus making possible an extensive and often even wasteful use of machinery to augment labor and, ultimately, almost to replace skilled craft labor in most jobs.[18]

From this background arose, in the years 1820–70, the notable specialized machine tool producers: Brown and Sharpe, Jones and Lamson, the Whitin works, and others. Alas that records no longer exist to detail just where, when, and at what wages and prices and profit margins the industry was drawn into being![19] Accompanying its development was the application, as in guns, of great mechanical ingenuity. The milling machine is claimed by several of the great names, notably Whitney and North. More certain in attribution are the stocking lathe and Blanchard's other patented and much sued-over inventions. The development of gauges, calipers, jigs, and fixtures is all part of the history of this precision machinery. The manufacture of parts for assembly required the precision of tools, and once such precise and controllable machine tools were made, with flexibility and adaptability to varied purposes, they could be used in turn to make copies of themselves. The generative organs of machine industry were thus created, in Connecticut and in the northeast's other machine tool center, north of Philadelphia – as later also in the areas of Cincinnati, Cleveland, and Detroit.

In the second half of the nineteenth century, the industrial tendencies displayed before 1850 were further played out. Textiles, machinery, brass, hardware, guns, machine tools – all continued to grow and flourish while New England's agricultural decline spread to the northern tier of states and out-migration continued. A new element was the financial wealth that was accumulated in New England and moved west, into land, minerals, and railroad and industrial stocks and bonds. But migration alone – of labor, of capital funds, or even of the stream of light machinery the region

[18]See Chapter 12, Section I, where the same point is made with respect to increased capital intensity in light and heavy manufactures in the Middle West after 1870.

[19]J. W. Roe, in *English and American Tool Builders* (New Haven: Yale University Press, 1916), draws on his earlier Yale dissertation and on such records as were available then. I have found no general treatment published since then to replace it, despite good specialized studies of the Saco–Lowell mills, the Whitin Works, and others.

exported – did not by itself accomplish the industrial miracle of the Middle West. There a late New England Puritan culture mixed with the migration streams from Pennsylvania and the southern uplands to the point where, in the presence of vast new mineral resources, the frame of a complete industrial structure began to arise, encompassing light industry, heavy industry, an agricultural base, and an overlay of commercial and legal institutions and practices. With the midwestern industrial development, the story moves into the twentieth century and New England's own industry moves into the cycle of abandonment, conversion, and partial revival that has characterized its life in recent decades.

SOME REFLECTIONS ON THE HISTORY

A la fin de toute pensée, il y a un soupir
– attributed to Paul Valéry

Between 1790 and 1840, along its rivers, its streams, and its coastline from Salem to Bridgeport, southern New England experienced a notable industrial revolution, lagging behind England's by only a few years. By the standards that economic historians – bourgeois or Marxist – apply, New England's industrial revolution was a success. To a Marxist it appears to have broken the mold of a pre-capitalist form: that of the patriarchal family economy or, some would hold, that of an equally ancient form, the communal village. A new class, merchants and petty capitalists, exhibiting its ingenuity in workshop and marketplace, replaced priests and a king – the latter by a violent revolution that proved to be the forward shadow of its great counterpart in France. In Yankee countinghouses and mills, American business civilization was born and began its giant-like growth into a bourgeois society still today awaiting its proletarian revolution. To the bourgeois historian, lacking the Marxist's story line, New England represented a region of that Britain whose culture and industrial revolution it shared, or a second "follower country" to which, in its technology, society, economy, religion, and politics, the impulse of the British "modernization process" had transmitted.

The history of success is, of course, a bore when repeated over and over again. Tolstoy observed and extended the observation to a long novel – that all happy families are alike; only the tragic, miserable ones have stories. Without a personal involvement, one's interest in the history of a locality or a firm or even a business leader is short-lived. To paraphrase a notorious comment, when you've seen one textile mill or one machine shop, you've seen 'em all – unless you are yourself in the trade. Even the scale on which the history is played out does not much matter. Textile mills for cottons or woolens, brass foundries or rolling mills, iron works, machinery and machine tool shops – the industrial histories have much the same form, with small idiosyncracies arising from peculiarities in the raw material, the market, or the circumstances of the specific time when the growth began to occur.

In the industrialization of a region, these industries are interlinked. At that level of learning and generalization, the observation of those link-ages, implicit in the relation of the technologies to one another and to the human culture out of which they all arise, may arouse interest, curiosity, and even admiration. Town histories come to life when, brushing over them as if rubbing a tombstone, one sees geographical patterns that have an economic or sociological explanation. Histories of firms, arranged by industry and stacked up according to the structure of production, show the "Rosenberg effect."[20] Such a generalization could have been deduced, even "predicted," from a knowledge only of the technologies and the rate of market growth. But it almost certainly would never have been thought of without a large measure of induction – an examination of the actual histories of firms and inventions.

The dynamics implicit in the physical nature of the environment and materials – the "challenge" side of the Toynbee thesis – is one-half of the story that lies hidden like a sea monster, immanent in the history and rewarding long hours of observation. The other half of the story – the "response" by which that potential dynamic is activated – lies in the all-pervasive and complex character of what one is forced to call, for want of a more precise and suggestive term, culture: culture of the artisan, the mechanic, the merchant-entrepreneur, the self-educated inventor, but a culture also of rationality, of close observation. That culture channeled its creativity along practical, material lines, combining with its materials a spiritual sense of both self- and civic righteousness – a self-confidence and self-esteem that came to the descendant of the Puritan, often all too easily, when the sense of sin dissolved into the consciousness of probable election. Foremost in this culture was a sense of pride in what was deemed worthy achievement: the determined effort, by farmer, workman, and businessman alike, to make money in clever trade and in useful production. It is this culture that forms the substream from which every town history, the history of every firm, of every locality or industry in the region draws its life.

Just as the history of towns or firms in a region, endlessly repetitous, gains meaning only when seen in a pattern, so the histories of one industri-alizing region after another in the nineteenth century exhibit similar traces of monotony. The textile industries march, endlessly it seems, in wearying parade from one new industrial region to another, like the dove

[20]Rosenberg, "Technological Change."

sent out from the ark, finding no spot on which to land. In North America, New England's textile phase finds repetition in the southern Piedmont nearly a century later. There the interesting question is a negative or hypothetical one: Why did that development fail to occur there earlier as part of the boom times of slavery and cotton? In the Middle West, New England's mechanical industries grew not on harsh soil, but on a rich agricultural base, and pre-industrial mentalities, if they ever existed in early colonial times, had long since been replaced by concepts of endless horizons and illimitable wants as a permanent and self-renewing "challenge." At the same time, these light and craft-like mechanical industries fuse after 1870 with the rather different history of the Pennsylvanian heavy industries to form at last, with the huge discoveries of coal, ore, oil, and gas, and in the presence of lake shipping and the railroad, the great belt of American heavy industry. The industrialization of the American economy, broken down by industries and regions, thus forms a history whose outlines are found also in those of the other self-contained national economies of the nineteenth and early twentieth centuries – the German, the French, eventually the Russian, and even, with the exception of the agricultural base, that of Britain. Smaller economies – Switzerland, Sweden, northern Italy – exhibit the entire history in miniature or pieces of it, depending on their positions in world trade.

Still to American and world industrialization, the New England episode is commonly said to have contributed at least one new idea, exhibiting it in so exaggerated a form as to make it the unmistakable and readily imitated hallmark of modern industry. This contribution was the ideal of interchangeable parts and of the thorough organization of machines and labor to create "mass" production. This was the trait of American manufacture that attracted attention from visiting Englishmen and at international fairs at mid-century. Obviously it was not simply in application to guns and clocks that the idea made history. It was the thoroughness, zest, and variety with which the principle was applied when the truly mass market and massive resources base opened up the Midwest that turned Yankee ingenuity into Taylorism and Fordism. The history of the New England episode, taken in the whole context of antebellum American economic history, should illuminate the reason why this development could take such firm hold and could prove so fruitful in so individualistic a society.

Where in colonial history is the origin of this taste for organization to be discerned? One hesitates to trace so complex a history back into the thorny brambles of the Puritan mind. But for the history of American industrialization in the nineteenth century, an anomalous, if not self-contradictory, aspect of the American character, or at least of our view of it, remains to be resolved. It is a question that has been broached at several points in this volume. How did a nation of individualistic farmers and small-time entrepreneurs move with such ease into the modern world of the large corporate organization? Part of the answer may lie in the traditional sympathy of nineteenth-century Americans, noted by de Tocqueville, for community organization. The small town was itself controlled by a neighborly vigilance as close as that of the factory foreman's eye. Evident, too, is the tendency of Americans, spanning a continent, to think big and to admire bigness. Something of the self-assured Texan permeates our picture of the enterprising part of the population everywhere. Yet community life and large settlement projects were organized essentially on a small scale. Nothing about them shows the nature of a centralized corporate management. Waste, not rationalized efficiency, was the hallmark of their success. What trait is it that the individualistic entrepreneur and the production manager and engineer have in common? How do we move so easily from the world of F. J. Turner to the world of A. D. Chandler?[21]

The answer, I suggest, may be found in seventeenth-century English Puritanism, as its doctrines and sensitivities were transformed by selective evolution into the several New England varieties and thence into the secular ethic of a nineteenth-century Protestant population. For the trait in question is simply an unusual insensitivity to human society, considered as a structure of emotion, vitality, and artistic sensibility. The Puritan drew energy and intolerant self-confidence from the knowledge not merely that he might be saved, but that in Christ he had found the only way to salvation. And he drew direction and guidance from an equally firm belief in the rationality both of the covenant with God and of God's revelation of His order in the physical universe. By the eighteenth century, faith in science was as strong as faith in God; indeed, the two faiths had fused together. The Puritan could proceed, then, to inflict an engineering order on the physical world with the same passion with which he had tortured his individual conscience in its search for faith and grace. In the language of two other cultures, the Yogi and the Commisar were two faces of the same soul.

But to convince puritanical economists of the essential Puritanism of their own ways of looking at the world is not the task for a short paper, or for a short life, particularly that of one born in that culture and sharing its values, its inspiration, and its blindness.

SELECTED BIBLIOGRAPHY

Even a history that has been relatively neglected has managed over the years to acquire an appreciable bibliography. The list that follows gives

[21]See Chapter 12, Sections IV and V, where some of this same ground is traveled and some of these same questions raised in connection with the development of heavy industry in the Middle West after 1870.

only sources on the industrial history itself. A bibliography of sources on
(1) social and legal history (including village studies and travelers' accounts, mostly well known to American historians), (2) the relevant intellectual history (the usual sources on Puritanism), and (3) the issues of
economic theory raised in the final section is available on application to
the author.

I. MANUFACTURING INDUSTRY

A. Textiles and shoes

Burgy, J. Herbert. *The New England Cotton Textile Industry*. Baltimore: Waverly
Press, 1932.

Faler, Paul G. *Mechanics and Manufacturers in the Early Industrial Revolution:
Lynn, Massachusetts, 1780–1860*. Albany: State University of New York
Press, 1981.

Goldin, Claudia, and Kenneth Sokoloff. "Women, Children and Industrialization
in the Early Republic: Evidence from the Manufacturing Censuses." *Journal
of Economic History* 42 (Dec. 1982): 771–774.

Hazard, Blanche Evans. *The Organization of the Boot and Shoe Industry in
Massachusetts Before 1875*. Cambridge, Mass.: Harvard University Press,
1921; reprint ed., New York: Johnson Reprint, 1968.

Lincoln, Jonathan Tayer. "Material for a History of American Textile Machinery:
The Kilburn–Lincoln Papers." *Journal of Economic and Business History*,
Vol. 4 (Feb. 1932).

Oxley, Jeffrey. *The Textile Manufacturing Corporation and Boston Capital, The
Era of the Lowell System, 1813–1880*. Doctoral dissertation, Stanford University, in process.

Shlakman, Vera. *Economic History of a Factory Town: A Study of Chicopee,
Massachusetts. Smith College Studies in History*, Vol. 20 (1934–35).

Ware, Caroline F. *The Early New England Cotton Manufacture*. Boston & New
York: Houghton Mifflin, 1931.

B. Clocks

Barr, Lockwood Anderson. *Eli Terry's Pillar & Scroll Shelf Clocks* (n.p., 1952).

Camp, Hiram. *Sketch of the Clock Making Business, 1792–1892*. New Haven,
1939 (pamphlet), in the Yale University Library.

Hoopes, Penrose R. "Early Clockmaking in Connecticut." In *Historical Publications of the Tercentenary Commission of the State of Connecticut*, Vol. 3.
New Haven: Yale University Press, 1933–1936.

Ingraham, Edward. *Connecticut Clockmaking* (pamphlet). Reprinted from 56th
Annual Report, the Connecticut Society of Civil Engineers, in Yale University
Library.

Jerome, Chauncey. *History of the American Clock Business for the Past Sixty
Years, and Life of Chauncey Jerome*. New Haven: F. C. Dayton, Jr., 1860;
reprint ed., Bristol, Connecticut: American Clock and Watch Museum, 1983.

Molan, Scott. *The Origin of the Machinery Industry in the United States: A Regional History of Mechanization in the Nineteenth Century.* Doctoral dissertation, the New School for Social Research, New York, in process.

Murphy, J. J. "Entrepreneurship in the Establishment of the American Clock Industry." *Journal of Economic History,* Vol. 26 (June 1966), 169–186.

Roberts, Kenneth D. *The Contributions of Joseph Ives to Connecticut Clock Technology, 1810–1862.* Bristol, Conn.: American Clock and Watch Museum, 1970.

C. Brass and brasswares

Bridgeport Brass Co. *Seven Centuries of Brass Making.* Bridgeport, 1920.

Brecher, Jeremy, Jerry Lombardi, and Jan Stackhouse, eds. *Brass Valley: The Story of Working People's Lives and Struggles in an American Industrial Region.* Philadelphia: Temple Univeristy Press, 1982.

Coyne, Franklin, E. *The Development of the Cooperage Industry in the United States, 1620–1940.* Chicago: Lumber Buyers, 1940.

Greeley, Horace, et al. *The Great Industries of the United States.* Hartford: J. B. Burr & Hyde, 1872.

Howell, Kenneth T., ed. *History of Abel Porter & Company from which Scovill Manufacturing Company is the Direct Descendant.* Waterbury, Conn.: Scovill Manufacturing Co., 1952.

Lathrop, William Gilbert. *The Brass Industry in Connecticut.* Doctoral dissertation, Yale University, 1909.

——. "The Development of the Brass Industry in Connecticut." In *Historical Publications of the Tercentenary Commission of the State of Connecticut,* Vol. 6.

Marburg, Theodore F. *Management Problems and Procedures of a Manufacturing Enterprise, 1802–1852; a Case Study of the Origin of the Scovill Manufacturing Company.* Doctoral dissertation, Clark University, Worcester, Mass., 1942.

Scientific American. Articles on brass manufacture: Vol. 41 (Dec. 13, 1879), p. 380; Vol. 42 (May 1, 1880), p. 277.

Scovill Manufacturing Co. *Brass Roots.* Waterbury, Conn., 1952.

Scovill Manufacturing Co. pamphlets – economic aspects, in Yale University Library: (1) *Scovill Manufacturing Co.,* Waterbury, 1802–1935; (2) *Historical Analysis of Scovill Manufacturing Co.,* "Scovill World-Famed Pioneers in Brass," E. L. Newmarker, 1928; (3) *Scovill Manufacturing Co., The Oldest Brass Company in America,* (reprint from *The Metal Industry of NYC,* Aug. 1923). Publications of the Scovill Manufacturing Company: (1) *Scovill Manufacturing Company* (n.p., n.d.); (2) *The Mill on Mad River,* Waterbury, Conn., 1953.

D. Arms

Cain, Louis P., and Paul J. Uselding, eds. *Business Enterprise and Economic Change.* Kent, Ohio: Kent State University Press, 1973.

Cooper, Carolyn C. "Eli Whitney's Armory: Myth, Machines and Material Evidence." *Journal of the New Haven Colony Historical Society*, Vol. 31 (Fall 1984), 19–34.

Deyrup, Felicia Johnson. *Arms Makers of the Connecticut Valley: A Regional Study of the Economic Development of the Small Arms Industry, 1798–1870. Smith College Studies in History*, V. B. Holmes and H. Kohn, eds., vol. 23 (1948).

Green, Constance M. *Eli Whitney and the Birth of American Technology*. Boston: Little, Brown, 1956.

Mirsky, Jeannette, and Allan Nevins. *The World of Eli Whitney*. New York: Macmillan, 1952.

North, S. N. D., and Ralph H. North. *Simeon North, First Official Pistol Maker of the United States*. Concord, N.H.: Rumford Press, 1913.

Smith, Merrit Roe. *Harper's Ferry Armory and the New Technology*. Ithaca: Cornell University Press, 1977.

Uselding, Paul. "Elisha K. Root, Forging, and the 'American System.' " *Technology and Culture*, Vol. 15 (October 1974).

E. Machinery and general industrial history

Bishop, John Leander. *A History of American Manufactures, from 1608 to 1860*, Vol. 1 *1608–1860* Vol. 2, *1789–1860*. Philadelphia: Edward Young & Co., 1864. London: S. Low, Son & Co., 1964.

Blackall, Frederick S., Jr. "Invention and Industry – Cradled in New England!" Address to Newcomen Society of England, American Branch, New York (pamphlet), 1946.

Bridenbaugh, Carl. *The Colonial Craftsmen*, New York: New York University Press, 1950.

Clark, Victor Selden. *History of Manufactures in the United States*, Vol. 1, *1776–1860*. Washington, D.C.: Carnegie Institution of Washington, 1916–1928. Published for Carnegie Institution of Washington by McGraw-Hill, 1929.

Cooper, Carolyn C. *The Role of Thomas Blanchard's Woodworking Invention in 19th Century American Industrial Technology*. Doctoral dissertation, Yale University, Program in the History of Science, September, 1985.

Day, Clive. "The Rise of Manufacturing in Connecticut," in *Historical Publications of the Tercentenary Commission of the State of Connecticut*, Vol. 5.

Fuller, Grace Pierpont. *An Introduction to the History of Connecticut as a Manufacturing State. Smith College Studies in History*, J. S. Bassett and S. B. Fay, eds., Vol. 1. Northampton, Massachusetts, October 1915.

Gibb, George Sweet. *The Saco–Lowell Shops*. Cambridge, Mass.: Harvard University Press, 1950.

Grant, Ellsworth Strong. *Yankee Dreamers and Doers*. Chester, Conn.: Pequot Press, n.d.

Hounshell, David A. *From the American System to Mass Production, 1800–1932*. Baltimore: Johns Hopkins University Press, 1984.

Hubbard, Guy. "The Influence of Early Windsor Industries upon the Mechanic Arts." *Proceedings of the Vermont Historical Society*. 1921, pp. 159–182.

——. "The Machine Tool Industry." In *The Development of American Industries*, John G. Glover, ed., Ch. 26. New York: Prentice-Hall, 1936.

Parton, James. *Famous Americans of Recent Times.* Boston: Fields, Osgood & Co., 1869.

Roe, J. W. "Connecticut Inventors." In *Historical Publications of the Tercentenary Commission of the State of Connecticut,* Vol. 4.

———. *English and American Tool Builders.* New Haven: Yale University Press, 1916; reprint ed., New York: McGraw-Hill, 1926.

Rolt, L. T. C. *A Short History of Machine Tools.* Cambridge, M.I.T. Press, 1965.

Rosenberg, N., ed. *The American System of Manufactures.* Edinburgh: Edinburgh University Press, 1969.

Steeds, W. *A History of Machine Tools, 1700–1910.* London: Oxford University Press, 1969.

Taylor, George Rogers. *The Transportation Revolution, 1815–1860.* New York: Harper & Row Torchbooks, 1968.

Tryon, Rolla Milton. *Household Manufactures in the United States, 1640–1860.* Chicago: University of Chicago Press, 1917.

Weaver, Glenn. "Industry in an Agrarian Economy: Early Eighteenth-Century Connecticut." *The Connecticut Historical Society Bulletin,* Vol. 19 (July 1954).

Williamson, Harold. *The Growth of the American Economy,* 2nd ed. New York: Prentice-Hall, 1951, Chs. 9–12.

Wolf, Ralph F. *India Rubber Man: The Story of Charles Goodyear:* Caldwell, Idaho: Caucton Printers, 1939.

Zimiles, Martha, and Murray Zimiles. *Early American Mills.* New York: Bramhall House, 1973.

II. RESOURCE INDUSTRIES AND TRADE

Bailyn, Bernard. *The New England Merchants in the Seventeenth Century.* Cambridge: Harvard University Press, 1979.

Bidwell, Percy, W., and John I. Falconer. *History of Agriculture in the Northern United States, 1620–1860.* Washington, D.C.: Carnegie Institution of Washington, 1925.

Cowles, Alfred A. "Copper and Brass." In *1795–1895. One Hundred Years of American Commerce.* New York: D. O. Haynes & Co., 1895, Ch. 47.

Cronon, William. *Changes in the Land.* New York: Hill and Wang, 1983.

Defebaugh, James Elliott. *History of the Lumber Industry of America,* Vol. 2. Chicago: The American Lumberman, 1907.

Johnson, Emory R., T. W. Van Metre, G. G. Huebrier, and D. S. Hanchet. *History of Domestic and Foreign Commerce of the United States,* Vol. 1. Washington, D.C.: Carnegie Institution of Washington, 1915.

Innis, Harold A. *The Cod Fisheries: The History of an International Economy.* New Haven: Yale University Press, 1940.

———. *The Fur-Trade of Canada.* University of Toronto Studies, History and Economics, Vol. 5, No. 1. Toronto: Oxford University Press, 1927.

Johnson, Richard R. *Adjustment to Empire: The New England Colonies, 1675–1715.* New Brunswick, N.J.: Rutgers University Press, 1981.

Martin, Margaret E. *Merchants and Trade of the Connecticut River Valley,*

1750–1820. Smith College Studies in History, W. D. Gray, H. Kohn, and R. A. Billington, eds., Vol. 24 (October 1938–July 1939).

Moloney, Francis X. *The Fur Trade in New England, 1620–1676.* Cambridge, Massachusetts, 1931; reprint ed., Hamden, Conn.: Archon Books, 1967.

Pabst, Margaret Richards. *Agricultural Trends in the Connecticut Valley Region of Massachusetts, 1800–1900. Smith College Studies in History,* Vol. 26 (1940).

Parker, William N., and Judith L. V. Klein. "Productivity Growth in Grain Production in the United States, 1840–60 and 1900–10." In *Output, Employment, and Productivity in the United States after 1800.* New York: National Bureau of Economic Research, 1966, 523–582.

Rothenberg, Winifred. "The Market and Massachusetts Farmers." *Journal of Economic History,* Vol. 51 (June 1981): 283–314.

Weaver, Glenn. "Some Aspects of Early Eighteenth-Century Connecticut Trade." *The Connecticut Historical Society Bulletin,* Vol. 22 (January 1957).

APPENDIX

Table 1. *Approximate consumption requirements and land and labor requirements for grain and meat for family of six on a New England farm, 1840–60 (source data for Figures 1 and 2)*

Consumption Requirements

			Family
Daily	1.5 lb meal:	.75 lb flour	4.50 lb
		.75 lb corn	4.50 lb
	⅓ lb meat		2.00 lb
Annual	wheat flour	1,600 lb	
	corn flour	1,600 lb	
	meat	730 lb × 10^a = 7,300 lb corn	

Factor Input Requirements

Land:	wheat 1,600 lb at 50 lb/ bu = 32 bu	= 2 acres at 16 bu/acre
	corn 8,900 lb at 50 lb/ bu = 178 bu	= 6 acres at 30 bu/acre
	hay	10 acres
Labor:	wheat 2 acres at 50 m-h/acre	= 100
	corn 6 acres at 113 m-h/ acre	= 678
	10 acres at 28 m-h/acre	= 280
		1,058 m-h
	= 106 10-hour days = 18 6-day weeks = 4.5 months	

Source: Land and labor requirements from Parker and Klein, "Productivity Growth in Grain Production in the United States, 1840/60 and 1900/10," in NBER, *Studies in Income and Wealth*, vol. 30, (New York: 1966). Consumption requirements are simply arbitrary estimates, supported by scattered references to diets. Among omissions in these calculations, the most notable are wild game and fish, milk, wild forage, straw, cornstalks and tops, orchard crops, poultry, etc. Account is also not taken of labor used in home manufactures or in farm capital formation.

[a]Rough estimates: Hay acreage for two animals, 10 acres; corn–meat ratio for cattle or hogs, 10:1. Under pioneer conditions, wild forage, not accounted for here, could replace two-thirds or more of the corn acreage.

Table 2. *Distribution of labor by operation over the crop year*

	Corn	Wheat	Hay
(a) Acreage	6	2	10
(b) labor requirement per acre			
Plow (m-h/acre)	18	18	18
Plant (m-h/acre)	14	2	–
Cultivate (m-h/acre)	15	–	–
Hoe (m-h/acre)	52	–	–
Harvest (m-h/acre)	14	15	10
Thresh (m-h/15 bu)	–	15	–
Total	113	50	28
(c) Total labor required (a × b)	678	100	280 = 1,058

(d) Per worker total = 529, or 53 10-hour days, spread over 180 day growing and harvesting season.

(e) Livestock care for two draft-meat animals estimated at 15 minutes a day each.

Source: As in Table 1.

12

The industrial civilization of the Midwest

I. RESOURCES AND TECHNOLOGY

After 1860, colonization in the American Midwest proceeded rapidly across the Mississippi River and by 1890 had encompassed the Prairies and Great Plains. At the same time, the population east of the Mississippi grew thicker, and the agro-business culture, with its small towns and manufactures, grew denser and more complex. This was accompanied by the growth of geographical and technical knowledge – a knowledge which, under the rules and forms of capitalist enterprise, was rather quickly translated into economic opportunity. In the Far West prospectors were alert for news of a minerals strike and responded with the classic "rush." On the Plains, beginning in Texas and moving north, cattlemen organized drives through newly opened grasslands and developed within the next few decades complex combinations of ranching, transportation and stall feeding to move the meat to middle western markets. Farmers, set loose into free land by the Homestead Act of 1862 and into cheap land on the enormous domains of the railroad grants, overcame an initial hesitation at venturing away from the forested areas and rapidly threw together whatever shelter they could build to make farms on the Plains and Prairies to raise corn and wheat on the rich soils beneath the grass.

Most of this new farming and mining opportunity was linked to what-

Most of this essay except for the portion on the sources of capital, have appeared in D. C. Klingaman and R. K. Vedder, eds., *Essays on The Economy of The Old Northwest* (Athens: Ohio University Press, 1987), Ch. 2. In its present version, it has benefited much from the chapters on banking (Ch. 9, by Eugene Smiley), manufacturing (Ch. 12, by D. C. Klingaman), and the regional aggregate growth (Ch. 12, by R. K. Vedder and Lowell Galloway). See "A Note on the Sources" after the conclusion of Section V. For research assistance and footnoting of the whole essay, I benefited from labors of Scott Redenius of the Yale Department of Economics.

ever means of transportation were at hand. In the 1830s this had meant the steamboat, rivers, and canals; now the railroad, having thrust itself to Chicago and the Mississippi, continued its spectacular advance on the Indians, the buffalo, the Rockies, and the Pacific. Local lines were within the capacity of local and private capital, assisted by many ingenious schemes of finance; where these fell short, and across unsettled lands, the corruptibility of legislatures, the federal Congress's eagerness to grant land for the purpose, and the burgeoning bond market in the East and in Europe completed the financing. In the Old Northwest, one notable study shows, settlement had predated the laying of rail lines, which then followed into the richer and more accessible localities that the knowledge of first settlers had pointed out.[1] But in the flatter, more homogeneous West no such nice discriminations were needed. Settler and railroad entered together into the unknown. In the northern Midwest, Yankees, along with the Germans, Scandinavians, and central Europeans, flowed smoothly into the lands west of the Great Lakes between the 1850s and 1890s.[2] At the same time the prior settlement of Utah, California, and the Oregon Country gave the transcontinental lines a place and a market in which to terminate. It was a high-risk venture, not only in physical terms, but as a business proposition. The physical and human capital were in place even while the market and an articulated system of distribution and credit were still a-forming. But westward expansion could not have been carried out so confidently or so fast had it not been for the uniquely simultaneous appearance of industrial opportunity in the Middle West's settled eastern region.

Light industry in the East

By 1840 in the settled portions of the Old Northwest, in farming villages and at transport junctions along rivers, small craft shops and manufac-

[1]Albert Fishlow, *American Railroads and the Transformation of the Antebellum Economy* (Cambridge, Mass.: Harvard University Press, 1965), Ch. 4.

[2]Some recent research by the geographer John Hudson at Northwestern University shows the lines of settlement, working from county histories out from the distribution in the Census of 1880. According to Hudson's preliminary report to the Social Science History Association's 1986 meetings, internal migrants moved in belts from the East. Upper Minnesota and Wisconsin got Yankees from the St. Lawrence Valley, upper New York, northern New England, and southern Canada. The Massachusetts – central New York zone extended across southern Michigan and Wisconsin and the whole lake shore. Pennsylvania and Maryland accounted for the bulk of settlement across the central plain from Ohio to Iowa. The influence of Southern (Kentucky–West Virginia) migration over the Ohio River was seen nearly halfway up in south–central Ohio, and the southern half of Indiana and Illinois. Across the Mississippi, northern migration with a strong New York/New England component was heavily dominant in Iowa, Kansas, and Nebraska.

tories lay woven in repeating patterns across the regularly ordered lines and tiers of the sections and townships of the agrarian landscape. Along the Miami River up from Cincinnati, in tiny spots along the canals and lower lake shores, where later large cities would grow, slightly denser clusters had appeared. At the great Territory's eastern end, a small scattered charcoal iron production had grown up, and at a few points where the vast Appalachian coal field surfaced in the hills in Ohio, coal was mined.[3] Beginning in 1828, production had risen to two million tons by the end of the Civil War.

With these few and scattered exceptions, the industry of the vast farming area to the Mississippi was light industry, nearly all of it, like the village industry of New England, combining a few tools and materials with some skilled labor and local raw materials – flour milling, saw milling, tanning, shoemaking, butchering and meat packing, brewing and distilling, blacksmithing, harness and carriage making and repair, boat building for the lake and river trade. Where the countryside, and with it the towns, grew a bit more prosperous – a thin prosperity, punctuated by speculative booms and breaks – some complex manufactures and services appeared. Printers, barbers, hotel-keepers, bankers, lawyers, ministers and professors, doctors, dentists, and politicians set up shop. Pianos, saddlery, furniture, china, bricks, farm implements and rudimentary machines, even steam engines for the river boats found facilities and markets.[4]

All such craft activities filled in readily alongside the main business of the small towns, i.e., simply "business" – buying and selling, arranging land transfers, lending and financing the production and movement of the farmers' crops. As settlement spread across to the Mississippi and the canals and railroads gave huge stimulus to agricultural production, the volume of such transactions was multiplied. The easy drift of the corn, barreled pork and beef, and timber southward along the rivers began to turn to the East, for at least the northern two-thirds of the area within reach of a direct rail and water link with the seaboard cities.[5] But this linkage did not immediately stimulate local industry; indeed, it brought in the competitively cheap manufactures of New England, New York, Pennsylvania, and Britain. This, along with the lack of water power, kept local industry scattered and of small scale through the Civil War. Unlike

[3] H. N. Eavenson, *The First Century and a Quarter of the American Coal Industry* (Pittsburgh: published by the author, 1942), especially 155–203, 264–292; for the very early history, see H. N. Eavenson, *The Pittsburgh Coal Bed* (New York: The American Institute of Mining and Metallurgical Engineers, 1938), 6–30.

[4] Clarence Danhof, *Change in Agriculture: The Northern United States, 1820–1870* (Cambridge, Mass.: Harvard University Press, 1969), 1–31.

[5] A. L. Kohlmeier, *The Old Northwest, as Keystone in the Arch of the Federal Union* (Bloomington, Ind.: Principia Press, 1938), Chs. 2–3.

the eastern seaboard, the Old Northwest did not industrialize under the easy guidance of experienced merchants; it had no textile "phase" and no putting-out system. The flatness of the terrain made it a stranger to the water wheel; horse power on the farms, steam power on boats and trains, and steam and manpower in the mills pulled it into the age of electricity and the diesel engine. Flatness, indeed, was the defining feature of the geography – that and the richness of the soil and its ability to sustain high yields in corn and the major North European crops.

Fuel and iron below the Lakes

So matters might have stood throughout the nineteenth century. Chicago would have developed as it had begun, as a rail junction, a point of agricultural processing and agricultural equipment manufacture, and a financial center. Milwaukee, Toledo, and Cleveland would have been simply – as they were in part in any case – the processing points or exit ports for grain and meat. In the absence of the bituminous coals south and southwest of Pittsburgh, the ores of the Mesabi, Marquette, and other ranges along the upper Lakes, and the system of cheap transport which ran between them and among the developing heavy industries, fuel-using, steel-making, steel-using, the midwestern area east of the Mississippi after 1860 would have remained like that to the west, almost entirely a land of farmers, grain merchants, ranchers, meat processors and a rich market for eastern and European manufactures. But by 1860, Pittsburgh, with several secondary smaller sites in southeastern Ohio, had become a significant coal- and iron-producing area. The famous Connellsville seam of coking coal, discovered in the 1840s, came into full exploitation after 1860.[6] The steel inventions of the 1850s and 1860s raised even higher the profits and the expectations. Oil, discovered in a salt well, was taken up by New Haven capitalists who hired "Colonel" Drake to dig the first drilled well in 1859, and the ensuing oil rush around Oil City added to the wealth, the excitement, and the rail net of the area between Pittsburgh and Lake Erie.[7] Already in the 1850s Michigan ore was being brought in by lake and canal shipping; the opening of the iron ranges in the Lake Superior country, one after another to the giant Mesabi deposits in the early 1890s, capped the opportunity.[8] On so rich a resource base, with such ready means of cheap access, it was a simple

---

[6]Peter Temin, *Iron and Steel in Nineteenth Century America, An Economic Inquiry* (Cambridge, Mass.: M.I.T. Press, 1964), 79, 94.

[7]Paul H. Giddens, *The Birth of the Oil Industry* (New York: Macmillan, 1938), 59; Charles D. Martens, *The Oil City* (Oil City, Pa.: First Seneca Bank and Trust Co., 1971), 21–58.

[8]Temin, *Iron and Steel*, 92–93.

matter for the heavy industry complex to unfold out from Pittsburgh from 1880 on, with lake shipping and rail connections to serve both eastern and middle western markets. According to the strictest locational principles, the American steel industry appeared, first, in the coal mining area itself, then between there and the lake shore, then in 1900 just below Lake Michigan, midway between the coal and ore, to serve the markets west and south of Chicago and the Lakes.

Accompanying the development in basic fuels and metals, as early as 1870, machinery and heavy engineering plants grew up to service and supply the mines, the railroads, and one another, as well as the iron and steel mills, creating small cities in the Mahoning and Cuyahoga valleys of northern Ohio between Pittsburgh and Cleveland and along the lower lake shore.[9] At the same time coal, oil, and electricity broke the Middle West's power bottleneck for light industry, and as the population and market thickened and the demand in growing cities multiplied, metal-fabricating plants, machinery, and tools in familiar succession developed in competition to Yankee and British imports. Thus the industrial region below the Lakes by 1900 had become nearly self-sufficient in all except textiles and some specialized equipment, and it had begun to export basic metals and light and heavy manufactures in large volume.

Feedbacks within the industrial matrix

To the historian dissecting a great complex movement in human society, natural opportunity does not mean simply the discovery of lands, lakes, and ores by a population sensitized through its culture to turn them into money. Opportunity consists also in certain necessary physical relationships between one natural substance and another, one natural force and another, such that their incorporation into a complex technology provides reinforcements, scale economies, cheapening of production which adaptations of the existing technology can encompass. The input—output relations among the main industries in the Middle West's developing agro-industrial matrix and the composite effect of certain special natural features of the environment cannot fail to strike the eye. It was cheaper to

[9]Harold J. Williamson and Kenneth H. Myers II, *Designed for Digging* (Evanston, Ill.: Northwestern University Press, 1955), gives an excellent account of one of the largest of these firms, the Bucyrus Erie Company. David R. Meyer's research into the "systems of cities" in the American manufacturing belt has begun to delineate the lines of regional manufacturing growth in the entire Midwest, emphasizing the strong start even before 1860 and pronouncedly in 1860–80. See David Meyer, "Emergence of the American Manufacturing Belt: An Interpretation," *Journal of Historical Geography*, Vol. 9, No. 2 (1983): 145–174, and "Midwestern Industrialization and the American Manufacturing Belt in the Nineteenth Century," *Journal of Economic History*, Vol. 50 (1990).

lay rails across flat land, and shippers had the cumulative advantage of both the flatness of the land and the superior speed of rail transport. The same was true of the adaptation of the reaper-binder to the grain fields. Productivity rose both because the land was flat and easier to farm by any technique and because the farm machinery worked especially easily on such a terrain. In elementary statistics, this is known as an interaction effect and the Midwest's fortunate history is crowded with notable examples. West of Chicago to the Rockies, two of the nineteenth century's great inventions for covering distance – the reaper and the railroad – found as it were, their ecological niche, their natural home.

Grain and meat flowing in large volume from the Great Plains utilized then the railroad's main feature, its large carrying capacity, and avoided its main obstruction, the cost of climbing hills. These features worked differently for the traffic in coal and ore. Minerals, except for oil (and here Pennsylvania oil was the exception to the exception), are usually found in hilly places, though the steepest gradients must often be ascended only on the return haul of empty cars. But the transport features of the industrial minerals have one great advantage over agricultural products: They flow the year round, while the crops present a serious peak load problem which can only be avoided by the strategic location of storage facilities, involving additional off- and on-loading expense. Despite such refinements, the main point is obvious: The railroad finds its natural best use in hauling bulky farm products, preferably over flat lands, and in hauling bulky minerals downhill. Steady prospects of such a trade will permit lines to be built which will then have the capacity to carry the lighter manufactures and passengers, almost as a by-product, at no risk and at rates covering only operating costs.

The railroad furthermore had an almost insatiable appetite for coal as a fuel and for iron in the construction, double tracking, and renewal of lines and rolling stock, as well as in the construction in the cities of great terminals, roundhouses, and storage facilities. And coal fed the industrial furnaces of the "further-working" industries of iron-rolling mills, forges, foundries, and machine shops. In so dense a tangle of inter-industrial linkages and feedbacks, economies of location, agglomeration, and large scale were prominent. Between 1880 and 1910 the Midwest generated a dense industrial district between Pittsburgh and Cleveland and another on the lake shore below and around Chicago. Even the old Cincinnati strip along the Miami River, the agricultural market towns and state capitals, Columbus and Indianapolis, and the smaller cities in the whole belt 150 miles below the Lakes felt the dynamic impulses and responded with an array of specialized manufactures, food processing, and light and heavy machinery. This widespread urbanization in turn made its demands on investment in construction and inter-urban transport. Scale and specialization based on cheap food, cheap minerals and cheap transport grew almost without limit to weld together an area of nearly a million square miles and to cover it with the tools, the artifacts, and the organizational units of a modern financial and industrial economy.

New technology: importation, invention, and adaptation

Obvious scale and locational economies do not exhaust the generosity of nature to the industries of the Middle West. Technology is a social product, like minerals exploration or land settlement, which nevertheless deals with natural facts and forces. Midwestern manufacturers or would-be manufacturers had knowledge of, and access to, a certain body of productive equipment and certain long-known formulae and techniques ready for application in the specific situation of costs and potential markets in which they found themselves. There were a few "basic" inventions developing in Europe, notably in Germany, in these decades, and the transmission of knowledge of them came through many routes – newspapers, technical journals, embodiment in pieces of equipment, visits abroad, and most of all visits and immigration of foreign workers and engineers.

In the realms of chemistry and thermal or electro-dynamics, certain of these inventions created a small Midwest chemicals industry[10]; others could be called "enabling inventions," permitting the mechanical revolutions to unfold. Important for the region's development were the steel inventions of Bessemer, Thomas, Siemens, and Martin, the English developments in the management and generation of electricity, the German research in coal chemistry and – most notably – the internal combustion engine. The American strain of invention at least before 1920 was still mechanical, focusing on devices for utilizing and transmitting energy – whether steam, electricity, or the chemical forces of internal combustion. Native invention in the Middle West was still in large measure the cleverness of tinkerers – a continuation of Yankee contrivance with purely empirical techniques. The state universities as they grew after 1880 set up schools of engineering with many specializations, but here, as in agricultural research, the emphasis was more often on the immediate practical problem and the quick payoff. Immigration, it is said, made employers neglect to train their own skilled workmen,

[10]A doctoral dissertation by Margaret Levenstein, now in progress, has begun to exploit the rich archive of the Dow Chemical Company at Midland, Michigan, on some aspects of this growth beginning in the mid-1890s. The firm, which grew to be second to Dupont in the industry, was based originally on the products derived and processed from a large salt mine. Its expansion was financed almost entirely by Cleveland capitalists with funds derived from the ore, coal, and steel trade.

and the same is true of the task of pursuing technology deep into the underlying structure of knowledge.

But the inventions were numerous, each often forming the basis of a separate firm and manufacture. The crowning achievements were Edison's famous and useful accomplishments setting electricity to work and Henry Ford's "invention" of mass-production techniques in manufacturing the automobile. The latter was, of course, for the Midwest a gigantic renewal of opportunity. Appearing in the rich culture of mechanics both in the Midwest and New England, the American industry became centered by 1910 in Detroit, possibly, it has been suggested, because of the prior development of boat engines there.[11] Like the railroad, it spawned a vast brood of ancillary manufactures, and produced even more cataclysmic social change in the countryside and the suburbs of cities after 1920. Again, it too was ideally suited to the western terrain, and it too consumed quantities of steel. Oil had already been found in western Pennsylvania and scattered across Ohio and Illinois, and the refining techniques were far advanced when the gasoline motor came on the market.

Other developments followed naturally from the development of motorized transport and haulage. In agriculture, first, in flat wheat and corn areas, the horse was abolished, with astonishing factor-saving effects after 1920, derived from the elimination of the acreages of feed grains and cultivated pasture.[12] The development was coincidental with the uncovering of the enormous mid-continental oil field, designed, again, almost as if by God, to fuel the new transport. And the auto's assembly was a sufficiently complicated job that it could yield to the breaking down of the operations along an assembly line, a technique inherited from meat packing and to a degree from the Yankee watch, gun, and shoe manufacture.[13] When the opportunity was perceived by the obsessively narrow village mind of Henry Ford in the first decade of the twentieth century, the rest was history.

[11] I owe this thought to Dennis Smallwood, who looked into the question in a course paper as a graduate student in 1965–66. The same suggestion is made by Abner Greif, now of the Department of Economics at Stanford, in a paper prepared for Professor Joel Mokyr at Northwestern in 1988.

[12] The elimination of hay and oats consumed by farmwork animals added ninety million acres to the land available for food crops and accounts for over half the increase in net farm output between 1920 and 1940. Dale E. Hathaway, *Government and Agriculture* (New York: Macmillan, 1963), 97–98, from data compiled by D. P. Durost and Glen T. Barton, Research Report no. 36, USDA/ARS, 1960, Table 4.

[13] David A. Hounshell, *From the American System to Mass Production, 1800–1932: The Development of Manufacturing Technology in the United States* (Baltimore: Johns Hopkins University Press, 1984), Chs. 1, 6.

II. LABOR POWER IN INDUSTRIAL MARKETS

All these natural opportunities for cheap production in terms of physical cost appeared to Midwest manufacturers operating within a capitalistically organized market structure, clothed, as it were, in the garments of labor and capital costs. Labor, a raw brute human force, was a natural force, too, and the supplies of it and the terms on which it could be made available, along with labor's skills or labor's ability to acquire skills, were essential in transforming fields, mines, and industrial processes into the stream of commodities.

Now labor for industrial occupations in a region derives historically from two lines of descent: earlier industrial laborers, of which the line stretches far back beyond neolithic times, and labor diverted from other occupations, i.e., since agriculture is the almost universal occupation of earlier times, almost wholly from farms. The first of these groups brings with it specific skills and aptitudes acquired as it develops in artisan households and an urban or village setting. But industrial activities were also pursued on American farms, particularly in earlier stages of settlement before specialized workers could find a market dense enough to support their skills. By 1860, agricultural settlement at this stage was virtually completed in the Middle West east of the Mississippi and south of central Wisconsin. Mechanical crafts were widely disseminated in tasks closely allied to the agriculture itself; the railroads had created their own body of machinists and repairmen, and the rapid spread of mechanical harvesting in the 1850s and 1860s acquainted more and more farm boys with machinery. At the same time, the first source of skilled industrial labor – the professionals – millwrights, carriage makers, blacksmiths, carpenters, machinists – coming in from the Northeast or directly from northern Europe, notably Great Britain and Germany, found occupation in the growing market towns and transport junctions of the region. With the growth of agricultural wealth and the appearance of local industrial opportunities for manufactures on the scale of the small factory, the demand for such semi-skilled industrial labor increased, and the supply from both industry and agriculture grew by steady increments.

Within the region, the generation of young men and women growing up on the farms after 1860 faced a particularly difficult choice. The unsettled "frontier" had moved beyond the Mississippi; half the American population indeed already lived to the west of a North–South line passing through western Pennsylvania, and half that western population lived north of the East–West parallel through that same point.[14] Land in

[14]Charles O. Paullin, *Atlas of the Historical Geography of the United States* (Washington, D.C.: Carnegie Institute of Washington, 1932), Plate 80A.

the Old Northwest was still available, especially in the upper and cold states and elsewhere as ranching gave place to grain and grain to a more labor-intensive mixed corn–hog or hay–dairy farming. But the farm population was used to taking up western lands by a series of small leaps – from one tier of counties to the next so that family ties might not be completely broken. Western movement from the long-settled regions to Wisconsin or Minnesota under new conditions of soil and climate and into new patterns of cropping was a more serious leap. The move to the treeless plains from Kansas to the Dakotas, where knowledge of new tools, new seeds, new insects, a new climate had to be acquired, posed obstacles that must have seemed insuperable for many, even the very young. Still, ample supplies of settlers pressed on to take up these lands – and in the 1860s and 1870s the stream was augmented by the great trek of the Scandinavian peoples across the same climatic belt to take up grain farming and dairying in the upper Middle West, while some Czechs, Hungarians, Ukrainians joined the mass of Yankee and southern migrants to the Plains and semi-arid regions. But there remained still a natural increase of the lower Midwest farm population to stay behind and to move at some point – and for many discontented farm youths, very early in their careers – off the farm.[15]

Nearly all these internal migrants were literate in English, knew arithmetic, and had been exposed to the elements of Anglo-Saxon culture in its American version as absorbed in the public rural schoolhouse, the rural church, in evenings in the farmhouse, and at the country store and courthouse. The women had formidable skills of housekeeping and family management, and the men generally knew something of carpentry, construction, animal care, and simple machinery. The move off the farm was generally not far – to a growing village, to the county seat and commercial center, to a job in a warehouse or in apprenticeship in a building or a machinist trade. But Midwest farmers, however hard they worked, however menial and physically demanding many of their tasks, were not simple laborers. The strong entrepreneurial streak, a taste for business, for gambling on land and crops, which might be absorbed as a boy observed his father, was not lost when the boy moved off the farm. He might work at the feed and seed store or take up selling fertilizer or

[15]A careful quantitative study remains to be done to trace the diaspora of this farm youth, particularly after 1870, when the agricultural land of the three lower states of the Old Northwest had become thoroughly settled. The statements here are surmises based on logic and impressionistic examination of census records, farm journals, and the popular literature. Content analysis of the farm press, on the lines of Louis Galambos's efforts on other issues, might yield some results. Louis Galambos, *The Public Image of Big Business in America, 1880–1940* (Baltimore: Johns Hopkins University Press, 1975).

machinery or insurance on commission. Aided a bit by the Morrill Act of 1863, which gave public lands to state colleges for the agricultural and mechanical arts,[16] a certain number of farm youth went on through a secondary education to agricultural colleges, teacher training schools, or even the state university. The culture and its formal institutions provided access to the professions, dentistry, the ministry, the law; the sector servicing agriculture, and so servicing also itself as well, provided employment, and by the 1890s women, from farms or more likely from the first genera tion off the farm, having long since professionalized school teaching, began to enter the clerical occupations.

The move from farm to city in the Midwest was thus not sudden, drastic, or complete. The youth might live at first in rooming houses or with an established relative; soon after marriage it was possible to rent, then to buy from a developer a new house with a bit of land. Women's work was lighter in town than on farms, with more opportunity for social activity, but gardens and home food processing were common. Even in 1900, a substantial number of dairy cattle, pigs, and chickens were urban or village residents. The isolation of the countryside itself was broken a bit by the inter-urban electric cars that spread over the area after 1890;[17] by the 1920s country roads and the Model T had made deep inroads into the sharp separation of rural and urban life.

The supplies of labor – of skills and of labor power – from these traditional sources might have filled to completion the array of labor needs of the Midwest's growing industrial plants. In the earlier industrializations in Europe, factory labor was drawn from the surrounding countryside. Numbers of Irish peasants were brought across the Irish Channel to Liverpool and other British industrial cities,[18] but otherwise the English industrial revolution and its counterparts before the 1840s in North France, Belgium, the Rhine Valley, and New England rested on local and largely rural – though not exclusively farm – labor. But the industrializations after 1850, in the German Ruhr, the American Middle West, and in North Italy, differed from the earlier, more gradual transformations in three respects. First, they did not always have access to a rural industrial work force, already specialized in industrial work. Second, a significant part of the work required was heavy work, "sheer" labor power – digging, lift-

[16]E. D. Eddy, *Colleges for Our Land and Time* (New York: Harper and Brothers, 1957), Chs. 4–5.

[17]George W. Hilton and John F. Due, *The Electric Interurban Railways in America* (Stanford: Stanford University Press, 1960).

[18]Jeffrey Williamson's recent article, "The Impact of the Irish on British Labor Markets," *Journal of Economic History*, Vol. 44, No. 3 (September 1986): 693–720, contains an interesting new treatment of the role of the Irish migrants in the English Industrial Revolution.

ing, pushing, handling coal, metals, and heavy machines. It was no more strenuous than farm work, but it was not the work of an auxiliary labor force. Third, the demand seemed to come all in a rush.[19] It was a demand for the heavy work of initial capital formation, for building rail lines, erecting heavy equipment, extending mines, creating canals and docks. North Italy drew on South Italy for this labor; the Ruhr drew on East Prussia and Poland. These were not tasks for farmer-businessmen accustomed to machines and generous supplies of horsepower, but for a laboring peasantry inured to a life of heavy toil.

Earlier in New York and Ohio, when canals and rail lines were to be built, some local labor appeared along the routes, but the bulk of the digging and hauling was done by teams of Irish migrants who followed the line. Now the building of plants and cities south of the Great Lakes gave rise to a similar burst of demand. After 1915, such demands, and demands for factory operatives as well, were supplied to the Midwest by the southern hills. With the shut-off of immigration particularly from eastern and southern Europe by the Act of 1923, these were the only sources of supply. But southern farm labor became unstuck only during World War I; before that, uncertainties as to its reception in the North and the immobilizing forces of ignorance, poverty, and fear in the South inhibited such mobility. Swelling rural populations in Europe had already created the push for the rural migration of Germans and Scandinavians and the rural–urban migration of Irish to the Northeast, and later of central and eastern Europeans and Italians. By the mid-1880s the forces of expulsion from eastern Europe and the suction of industrial job opportunities in the American Midwest tilted the balance, and the streams of laboring men from Slovakia, Poland, the Baltic provinces began to arrive.[20] As in the East Coast cities, the migrations had a cumulative qual-

[19]Alexander Gerschenkron, *Economic Backwardness in Historical Perspective* (New York: Praeger, 1962), 5–52, 353–367.
[20]The literature on immigration does not seem to give much detailed help on the matter. It appears that the labor force before 1895, if not off the farms, was English speaking with an admixture of Germans, especially in skilled categories, and some Italian labor. Critical to the process in its earlier phase was the arrival of many Scandinavian immigrants to the ore-mining regions of Lake Superior from the 1870s on. Michael G. Karni, Matti E. Kamps, and Douglas J. Olliln, Jr., *The Finnish Experience in the Western Great Lakes Regions: New Perspectives* (Turku, Finland: Institute for Migration, 1975), 55–69, by M. E. Kamps. In the Mesabi range towns in 1905, foreign born constituted 55.4 percent of the population, mostly Finns, Italians, and central Europeans. William B. Gates, *Michigan Copper and Boston Dollars* (Cambridge, Mass.: Harvard University Press, 1951), 95–109, gives interesting figures for the Michigan copper area far to the north after 1845. In the Pittsburgh and western Pennsylvania area generally, with its immense expansion, the "new" migration began earlier. The great study of Simon Kuznets, Dorothy Thomas, et al., *Population Redistribution and Economic*

ity. Once an ethnic group had gained a beachhead in a section of Buffalo, Pittsburgh, Cleveland, Detroit, Chicago, news traveling back through intimate channels attracted more migrants from the same region, often from the same village or town. The reverse flow of earnings to finance the voyage for others became a visible factor in some small nations' balance of payments. And the presence of countrymen, in a community, with church and social circles established, vastly reduced the appearance of risk and strangeness which was for non-English-speaking nationalities the greatest barrier. The movement was rapid and immense. By 1910, the foreign-born constituted 27 percent of the Midwest's population in cities of over 100,000.[21]

The Midwest thus acquired an urban industrial population layered much as in the cities of the Northwest. The important fact in both cases was that by the time the immigrants arrived, the region had already established the institutional frame, the behavioral characteristics, the fundamental values of the Northwest European business culture. The new arrivals were not "settlers" taking up land, trades, and offices, recreating a variant on the societies of Pennsylvania, New York, and New England.[22] That had already been done; indeed, a bloody Civil War had been fought

Growth, United States, 1890–1950, Vols. 1–3 (Philadelphia: American Philosophical Society, 1957–64), bases estimates by state for net migration in intercensal intervals from estimates of birth and death rates and natural increase of native and foreign born compared to census totals. The relevant tables show that the in-migration of foreign-born white males, decade totals (in hundreds), are:

	1870–80	1880–90	1890–1900	1900–10	1910–20
Ohio	414	711	541	1,479	1,087
Indiana	128	158	181	381	124
Illinois	639	1,760	1,413	2,392	1,014
Michigan	781	1,027	439	902	1,434

Kuznets and Thomas, Vol. 1. (1957), Table P-1.

[21]This statistic is based on the data concerning the population and the number of white foreign-born residents in cities of more than 100,000 population. Bureau of the Census, *Thirteenth Census of the United States, 1910,* Abstract (Washington, D.C.: Government Printing Office, 1913), 95. The cities included for this purpose were those of the West North Central and East North Central regions with the addition of Pittsburgh.

[22]Disquiet about the effect of the "new" immigration on the fertility of the "native" (i.e., North European) stock and on the cultural institutions and spirit already created was expressed by two great authorities: Francis A. Walker in 1891 and John R. Commons in 1907, quoting Walker. Francis A. Walker, "Immigration and Degradation," *The Forum,* Vol. 2 (1891), 634–643, reprinted in D. R. Dewey, ed., *Discussions in Economics and Statistics,* 2 vols. (New York: Henry Holt, 1899), Vol. 1, 417–426, 429–448. John R. Commons, *Races and Immigrants in America* (New York: Macmillan, 1907), especially Ch. 9, 198–238.

in defense of that culture's existence and in assertion of its right to dominate the national economy across the continent. The new ethnic groups
were splintered, too, among themselves, even where as a group they constituted a majority, but within each, certain family and social structures
became evident. Language, religion, church schools, endogamy, and the
settlement in neighborhoods gave them an integrity even as from one
generation to the next their wealth and the variety of their occupations
increased. They furnished labor power, working long hours at as low a
wage as the market required, and their net effect was to advance the
industrialization perhaps several decades beyond the rate which the native
population could have sustained. The cultural difficulties of their assimilation which might have encouraged their unionization in fact delayed it
until the social and economic revolution of the period 1933–45.

III. CAPITAL: REAL AND FINANCIAL

In midwestern agriculture, the growth of capital had been a laborious
process; land clearing, fencing, stump pulling, road construction required
in a region a generation of back-breaking toil, and implements were not
much improved in the nineteenth century to hurry the process along.[23]
This was only slightly less true for the industrial crafts before 1850, when
the fashioning of tools and primitive machinery required much hand
labor and skill. The eighteenth-century tools, largely hand made and
hand operated, were a precious heritage passed on from father to son.
Power – first, foot power, then water power, then after 1880 the gas
engine and electric motor – changed all that. Tools could be made by
powered tools, and when worn out, they could be readily replaced. These
possibilities were apparent by 1820 in New England and outside Philadelphia and later above Cincinnati and below Cleveland. They met their
supreme demonstration after 1900 as the automobile industry grew up
outside Detroit.[24] The area became alive with machine shops, to produce

[23]Martin L. Primack, "Land Clearing Under Nineteenth Century Conditions:
Some Preliminary Calculations," *Journal of Economic History*, Vol. 22 (December 1962): 484–497.

[24]The financing for the large car assembly enterprises—Ford, Dodge, Chevrolet,
Olds, and all the rest—was a notorious case of a shoestring operation in every
instance. Just as in the southern textile mills in the 1880s, machinery and parts
suppliers, dealers, small local bank loans, the personal funds of partners and
family stockholders bridged the gap until the huge profits became realized for
reinvestment. See Lawrence H. Seltzer, *A Financial History of the Automobile
Industry* (Boston: Houghton Mifflin, 1928). Research by Levenstein into the
archives of the Dow Chemical Company at Midland, Michigan, tells a similar
story. In this case, the "original accumulation" came from Cleveland capitalists,
with surplus funds from the lake trade in ore and coal.

not only parts to be fed into the assembly lines, but machinery to make the parts.

With the reductions in costs and improvement in qualities of the heavy metals, there was a fall in the cost of machine tools.[25] The impact of cheaper and better iron and steel was then felt doubly in the machinery products – mining and railroad machinery, typewriters, presses, boats, bridges, and urban buildings. A steady and reinforced fall occurred then in the real costs of capital equipment. It was this beneficial spiral, and not simply the various ingenious inventions of financial instruments that stood at the heart of the Midwest industry's real capital formation.

The channels of local finance

In a capitalist economy, capital – the produced means of production – leads a complicated and curious life. It must indeed be "financed," which means that before it is produced, or perhaps it is more accurate to say "while it is being produced," someone must pay for it. This is in itself a fact of nature – as true in a socialist economy as in a capitalist one. It occurs because trade and production take time, and during that time, workers must be fed and materials and equipment must be accumulated and uti-lized. The unique feature of a capitalist economy is that this function – the provision of resources or of the money that will buy resources – is divided among three agencies:

(1) Private individuals, who may simply lend resources (e.g., land from father to son) or who may spend their own accumulated resources, whether a farmer sowing seed or a household or business firm drawing on previous savings in current use;
(2) A banking system that can make loans paid out by notes or as checks on the borrowers' accounts;
(3) The state, which coins or prints moneys of its own and inserts them into the streams of exchanges in the private economy, on terms set by the system of prices created there.

[25]To explore this hypothesis world, of course, require an extensive research into the evolution of the industrial price structure from 1870 to 1914. I have made at this time only one back-of-the envelope calculation drawn from the series for steel rails, divided by the commodity price index as given in the Census's *Historical Statistics* (Series E130; E2, E40). Though the real price of rails varied over the period, the trend was clearly downward, as an index of the real prices for the five years at each end of the series attests:

1867 = 100.0	1871 = 77.0	1911 = 28.9
1868 = 97.9	1909 = 27.7	1912 = 27.1
1869 = 85.5	1910 = 26.6	1913 = 26.8
1870 = 77.2		

In trade and light manufacturing, it was the second of these three sources of finance – bank-created credit, based on private debt – which was the most important.[26] A new region desperately needed something to use as money to replace the inconveniences and clumsiness of barter trade. Supplying that need could permit wealth to grow and production to increase, so that a price level and the liquid means for saving and investment spending could form. The money so created did not inflate prices; it established them, being absorbed in the balances that individuals, stores, small firms held to conduct daily transactions and to even out receipts and expenses over a week or a month. Charge accounts (book credit) furnished not only by merchants, but also by manufacturers who sold to jobbers on consignment, helped to bridge the gap between purchase and sale. In these circuits of credit, the role of banks was the traditional one, to "discount," i.e., buy in exchange for bank notes merchants' or manufacturers' own notes at less than their face value, turning them in effect into money that could more readily pass from hand to hand and firm to firm.

Before the National Banking Act of 1863, banks chartered by the states created circulating medium, or rather a collection of circulating media, each set of notes valid at face value over a fifty- to hundred- mile radius, then exchanging themselves at central points at varying rates of discount like foreign currencies in wider trade. The time and trouble of collecting funds at a distance, and even more, the imperfect knowledge of a distant bank's portfolio, created costs and risks that the users of the system had to bear. The individual states chartered banks as stock corporations, either individually, or under the so-called free banking acts of the 1850s, and rules and safeguards erected were supposed to be enforced by state

[26]The role of banks in the development before 1860 is realistically discussed in Donald R. Adams, Jr., "The Role of Banks in the Economic Development of the Old Northwest," in D. C. Klingaman and R. K. Vedder, *Essays in Nineteenth Century Economic History* (Athens: Ohio University Press, 1975), Ch. 9, 208, 246. A companion study for the postbellum period is offered in Gene Smiley, "Postbellum Banking and Financial Markets in the Old Northwest," in Vedder, *Essays*, Ch. 9, 187–224, containing good summaries of the controversies about the national capital market in the recent literature. See also Richard E. Sylla, *The American Capital Market, 1846–1914* (New York: Arno Press, 1975). The whole period for the midwestern states has been re-examined, with use of extensive quantitative data, by Hugh Rockoff, "The Free Banking Era, a Reexamination," *Journal of Money, Credit, and Finance*, Vol. 6 (May 1974), 141–167, and more recently in an informative article by A. J. Rolnick and W. E. Weber, "New Evidence on the Free Banking Era," *American Economic Review*, Vol. 73 (December 1983): 1080–1091. Both studies indicate that the state-chartered and "free" systems worked with much less loss and inconvenience than earlier studies, based only on stories of "wildcat" banks and frauds, had concluded.

inspectors.[27] But in the antebellum period, where the state government itself was so often looked on as the object, rather than as the policeman, of private promotional schemes,[28] these rules in many cases must simply have kept out competitors to the insiders who controlled their enforcement. Purely private banks, partnerships, or individuals, or companies accumulating cash reserves in the course of some other business, served too as a source of credit and on a few occasions appeared to have held deposits and issued notes.[29]

This confused tangle was only partly set straight by the National Banking Act of 1863.[30] That system did indeed set up a uniform system of

[27]Bank balance sheets available in the works on the period uniformly show deposits to be a small percentage of total liabilities. See, for example, Fred D. Merritt, *The Early History of Banking in Iowa* (Iowa City: University Press, 1900), with balance sheets from different points in the checkered history of the Miners' Bank of Dubuque, 21, 25–26, 27–28, 41, 50, 52, 69. Although there is great doubt the full authorization of capital stock was ever paid in, the balance sheets show that at no time did deposits exceed 8 percent of the bank's liabilities. Charles C. Huntington, *A History of Banking and Currency in Ohio Before the Civil War* (Columbus: F. J. Heer, 1915) contains some aggregate data and balance sheets for antebellum Ohio; see 76, 81, 160, 163, 179, 204, 276–282, 289–290.

[28]The Illinois bank incorporation law of 1851 was based on the New York incorporation law requiring banks to deposit with the state auditor national or state bonds as a backing for their notes. A bank could be forced into liquidation if it failed to redeem its notes. The bill did not rid the state of illegal paper issues as intended; the newly incorporated banks continued to fight in the courts the unchartered institutions which issued currency. The original incorporation law was supplemented in 1853 to provide a heavy penalty for illegal note issue and, due to the cooperation of the Board of Brokers of New York City, proved largely effective. Notes from Georgia and other states became an important part of the circulating medium after this time – largely through the efforts of Chicago firms which had set up the banks for this purpose. The Illinois banks made concerted efforts to force these institutions into liquidation by presenting their notes for redemption. George W. Dowrie, *The Development of Banking in Illinois, 1817–1863* (Urbana: University of Illinois, 1913), 135–142, 146.

[29]To finance their operations in the winter, Burrows and Pettyman, an Iowa flour mill and pork packing company, issued checks payable in the spring when they could ship their goods south to market. These checks, as well as the notes of other Iowa firms, circulated as currency. Erling A. Erickson, *Banking in Frontier Iowa, 1836–1865* (Ames: Iowa State University Press, 1971), 71–73. From May 1837 until its voluntary liquidation, the Chicago Marine and Fire Insurance Company, along with many unincorporated Illinois firms, made loans and received deposits despite the prohibitions in the corporation's charter. Its deposit certificates circulated as currency. The Wisconsin Marine and Fire Insurance Company was modeled after the Chicago company, issuing notes, called "George Smith's money," from its incorporation in 1841 until the legislature forced them out of circulation in 1852. George W. Dowrie, *The Development of Banking in Illinois, 1817–1865* (Urbana: University of Illinois, 1913), 129–131.

[30]On the National Banking Act, see Davis R. Dewey, *Financial History of the United States*, 12th ed. (New York: Longmans, Green and Co., 1936), 326–328;

banks chartered by the federal government on uniform terms and inspected by the office of the Comptroller of the Currency. The state bank notes were put out of business by a 10 percent tax and disappeared from circulation, but the state-chartered banks continued their lending activities nonetheless, dealing in the notes of the federal banks and of the federal government, and supporting a large volume of deposits drawn on by check. The role of the federal government, of specie reserves, and the international capital movements coming to the Midwest through New York become more evident, but perhaps less important, as the nineteenth century goes on.

The financial problems of the large construction projects and of heavy and expensive manufacturing were of quite a different character from those of trade and light manufactures. In the latter, wages and advance payment for goods in transit or in inventory constituted the main credit needs. Such debt tended to be self-liquidating in the sense that the real capital – an inventory plus the value added by manufacture – once acquired, was turned into cash as the goods were sold and the proceeds used in the next cycle of replenishment. In the face of the vastly growing body of such trade, the annual increment of such needs was nevertheless very substantial. On the other hand, the large construction projects – canals, harbor improvement, and, of course, notably the railroad – could depend only to a very limited degree on such small-scale sources of finance. This need was not always so large-scale and immediate as one might suppose. Even a canal or a river improvement could be effected a small part at a time and, provided it led somewhere, could begin to accumulate revenues. The same was true of the railroads before 1850 and of the numerous improvements and extensions of the railroads – double tracking and spur lines – throughout the entire period. But the Midwest, lying between the Alleghenies and the Rockies, offered scope for transportation projects conceived as systems, joining points several hundred and (in the case of the transcontinentals) several thousand miles apart.[31] Something of the

Paul Studenski and Herman E. Krooss, *Financial History of the United States* (New York: McGraw-Hill, 1963), 154–155. See also Eugene R. White, *The Regulation and Reform of the American Banking System, 1900–1929* (Princeton: Princeton University Press, 1983).

[31] The following passages from the classic survey by William Z. Ripley, *Railroads: Finance and Organization* (London: Longmans, Green, and Co., 1915), 10–11, give the flavor of the history as it appeared to the leading railroad economist-historian of the 1920s: "The first railways in the United States were built from the proceeds of subscriptions to capital stock. . . . Even as late as 1868, after new styles in railroad finance had come into vogue, the capital stock of the railways of Ohio considerably exceeded in amount the aggregate of their outstanding bonds. But no sooner did construction begin to extend into undeveloped territory than a new situation arose. . . . [S]uch enterprises, instead of being solid investments appealing to a substantial local constituency, were essentially specula-

same is true on a miniature scale of the electric car lines that became popular in the region between 1890 and 1930, the street railways and other municipal public works. In all such semi-public projects, the instrument for raising money was not a bank loan but a bond, and though banks might "underwrite" such issues and furnish the notes or deposits by which the amounts were transferred, they were not, as in Europe, active, but passive instruments of the development. The basis of the "security" was the expectations of the promoters, supported by the taxing power of the community in the case of public issues and, for the land grant railroads, the expected revenues from land sales and the subsequent operation.[32]

The creation of large industrial plants was similarly distanced from dependence on a commercial banking system. The pattern clearly for small- and middle-sized manufacturers must have been to grow through the reinvestment of profits, at least till the 1890s, when whole industries became ripe for "reorganization." Here (perhaps partly the result of the Sherman Antitrust Act of 1890) the enterprise of bankers could intervene to float new issues of stock and bonds, based on expectations of profits from the consolidated firm.[33] This was notable also in the case of public

tive. However great might be the local interest, most of the funds, except the land, must be obtained from remote capitalists in the eastern states or in Europe."

After the main lines were built, a railroad's construction company would raise funds, often locally, for branch lines. Ripley, op. cit., 14. Often an extension was organized as a separate company, the form of organization conditioned on the financial strength of the parent road. The parent company frequently backed the bonds of the local road. Ripley continues, "Many independent short roads and feeders, particularly in prosperous communities like Wisconsin, have been constructed by local enterprise and credit through the activity of farmers, thus seeking an outlet to markets. The right of way costs little; the labor is contributed by the subscribers; and the first light construction is financed by local borrowing. Be the enterprise a little more ambitious or, as in the Southeast, local funds less ample, the aid of city bankers may be necessary. These bankers contribute funds, such as possibly $8,000 per mile in bonds, having as equity the labor and right of way put into the property prior to the loan." (Ripley, 32, 33)

For the development and financing of the extensive inter-urban electric rail systems, see George W. Hilton and John F. Due, *The Electric Interurban Railways in America* (Stanford: Stanford University Press, 1960), Chs. 1, 6.

[32]Increasingly after the 1870s, bonds were sold to banking syndicates for a commission. "Anticipated profits from speculation in land along the proposed right of way were an important inducement to the construction of railroads in the early days. . . . It is indubitable that without the profits from land sales, the construction of railroads would have been greatly delayed in the early days" (Ripley, op. cit., 18–19, 135). Paul W. Gates, *The Illinois Central Railroad and Its Colonization Work* (Cambridge, Mass.: Harvard University Press, 1934), 26–27, Ch. 4.

[33]Gene Smiley, "Postbellum Banking and Financial Markets in the Old Northwest," in D. C. Klingman and R. K. Vedder, *Essays on the Economy of the Old*

utilities in the late 1920s.[34] But the earlier constructions were not carried out under such ambitious aegis, and the banks' role was very likely to provide loans against such securities so that the development was not held up by a shortage of liquid funds.

The situation was not much different with the financing of agriculture. To one acquainted only with a sophisticated industrial and commercial system, the volume of farm capital formation created by farm labor, and so in a sense self-financed, is truly astonishing. Beyond the Alleghenies, 15 to 20 percent of the farm labor force alone was used in the 1850s in clearing land, and the "saving" that matched such investment was simply the withdrawal of time from other farm tasks or from "leisure."[35] The motive, after the first essential constructions and clearing, was to increase the value of the family's assets, and this way of looking at the farm, as an asset to grow in value over the years, accounts for farmers' willingness to acquire mortgage debt. The financing of land holding and land transfer created indeed a body of debt which was no part of real capital formation but formed the raw material for speculation and an involuted financial structure. Fortunately, agriculture did not depend on the outside economy to provide for the larger part of the mortgage loans. As late as 1920 as much as 70 percent of the farm mortgage debt was held by farmers – mostly parents who had transferred land within the family under such an arrangement – or derived from loans by local rural moneylenders.[36] The "pressure" of this debt did not do much to improve efficiency on farms, except to finance the landholding, which kept up farmers' hopes, and to raise land prices, even during periods of falling commodity prices. But its mode of financing removed pressures and opportunities that might have been encountered in the industrial credit system at large.

Northwest (Athens: Ohio University Press, 1987), Ch. 9, 192. Vincent P. Carosso, *Investment Banking in America* (Cambridge: Harvard University Press, 1970), Ch. 2.

[34]M. L. Ramsay, *Pyramids of Power: The Story of Roosevelt, Insull and the Utility Wars* (Indianapolis and New York: Bobbs-Merrill Company, 1937), 14, 47–49, Chs. 6, 7, 11.

[35]Primack, "Land Clearing . . . ," 492.

[36]Alvin S. Tostlebe, *Capital in Agriculture: Its Formation and Financing Since 1870* (Princeton: Princeton University Press, 1957), Chart 15, 155. See the excellent detailed discussion of tenancy as a stage in the "ladder" to full ownership in Allan G. Bogue, *From Prairie to Corn Belt* (Chicago: University of Chicago Press, 1963), and of mortgaging in Ch. 9, 171–181. While taking due note of the importance of eastern money-lenders and of the life insurance companies after 1860, Bogue cites studies of Illinois and Iowa in which "more than half the funds loaned on farm security came from within the state concerned." He points out that the outside funds injected new money into the region (though draining it out later in the form of interest and principal repayments), while the local finance often came from a seller who was willing to receive the sales price in installments.

For the other part of farm credit, the medium-term livestock loans and the annual production credits for covering expenses and moving crops, dependence was on the commercial banks, as in the case of all mercantile trade. Only indirectly is this problem, the most politically explosive in American financial history, related to industrialization. It is enough here to say that the farmers could never get out from under it. In the South it was the basis of the crop lien system, and there and in the Midwest it was one of the bases of Populism. And at the other end of the credit ladder was the financing of the holding of the marketed crop, which had been harvested over a few weeks, during the entire year of consumption. By and large, farmers got paid early in the chain. Dealers could hold warehouse or elevator receipts which they could discount at a bank, and ultimately titles to the crop could be traded in the grain pits in Chicago to serve as the basis of an immense speculation.[37] At some point such trading served no productive purpose but carried on a life of its own. The separation of finance from production, like the separation of sex from procreation, allowed it to become an activity carried out for its own sake. Indulged in in moderation, it improved the functioning of markets, but indulged in excess, its effects were destabilizing, disruptive, and depressive.

The relation to specie and the East

What has been said up to this point concerns largely the financial requirements of the several sectors of the Midwest's growing economy, and the presence of natural surpluses derived from that growth to supply the "savings" for them, under the assumption of a very simple, independent system of finance. Such a procedure has the advantage of emphasizing the indigenous quality of the growth and even of the investment once the soils and minerals were uncovered, the techniques borrowed or invented, and the production units organized within markets, with access to labor supplies and with the prevalence of a mixture of recklessness and caution among businessmen.

But just as immigrant labor, imported equipment, and export markets were to be found through the connection to the East and to Europe, so also the formidable system of financial arrangements organized from London by way of New York to make loans, supplied an internationally valid money and collected interest and dividends as the development paid off. If we had enough evidence on the actual size of these flows, it would be interesting to consider how the development would have proceeded had they not been available. The midwestern banking and credit system

[37]Jeffrey Williams, *The Economic Functions of Futures Markets* (Cambridge: Cambridge University Press, 1966), 18–19, 58, and his Yale Ph.D. dissertation (1985) of the same title, 88–100, 119–122.

was laced with gold from the very start through its use for bank reserves and to settle transactions between distant places.

Before the Civil War, the western banks were restricted in the volume and types of loans by state laws, but even more by prudence, so as to maintain "convertibility" of their notes. By the Act of 1862, the national banks kept holdings of government bonds as security for their issues, but except for the wartime issue of irredeemable paper currency (the greenbacks), these were convertible or redeemable in coined gold and silver at stated ratios.[38] Irredeemable bonds issued by the Civil War government had to be sold at a discount. To be sure the ultimate basis for confidence in a bank was the soundness of its investments, or in a government, its taxing power. But gold acted as the symbol and pledge of financial solvency, and bank reserves of the order of 15 to 30 percent against notes and deposits were universal.[39] The international and eastern system did not provide the savings for Midwest industrialization or agricultural investment, except for some mining and cattle-raising ventures at the outset, and to an appreciable degree through the purchase of canal and railroad bonds. Those early investments were important, and the capital market served as the channel. But steadily as the Midwest grew, it exhibited a growing volume of credit exchanges with the East and with England.[40] The net of that balance affected the availability of bank reserves in the area. Loans came in and returns and repayment went out, and as the Midwest added to its food exports a large measure of self-sufficiency in manufactures, the role of real capital imports greatly diminished, but the financial flows continued on.

The link with the international and national economy through specie shipments and capital flows had complex effects, however, of prime importance on the regional growth. First and foremost, it connected the course and level of prices to the economy of the internationally trading world. The whole price level rose and fell on the rhythms of bank credit and contraction, and on these fluctuations, sometimes analyzed as cycles

[38]Bruce Phelps, *A Finance Approach to Convertible Money Regimes: A New Interpretation of the Greenback Era* (Ph.D. dissertation, Yale University, 1985), 83–84, 92, 111, 113.

[39]For the period 1820–58, the reserve ratio of the banking system fluctuated between a low of 14 percent in 1856 and a high of 35 percent in 1843. Peter Temin, *The Jacksonian Economy* (New York: W. W. Norton, 1969), 71 (Table 3.3), 159 (Table 5.2).

[40]Harry H. Pierce, "Foreign Investment in American Enterprise," with comments and discussion in David T. Gilchrist and W. David Lewis, eds., *Economic Change in the Civil War Era* (Greenville, Del.: Eleutherian Mills–Hagley Foundation, 1965), 41–61. Gene Smiley, "Postbellum Banking and Financial Markets in the Old Northwest," in D. C. Klingaman and R. K. Vedder, *Essays on the Economy of the Old Northwest* (Athens: Ohio University Press, 1987), Ch. 9, Sec. 5.

of three, ten, twenty, and forty years, producers' calculations and expectations were hinged. Whether this hastened or hindered the growth of investment, clear-sighted economic analysts may be able to say. Those who made the most out of these fluctuations were those who, like Andrew Carnegie, were able to remain independent of the capital market and expand when investment was cheap.[41] To do that, they required a confidence in the trend that overrode the ups and downs.

Now in the Midwest's great secular growth, physical productivity did not, of course, rise proportionately in all sectors and occupations. Nor did relative prices all change with changes in relative costs and relative demand. In two striking cases, farm prices and the price of labor, the machinery seemed to work in such a way as to outrage many contemporaries' sense of justice, but to be in retrospect nonetheless unusually favorable to industrial investment. Farm incomes surely would not have benefited by isolation from the export market; without it, food to the cities would have been even cheaper. But prices of manufactures were protected to a degree by the Republican policy of a high tariff, especially when sustained behind the tariff through industrial combinations. Whatever effect this had on the terms of trade between the sectors, it was compounded by the greater inflexibility of farm supply adjustments. The matter is still unsettled, but there appeared at the time to be pressure on agriculture's share in the period of falling prices which dominated the 1870s and 1890s.[42] The same phenomenon has been alleged in different guise in the market for labor where immigration should, it would seem, have persistently undercut the possibility of wage rises commensurate with productivity growth. On balance, the connection to world prices may have put a squeeze on farmers, which both kept food cheap and pushed some population off the farms and, combined with free immigration, shifted a certain portion of the productivity gains in manufacturing from wages into profits. But though those were the phenomena that caused most attention at the time, the result was not restrictive of economic expansion. The capital market with its many devices kept credit cheap to businessmen and encouraged investment. This meant that the general price level did not fall in proportion to long-term productivity gains. Through complex sets of waves, and many sharp peaks and troughs, it came out at the end of the whole period 1820–1910 showing little trend in the face of a continuously growing volume of output and transactions. Such stability meant that a portion, but not all, of the productivity gains – at least after 1900 – did go to farmers and workers

[41]Jonathan Hughes, *The Vital Few* (Boston: Houghton Mifflin, 1966), Ch. 6; Joseph F. Wall, *Andrew Carnegie* (New York: Oxford University Press, 1970).
[42]Douglass C. North, *Growth and Welfare in the American Past* (Englewood Cliffs, N.J.: Prentice-Hall, 1966), Ch. 11, esp. 145–148.

in the form of higher money incomes. And that, too, was necessary to create a growing purchasing power to match the growing output.

The Midwest's industrial credit system thus walked a knife edge between an excessive stringency, locked to the supplies of gold and rigid rules of the gold standard, which would have kept prices low but interest rates high, and an excessive inflationary leniency which would have choked off mass demand through higher prices. These are matters that take the discussion into the economic rules and practices of the world economy at the time of the Midwest's growth and into political issues – the tariff and the gold standard – that featured in platforms of the two political parties at the time. The important fact here is that the connection to world markets did not destroy the region's growth potential even if it may not have done much to help it along. The "natural" sources of savings and investable funds in the region were ample and, given a moderate supply of money, could be turned into real investment.

An ideal credit system may be said to be like a river: "though deep, yet clear, though gentle, yet not dull; strong without rage, without o'erflowing, full." Such a supply the Midwest had, and through the devices of the tariff and open immigration, its political leaders could allow relative price distortions to occur, with accompanying accumulation of profits, without carrying the game so far as to kill the goose that laid the golden eggs.

Money and federal mercantilism

An historical approach to money and credit takes them as folk customs, developing of their own motion for the convenience of merchants, and then for all others who hold natural surpluses that they wish to exchange. Rules were evolved in the world community, standards set, an ethic of faith and trust elaborated and objectified and symbolized by gold. So powerful a current was the world's stream of money that the strongest states, beginning in the sixteenth century, were not able to set themselves against it. To create a money was, next to an army, the most spectacular achievement of a national state. It could ordain a currency unit, coin metals with the impression of the head of the prince, and could in such units pay soldiers and collect taxes. The royal household, like any self-sufficient unit, could live within its own self-confirming structure of money and prices. Since it had a monopoly of the courts of justice and put its armed force at their disposal for settling disputes and enforcing obligations, it could create the doctrine of legal tender and make available its police services only to such moneys as conformed. But as we have seen for the economy of the Midwest, the game was up once a bank sought to go beyond the limits of its own exchanges, or the state, beyond its own power. To enter the markets of the world, even the kings of France or

Spain had to trade, to adopt merchants' standards, pay merchants' prices, and use the merchants' metals at merchants' rates.

In the end, governments were left with the largely accounting function of naming a currency unit and defining it in terms of metal, so that prices formed around it in response to its trading value. The monetary history of the United States is a history of efforts to gain the advantages to the state of a connection with world markets, notably in the ability to borrow during wars, while retaining some degree of independence of policy. In the pre-Jacksonian period, through the Banks of the United States, the federal government was largely responsible for the spread of the uniform gold-based system of reserves and convertibility. Following the National Banking Act of 1862, the Civil War government married itself to the system, though by substituting bonds for gold as a reserve it did get some accommodation to its needs. The issue of greenbacks by the federal Treasury under the Ohioan, Salmon P. Chase, too, was an expression of independence, almost of defiance of the money market.[43] And by the same token, the agonized and early resumption of specie payments brought the system back under the influence of the supplies of the precious metals. So strong was this current that even the government's efforts under strong populist pressures to monetize silver in the 1890s could not swim against Gresham's law. The credit system's only defense against the dominance of gold was its ability to economize on reserves through the invention of financial intermediaries in great profusion. These, however, did not really bypass the banking system, but tailored its varieties and forms of instruments – stocks, bonds, investment banks, life insurance companies, savings banks, etc. – to the demands for convenient forms that an economy of growing wealth was able to afford.

In the course of the Midwest's growth, then, natural surpluses of labor and commodities appeared, and the system of money and credit called capitalist was able to place these at the disposal of those who could use them while carrying on production over a cycle of crops and manufactures and while constructing public works and private plants and equipment that accomplished production with more effectiveness and less waste. An intensely time-conscious production system was made possible and, once possible, became compulsory on the individual and the firm. The connection to the world money flows and the controls and rules of the federal government by and large facilitated this regional achievement, though those connections were not an unmitigated help. Most crucial was the ability of what was called the region's business interests to domi-

---

[43]Wesley C. Mitchell, *A History of the Greenbacks* (Chicago: University of Chicago Press, 1903). For the National Banking System as a means of war finance, see 37, 44–46, 103, 109. For the first legal-tender act and bankers' objections to this expedient, see Ch. 2.

nate the mercantilist policies of the federal government, particularly so as to isolate a growing manufacturing from the European competition and to keep labor flows going through Ellis Island. From this view, the Republican Party and its programs were an essential ingredient in the Midwest business culture.

IV. INDUSTRIAL AND MARKET ORGANIZATION

In the world's industrial regions, economies of scale appeared at many points in the organization after 1870. In some branches of production, the economies were external to the individual firm and so offered no problem to the growth of a competitive economy. In agriculture, for example, the productivity advantage to the Midwest of the huge volume of its production – the falling costs in cheap storage, transport, handling and processing facilities, and its input industries, especially machinery – was notable. But in individual plants, too, economies of scale and systematic operation also appeared, and in the organization of such industries – transportation, smelting, continuous processing and assembly – the large corporation made its appearance. Whether cost advantages alone made such economic monsters able to outcompete their smaller rivals, or whether they made their way in the world like village bullies, by threats and shows of market power, they became a fact, and established themselves by 1900 in many major industries, not only in railroads, where their cost advantages were obvious, but also in steel, meat packing, farm machinery, oil refining, and within a decade of 1900, automobiles. Many industries where large firms offered no special advantages came to be organized in unstable, and after 1890, occasionally illegal, producer combinations – the "trusts" and monopolies on regional or national scale.[44]

Large plants and large firms faced a serious and novel problem of internal organization. The family farm had had the problem of control of

[44]A recent, and most judicious, re-examination of the "trust problem" is by Naomi R. Lamoreaux, *The Great Merger Movement in American Business,* 1895–1904 (Cambridge: Cambridge University Press, 1985). The whole history is now undergoing painful reassessment stimulated by the massive researches of Alfred D. Chandler, Jr., *Strategy and Structure* (Cambridge, Mass.: M.I.T. Press, 1962), and *The Visible Hand: The Managerial Revolution in American Business* (Cambridge, Mass.: Harvard University Press, 1977). Chandler's work is addressed not to the trust problem (horizontal combination) directly, but to the extensions of vertical integration forward into marketing and distribution. The lower costs achieved in this way by a steadier and more assured throughput from raw materials to final consumer derive from economies of scale and systematic operation in the production activities and appear in every case to rest on the spreading of fixed costs through a full and steady utilization of a work force already assembled and of heavy and expensive equipment.

its family members. Sons had to work in the field, and daughters in the farm kitchen. The sexual division of labor was clear and unequivocal and enforced by individuals' images of roles, of sexuality, and of self-worth. Affection, discipline, the promise of reward, finally habit confirmed the countryside in its system of labor management. In small shops, proprietorships, and partnerships, the system of semi-filial apprenticeship sometimes worked, though much less extensively than in the stabler societies of the East and of Europe. The independence and individualism of the indigenous labor force, its mobility and restlessness, were notable. But as firms and plants grew larger, more formal systems of control were required. The competitive advantages of size – whether real or merely financial – were evidently great enough to sustain such organizations, if the labor could be obtained, organized, and controlled.

Here then was a dilemma. How would a society of small-scale units, competitive farming, and industry organize itself to encompass the presence of giant intruders on its markets and the enforcement of semi-military systems of internal control, of bosses and workers within them? Other industrializations – in Russia, for instance, and in Japan – counted on feudalism or militarism or the regulations of ancient bureaucracies to provide the answer. Workers lined up like peasants on the estate or soldiers in the army to march into the factory. To a degree, the American workers, native and immigrant, fell into this pattern with surprising readiness. The problem of worker discipline was no harder to solve, nor, until the 1930s, was its solution any more controversial than the problem of the market discipline to be enforced on the large enterprises themselves.

Shop management began in fact, as in the early textile mills in England and Rhode Island, by an adaptation of the system of piece rates or subcontracting to homes or small-scale shops. In the iron- and metalworking industries, a portion of the labor was contracted for by the firm through master mechanics who brought in their own staff on contract. The mill then was not a monolithic centralized structure, but a network of small units. The difficulties with the system were many, not only in the relation of sub-contractors to workers, but in the independence of the sub-contractors themselves, particularly where, as master workmen, they were few enough to organize in unions and go out on strike. Centralization of control promised to yield higher profit once a firm was organized and its workers had given up other options in order to join it. As the political possibility of centralized management came in view, the inducements to employers to enforce it were raised by the research into industrial management development by Taylor.[45] The importance of Taylorism

[45]I have greatly relied here on (and perhaps misused) the essays of the labor historian, David Montgomery, *Worker's Control in America: Studies in the History of Work, Technology, and Labor Struggles* (Cambridge: Cambridge Univer-

has never been measured, and his methods represented an ideal type of technocratic efficiency that lends itself to caricature. But the simultaneous discovery of "efficient" management independently in many locations created the typical midwestern factory system – not differing greatly from that of the Waltham system in New England textiles. Productivity was strikingly increased by such methods, and this was the easier to do in that expanding markets allowed productivity gains to be translated into more, rather than fewer, jobs.

The result was not only productivity gains, but an increased authority of management over workers and a clear division of labor and function between the two. How could a society that was based on individual freedom produce such a result? The answer, once again, lies in the "Puritan" component of the Middle West culture's concept of freedom and the individual. Puritanism was characterized by two elements relevant in this context: (1) the individual's faith in himself, his responsibility only to himself and to God, and (2) the respect for the logic of the natural world, for science as the revelation, jointly with the Bible, of the hand of God. Individual drive and an engineering mentality created a society with an attenuated sensitivity to the human condition, to weak and erring mortality, to the sins and inefficiencies of the flesh. *Fordism*, as the system of efficient factory management came to be called in the 1910s, was its culmination. But it was a system applicable not only to workers on the factory floor but to all phases of corporate operation – inventory management, buying, selling, and finance. It represented a triumph of the accounting mentality over unbridled human creativity. In the Puritan and liberal views, human freedom was derived from and exercised in a world and a society of laws, not of men. Freedom in society is the willing acceptance of an orderly and impersonal discipline. Why should this not be true in a factory or a corporation? Where markets were wide and homogeneous, products simple and capable of production en masse, and workers available and malleable, the Midwest system, which in its origins in New England has been called the American system, passed the supreme test of its own devising: It produced immediate, tangible, measurable results.[46]

An analogous problem was created by large firms externally on the markets for products, materials, and labor. Agricultural producers were

sity Press, 1979), esp. Chs. 1–2, and some of the abundant literature on work organization and on Frederick Taylor and "Taylorism," cited there. On New England, see Caroline F. Ware, *The Early New England Cotton Manufacture* (Boston: Houghton Mifflin, 1931), Ch. 4.

[46]These observations are based on reading, and reflections on reading, done for the sketch of New England's early industrialization in Chapter 11 above. See references there cited.

as numberless as the sands of the sea and sold their goods through channels in which no one could much influence the prices received. Above
them in the chain of distribution stood meat and grain dealers, elevator
operators, the flour mill and the slaughterhouse, and the railroad, canal,
and lake shippers. These were fewer in number, and in any given year
could drive bargains from which a farmer, with crops planted or even
harvested and animals on the hoof, found it hard to escape. Tiny pockets
of monopoly, local shakedowns, appeared everywhere in the system of
marketing; where a farmer tried to escape by changing his crop mix or
seeking out a rival deal or shipper, they reappeared somewhere else. But
each handler or processor of a crop on its way to market found himself in
a similar situation at the next level. For shipments beyond a very local
market, there were competitors, and this layering built up to the great
regional centers at Omaha, Minneapolis, and the lake ports, notably
Chicago. Here the titles to commodity shipments were bought and sold,
pieces of paper changed hands, complicated futures and forward transactions were accomplished, and prices fluctuated hour by hour with
expectations – sometimes based on information about the future course
of supply and demand. Agriculture, then, though honeycombed with tiny
and transient local monopolies, was taken as a whole as a textbook
model of what economists far away in the East and in Europe described
as perfect competition.

The sturdy though delicate web of markets and commodity prices that
connected farms to distant markets was partly the creation of steam
transport on land and sea, which had reduced the real costs of hauling
freight over land and had increased over both land and water the range
and speed, reliability, and predictability of shipments. The telegraph and
cable set the capstone on the system, enabling market information to be
diffused instantaneously over wide areas and so extending the range of
arbitrage and potential competition. But the railroad also furnished bru-
tal instances of local monopoly power at every station it served. The high
fixed costs of a new railroad and the undeniable cost economies of extensive and systematic operation gave railroads local market power; hence
the railroads from the 1870s on provided the Midwest with the first
incentives to regulate monopolies and producers' combinations. The opportunity was not missed by politicians, and it served as a target for the
zeal of civic-minded idealists. Railroads first brought out in a substantial
way the reforming streak in midwesterners, among farmers, businessmen,
journalists, and professional men and among liberal ministers and their
heirs: the teachers and professors of the moral – now increasingly called
social – sciences. Railroad regulation at the state level was followed in
cities by regulation of the "natural monopolies" of franchised public
utilities. The movement, which owed much to German-derived social

democracy in Wisconsin, spread rapidly after 1900, if often not very effectively, and showed that private property and laissez-faire were no sacred cows if they created monopoly, allowed discrimination among users, and resulted in the misallocation of productive resources.

Manufacturing industry stood midway between the extremes of agriculture's competitive organization and the public utilities' natural or state-created monopoly. Here, as in commodity distribution, in artisan shops and small plants using local materials and serving local markets, pockets of monopoly could exist. Usually, however, without heavy fixed costs or some rare aptitudes or skills, a producer pricing too far above costs found himself undercut. Competition came less in the anonymous, faceless form it exhibited on commodity markets and more often in specific rivalry among a few shops or producers. Here the incentive to combination was always present; in the skilled trades, as we have seen, local unions formed. Still, new labor and new entrepreneurs constantly undermined the effectiveness of such combinations.

But the Midwest's industrial burst after 1880 was built on scale economies of large regional markets. In some of the industries where it occurred, optimal plant size was far greater than that of a local shop or smithy, and the large plants serving the wide market tended for reasons of transport cost minimization to be located near one another. The industries had high capital costs, too, and acute needs for financing in large lumps. And since finance and all successful asset management is built on the insurance principle of diversifying risks, its pecuniary economies of scale were themselves very great, though many devices developed later for spreading these among small investors, banks, and funds.

So from 1880 on, large plants, large collections of plants, large firms, large producer combinations, large networks of centralized financial control grew up – organizations in which physical cost saving, the benefits of a superior stability, continuous throughout, were inextricably intertwined with the bargaining power of the large customer or the large supplier. It was a system in which within firms many market relations were internalized, and the tests of the market bargaining were supplanted by internal accounting controls and by the internal power politics of the large organization, in which routine could enforce discipline and measurement could rationalize routine.

The movement to industrial concentration was the Midwest's thorniest problem – the one most at odds with its proclaimed ideology, while at the same time it seemed to be a source of its industrial strength. Once again, pragmatism furnished the test. So long as the system, supplemented by bursts of "reform" and half-hearted "trust busting," worked, so long as industrial expansion went forward, so long as the national product rose and a substantial majority shared in its rise, democracy asked for nothing more. It did not seek to know whether the growth came in the face of the abundant opportunities offered by larger markets and ingenious technical change because of the system of production organization and distribution or in spite of it – or what hidden operating costs or social inequities its dynamic operation concealed.

V. SOCIAL ORGANIZATION AND VALUES

History, religion, and political theory had combined to instill in the midwesterner the doctrines of the equality of man and the supreme worth of human ingenuity and labor. The history derived not only from the famous "frontier," but also from the experience of the succeeding generations of agrarian life. Rural development was a group effort, as well as an individual one, and the man who did not work at it, making use of the opportunities that came his way, put the issue of the whole risky enterprise in doubt. All labor yielded wealth and so commanded respect, but skill, ingenuity, or brains in handling physical materials or in managing assets and transactions – all qualities that could make labor yield new wealth – commanded admiration. It has often been observed that the midwesterner did not worship wealth, but something called success, of which wealth was the tangible token. Unlike the situation in societies based on the aristocratic principle, wealth seemed to lose rather than gain respectability as it passed from the original accumulation to the second and third generation.

The haunting echoes of Puritan theology in such a set of values – derived though it was from the experiences of the frontier community – are inescapable.[47] All men are born equal: equally free and equally ignorant of their destiny. Whether they are equal in sin or in innocence is less important than the fact of their equality and their ostensibly equal access to grace. In seventeenth-century New England as we saw in Chapter 11, above, the signs of grace were not wealth, but visible sainthood, the bearing, disposition, virtue, radiance that came from a godly public life and a sincere private faith in the goodness and justice of God. In that theology, assurance of salvation was never given. A man stood, in Milton's words, "as ever in my great Taskmaster's eye," and far from causing believers to despair, this uncertainty drove a Christian to try even harder and without remission. Of course, nineteenth-century midwestern Protestants admitted the existence of luck, as seventeenth-century Calvinists believed in the doctrine of election, but in both faiths, life was lived with an objective in view. Whether sainthood or more riches, the goal was open to all men to be reached for, and it was attainable, if at all, only by a lifetime of work, activity, intelli-

[47]See note 44, above.

gence, and striving. In midwestern America the opportunity to acquire wealth seemed suddenly to have opened wide, and its acquisition, if not an indication of saintliness, nevertheless earned a man an equivalent or even a superior renown.

This ethic, whether called Puritan or pragmatic, animated activity within the structure of midwestern social life – families, small towns, schools, social clubs, and business enterprises. It caused men to employ readily the capitalist forms of economy that were at hand – private property ownership, banks and financial instruments, free wage labor, contracts, and markets. But form – even the forms of government and public order – were not long allowed, as the phrase went, "to stand in the way of progress." Every social form and practice was measured by the iron test: Does it work? And the units of measurement, it was widely agreed, were dollars and cents.

The ethic was derived in equal parts, not only from the frontier and from God, but also from Thomas Jefferson. There was in it an ingredient from eighteenth-century Republican rationalistic humanism which could save so driven and greedy a society from the ultimate self-defeating idiocy of destroying its own human capital. Both children and immigrants had to be socialized and motivated and, if not wholly co-opted into the social enterprise, at least induced or obliged to pull their own weight and not to dissent. For this, two liberal institutions were at work: compulsory education and the system of law, justice, and open opportunity. Schools and law were the institutions which gave stability and continuity to a mobile population and a rapidly expanding social and economic organism. But to speak of their function in nourishing and perpetuating the conditions of industrial growth is not to denigrate the integrity of their own peculiar objectives: education and justice. Both schools and courts were the locus of a formidable cadre of skilled professionals commanding respect for their own sake as well as for the economic ends they served. They served those ends so well indeed because they were never wholly co-opted within them.

The Midwest, in short, although becoming wealthy in an economy of free and enthusiastic enterprise preserved the elements of a liberal society. Education and justice, subject as they might be to corruption and transitory public pressures, still preserved a human face, and by means far more effective than physical force gave hope to the streams of immigrants and to the succeeding generations of youth. To greater or lesser degrees, it "middle-westernized" them.

The effect on the quantity and flexibility of labor supply was significant. Off farms the indigenous population still was guided by the rural ideals of work, self-improvement, and achievement, settling at some point into the routines of an increasingly structured business civilization, carrying out white-collar jobs and specialized professions as required.

The industrial civilization of the Midwest

The immigrant population as it grew up in ethnic neighborhoods developed an increasing political influence. At the local level, the heritage of the Northwest Ordinance – schools, courts, and ballots – allowed new institutions such as the Catholic Church, the boss-controlled urban machines, the local labor unions to break through the small-town oligarchies of wealth, virtue, and Protestant uniformity. The location of urban government within the sovereignty of the state legislature insured the maintenance of many rural norms. But any group was free to run its own affairs, to seek a job, to send its children to a recognized school, and to aspire to rising incomes.

The semi-feudal class consciousness instilled in the immigrants from Europe was shed, and a new one, based on the conditions of industrial society, was acquired only slowly and with great uncertainty. Local labor unions organized in the skilled trades to establish monopolies in local markets, but in the great and growing new industries, organizations of unskilled or semi-skilled labor broke against the internal divisions in the labor force and were floated away after 1900 on the flood of new arrivals. Labor as such was respected, and laboring men seeking their fair shares in the system were not stopped from group action. But when labor put on a political face of its own, particularly when the demands threatened property, public order, and the inviolability of contracts, all the pressures of law and public opinion that had preserved and regulated the bourgeois life of the small town were brought down upon its head.

* * * * *

Between 1830 and 1880, the midwestern farm region from the Alleghenies to the Rockies expanded in size and in volume and variety of output. The growing industrial districts of the Old Northwest – both those that shipped and processed the farm output and those that supplied its inputs – the items of farm capital and farm consumption – grew as well, and with the swelling size of the whole mass of production and trade, efficiency, income, wealth, and thence markets and production further increased. Initially after 1860 there was the simple substitution of regional products for British and East Coast imports. Since agricultural exports remained at high volume, such substitution presumably made the region richer in holdings of external assets and less dependent on eastern capital. Demand on farms was high, but more important was the share of income going to labor in the industrial population itself. Much deep research is needed to get at the determinants of the wage rates in all the markets and for all the varieties of labor. Somehow, a division of income between spending and saving was created which, when supplemented by the financial flows from local banks and the East, was satisfactory for continued growth. The concern for adequate market outlets is evident in

247

the great emphasis by mail-order firms and shopfront stores alike, as well
as by great firms, on selling. Salesmanship became notoriously the hallmark of the midwesterner.[48]

The heady spiral of solidly based growth in supplies and in demand
gave to the Midwest's economy and culture in the late nineteenth century
a vigor, a zest, an optimism and self-assurance which made further accomplishment easy and growth apparently endless. The stimulus raised the
value of time even as the good living and cheap protein diet increased
physical energies. Never perhaps in the history of the world have nomi-
nally free and prosperous farmers, businessmen, and laborers worked so
hard, such long hours, so energetically, and with such visible reward.[49]
The Northeast had been "cabinned, cribbed and confined," by valleys
and hillsides, by peculiar beliefs, by history and class structures; the
South by the foul blight of slavery and racial prejudice, an ill-motivated
work force, and an idle and ignorant aristocracy. From 1880 to 1930, the

[48]The history of the traveling salesman is a long one, going back to the Yankee
peddlers of the early nineteenth century, the sales forces of large commission
houses, and the integration of them into the sales agencies or distributions of
manufacturing firms, insurance companies, and the like. Alfred D. Chandler, Jr.,
The Visible Hand: The Managerial Revolution in American Business (Cambridge, Mass.: Harvard University Press, 1977), Ch. 9. Current research by Oliv-
ier Zunz is underway on the shift by Dupont from selling through local agents to
a cadre in the field of specialized agents operating out of branch offices and
moving from one to another. In rural areas the Agricultural Extension system,
organized under the Smith–Lever Act of 1914, represents a similar organization
distributing knowledge of crops and practices. A peculiarly midwestern development, which spread elsewhere, is the mail-order house, beginning after the introduction of rural free delivery on the farms. Wayne E. Fuller, *RFD: The Changing
Face of Rural America* (Bloomington: Indiana University Press, 1964), 249–254.
With wider mail service came growth of an advertising industry with advertisements in periodical literature. With highways and cities in the twentieth century
came billboards, and with radio and television, the commercial. The salesman is a
folk type in the popular literature from George Ade's *Fables in Slang* to Arthur
Miller's *Death of a Salesman*.

[49]For an interesting discussion of a lengthening of the workday in the United
States and Europe as a source of increased output, often paraded as increased
productivity, see Gregory Clark, "Productivity Growth Without Technical Change
in European Agriculture Before 1850," *Journal of Economic History*, 47 (1987):
419–432. For the Midwest, I found evidence on a longer average day in some
earlier research that measured man hours in farm operations relative to the farm
labor force employed. See also the interesting remarks of Clarence H. Danhof,
Change in Agriculture: The Northern United States, 1820–1870 (Cambridge,
Mass.: Harvard University Press, 1969), 141–144, on economizing time.
The shift from horse to tractor between 1920 and 1940 must have relieved the
pressures that the time constraints in the presence of abundant land and market
pressures and opportunities presented. But that shift itself, by releasing one-
quarter or more of cropland from hay and oats, further raised the strain on
farmers to work more land, even as it speeded up operations.

Midwest *was* America. Its vision of itself, its self-confidence, had a physical basis in rich resources and the fortunate self-reinforcing efficiencies of a production scale easily won over a flat terrain and by the homogeneous culture of what radicals suspiciously called market capitalism and bourgeois democracy. Midwesterners, if ever exposed to these phrases, put them in quotations marks and could hardly repeat them without a pang of bad conscience as if even the very use of such terms were a betrayal of the only form of economy or society worth mentioning anywhere on earth or in history. The complement of an expanding agriculture and expanding mines, transport, and manufactures and of a correspondingly expanding internal demand made the midwestern economy a large operation. It had to be large if it were to exist at all, and its size and success rested not only on physical sources but on the optimism generated by the prospect of continued expansion. Import substitution and prosperous farms and cities could provide the expanding markets, but like resources, these sources of growth contained in themselves a tendency to exhaustion and self-limitation. Eventually, creative technological changes and a closer attachment to the world markets would be needed to support the demand and supply conditions that a growing output would require.[50]

Midwestern small town society by 1900 had created a gigantic industrial structure across the northeastern edge of the vast region of small farms, rail junctions, and crossroads towns. At the foundation was a drive to produce, and in producing to get rich – not for wealth, not for comfort, not even for power, but simply for the use of talents and energies, simply not to waste the greatest opportunity in the world on the part of common men to increase their earnings by tending to their job and on the part of an uncommon or lucky few to create little empires as energies, wit, luck, or fate might dispose. Deep in the folds of this single-minded culture lay the discipline needed to create, tolerate, and enforce efficient commmand structures within corporations and to threaten to overtop even large corporations by state or federal regulation where the ingrained

---

[50]Technological change is an aspect of midwestern industrial development not examined in this essay. A plausible hypothesis is that fundamental scientific research was undervalued and neglected for engineering and inventive activity with a quicker payoff. The temptation for private and public agencies and popular attitudes to favor a shallow and shortsighted pragmatism is great where resources and markets are ample and vigorous growth occurs on a very limited technological basis. The possibility has never been examined for the Midwest, but the discussion of England's nineteenth- and twentieth-century development vis-à-vis the continent may be to the point. See an allusion to the problem of technological diffusion and technological creativity in an earlier treatment of the European experience: William N. Parker, "Industry," in *The New Cambridge Modern History*, Vol. 13, ed. by P. Burke (Cambridge: Cambridge University Press, 1979), 78–79, reprinted in Vol. 1 of the present collection.

rush toward monopoly ran counter to the social purpose. That purpose was not so much to allow society to acquire wealth as to leave open opportunities for individuals to engage in its further acquisition.

In this way, effective though surely not ideal, through the doorway that lay along the line between Pittsburgh, Cleveland, and Chicago came American industrial prosperity in the Republican half-century before 1930. Here, too, originated many of those transformations of the Midwest's underlying layers of civilization that gave the region and the country a second further expansion and a drastic cultural transformation in the four liberal Democratic decades that followed. Then the spotlight of industrial opportunity shifted from this immense heartland region of farms and furnaces and the response appeared in the American periphery – toward the continent's seacoasts, in the already densely industrialized Northeast, the stubbornly agrarian rural South, and the ranching and lumbering regions of the Far West and the Pacific rim. Since 1950, under the name of *Americanization*, this whole body of agrarian and industrial activity with its accompanying organization and ethos has blended with native cultural traditions in the wider stream of world history in many portions of the world beyond the Rockies and the Alleghenies, and indeed far beyond the political reach of the United States of America.

EPILOGUE: DENOUEMENT AND DECLINE

By 1929, midwestern industry had grown on its rich agrarian and resource base to a scale which amply utilized those scale economies described above. The farming regions had been extended, even overextended, in World War I; their loci were firmly established; the theory of comparative advantage had worked itself out over the landscape. American resources had yielded oil, technical change had yielded the automobile, and in classic nineteenth-century fashion the states with federal support were providing roads. Model T's and Model A's gave unheard-of social mobility for the farm population, whose absolute numbers had by 1920 reached roughly their historic limit. Despite a growing "farm problem," the rural small town and the elite culture of the Midwest and Northeast was as firmly Republican as it had been since the Civil War.

On the national level the Republican program had developed under heavy influence of "bosses" who were close to the basic steel, mining, and refining industries of Pennsylvania and Ohio. Since the 1880s, it had combined elements favorable to "big business" with just enough progressivist counterpoise to maintain the public trust. The program to be described in Chapter 13 was in full operation. The tariff, unrestricted immigration, and a "sound" dollar were at its heart. The tariff, it was said, permitted high wages, unrestricted immigration gave a continuing labor supply, and the gold standard detached "money" from local "politics" and left control of its supply in the hands of bankers in financial centers whose mysterious skills and interest could give it necessary guidance. At the same time, the Republicanism even of the 1920s did not base its appeal ultimately on ideology, on laissez-faire, free enterprise, or self-regulation in markets or in the money supply. These things were good because they worked and in working confirmed the social virtues and the natural law which their working seemed to reveal. Moderate regulation, at least at state and local levels, and government sponsorship of important public works which set the frame for the private economy and did not compete with it were part of the package. But the progressivist antibodies the system contained were in no way equipped with techniques or an ideology which could produce thoroughgoing institutional reform. When the system failed to work, it had no option but to collapse, and it was vigorously, if not violently, repudiated.

One need not be much of an economist to note the Old Guard Republican's blind spots or to see in whose relative benefit the system operated. Nor need one be much of a Hegelian or an historian to see that even if not containing the seeds of its own destruction, its success was based on elements which were disappearing over the course of time.

Take, first, the tenet which equated high tariffs to high wages and a large home market. No economist and probably not many knowledgeable politicians, editors, or businessmen believed that the American wage structure in the 1920s depended purely on the tariff. It depended fundamentally on the access to cheap food, on the ready use of new inventions, and on the efficiency of the organization in space and in the factory – all this in the presence of countless obstacles to factor mobility. The time was long past when American industries were infants in need of protection.[51] To understand how the slogan had an appeal, one

[51]But the tariff had a moment of its own. It was raised to what became protective levels in the Civil War, where, in the absence of domestic import-competing industries, demand was inelastic and higher rates meant more revenues. After that it served two purposes – as a political football, an apparently painless way for competing local interests to balance protection for one against that for another – and, as the "mother of trusts," a cover for collusive price rises and, where entry could be restricted, higher profits. So long as farm exports were strong, capital inflows considerable, and import-competing manufactures had failed so far to make the country self-sufficient or a net exporter of manufactures, the tariff managed to combine its two contradictory objectives, providing some revenue and some encouragement to domestic industries, without curtailing excessively the flow of imports. But in the 1920s America was trying to export both farm products and manufactures, with surpluses of foreign exchange permitting a large volume of monetary investment abroad, particularly in Germany and Latin America. To have removed or lowered the manufacturing tariff at this point would certainly have increased domestic welfare and provided some healthy competition to Midwest producers.

must examine how it fitted into the wage structure. Wages were high, but for whom and relative to what? Farmers, it should be noted, did not hire much labor, so the urban wage rate was largely a matter of indifference to them in daily operations. However, in the wage categories into which off-farm migrants had gone, industrial wages were notably higher than farm earnings, and the gap was probably widening. Farmers' escape, then, was seen to lie not in populistic agitation against the industrial price level but in the sale of surpluses abroad and in the move to city jobs. In the cities, immigrants' wages in common labor, too, were higher than they had been in Europe. Overall, competitive labor markets worked well under the tariffs but were not supported by them. Interferences in the labor market were two: the wage bargains driven by the Republican trade unions, which by restricting entry into local markets had acquired some power, and the special advantages of English-speaking white workers, especially Americanized ones, compared to the new immigrant labor. So long as free immigration persisted, everyone got higher wages than he was used to, but only in relation to its reservoirs of origin – Europe and the farm – was labor artifically "short" and some wages unnaturally high.

Into this situation came the move in 1923 to end foreign immigration, which nativist sentiment – and the interests of labor already here and at work – finally accomplished. That it had not happened thiry years earlier is testimony to the power of employers when supported by the national myth of the land of opportunity. Certainly the opposition of the "old guard" and of urban developers was diminished by the appearance at this time of the population movement off the southern farms. The movement of blacks had begun during World War I, and in the 1920s the hill people from the border states began their invasion, in numbers which had not been seen since the days of first settlement and southern slavery. But this component of the labor force was to prove not as docile as the ethnic East Europeans, not as equipped with internal cultural controls, not as ready to seek to exert influence at the local level through church and the Democratic Party. They, too, were largely Republicans; they, too, were old Americans. The racial issue made the problem a very complex one, and in addition unions were not very strong or successful during the 1920s. But there can be no doubt that this new element in the Midwest's labor force represented a prospective threat to the Republican system of unionized native trades and non-unionized immigrant industrial workers – one that was to prove far more serious than the socialism of Debs or the anarchism of Emma Goldman.

Finally, the financial "crash," when it came, and the four downwardly spiraling years that followed, destroyed the credibility of the Republican financial orthodoxy. In an area which has been so expertly and so inconclusively covered, one would be rash to venture very far in stipulating the exact chain of causation. The novelty in the situation was not only the depth of the collapse, which showed how the Midwest's financial structure had become entangled with that of the world at large, but also, as the 1930s wore on, its duration. Despite all the political changes, the monetary and organizational experiments of the New Deal – even despite the rather rapid recovery from the lows of 1933 to the new break in 1937 – a hard core of unemployment of 15 to 17 percent, double that of any previous decade's experience, hung over the economy, and much of it lay in the once new and now aging industries of the Midwest. It is difficult not to see here weakness at levels deeper than economic policy – both in what I label opportunity and in "response." We may suggest three.

For one thing, the drying up of the domestic rural market was partly the result of the farms' own depression in the 1930s and of the shrinking of the export market after 1929. But even a prosperous agriculture would have continued to shrink in relative size and importance as a market for manufactures. The Midwest's home market in this sector had become the victim of its agriculture's growing efficiency, of the low income elasticity for food, and the farm sector's own competitive organization. This market for farm exports could be maintained only by the growth in the manufacturing exports of the Midwest's industrial competitors. Farms and industry in the Midwest no longer formed a self-contained system. One of the advantages of the large-scale inland empire protected by industrial tariffs had merged imperceptibly into the advantages of free international trade.

Secondly, the weakness of the native structures of technical change became evident as technology paused on the brink of the great discoveries of the 1940s and 1950s. This is far too vast and shadowy a matter to be covered here. I allude to it in some reflections confined for the moment to Annex B.

Third, the crazy-quilt of industrial pricing, half monopolized, half randomly competitive, occasionally controlled, and incompletely free needed rationalization, and macro monetary and credit policy needed to be supplied. As suggested above, the structural and institutional changes required as the base of a new national prosperity were more thoroughgoing and sophisticated than any the Progressive or Socialist program had ever formulated. The Midwest's old Republicanism was no more; the needed activist and progressivist programs were far beyond what had been dreamt of in its philosophy. New slogans, new personnel, and a new political party were required. The old Democratic Party was not the origin of this policy revolution, but under FDR after 1936 it became its political instrument.

The North: dynamics of an industrial culture

The Midwest under Democratic progressivism

To describe the cycle of Progressivism, which began as part of liberal Republicanism and culminated in Vietnam and Johnson's "Great Society," is the task of a whole book – indeed, of a whole library. The New Deal was its time of crystallization. The welfare programs and Social Security, the monetary isolationism, regulatory reform, the Wagner Act and the formal establishment of unions alongside corporations in the society, the farm programs, the growth of the huge federal budget, the inventions of monetary and fiscal management grew up in response to specific needs and pressures. To a degree reform addressed itself to obvious and expressed grievances. It extended Republican progressivism from antitrust and token regulation of monopoly in three directions: (1) to the task of maintaining employment, (2) to the closer regulation and establishment of counterforces to business (farm programs and unions), (3) to the welfare of disadvantaged groups.

As its programs developed, and particularly by virtue of World War II, in which America's participation itself, though in self-defense, had elements of progressivist activism, institutional change developed a logic and dynamic of its own. Monetary management led to ever "finer tuning" and to budgetary management. Regulation led to more regulation. Programs for the poor and the aged led to the massive efforts of the 1960s and the Great Society to secure justice and equality for blacks, women, and ethnic minorities. In the Republican era, the Democratic Party – a strong coalition of urban immigrants and Southern white masses – had no real alternatives for a platform of its own. So in a Democratic era the residual Republicanism had nothing to say or to offer. In both cycles, the established system produced results by the two basic American tests: the maintenance of reasonable and growing prosperity and the provision of a measure of open opportunity. The main differences were that the Democratic years seemed to require big and active federal government to produce these results. And in both cycles of policy, pressures were generated and inadequacies revealed with which the program could not cope. These pressures in 1929 were generated partly from the collision of American expansion with a world economy which was itself falling apart, and partly from purely domestic developments and maladjustments. In 1969–76, the pressures came more largely from abroad. But that in itself demonstrates the drift of the whole society into closer touch and interaction with the wider world.

The years of Democratic progressivism did not deal kindly with the older America of the Midwest. The impact of the Depression in the region was the first blow. Revival came in the war and the immediate postwar recovery. But the restoration of the old dominance, the regaining of the region's old relative position and its inner integrity and political strength did not occur. The new social and political forces which the failure of Republicanism had set free, the further relative decline of farming, the growth of unions, the new composition of cities and the labor force, even the excesses of war and postwar prosperity, ate at the foundations of its regional character. Its virtues, its religiosity, even its self-confidence seemed old-fashioned and outmoded. And at the same time, the region's classic locational advantages as an industrial site had been destroyed. Iron and coal no longer dominated the industrial structure; the "inter-urban" had long since disappeared and now the railroad itself was on the way out. Instead, new points of expansion offered themselves in the non-unionized atmosphere and warm climate of the West and South. The great internal free trade market, the national union that midwesterners had fought to preserve and exploit, had turned against it. As part of that union and that market, the region was defenseless. It could not restrict interstate commerce, it could not erect tariffs, it could not secede into a regional nation-state. Most ironic, the punishment of the Midwest took place under the very slogans that had made it great. Enterprise, new industry, new growth, expanding horizons worked as well under the Democrats and the liberal Republicans of the 1950s and 1960s as under McKinley, Taft, and Coolidge. In the first era, these things had made the region; now they destroyed it. The New Deal and the Great Society had produced new stimuli and erected new protections to races, classes, and the levels of national income and employment. For the Midwest in the 1970s, as for New England in the 1920s, no one cared for an aging industrial region or the integrity of its regional society and character. There were programs and funds to save whooping cranes, seals, the national forests, historic buildings; there was none to save the function-ing life, the families, and the historic character structure of the region that had called itself the Heartland of America. The Midwest had exported to the internal market not only its grain and iron and manufactures, but its spirit, its ethos, its very soul. Now its older natives and newer immigrants alike were to see the life drained away around them, while the new regions, and even New England and the Southeast, were being midwest-ernized. In the 1950s and 1960s the boosters were no longer in Chicago or Omaha or Cleveland; the spirit had departed to Atlanta, Houston, Los Angeles, even at last back to Boston, and the terrain was not the great internal market, but the markets and societies of the whole planet. A new nation of Republicans had sprung up in those regions, richer, harsher, less constrained by the civil conscience and the progressivist ideals or sensitivi-ties which the earlier, farm-based Republicanism had bred. As the Demo-cratic programs broke against the impossible task of Americanizing the world, these new Republicans would show themselves, in classic Oedipal fashion, pitiless toward the old Republicans who had completed the cycle and now begged for shelter and mercy.

A NOTE ON THE SOURCES

This essay marks the beginning and not, I hope, the end, of a cycle of research on this history. The topics so lightly treated here, and many more, demand sharper definition so as to isolate the relative weights of the factors (such as religion, schooling, resources, entrepreneurship, markets, scale economies) in the development. Only such an Olympian view would allow the construction of counter-factuals (e.g., how fast would the development have proceeded had the eastern European immigrants not come in?). The effort is like the race of Achilles and the tortoise. The goal of full understanding is never reached, but each new research may narrow the distance.

The present manuscript began as a vastly overambitious effort to survey the route and to test my own intuitions on the subject. It was written in first overextended draft under rather odd circumstances in a foreign country at a distance from my books and students and with no other pressing occupation. The intuitions exploited were derived from growing up (through high school) in Columbus, Ohio, and from studying in later life similar heavy industrial developments in Britain, Germany, France, Belgium, the light industrial development in New England, and the Old Northwest's agrarian expansion before 1860 and its resultant agrarian civilization and economy.

It is particularly deficient through the superficiality of my knowledge of labor history, urban history, women's history, Afro-American history, and many topics that have greatly engaged young historians since the late 1970s. The effort is made here to look forward toward the twentieth century from the eyes of the 1870s, not backward with the eyes of the 1990s or even the 1930s. There is good reason for beginning in history at the beginning; chronological order is the historian's only monopoly, with all the surprises and distortions it creates. The Republican business society that ran America until 1930 underwent shattering changes in the four decades of depression, war, and liberalism. But it would be hard to argue that its vitality and expansive power in transformed form are played out in the world of the 1990s.

A partial bibiliography is given in the Klingaman and Vedder volume referred to above. In general, the sources for the history are not well organized for easy access. Good collections of state documents, business publications, and social studies exist at the several state universities and in the state and local historical societies' libraries, and a few state histories of varying usefulness have been written. Even business histories, as catalogued in the Harvard Business School bibliographies, are not as abundant as one would expect. No good bibliography of the materials for a regional economic history has been uncovered. A few valuable industrial histories have been written.[52] The moderately abundant quantitative materials in the state and federal censuses are only now beginning to be exploited. I could find no studies of internal migration from farms to nearby towns and cities from which to estimate the sources and size of the streams.

Two areas somewhat better endowed with scholarship are the history of the immigrants and the labor movement in the cities and large plants and the stories of a few of the great entrepreneurs and politicians, notably for this period Carnegie, McKinley, Hanna, Rockefeller, and the early days of Henry Ford. This emphasis in the historiography since 1930 reflects a creditable concern with the central struggle of big capital with labor in the mid-twentieth century, and the nineteenth-century and early twentieth-century problem of assimilating both into the structures and ethos of American capitalism. The less sensational history of how those structures and institutions developed on the basis of a native culture has been ignored.

One need only compare these works with the rich and sophisticated studies of the New England mills, the libraries on the South, the tales of the ranching and mining frontiers in the West to realize the poverty of the central region's literature. To explore the reasons for this would take us far beyond the scope of this note. Perhaps the Midwest has been the norm against which other regions have been seen. Among most of us modern scholars, it is not norms but aberrations that seem intriguing. The dearth of economic studies on Midwest industrialization is thus, in a sense, a confirmation of the final thesis in this paper.

The essay should be regarded as a tissue of intentions, impressions, or, at best, hypotheses. Where the text refers to a specific author or event, I have provided the reference, but have made only a frail attempt to document general statements or to do justice to such sources and studies as I have found. This is especially true of Section III, on capital, which was written in recent months. My choice was either to omit the entire essay from the collection or to present it in a somewhat primitive form. Readers and reviewers must decide for themselves whether in publishing it in this state, I have made a wise choice. I hope that for me it will prove an instructive and constructive one.

[52]See Lorna M. Daniells, *Studies in Enterprise,* a selected bibliography of American and Canadian company histories (Boston: Baker Library, 1957), and Supplements (1959–64), esp. Sec. 3: H, J, L.

PART V

American values in a capitalist world

13

Political controls on a national economy

I

Since the first seaboard settlements, practical affairs in America have been conducted within two rather different economic and legal forms: the corporation and the free market.[1] Each is of ancient lineage, but on these

This paper was delivered in its original version, entitled "American Attitudes Toward Business," at a conference at Sangamon State University, Springfield, Illinois, in April 1975, organized by James Worthy and Clarence H. Danhof. The version was reproduced and given limited distribution at that time.

[1]The contract, enforceable in law, and the implied contract, agreement, or promise, enforceable by serious social or inter-personal sanctions, lie between these two ideal types. Either may be looked on as a network of contracts, all resting on the concept of individual "ownership," i.e., free disposal of one's own person and effects legally acquired and on the state's guarantee and protection of this right from force and fraud. On the free market, the contracts are momentary, acting only until an exchange is made, and are subject to continuous and instantaneous renegotiation, either between the parties or on special markets for that purpose. In the corporation, the contracts are more complex; they are ordered into a structure of roles, rights, and duties, i.e., a "bureaucracy." The enforcement is still by economic sanctions, i.e., not through force as in a "state," but, as in society at large, status, dignity, and power, i.e., customary behavior in several dimensions, are important elements. Into the free market, custom and contract then introduce constraints ("rigidities" in economists' language), and these are, as it were, written in the corporation not in the water of free and rapid bargaining, but in cement. Ultimately it is the state's assurance of the "inviolability" of ownership and contract from which all such "rigidities" stem. Without it, the economy is organized like a state, i.e., through force, threats, and the elaborate persuasions of politics. The literature on all this, from Sir Henry Maine to Oliver Williamson, Harold Densetz, and among contemporary legal and economic historians – Morton Horowitz, J. R. T. Huges, and Douglass North and his students – is vast and not infrequently illuminating. See especially the most recent collection of papers edited by Erik G. Farubotn and Rudolf Riditer in cooperation with D. C. North and Richard H. Tilly, "The New Institutional Approach to Economic History," *Journal of Institutional and Theoretical Economics* (*Zeitschrift für die Gesamte Staatswissenschaft*), Vol. 145, No. 1 (March 1989), containing contributions by Gary D. Libecap and others.

shores the corporation was first on the scene. Jamestown, Plymouth, Massachusetts, and Providence Plantations were settled by semi-private corporations chartered by the crown to perform private and public economic and political functions. They had their precedent in the chartered corporations of medieval towns and their artisan guilds, outside the domain of territorial lords, which controlled manufacture in the towns and governed them. They were akin to the royal grants of monopoly made between the sixteenth and nineteenth centuries to companies of merchants to conduct trade on foreign soil and seas, to govern an enclave at home or abroad, and to deal with foreign princes. Canada in the eighteenth century was the site of several such companies (the Northwest Company and the Hudson's Bay Company); the famous Dutch and English East India Companies were even more powerful and more prominent examples.

These early corporations, though concerned with trade and settlement, were in fact quasi-states, exercising some of the powers of a sovereign over their territories. The land they held in colonial America had been granted by the King under the least restrictive of feudal tenures. In Virginia, Georgia, and the Carolinas they disposed of land directly to individuals, granting portions both to shipowners who had brought over settlers and to the settlers themselves. In New England, lands were assigned by the company to individuals or groups of incorporators or proprietors of a township, with provision for common pasture land and common regulation of town life through the church and town meeting of the proprietors. The control of the political functions of these towns was derived from the distribution of the shares among proprietors, while the assembly of the company's shareholders, much like the shareholders in a modern business corporation, provided the foundation of the colonial assemblies. But control of government by landowners and colonial assemblies was modified by the rights and powers of the original grantees in the proprietary colonies and by the crown, from which power ultimately derived.[2]

The distinction between settlement companies and monopolistic mercantile companies was not clearly made in the seventeenth century. Mercantile companies were an extension of the medieval industrial guild, and the colonization companies were extensions of mercantile enterprise. At the same time, some North American lands were granted by the king, not to companies of "adventurers" or "planters," but to individual noble persons, in much the same way that William the Conqueror six hundred

---

[2]A useful source tracing the title to land from the Indian tribes to the British royal and proprietary colonial governments to the final European settler for each colony is Marshall Harris, *Origins of the Land Tenure System in the United States* (Ames: Iowa State University Press, 1953).

years earlier had divided the Anglo-Saxon kingdoms of England among his knights and lords. Like the corporate colonies, the so-called proprietary colonies – Maryland, Pennsylvania, Delaware, and several others in a modified form – granted or sold land, retaining in the proprietors only a faint shadow of rights. In Pennsylvania, for example, the right to collect a small quitrent was retained in the Penn family until the Revolution and persisted even afterwards in Maryland.[3]

As settlement proceeded, the colonies became not simply merchants' plantations, or proprietors' estates but full-scale social organizations. The political authority held by an English trading company or by absentee landholders became transferred to the colony with the increasing importance of Indian defense, the growth of population and trade, and regulation of trade by the crown itself under the Navigation Acts. After 1680, the crown took back or revised most of the charters, established royal governors, and transformed the assemblies of corporate landholders into elected assemblies, retaining a property qualification for voting and holding office. Since mercantile corporations had had the right to make a levy on their members for corporate purposes, and since the English Parliament had kept control over direct taxation, the colonial assemblies levied land and property taxes, whereas the king's revenues were derived from customs duties and excise taxes. The transformation of the corporations into political units opened the way for nineteenth-century participatory democracy. It also freed landholding, trade, and manufacture from most corporate and feudal controls. It is important to realize how early this occurred in America. In Prussia, for example, it was not until 1858 that the state decreed *Gewerbefreiheit,* the right to engage in a trade, untrammeled by guild or other corporate restrictions.[4]

The market, or business, system, otherwise known as "the competitive economy" or "laissez-faire capitalism," the paradigm of neo-classical economics, began to grow away from corporate and mercantilist forms in the North American colonies almost from the beginning. By 1700, the economy in the northern states was organized largely by small-scale units – a master workman, his tools, and a few apprentices, working at home or living above or behind his shop; a merchant owning a ship or two and a countinghouse; a farmer with fifty or a hundred acres, mostly in woodland and pasture, a trapper or fur trader with a cabin as headquarters and an annual catch of skins. Among the larger-scale eighteenth-century enterprises were the rice and sugar plantations of the deep South; they were individual proprietorships, with slaves as capital reproducing

---

[3]Philip S. Klein and Ari Hoogenboom, *A History of Pennsylvania* (University Park and London: Pennsylvania State University Press, 1973), 25, 36–38, 107.

[4]J. Conrad et al., *Handwörterbuch der Staatswissenschaften,* 4th ed., 9 vols. (Jena: G. Fischer, 1909), Vol. 4, 897–901. Article on *Gewerbegesetz.*

themselves without the need for outside financing.[5] The corporate form, driven out of land holding and trade by the intense individualism of settlers and merchants, responding to the abundant opportunities for free and untrammeled enterprise, remained in enterprises of a semi-public character serving business – i.e., in banks, insurance companies, public works, charitable and philanthropic organizations, colleges, and other non-profit institutions. The corporate form for the distribution of land enjoyed a temporary revival when the Old Northwest was first opened up for settlement. Congress revived for a brief period the land and settlement companies of earlier times. Several such – the Holland Land Company, the Ohio Company, the Scioto Company – received or purchased large blocs of land which they held on speculation and resold at retail to settlers. And several, in particular the notorious Yazoo companies in Alabama and Mississippi territory, operating as purely speculative ventures, close to the borderline of fraud, illustrated the illegitimate purposes to which the corporate form could be put. But once again, this use of the landed corporation disappeared before the political thrust of a growing population, hungry for land and profits.[6]

The economies of the regions that made up the United States and the links that bound them together before the Civil War operated then within the structure of a market economy, rather than under that of a state or corporate capitalism. The numerous small households were its "firms," restrained from pure profit maximization in market activities only by the admixture of family considerations with those of a business nature. This structuring of the economy comes through, with slightly different seasonings of values, in the visions of Jefferson and Hamilton often alluded to in these essays, for the American economic future. An agrarian democracy of freeholders, selling such products as exceeded the needs of subsistence, and with land as a private, disposable commodity, requires only minor modification of the ideals of a business system. All corporate organiza-

---

[5]L. C. Gray, *History of Agriculture in the Southern United States to 1860*, 2 vols. (Washington: The Carnegie Institution, 1932; reprinted, Gloucester: Peter Smith, 1958), Vol. 1, Chs. 14–16. On Louisiana sugar, see further J. C. Sitterson, *Sugar Country* (Lexington: University of Kentucky Press, 1953), Ch. 3, for the early nineteenth century. Plantation size in the Chesapeake tobacco-growing areas in 1740–90 is shown in Alan Kulikoff, *Tobacco and Slaves* (Chapel Hill: University of North Carolina Press, 1986), Table 37, p. 38. None of these was large by European standards of serf estates, holdings of twenty or more being considered plantation size.

[6]Ulrich B. Phillips, *Georgia and State Rights* (Yellow Springs, Ohio: Antioch Press, 1968), 29–37. Milton S. Heath, *Constructive Liberalism: The Role of the State in Economic Development in Georgia to 1860* (Cambridge, Mass.: Harvard University Press, 1954), 74–75, 108–109. Paul D. Evans, *The Holland Land Company* (Buffalo: Buffalo Historical Society, 1924)

tion and functions outside the family are – in Jefferson, as in Adam Smith – transferred to the supreme corporation, the state, governed by the assembly of landholder-citizens, and with functions as minimal as Smith would have desired. Hamiltonian democracy differed from this Jeffersonian ideal in admitting an alternative form of wealth – mercantile and industrial property – and in envisaging a state responsive to the needs and advantage of this property as well as to those of land. The state did not participate in a corporate capacity in economic life, but set the rules – the tax and legal systems, the funded debt and coinage – within which the private business system could function.[7]

It is an open question whether the Hamiltonian version of federal mercantilism was more or less "interventionist" than the petty mercantilist policies pursued in the 1820s, 1830s, and 1840s by the several states. Banks, turnpikes, canal companies, schools and universities, railroads, depot and harbor companies, steamship lines – all were state-chartered enterprises readily created as instruments of the public purpose. The motivation was in no way doctrinaire, but wholly pragmatic. Symbiosis between state and corporate "business" was so close as to leave unclear whether the corporations were public or the state was private. Both were instruments of a vast popular will, the will to expand, and to make abundantly available to all the opportunities and fruits of expansion.

II

Before the Civil War there is little, if any, evidence of any fundamental distrust or collision of interest between either business (or the corporation) and the community in its other forms and interests. To be sure, sectional interests clashed. The great national issues were slavery, the disposal of public lands, the role of the *federal* government in canals and railroads, and the balance between manufacturing and agricultural-mercantile interests in the issue of tariffs. These were quarrels between groups of small capitalists and landowners on how to shape the course of national economic growth to their own advantage. In the North, both Northeast and Northwest, the society was the business community and the business community was the society. The petty capitalists themselves constituted the bulk of the citizenry. No one argued that "the government" should stay out of business or that "the government" should enter a business or "take over" any given function. The federal government was small and weak, with slender revenue sources – mostly from the

[7]A nice discussion of the Hamiltonian program and the feud with Jefferson is contained in John C. Miller, *The Federalist Era, 1789–1801* (New York: Harper & Brothers, 1960).

tariff and the sales of public lands. The state governments, supported by property taxes, might look to state enterprises as sources of revenue. Their principal development function in the canal era was to underwrite with their own shaky credit the issues of private bonds. Certainly there was no widespread suspicion of the state by "business," or of "business" by citizens and voters.

Yet one ought to mention at least four incidents or elements in this period which foreshadowed what was to come. First, there is the notable matter of the non-capitalist classes. Except for the slaves and poor whites in the South, these classes were less numerous and weaker in early nineteenth-century America than in any other place and time in the world's history. One major study in the 1970s of antebellum slavery even treated the slaves almost as petty capitalists since, it was contended, they had some opportunity for advancement.[8] But it is of the essence of slavery that advancement could proceed only a few steps and, once achieved, was never assured, but might dissolve on the whim of the master. From the planter's point of view, slaves were a chattel part of the system of small-scale business and property. From the slave's own point of view, he was a proletarian, an object bought and sold for his labor power. Was the anti-slavery movement, then, a protest against the principles of the business system when carried here to an extreme? I do not quite think so. I wonder instead whether much potentially effective protest against business, land-grabbing, continental expansion, even against "male chauvinism," was not drained off into the anti-slavery movement just as later it was deflected by the temperance movement, and the crankish agitation for a bi-metallic standard. But the moral fervor of abolitionism went well beyond a protest by one form of capitalism against another. I think one cannot understand the movement without appreciating the vein of sheer anarchism that threaded through it. No man should have *any* power over another: That is radical Republicanism, or republican individualism, the spirit of the frontiersman driven by a distaste for human society, the spirit of Jefferson absorbed from the French revolutionary philosophers. Slavery was the most patent, the most extreme, the most unbridled of all the forms of un-freedom. The spirit of radical Republicans was the spirit of 1789: *Ecrasez l'infâme!* Directed against slaveholders in 1861, this cry of bourgeois liberty was to be directed later against an even more giant-like opponent, the monopolistic corporation, and with more equivocal results.

Slaves apart, there lay in the American scene before 1860 other non-business elements which did not share the ethics, the aspirations, or the

[8]Robert W. Fogel and Stanley L. Engerman, *Time on the Cross*, 2 vols. (Boston: Little Brown, 1974).

opportunities of the business class, even at its poorest. These were wage-earners in the cities, hired hands and servants in villages and farms – all just graduating from the quasi-familial status of eighteenth-century domestic and artisan labor. They included as well manual laborers, the kind needed to dig canals, throw up levies, harvest wheat and hay, fell forests not as farmland clearing, but for commercial lumber. They were a proto-proletariat, voiceless, inchoate, but also assuming those odd organizational forms of workingmen's associations and friendly societies that populate the early chapters of books on labor history.

A second group was the famous "poor whites," the up-country subsistence farmers of the southern and border highlands, whom the historian, Frank Owsley, called the "plain folk of the old South." At what point in the spectrum of self-sufficiency does peasant agriculture end and commercial farming begin? No one can say, but certainly many of these farmers were closer to Scottish clansmen than to petty capitalists. They made no anti-business protests, but like peasants everywhere, they hated government, and particularly remote government. They rallied in 1861 to the southern cause, not in defense of slavery, which they also despised, but out of hatred for remote authority.[9]

To claim to find in the non-capitalist classes any anti-business movement or attitude surfacing in the Civil War does violence to the historical record. Was the war a crusade against planter-capitalism, or was it a struggle against northern business by a patriarchal agrarian society? Neither formula quite fits. But there was another sectional struggle before the Civil War which fits the model a bit better: that of the West against the East, or the backcountry east against the seaboard. Here again one has hardly an anti-business, or anti-corporation movement, but rather a contest between two types of property: the commercial and financial property of bankers, merchants, and speculators and the landed property and human capital of skills and social organizations embodied in the settlers, ranchers, and farmers of the Old and the New West. This split animated the pre-federal "rebellions" of Bacon and Shays, and the "Bank War" under Jackson. In any case, all such movements were to be submerged and engulfed in the agitation over slavery. One has the picture of a class and regional struggle absolutely diverted between 1840 and 1870 by the struggle over slavery. The Whig and Republican attack on the slave South was supported by the business-agrarian class of the Northwest, though *not* by a certain anti-black and anti-business, hillbilly element, the "Copperheads." Curiously, a "nativist," proto-populist, pro-southern Democrat in Indiana found himself supporting slaveowners in much the same

[9]Eugene D. Genovese, "Yeoman Farmers in a Slaveholder's Democracy," *Agricultural History,* Vol. 49, No. 2 (April 1975): 331–342, esp. 333–336.

way as a Tennessee or Kentucky upland farmer. Here indeed is the origin of the southern Democrat of 1880 to 1940, who combined anti-black slogans with an agrarian, anti-business heritage. It made real populism impossible to achieve.

Still, in retrospect we can see even before the Civil War that inchoate mistrust of "bigness" which was so prominent a feature of the period of populism and progressivism. Here, again, is a curious American paradox. Americans were and are notorious for their boasting worship of the large-scale – their equating of the biggest with the best. The tall stories of the West make up one of the country's notable contributions to folk literature. Yet it is physical bigness rather than the large organization that has been the chief source of pride. Americans have admired large aggregations of wealth, but the power that wealth brings has on the whole been disliked and feared. In the small town, a certain undercurrent of nihilistic dislike of the local worthies, the banker, the large and successful farmer, the successful manipulator, might be written down to sheer envy or to the exhibition of those basically anti-bourgeois values which intellectuals also exhibited. But the mistrust of the federal government was the strongest political current before the Civil War. It was, in effect, a mistrust not of business or of politics as such, but of the remoteness of its power, of its susceptibility to manipulation, of its ability to reduce the free individual to a state of insignificance.

Slaves, wage-workers, western frontiersmen, and mountain hillbillies did not form a very effective anti-business movement before the Civil War. A fourth type of dissent from the values and purposes of a business society was exhibited more widely in pre–Civil War America. In a long-run which includes the American future, it may prove to be the most enduring and important – the attitude on which American civilization may split apart like a ship against the rocks or on which its new structures may be built. It has been an attitude of protest, a cry of the powerless, the weak, the dependent, the frustrated. It has, in consequence, appeared largely as a negative, a destructive force. Yet at bottom it derives from a feeling of common humanity. It involves a total repudiation of the business ethic and values, including in its frustrated rage even the ethics of a scientific rationality. It is expressed as an irrational emotionalism, a transcendant idealism that has surfaced in much of American literature and American religion.

Life, even in America, has always been bigger than business, no matter how much of the time and energies of men have been absorbed in dollar chasing and profit calculation. So strong, however, has been the business ethic, that those residual energies and values, when blocked, dammed, or diverted, have assumed bizarre, crankish, and impotent forms. In early American religion they appeared in sectarianism, accompanied by either emotional "revivals," or by an enduring, hard, gemlike pietism. What are we to say of the "Great Awakening" of the 1720s, of the second "Great Awakening" of the early 1830s and 1840s, and of the repeated awakenings that frontier revivals institutionalized in the Victorian camp meetings and city church revivals, as represented by Finney, Moody, Billy Sunday, and at last by Billy Graham and his less reputable counterparts, the latter-day Elmer Gantrys spawned by television? Surely they expressed, as did Wesleyan Methodism in England, not a reinforcement of the business system, as some would have it, but an emotional protest, and a temporary escape, a violent release from it, a scream against it, an atavistic barbarian yawp against the tidiness of accounts, the neatness, the gentility, the hypocrisy – as some saw it – of respectable Protestantism.

A similar spirit, more measured, much more literate, animated much of early mid-nineteenth century American literature. Where are the novels of American business, the novels of bourgeois life, of the country house, the artisan's shop, the law office, the speculator? Where is the American Balzac, Dickens, or Trollope? American fiction in the antebellum period of great regional literature is either romantic (Cooper or Poe) or symbolic (Hawthorne and Melville), a literature either of adventure or of morality, never of calculation and manners. Indeed, it is this profoundly moral tone that sets American writers, even Mark Twain, apart from French realism and Russian psychologizing and from the English novel of manners and society. The closeness to nature which American writers felt drew them from business and society. Literature before the Civil War is not a protest against business society; it treats it in a far more demeaning way by simply ignoring it. It focuses on higher things – on man, God, sin, nature and the supernatural.

We may identify then at this point several strains in the history of pre–Civil War America that bear on our topic:

(1) The rivalries among groups of capitalists (farmers against merchants, free farmers against slave holders, manufacturers against both), rivalry often mistaken for anti-business sentiment

(2) A mistrust of the large corporation, whether of an economic or political nature, apparent among small businessmen and farmers, but shared by groups on the edge of business – slaves, wage earners, and subsistence farmers

(3) Early evidence of a true "class struggle" along Marxian lines in the formation of early labor organizations

(4) A deeper cynicism about – or obliviousness to – the business ethic, an attachment to other, more romantic values that can be read into both popular religious attitudes, some inarticulate and some overly articulate, and into the famous works of the great American regional literature of those decades

Yet neither business attitudes nor anti-business attitudes had crystallized into explicit philosophical positions. Religion, human freedom, political power, even economic growth, hold the center of the stage. Organizational forms and ethics in economic life are the backdrop, the unexamined background of the historical pageant.

III

The Civil War has been called the watershed of American history so often and for so long that the temptation for modern-minded social and economic historians to downplay it is almost irresistible. We no longer see it, as Louis Hacker and Charles Beard did, as a triumph of northern capitalism over southern agrarian society. The South had been capitalistic in its own way, too – one of the few societies so capitalistic that it had even capitalized its labor force as a commodity to be bought and sold. Slaves, we know now, were an investment as profitable as any other in the last antebellum decade. And there is nothing in the growth statistics to indicate that the war itself was anything but a destructive interruption in a rather steady path of industrial development from New England as early as the 1810s into the Midwest after the canals and railway improvements of the 1820s, 1830s and 1840s. But we are not talking here simply about growth rates or productivity. We are talking about a much more nebulous thing, the business civilization, as described in Chapter 12, and popular attitudes toward it. Can anyone doubt that the railroads, even before the war, the trunk lines and particularly the transcontinental railroads after 1865, formed the model for business and economic organization on a new scale? No one can read Paul Gates's history of the Illinois Central or Richard Overton's book, *Burlington West*[10] without gaining an appreciation of the fact that in the railroad the corporation was revived on a scale far surpassing the colonial and early federal land companies, with social and political influence to match. The economic history of Germany provides some interesting parallels between military and industrial organization and a state bureaucracy and corporate controls. Surely in America, too, the organization of men and materials in war had its effect on the imagination of those who wished to develop industrial empires. The stretching of rail lines across the continent and the control and operation of trains to a close time schedule involved organization of a wholly new order of magnitude in American life.[11]

[10]Paul W. Gates, *The Illinois Central and Its Colonization Work* (Cambridge, Mass.: Harvard University Press, 1934); Richard C. Overton, *Burlington West: A Colonization History of the Burlington Railroad* (Cambridge, Mass.: Harvard University Press, 1941).

[11]Alfred D. Chandler, Jr., ed., *The Railroads* (New York: Harcourt, Brace & World, 1965), Part 3; Alfred D. Chandler, Jr., *Henry Varnum Poor* (Cambridge, Mass.: Harvard University Press, 1956), Ch. 7; Alfred D. Chandler, Jr., *The Visible Hand* (Cambridge, Mass.: Harvard University Press, 1977), Ch. 3.

Political controls on a national economy

How strange it is that so many things in a period often appear to conspire together to establish its characteristic form of economic action! For as railroads – the first great industry of fixed costs and increasing returns – were developing, new technologies in power, in machinery, and in raw materials fabrication and handling, notably in steel, were also tending toward large scale. Toward the end of the nineteenth century electricity appeared, involving large scale in generation and distribution even though it gave some opportunities for the powering of small machinery and small work shops. And the automobile, though it encouraged small-scale transportation and haulage, was susceptible to great economies of scale in its manufacture through the use of assembly-line techniques and the assembly of prepared parts and required also, of course, immense highway projects. At the same time that these real opportunities for large plants in transportation, public utilities, earth-moving, steel and metal fabrication, and chemicals were presenting themselves, the technology of communications and control was also in development. The telegraph, which accompanied the railroad, stretched out like the nerves of the business system to raise at distant points the sensitivity of prices and expectations to the state of markets in Chicago and New York. The telephone had similar effect, and within corporate organizations the development of systems of management, particularly of systems of control through accounting practices, helped large-scale enterprise to take advantage of its technological and natural opportunities. Capital markets evolved, permitting the aggregation of small capitals for use by a single large enterprise; the ingenuity of financiers developed numerous types of bonds and other debt instruments to finance mergers and consolidations. The shadow of the great life insurance companies unfolded like the wings of the angel of death across the credit system. National banks, clearing houses, and the use of checks; grain, metals, cotton, livestock, and other commodity markets; the concentration of milling, slaughtering, and other processing in the cities – these and many similar developments created an integrated national economic system. In the interstices of the communications and financial network, the industries of the Midwest matured. Beginning in the coal-mining regions of Pittsburgh and West Virginia, spreading across the lower lakes to Chicago and reaching up into the ore and wheat regions of Minnesota, the giant heart of American industrialism began to beat. The resemblance to the corporate growth of Germany, which in the same decade centered around coal, ore, and communications by rail and water, is unmistakable.

The Civil War, the railroad, the technological changes in industry, communication, and agriculture, and the population growth of the decades from the 1870s to 1900 thus established in the Northeast and in the eastern and upper Midwest a structure of industries and a system of business organizations quite unlike anything that antebellum America had known. That such a synthesis in the real, tangible, material world should be accompanied by a similarly vast, well-structured, and harmonious development of economic and political doctrine and ideology is not surprising. The period was one of the dominance of the Republican Party and the development of a body of orthodox Republican doctrine, whose hold on the thinking of the American middle classes has been matched only by the ignorance and neglect of it on the part of professional American thinkers and intellectuals. Consider the astonishing synthesis, the amazing blend of opposing interests, that Republicanism achieved. The party won every presidential election from Lincoln through Hoover, with only four exceptions – and those (Cleveland and Wilson) not to men whose views differed very strikingly from those of their Republican rivals! Yet like so much of American thought and activity, Republican doctrine never received an able, full, and elegant exposition. It appears in Supreme Court decisions, in congressional speeches, in party platforms and keynote addresses, but none of the expounders, certainly not the presidents who led the party, could be called an eloquent or even a philosophical prophet. No Burke, no Marx, no Mao served to articulate this doctrine. As often in social and cultural history, a period of vigorous activity received its fullest statement only at its close; the writings of Herbert Hoover formulate, though rather ponderously, the conservative, orthodox Republican creed. Its positions and the reasonings behind them are deserving of far more careful and detailed examination than intellectual historians or political scientists have acknowledged.[12]

This ideology, which won elections and controlled American public policy for the seven vastly productive decades from 1860 to 1930, rested on several assumptions. Most fundamental was, of course, the well-known doctrine of laissez-faire and the privateness of private property. It is almost impossible for us to realize today what magic those words held in Europe in the eighteenth and nineteenth centuries. There the revolutions of 1789 and 1848 were fought not so much to free men as to free property, to destroy the economic policies of mercantilism and the control of wealth by royal and aristocratic power. The American Revolution and the Constitution put these rights of property high on its list of freedoms; indeed, the Civil War was fought not to ensure social equality or a full political franchise, but simply to give black men the right to own their own bodies and to enjoy the property deriving from their own labor. It was in these terms that Lincoln described his goal in

[12]Herbert Hoover, *American Individualism* (Garden City: Doubleday, Page, 1922); William J. Barber, *From New Era to New Deal* (Cambridge: Cambridge University Press, 1985).

emancipation.[13] In America this impulse to freedom was immensely strengthened by the availability of free land and the success of the common farmer in securing it.

The great achievements of Republican ideology in the decades we are considering continued, extended, and transferred the right to free disposal of property, including intangible forms of wealth, to that large-scale, fictitious creature of the mercantilistic state, the corporation. The Supreme Court declared the corporation to be a person, to be granted the freedoms of a natural person against state interference.[14] Symbolic of this transition, the Acts of General Incorporation were passed in all the states between 1850 and 1870. These Acts eliminated the need for special legislative charters of incorporation, allowing a simple application meeting certain standard terms to suffice. The Republican Party became the party of business, great and small; it linked the business affairs of the crossroads town to the huge complex aggregations of capital and power in the great metropolitan centers. Bryan spoke well when, in 1896, in his famous Cross of Gold speech he said that the farmer raising grain was as much a businessman as the man who went into the trading pit and bet on its price.[15] But that reasoning emphasized not the differences of interest between the farmer and the banker or the speculator, but rather the identity. The Republican Party was able to keep its control over commercial agriculture, to keep the vote of farmers and small merchants in the North and West while the modern system of corporate business grew giant-like and tall.

The ideological link between small-scale and large-scale business – and the party's resulting ability to enlist the growing classes of professional and salaried workers to support its financial and economic policies – I would call the first pillar of Republican strength. The second I would

[13]For an exposition of Lincoln's views on this, see G. S. Boritt, *Lincoln and the Economics of the American Dream* (Memphis: Memphis State University Press, 1978), Ch. 12. For Lincoln's writings and public statements on the subject, see Roy P. Basler, ed.; Marion Delores Pratt and Lloyd A. Dunlap, asst. eds., *The Collected Works of Abraham Lincoln*, 9 vols. (New Brunswick, NJ: Rutgers University Press, 1953–55), Vol. 2, 405, 520; Vol. 3, 16, 315; Vol. 4, 24–25. A typical statement from a campaign speech in 1858 says, "Certainly a negro is not our equal in color – perhaps not in many respects; still, in the right to put into his mouth the bread that his own hands have earned, he is the equal of every other man, white or black." (Vol. 2, 520).

[14]Harry Scheiber, "The Road to Munn: Eminent Domain and the Concept of Public Purpose in the State Courts," *Perspectives in American History*, Vol. 5 (1971): 329–404, includes a wide consideration of property rights and the status of the contract and the corporation in the later nineteenth century.

[15]William J. Bryan, *The First Battle: A Story of the Campaign of 1896* (Chicago: W. B. Conkey, 1896), 200.

identify as the ability of this doctrine to command allegiance in rural areas, leaving to the populists only a dissident minority, a disease in the body politic rather than its life blood. One would need to penetrate far into the sociology and ideology of rural districts to understand how such elitist leadership by Republican lawyers and businessmen in the North and Midwest and, in the Democratic direction, by their Democratic counterparts in the South was able to impose itself.

No less remarkable was the third pillar of Republican strength, the ability to get the votes of labor, particularly of skilled and organized labor. The doctrine employed here was, of course, the notion that high tariffs guaranteed high wages, and wages were certainly high enough and rising enough for seven decades to give this doctrine some credibility. Here, again, in the laboring population, some credit must be given to the force of a certain elitism. The successful merchant, farmer, or skilled worker set the goal; the hope of emulating his success helped to transfer his values, his business ethic, his politics to those who aspired to positions they might never achieve. The Democrats, with an ideology only marginally different from that of the Republicans, controlled the new laboring masses in the large cities, but they could not alter economic policy in the country at large. When they were in power, they had no alternatives except to work for modest reductions in the tariff.

Finally, as a fourth pillar of Republican strength, one must not neglect the doctrines of financial orthodoxy, the gold standard, the balanced budget, and economy in government: doctrines compatible with laissez-faire and the privacy of private enterprise. Here, too, as with corporate organization and private property, a doctrine of natural law and automatic self-regulating mechanisms was adapted from an earlier period to an environment where artificial money and credit instruments of the most bizarre sorts were proliferating.

IV

It remains now to examine the actual protest, and the overt actions, formulated in opposition to orthodox Republican doctrine as it developed during the century following the Civil War. In their inarticulate fashion, the doctrines of the Republican Party expressed ideals, ambitions, pieties, and estimations of social worth derived from a business civilization. Its policy for natural resources was to turn them over to private hands – to farmers and settlers and miners, but also to timber kings and oil barons. It was a policy that satisfied rich and poor alike. The policy toward industry was to let it alone, assuring through the courts the rights of property and contract and the right to organize in the corporate form to whatever degree such organization suited a private purpose. Its policy toward labor and all the many special industrial and regional groups was to maintain a high tariff and to hope that wages would rise with rising productivity. It was on immigration policy that the most noticeable difference of interests between labor and business might have made itself felt, since growing urban industries were eager for labor and the existing labor force had a considerable interest in protecting its wage level. Moreover, many of the immigrants became Democrats in the Catholic and ethnic enclaves of the eastern cities and along the lower shore of the Great Lakes. Yet the whole thrust of the national development favored a free immigration of labor. Many of the immigrants, once arrived, had relatives they wanted to bring over, and the economic expansion was sufficiently rapid in the 1880s and 1900s and 1910s to allow new immigrants to fill up jobs in new industries without noticeably depressing wage rates of skilled labor at large. So the usefulness of immigrant labor to industry quite overbalanced the way it voted. Finally, to the financial community the Republican Party promised order, an automatically controlled money supply linked with European financial markets through gold and limiting through a fractional reserve system the dangers of excessive expansion of the money supply in the West.

It is hard for us to realize fully today the artistry, even artfulness, of Republican policy. It accomplished the objectives of capitalism with a minimum of government action and effort. The high tariff had its protective effect in keeping out exports, but it also produced enough revenue to replace land sales as the primary source of federal finance. Its effect as an instrument of taxation was almost completely hidden from the public, visible at the ports but lodged otherwise within the folds of the price system. No income tax forms, no excise and revenue stamps existed to make it obvious. As a policy of minimal mercantilism, it worked as effectively for the federal government in the late nineteenth century and early twentieth century as it had for the Renaissance rulers of England and France or for the Prussian kings in the age between Frederick the Great and Bismarck. In the gold standard the business society had a similarly inconspicuous and almost automatic mechanism of exercising economic control. This Republican policy in all its features was enshrined most explicitly in the attitudes and person of William McKinley. By the time of Herbert Hoover, it had suffered the change which all nineteenth-century ideas experienced as they passed through the turmoils of the twentieth century.

It is impossible here to examine with any thoroughness all the influential and partially contradictory forms of opposition that conservative Republican doctrine began to encounter by 1870. For the period between 1890 and 1915 our textbooks have classified them under the headings of populism and progressivism. Populist and progressive are names for groups and classes rather than for separate coherent bodies of economic doctrine. One identifies the populists with the older, rural America, with the small farmers in the South and on the Plains, standing at the lower end of the agricultural ladder. Threatened by debt and industrial monopoly, they laid claim to the ideal of the yeoman farmers, at once narrowly religious and nativist yet thoroughly democratic in thinking. One identifies the progressives with city politics, with the growing numbers of urban salaried workers and upper-middle-class professionals with whom wealthier farmers and smaller businessmen might readily identify. These two characteristically American groups both shared the individualism, the morality, and the optimism of nineteenth-century America. In addition, there was an imported strain of socialist thought and agitation, both of the variety diffused by German social democrats and of a more stridently Marxist stripe, directed toward creating a class-conscious American proletariat. These strands in the history I will have to neglect here, though they have more importance than our history books used to give them.

I want instead to suggest a different way of cutting the doctrines and a different attitude toward the problem than is suggested by the terms *populism* and *progressivism*. I do this because I think that what we are faced with today is not a choice between populist and progressive policies but between something they have in common and something they both overlooked. Let me begin to consider the matter by posing what seems to me what a Marxist might call the essential contradiction in both populist and progressivist thought. The populist was a small farmer or small entrepreneur, and his ideal for America was not socialism, but a society of free yeomen. Yet the policies that populism advocated involved more state control of corporate wealth and monopoly, more state intervention, and government on a larger scale: the income tax to replace the tariff, the control of monopolies, and government ownership where necessary.

The progressive's ideal similarly required a considerable body of state and federal legislation. The point of most progressive legislation, as put forward by Theodore Roosevelt, at least, was to make the world safe for competitive individualism, to save, indeed, the very values that the Republican orthodoxy proclaimed, and through intelligent regulation, to keep it from digging its own grave.[16] It was ready to use government,

[16]Richard Hofstadter, *The Age of Reform* (New York: Vintage Books, 1955). It has never seemed to me that Hofstadter's work called for much revisionism; nevertheless, as always with work of this sweep and definite point of view, revision came. See G. Kolko, *The Triumph of Conservatism* (New York: Free Press of Glencoe, 1963; Chicago: Quadrangle Books, 1967), and Robert H. Wiebe, *The Search for Order, 1877–1920* (New York: Hill and Wang, 1967), a work more synthetic than revisionist. John M. Blum's *The Progressive Presidents* (New York: Norton, 1980) is an interesting and well-balanced assessment of the movement at the level of national politics continuing on through FDR and Lyndon Johnson. In

both local and federal, as a regulator of private activity, in the control of natural resources, in the planning of cities and transport systems. In the very large-scale industrial operations, such as power generation, it was ready to take a page from the book of socialism. Both the populists and the progressives, then, worked, I think, to retain the ideal of early nineteenth-century capitalism in the late nineteenth- and twentieth-century environment. Both contained elements of democratic socialism, and both are echoed in most of the measures of the New Deal. Both were built on the socialist notion that the line between public and private is more important than the line between large-scale and small-scale organization. Both were ready to bring in government as a counter-valence to private concentrations of power, whether of city bosses or of corporate monopolies.

Cutting across the liberal thought of populism or progressivism, with their differences as to the right mix of public and private enterprise, is the more fundamental distinction between organization on a small and that on a large scale. The developments of enterprise and of the corporation in the twentieth century have accentuated the importance of this distinction. What difference, after all, does it make whether socialized or private corporations run an economy? What difference whether bureaucrats are paid from the public or a corporate payroll? We are back, in a sense, to the sort of problem that obsessed the writers of the Constitution and animated the political struggles of the antebellum decades. How powerful and extensive should the federal government – or Exxon or U.S. Steel or AT&T – be? This was not a problem that the Republican orthodoxy really solved. Large concentrations of private economic power were its Achilles heel. It was this problem, among others, which brought orthodox Republicanism down in the crash of 1929–32 and gave for nearly the half-century following the flavor of hypocrisy, naiveté, or anarchic radicalism to all efforts to revive it. The norm was shifted in the decade of the 1930s from an assumption that a large-scale federal government was wrong to the assumption that a large federal government must be an active organ of economic life. In the 1980s the classic doctrine was revived as a slogan, but the size of the federal government and its spending expanded further.

Even the later Republican thought, enshrined in the policies and some of the utterances of Herbert Hoover, had moved away from the McKinley style of laissez-faire. Republican progressives showed less fear of intervention of large government than did Republican conservatives. Business influenced and helped to direct its own regulation in the Interstate Com-

politics and industry at the state and local level, for the period 1865–1900, Morton Keller's *Affairs of State* (Cambridge, Mass.: Harvard University Press, 1977) gives important insights at many points.

merce Commission, the Federal Trade Commission, and the Federal Reserve System. Certainly in the thought of Herbert Hoover, the great planner and engineer, there occurs a certain elitism, a certain technocratic bias that would do credit to an ardent socialist. The federal power projects, the federal farm subsidy programs, and the federal highway development system of the 1920s overturned more of the conservative Republican laissez-faire attitudes toward the economy. The New Deal completed the job, overturning the myth of self-regulating financial markets and transferring power from Wall Street to Washington and from the Federal Reserve Board to the Treasury.

As the German socialist Michels, in his interesting study of the German Social Democratic movement,[17] and Max Weber, in his major writings, reveal, an elite tends to arise in large organizations, an elite of managers undermining eventually any democratic base. The fact is that the concepts of small-scale and large-scale political control of one man over others are far more fundamental to human welfare and efficient human organization than the concepts of public and private, which, translated into large-scale context, have in fact very little meaning. We have long since awakened from the dream of nineteenth-century socialism, in which men may be expected to behave vastly differently when they hold their property not in tangible transferrable forms of capital but in the form of superior training, skills, prestige, and position. What really makes a difference in human behavior is the scale on which human interactions occur, the power that organizations give to individuals to influence human action. The fundamental distinctions are between the collectivist and the individualist mentality; whether the power in the collectivity is wielded through property rights and courts or through direct political force is of less consequence. The child born and growing up in the small family of locality and neighborhood acquires a certain character structure which the child growing up in the large institutional family of urban mass and bureaucratic organization does not acquire. This is why the distinction between rural and urban society and character has proved so fundamental in history. The improvement of means of communication has smudged that distinction, but the distinction remains between an environment in which relations are close and immediate and one in which they are extensive and remote.

None of our political orthodoxies or our political protest movements has really faced this dilemma. Yet there is a strain in American thought relevant to it – one which we identified before the Civil War, one which

[17]Robert Michels, *Political Parties*, Eden Paul and Cedar Paul, trans. (New York: Dover, 1959), a re-publication of the 1915 English translation of the Italian edition, based on the original German version. See esp. Part 6, Ch. 2, "Democracy and the Iron Law of Oligarchy."

has grown in strength in the twentieth century. The undercurrent of protest against business in American literature and sentiment in the late nineteenth and twentieth centuries has been part of a continuing suspicion of bigness and of the pompousness of public life as conducted by government or by "private" organizations. In the twentieth century the tradition has been carried on less as protest than as skepticism about the business system with even an intentional obliviousness to it. Except in the frankly progressivist writers, Frank Norris and Upton Sinclair, the novelists in the great tradition of American writers – Mark Twain, Theodore Dreiser, Sinclair Lewis – have tended toward the nihilism and cynicism of the frustrated idealist. The view taken toward the pieties of American life of politics, business, and religion is that of the village atheist. Can so anarchic and destructive an individualism be harnessed to contribute to making the forms for a good society?

In the protest movements of the 1960s this most radical strain in American thought came strongly to the surface. I recall a student from Portugal comparing for me the attitudes of European and American students as he saw them in those years. He said that in Europe everything, even protest, had been done for so long and repeated so many times that it fell into a tradition – a communist tradition, an anarchist tradition, a Catholic tradition, a fascist tradition, or a tradition of democratic socialism. In America, on the other hand, he found that students were engaged in really profound philosophical discussion of the first principles of human life and organization. In the fashion of Descartes, they seemed to accept nothing and to insist in their violent individualism on rethinking all institutions, even institutions of protest. Certainly they were engaged in rethinking the liberalism of the New Deal, the inherited progressivist and populist tradition, with its trust in the ability of the federal government to guide, control, counterbalance the economy and to remain under popular control itself. The positions arrived at were often closer to those of a McKinley Republican than those of a Franklin Roosevelt New Dealer. What had been a protest against business and large-scale concentrations of private property was transferred into protest against bigness and the large-scale concentration of power, whether wielded through law or through the marketplace. Private life, private values, values separated not simply from a government but from the public life of government or business, were cultivated.

How could society in its political and economic organs be organized to give voice and fulfillment to the sense of worth of an individual soul, which American civilization has continued to cherish? Could not a close examination of the functions of society reveal the variety of scales on which they might be organized, so that technical efficiency could be maintained without excessive subordination of individuals or small groups and the extinction of their unique and individual values? Surely young Americans ever since 1970 have been faced with a struggle involving a choice, not like that between Bryan and McKinley, Taft and Roosevelt, Hoover and FDR (perhaps a little like that between Goldwater and Johnson), but fundamentally in modern dress the choice between Hamilton and Jefferson. Certainly Hamiltonian ideas of enterprise, manufacturing industry, finance, and centralization appear to have captured our world – even Hamiltonian mercantilism has finally engulfed it. They were as much enshrined in populist and liberal Democratic thought as in Republican progressivism. But if Hamiltonian business values, with their strong dose of mercantilist centralism, dominate our business lives and the course of our affairs, political and economic, there is yet the shadow of Jeffersonian individualism that falls across our inner lives, our private values, and our fantasies. And the strange thing about human life and human history is that what seems fantasy to the hardheaded social scientist or the retrospective historian, so often dominates and shapes the reality. What men really are may be less important than what they think they are in making them become whatever it is that they will be. That is perhaps a typically American sentiment – optimistic, idealistic, strenuous.

14

Nationhood in a common market

I

The American nation, I was taught in school, was born in 1776 with Jefferson's Declaration of Independence and the Revolution that Washington led. It was given legal form in 1789 by the establishment of the Constitution. And it was most bloodily "tested," as we used to say, in the fires of the Civil War.

But a nation is not a set of laws, and its history is not a mere chronicle of military engagements. Political historians will be quick to point out that the Declaration of Independence was not addressed to the world as from a single nation. It does not contain the word "nation," and though it speaks of the People as the rightful source of government, it resolved "that these colonies are, and of right ought to be, free and independent states." A period of thirteen years ensued under the improvised government of the Continental Congresses and a weak Confederation. As those years continued into the 1780s, uneasiness was felt over the security of the structure. The Confederation's great achievement was one of internal diplomacy, to secure agreement among the states to pool the claims derived from their royal charters on the lands west of the Alleghenies. This meant most notably to secure cession of Virginia's claim, according to one interpretation of her charter, to the lands north and west of the Ohio River, which became the six states of the Old Northwest: Ohio, Indiana, Illinois, Michigan, Wisconsin, and Minnesota. A large tract was retained by the state to permit her veterans to establish claims on good farming land as redemption of the warrants, or IOU's, in which the state had paid many of them for their wartime service. When this was done, the leaders of the state, Washington, Madison, Jefferson, were ready to

Sections I and II of this chapter were delivered as part of the first Thomas S. Berry Lecture at the University of Richmond, on November 10, 1988, under the title "Nationhood and War in America's Development."

281

give the trouble of defending and governing the huge area to the new Confederation.

There were two partly conflicting reasons for this. Virginia was still governed from Williamsburg and by substantial tidewater planters. It was a government which was formed in structure, attitudes, and distribution of power much on the model of early seventeenth-century England. For this sort of government, whether the Scots north of the English border (the River Tweed) or the Scotch-Irish over the mountains in the Great Valley of Virginia, the back country meant trouble. This had been the case since the days of Bacon's Rebellion of 1676. Such a settled aristocracy, whatever its profession of republicanism or democracy, by no means looked forward to an invasion of its House of Burgesses, in its lovely eighteenth-century setting, by hordes of rough men, free and wild, obstinate and violent, in their muddy boots from the banks of the Ohio and beyond. The economy, the thinking, the culture for the Virginian commonwealth of farmers looked down its great rivers and across the ocean. We have become so accustomed to imperial modes of thought, to growth and expansion of wealth and power, that we find it hard to understand the idea of a limited, a peaceful, a well-arranged basically undemocratic vista. But these men were "little Virginians," and they readily yielded up their claim to an unruly, though imperial, domain. Connecticut was somewhat more obstreperous and kept fighting over a claim to the northern third of Pennsylvania and the southern shore of Lake Erie – a strip lying between her parallels of latitudes "as far as the Western sea," as her charter read. But she was too small to give her claim major significance.

There was one partial dissenter from these sentiments, Jefferson, who was by no means a little thinker. He saw the nation, in a sense, in Virginian terms, though not as the planter aristocracy it was, but rather as the republic of modest farmers it thought it was, its power centralized only to defend and extend its boundaries. So he was ready for these lands to be surveyed and conveyed into private hands, the sooner the better; whether the government was called Virginia or the Confederation was to him immaterial, so long as it was small and of minimal powers to accomplish its single purposes.

Even for these narrow purposes, the government of the Confederation was not a satisfactory instrument.[1] It lacked an army of its own, and it lacked a treasury. It could not protect the West against the English or the Indians. And it could not protect the comfortable social and political arrangements of the planters and the northern merchants, who thought

[1]The decade of the 1780s has been examined by, among others, Jackson Turner Main, *The Anti-Federalists* (New York: Norton, 1961), and Gordon S. Wood, *The Creation of the American Republic, 1776–1787* (New York: Norton, 1969).

they had won their independence and integrity by the Revolution from the "West" within their states, the growing populations remote from the state capitals, which were all, with a few minor exceptions, set on tidewater. The Annapolis Convention, which issued the call for the Philadelphia Constitutional Convention, was called by Washington and others under an acute sense of concern about dissension in the back country. In western Massachusetts, Shays's Rebellion had broken out openly, and in Vermont, New York, Pennsylvania, Virginia, and North Carolina, there were memories of the rent riots of the 1760s, which had only been appeased in some states by an emergency issue of paper money.[2] The nightmare of a lawless mob, whether urban or rural, obsessed the founding fathers.

It would serve no purpose here to open up the old debates among historians and scholarly lawyers about "original intent" in the framing of the Constitution. From what I have read of the literature, I come out with the clear impression that the Revolution was not waged and the Constitution was not framed, despite the opening words of its Preamble, by a great popular swell of patriotism, a popular will for nationhood. Revolutions are made and governments are formed, from that day to this – and long before, from the beginning of history – by a set of social and political leaders who seek to establish what they consider to be some acceptable terms for political life and to secure the control of military force to enforce them. The work is carried on with the silent complicity of the people, but not necessarily with their active connivance. Some inchoate sentiment of community may pre-exist, and it may be crystallized in the actual commitments required in a Revolution and the erection of a state. But certainly not in America, even less than in Europe can it be said that the national community antedated the government. Patriotism does not create the state; rather, the sentiment of nationhood develops under its roof – through common experience, the presence of common enemies, the shelter of a common indoctrination. Kings, politicians, charismatic leaders create states; those states then create a people whom they govern.

To say this is to give a cultural and political, not a mere economic explanation for the Revolution and the Constitution. The founding fathers did not act as mere "economic men" in the economist's usual definition of that doubtful term. Their lives, their property, their fortunes had, on any reasonably long-run view, prospered under the crown, under the military and naval protection it had afforded, and in the protected – though taxed and restricted – markets for staple commodities and for ships and shipping that the Navigation Acts had provided. Before 1776, British mercantilism had not seriously distorted the main lines of colonial settlement and invest-

[2]A satisfying recent treatment in David P. Szatmary, *Shays's Rebellion: The Making of an American Insurrection* (Amherst: University of Massachusetts Press, 1980), esp. Chs. 3 and 7.

ment from what free trade and the law of comparative advantage would have ordained.[3] The specific customs duties were high and for 150 years had formed the payoff to the crown for its control. But the colonial structure of production had grown up under this system, especially in tobacco, where both trade and duties were very large. The industry's market growth depended on the shifting of the European demand curve for tobacco from one decade to the next, not on any sudden movement along the curve that a withdrawal of duties might have occasioned. The stricter collection and local corruption in the administration were indeed specific grievances, but surely the Revolution was not a simple grab for the British customs revenues. Such economic gains are not the stuff of revolutions, but can become bargaining items with the government in place, particularly where the system has grown corrupt.

The Revolution, then, was a bit more than a palace revolution, the ousting of one king by a military or aristocratic junta. It was a long and hard war, but in the upshot, it was not really very revolutionary. In the state capitals, royal governors and officials who remained faithful to their oaths had to flee. The goods of a few hundred Tories were confiscated. In Pennsylvania the Penn family, like Indian princes, had already been expropriated. In Virginia, though not in Connecticut, the established church was disestablished. Otherwise, every act of the crown with respect to land and wealth was reaffirmed and became precedent for the common law which was formally adopted by statute or in new state constitutions as the standard of justice and the guide to the judiciary. In no state was the established form of government overturned. And when the Constitution placed that firmer arch over the federal union of the states and gave a new taxing power and the care of the public domain to the new government, with military power to enforce its sovereignty, it explicitly confirmed, as against that new authority in its first ten amendments, the rights of Englishmen won by centuries of legal decisions and by two English revolutions against the crown – including most notably the right to own and use private property. The state assemblies, too, were forbidden to indulge in the potentially irresponsible coinage or issuance of money, the remission of debts through easy bankruptcy, and the impairment in any way of contractual obligations. Later, in the famous Dartmouth College case

[3]See the early article by Curtis Nettels, "British Mercantilism and the Economic Development of the Thirteen Colonies," *Journal of Economic History,* Vol. 12, No. 2 (Spring 1952): 105–114. Measurement of the gains and costs of mercantilist policies, which began with an early article by the historian Lawrence Harper, was taken up and carried on by R. P. Thomas, Peter McClelland, and Gary M. Walton between 1965 and 1972. The concluding article in the group, with references to the earlier ones, is by McClelland, "The New Economic History and the Burdens of the Navigation Acts," *Economic History Review,* second series, Vol. 26, No. 4 (November 1973): 679–686, with comment by Walton and David J. Loschky.

(1820), a great Virginian, John Marshall, confirmed against democracy embodied in the New Hampshire legislature the inviolability in American law of the college's property and corporate existence based on royal (i.e., George III's) charter.[4]

With respect to property in its most anomalous form – the slaves – the Constitution expressed itself in studied – and ultimately fatal – ambiguity. It made possible the eradication of the slave trade after twenty years. Otherwise its compromises created the impression that the legal power over the form of property resided in the states. And there appeared to be among some of the delegates to the convention a certain odd hope that once the trade had been abolished, the institution would die out.

The Constitution created then the framework of a nation strong enough not only to express disturbances in the back country but to expand the back country to the Pacific Ocean by 1850. Under Jefferson's peculiar form of democratic imperialism, the country doubled its area by the Louisiana Purchase and in succeeding decades by two wars of expansion. The War of 1812 was waged both on sea and on the lands of the Virginia session in Ohio and Indiana against the Indians and the British to confirm the settlement of the Revolution. And finally the War of 1845–48 in the Southwest took that vast region away from Mexico.

But despite florid Fourth of July rhetoric, east and west, this federal union by 1860 had come to serve as the container not for one nation but for at least two. This was in large part the fault of democracy and of the party and principles of Jefferson and Jackson. No national party could base itself ultimately upon a purely negative program; a program of local government, of weak government and states' rights. (In the 1980s these negative sentiments were labeled Republican.) In the 1830s and 1840s, the Democratic Party had been the dominant national party, the party of nationalist expansion. But in the 1850s, its program of states' rights became a block to the settlement of the territories, the extension of coast-to-coast railroads, the creation of a national banking system, the provision of a national agricultural program and free land. The radicalism of the 1800s had become the fearful conservatism of the 1850s, just as later in American history the radical nationalism of Lincoln and Grant became the old guard conservatism of Coolidge and Hoover.

II

We come then to the involvement of the idea of nationhood in the interpretation of the Civil War, and of that war in the growth of the American nation. On this immensely complex topic in American history, so fertile in

[4]*Trustees of Dartmouth College v. Woodward,* Supreme Court of the United States, 1819, 4 Wheat, 518, 4 L. Ed., 629.

possibilities for the historical imagination, what have the economic historians of my generation had to say? They have said some very salutary things, injecting some common sense backed up by statistics previously disregarded or unexplored into the overheated rhetoric of traditional historians. Oddly enough, here, too, the net result has been to play down the importance of economic motives as a basis of the war and the importance of the war itself as any direct contributor to the subsequent economic growth. In the economic statistics, the war appears a dead-weight loss. This was shown to historians in 1961 when the economic historian Thomas C. Cochran brought to their attention the implications of Robert Gallman's recently compiled statistics on commodity output and value added by manufacturing. Gallman showed that commodity output in 1839–59 and 1869–99 grew at average decadal rates of 57 and 54 percent in the two periods, respectively, with only the serious fall, to a rate of 23 percent, in the 1860s.[5] The war did not accelerate the pre-war trend; it dropped a decade out of it. Intelligent calculations by Claudia Goldin and others showed further that the expenditures on the war, the incomes forgone, and the direct capital losses in men, material, equipment, and livestock far exceeded the cost of a compensated emancipation, even allowing for any possible stimulus given to northern factories by concentrated war orders for uniforms and iron and steel.[6] The war did remove the traditional southern political leaders from participation in the national government for nearly two decades, during which time railroads, national banks, and land disposal grew apace in the North, and certain institutions – notably a national debt and a bond market – developed facilities with a spin-off effect on industrial finance.

But does all this really mean that the war or its outcome made no difference at all to either North or South? One thing we may feel sure of. Without the war, slavery would not have soon ended, collapsed, as historians say, under its own weight. Slavery was not on the verge of economic collapse in 1860; far from it. It yielded a normal rate of return on the value of investment, and the costs of reproducing that investment, the slave industry if you will, were well below the slaves' capitalized value.

[5] Thomas C. Cochran, "Did the Civil War Retard Industrialization?" *Mississippi Valley Historical Review*, Vol. 48 (1961): 197–210. Gallman's original study is "Commodity Output, 1839–1899," in William N. Parker, ed., *Trends in the American Economy in the Nineteenth Century*, National Bureau of Economic Research, Conference on Research in Income and Wealth, Studies in Income and Wealth, Vol. 24 (Princeton: Princeton University Press, 1960), 13–73. This is the basic study, on which Gallman's revised national income series, published in Vol. 30 of the Income and Wealth series, was based.

[6] Claudia Goldin and Frank D. Lewis, "The Economic Cost of the American Civil War: Estimate and Implications," *The Journal of Economic History*, Vol. 35, No. 2 (June 1975): 299–326.

Here we can perform a very simple exercise in counter-factual history. Suppose the South had won her independence either through the prowess of Lee, Jackson, Beauregard, and all the rest, or more simply because the northern states and Lincoln had simply granted it in order to avoid war. Suppose the northerners had simply shrugged their collective shoulders, drawn a line perhaps from the southern border of Missouri to the West, thereby dividing California, and had said to the Confederates, "There's your country, if that's what you want; go to it!" There would have been difficulties with Kentucky, Missouri, Maryland, and Delaware, but they might have been adjudicated. Would the economic development of either North or South over at least the next seventy-five years, say until 1930s, have been much affected? As it was, the southern economy remained agriculturally focused on cotton, using black and some white tenant and free farmer labor, with minimal disturbance of production relationships. There is no reason that the slaveholders would have made any changes under independence. Of course, the South would have been hurt, as it was hurt, by the slowdown in the world demand for cotton. As a separate nation it could have started its cotton industry under a protective tariff. But it did not need tariff protection from the North in order to compete away the New England textile industry in the period 1880–1920, even as part of the federal Union. And in the North, with the political obstacle to the national legislation removed, westward movement and the industrialization of the Middle West should have proceeded much as they did anyway. The southern Confederacy in 1860 was a closer approximation to a national state on the European model, with a clearly defined social structure and ideology, than was the more amorphous and complex North. There, Jefferson's original republic of independent farmers had been fused with Hamilton's vision of a growing industrial power by three decades of water and rail links, by the streams of immigration and the vigorous inter-regional trade. The Republican petit-bourgeois ideology of 1860 was a powerful one; it was the ideology of the French revolution against aristocracy and privilege, an ideology which in 1848 swept Europe and stood behind the efforts of princely politicians to form European nations out of the German and Italian principalities. Perhaps, then, it was only the crusading zeal of this ideological movement, rather than any close regard for economic interests that made northern farmers fight for the national union.

A change in the political atmosphere of business behavior, in the disposition, as it were, of the central government toward ambitious industrial capitalists – a kind of freeing of industrial enterprise and a transfer of the power over the pace of capitalist expansion from aristocratic or agrarian hands to the hands of a business bourgeoisie – was the net effect of the war, intangible and inestimable in importance. Under British rule, before the Revolution, no matter how minor, how weak the British restrictions on colonial capitalism may have been, the industrialization which did occur after 1790 would, under a colonial regime, have been sharply curtailed. What New England merchant would have experimented with investments in cotton mills in competition with those of Manchester, against the express policy of the crown? And in the 1870s how much of land speculation, minerals development, railroad construction, small-scale industrial investment might have been withheld under a national government divided and quarreling within itself, a government where a handful of antique slaveholders with wholly contrary economic interests exercised appreciable power over legislation. "Rational expectations" we now learn, are everything, but they presume a governmental behavior that investors can count on at least as predictable, and preferably, as exhibiting loving concern for their welfare.

With the Civil War then, the American government made one choice: a technically free labor force and a technically united national state, one that included by force the formerly slave states, a large, bi-racial, socially distinct, largely agrarian society. For the continued growth of a modern capitalist economy in the North, Lincoln's instincts were correct: National union was more important than the slaves' freedom. The North's union need not have included the South. It is hard to find the principle in technology or in economics that compelled the industrializing North, with its excellent East–West connections to a booming agricultural and increasingly industrial area of the Midwest, to drag behind its cart this large, depressed, troubled, and troublesome southern society.

Of course, if Lincoln could have looked ahead a hundred years, it would have seemed different. He would have seen, beginning in the war years just before 1920, the miracle of black mobility, and beginning in 1950, following the federal military and air/space projects, the co-optation of northern technicians, capital, and enterprise in exploitation of the resources and rich locational advantages of a sun-and-oil-belt. He would have seen the initiation of a new regional history from the central South to the Southwest and southern California, replacing the old Midwest as the focus of American hope, exuberance, and growing wealth. But we cannot credit the fathers of modern America with that sort of vision. Indeed, we can hardly believe it now that it has happened. Had he been an economist, Lincoln would have had to reckon that the expected gains to the North from a North–South trade and from investment permitted by free capital and labor movement across the border – those future returns, discounted back to 1860 – exceeded the war's expected costs. It is not likely that he carried cost/benefit analysis and counter-factual history that far.

It would seem easier for a historian simply to decline on the recorded fact: The North, through all its institutions – churches, farms, families, local governments – would not let the slaveholders get away with breaking up the nation. Lincoln – intuitive, astute, cautious, and politic enough to know when to be bold, like FDR in the second great American transition – had known just when to touch on the national nerve – the nerve of democratic sentiment, intertwined as it was with a cautious affection for an American history that began in a schoolbook version of the American Revolution – the nerve, in short, of patriotism. It is the feeling of family loyalty that, along with draft laws, social pressures, threats of jail, and thirst for excitement, gives the last push to a nation's military adventure. Instinctively Lincoln felt its stirrings or saw its potential as he formulated his public stance on the issues in the late 1850s and felt his way as president, first, to a rejection of compromise on the issue of slavery's territorial expansion, then to war for the union, then to slave emancipation as the culminating extension of free Republican principles.

III

It is one thing to hold together a body of people, North and South, barely, through force, by the skin of your teeth, and quite another to create from the legalities of the unity a strong national economy, supporting a recognizable national society, and assuming a position on a planet of nations. Yet this occurred repeatedly within the many-nationed capitalist civilization in the West in the nineteenth century as the political structure of nation states took definite shape. The proof in every case was found in a sustained national rate of economic growth and in the development of a coherent class-structured society and a national culture that gave warmth and excitement and spoke, at least to the middle classes, with a stirring eloquence. That set of cultures in the Western world lasted through to the middle decades of the chaotic twentieth century. Then, all together, it began to fall apart.

In the nineteenth-century history of nation-forming in America, as in Europe, a single region moved into a dominant position politically, and achieved rather readily a central position in the national culture. In France, this had long been Paris and the Ile-de-France; in Italy, the Piedmont and Lombardy; in Germany, Prussia and its Rhenish territories; in Lincoln's United States, the Middle West. As I have suggested above, not merely a national economy, but the national society formed in a large degree around it. The ethic, social structure, and values that contained and infused its strong and aggressive business life reshaped the Northeast and ultimately the South and Far West in its image. Its products were not only hogs, beef, corn, coal, steel, and the automobile, but also the great social products which it derived from the Northeast: the extension of the essentials of schooling, justice, and livelihood in its cities to internal migrants from its farms and the Americanization of foreign immigrants from eastern and southern Europe.

In this cycle, where the Republican culture was formed, the country grew like a long, heavy animal, with its head perhaps in New England, its nerve centers in New York and Chicago, its body and chief productive organs in the Middle West, and – dare a Yankee add? – its sturdy lower parts in the South and the still untamed West. From a Northeast perspective, the economy of the creature functioned, and the creature put on weight and muscle, through controls from the nerve center by signals from financial markets centered in New York, transmitting in turn signals from Europe, and especially from London. There in the nineteenth century the messages and information indispensable for international capital movements, investment, and trade were brought together and dispersed ultimately in the form of gold movements that underlay price, currency, and credit systems in the world's different constituent national states and their respective units of account. This is the way capital is said to organize production, to create flows of resources and of labor, to adopt new production technologies, and to turn out its swelling river of products even in the most bizarre and miscellaneous variety.

But in size and shape, America in 1900 formed a new species of nation, something unlike anything the world before had seen. Certainly it was far removed from its past as a mercantile city-state, yet its governing ethos was still a form of elite republicanism. In four decades since the Civil War, its farmers and businessmen, statesmen and educators had guided the extension of settlement to the Rockies and Hawaii and from the California coast east. The Plains were thick with wheat and cattle, and the southern Plains with cotton. The older Midwest was swimming in hogs and corn; the Northeast was floating in butter and milk to supply the growing urban centers of industry, trade, and communication. The secret of industrial technology, too, had been unlocked, and with it the earth had been tapped for coal, iron ore, and oil from what seemed to be an inexhaustible reserve. The political, legal, educational, and business system descended from earlier time had remained intact, but schools had assumed the function of social integration, and at least half of industrial production was carried on in corporations of large scale. What the Anglo-Celtic majority had built, utilizing its civic and capitalistic ideals, was a vast, rich receptacle to contain and reshape the new 20 percent that had come from Europe and, beginning after 1940, the old, black 15 percent emerging from the aftermath of slavery. The process was called Americanization, or more recently, integration. Its impulse was derived from the self-conscious rectitude and the earnest, confident evangelism of the Protestant spirit, working in harness with the economy's demand for labor to realize rapid economic growth.

This new American civilization felt a definite, but slightly defensive, uneasy, half-truculent, half-indulgent superiority to its European parent.

The immigrants themselves, those who had remained here, and sometimes their children, too, felt a tie not so much to a country as to a village,
a locale where grandparents still lived and whence the ethnic culture, the
religion, the cuisine, the memories, and the vanishing language derived.
In the upper classes, there was still the provincial subservience to European "culture" in music, the fine arts, humane scholarship, and pure
science. The notion of royalty and noble title still carried a fascination
which European artists and titled persons could exploit. But American
patriotism defined itself by its dissent from the class system and the ethnic
homogeneity of European nations. A less snobbish image of Europe was
of a place where the common man did not have a chance. As in colonial
times, Europe was looked upon as wicked – the more so since many of
the immigrants had come to escape harsh political and religious persecution. This was, in fact, a time in Europe when mass society, if not liberal
democracy, was spread faster than ever before or since (at least until very
recent decades), while America had in truth grown far away from the
unstructured egalitarianism of the Jacksonian republic. But this irony
passed unnoticed.

America's participation in the two world wars revealed how these
attitudes crystallized under stress. Both in 1914–17 and in 1935–40 the
impulse to pacifism and neutrality was strong. Washington's Farewell
Address was a staple of the political rhetoric; Wilson's 1916 slogan, "He
kept us out of war," and Roosevelt's blatant 1940 promise, "I will not
send your boys to any foreign wars," helped mightily in the elections of
those years. Wars are never entered into, at least by democratic states, in
cold blood, and for several years before entering the wars America sustained an official cold-bloodedness while emotions were torn and national pride was shamed.

At the heart of this ambivalence lay a division within the WASP majority
which revealed itself in the complex shadings of difference between the old
guard in the Democratic and Republican national parties, and their respective populist and progressive wings. The isolationism of 1914–17 was a
popular policy. The ethnic minorities with a residual emotional attachment
to the Central Powers strengthened the anti-British sentiment that was a
staple of political rhetoric. Without the ignorance and arrogance of the
German Foreign Office and High Command, particularly in the resumption of unrestricted submarine warfare, it is very possible that the United
States might never have been drawn in.[7] Yet the moment war was declared,

[7]A fascinating study on this topic was delivered by Avner Offer of the University of York at the 1988 meetings of the Australian Economic History Society at
Canberra and published as "Economic Interpretation of War: The German Submarine Campaign, 1915–18," *Australian Economic History Review*, Vol. 24,
No. 1 (March 1989): 21–41.

there was total enthusiasm for it. It was as if the country knew that it had done the right thing. This enthusiasm and sense of rightness came in part from old loyalties to England and France and the feeling that American democracy was safer in a world where they remained great powers. But it was not simply to keep America safe for democracy but to make the world safe for its spread that Wilson called up his troops. Entry into the war marked the domestic victory of the progressivist image of America over populism, of Roosevelt over Bryan. Much of that struggle must have taken place in the complex soul of Woodrow Wilson, but in the end, the tie to Britain fought on the same side as the sense of national pride and honor, and how could a man of Wilson's character, of his weakness for exaltation, resist the call to spread the gospel of American democracy to all nations? And surely the emotional reception that this chilly Presbyterian received as the symbol of the American dream among masses of European people after the war seemed a confirmation of his call. Wilson gave the finest and most universal expression to American political ideals. As with a Greek hero, the gods – the people – beckoned him on, and in the moment of victory, they struck him down, and showed him to have been self-deceived, ridiculous, and pathetic.

The isolationism of the 1930s and the slide into war was something different from the sentiments of 1914–17. Populism was not extinct, as *The Grapes of Wrath* so plainly reveals. Yet the ideological nature of the European conflict developed almost for the first time a split in opinion along a more classic seam. There was a great deal of popular sentiment for the Loyalist side in the Spanish Civil War. In America even less than in England and France did the postures of the Fascist and Nazi leaders strike a resonant chord. The predominant American attitude was less active hostility, which might have implied a confrontation, than a disgust. English and French inactivity supported American cynicism. This, Americans could say, was the sort of thing that Europeans had always done to one another. The New Deal had co-opted nearly all liberal sentiment, and Roosevelt for all his instincts as a Dutch patroon was no Anglophile. A shallow neutralism was the country's mid-thirties mood. The situation was the more complex because conservative leaders of both parties were split between the Anglo–American financial "establishment" and the America Firsters, a collection of rich Roosevelt-haters with sympathies on the "right."

The two entries into world war thus present a curious and complex contrast in America's self-image and its attitude toward Europe and the world, and the place of America in that world. In 1917 there had been a sincere and deep-rooted desire to stay out of the war, yet when entry into the war came, it was seized almost as an opportunity and pursued with zeal. By 1941 war had for several years seemed inevitable and perhaps by a majority even desirable so as to align America on the right side. Yet when the war came, it was realized that it would be long and hard and that the Japanese enemy was as dangerous as the German one. The consequences of losing such a war were unthinkable. But to win it would, Americans knew, leave the United States and the Soviet Union face to face on a world theater. The war was not a crusade for democracy. It was an angry effort to turn back the three Fascist powers, whatever the cost might be and whatever the future might bring.

The two decades immediately following each of these wars also deserve much thoughtful comparative study. A conservative old guard persisted in both parties and Republican progressives and Democratic populists existed in many shades and flavors. In the 1920s, everyone – populists, progressives, and conservatives alike – had pulled back from Wilson's formula for American involvement in world government. The progressivist urge to spread American democracy, which radical historians label imperialism, did not contemplate that this should be done in concert with the feeble and corrupt states of western Europe. And in the prosperity of the 1920s it almost seemed as if progressivism had accomplished its "historic mission." The European immigrants had been absorbed and the gates shut on that episode in the development of the republic. The reforms, too, had been absorbed and functioned easily within a framework of a large-scale and growing capitalism. Herbert Hoover, the conservative social engineer, represented the impulses of both laissez-faire and humane intelligence in the Republican Party. The continuing depression in some sectors of farming, the Red Scare, Prohibition, and fears of the growing mobility of blacks, made nativist populism the only authentic undercurrent of the 1920s. But neither populists nor the conservative–liberal fusion of sentiment among Democrats and Republicans alike left room for an imperialistic foreign policy in Europe – or even for one doing credit to the world responsibilities that so large and strong a nation should have assumed. So World War I, which was entered into in a wave of evangelical enthusiasm, faded into an isolationism tinged, as American attitudes had never been before, with a slight sense of malingering, of selfishness and guilt. These attitudes were strengthened in the early 1930s when Roosevelt pushed for domestic recovery by domestic means. Far from being imperialist, he and Morgenthau took an almost perverse joy in breaking up the world economy and gold standard.[8] But this childish irresponsibility by a great power could not be sustained after 1936 – and certainly not after Pearl Harbor.

After World War II, for at least two decades, the problem and the

[8]Charles P. Kindleberger, *The World in Depression, 1929–1939* (Berkeley: University of California Press, 1986), 225–226, from J. M. Blum, *From the Morgenthau Diaries* (Boston: Houghton Mifflin, 1959), 70–73.

policies took a different shape. It is hard to imagine how the decades 1945–65 could have differed more sharply from the inter-war years. The new domestic economic structures, public and private, demonstrated their strength. The American South released a new migration of blacks from the cotton belt and farmers from the hill country, and the body politic wrestled manfully with the special problems presented, while the South began its ascent into income parity and cultural homogeneity with the rest of the nation. The grandchildren of the European immigrants infiltrated all the kingdoms of the WASPS, while the latter sought to regulate the terms of coexistence, endeavoring to combine self-consciously liberal attitudes with some minimal maintenance of the forms of their familiar institutions. Again, as in the 1920s and 1930s, except for a residue of fearful conservative Republicans, there was in the 1940s, 1950s, and 1960s a rough national consensus about foreign and domestic policy alike. But how different – and how much better – was that consensus from the earlier one! How happy indeed might history have been had those inter-war decades of overheated domestic prosperity and frightful depression been simply cut out of the history like a piece of leaky pipe, and the attitudes, programs, and national balance of the Truman–Eisenhower years been joined directly to the Peace of Versailles, to Wilson's program, of which in fact they were a logical continuation!

To see the historical landscape from so great a height is to see indeed many such exciting paths down which history might have moved. But, of course, it is an illusion. Historians travel over history by air, but men, as they make history, travel on the ground. The dream which guided their steps after 1965 led them to follow the Japan of the 1930s in a foray into the jungles of Southeast Asia, a land where America's dream of creating a universal *pax Americana* went down in the frustrations and flames of a politically unwinnable war. The policy consensus in America broke up, and both political parties fractionated into a warring chaos of interests and ideologies, ideologies themselves largely false and contrived to cover the interests of the rich, the poor, the educated, the ignorant; of libertarians and proto-Fascists, of separate industries and regions and portions of the landscape; of those who set zeal on a single issue above peace and the general welfare. Americanism was dead at home, even as many of its values spread across the cultures of Europe, Asia, and the continents of the tropics. At home the word itself was no more than a verbal weapon in a civil war, and the language of that war reached its lowest point when the word *liberal* could be used, and used effectively, as an antonym to *Americanism* and a term of political abuse.

* * * * *

Nationhood in a common market

The astonishing materialism of the 1980s, the deterioration in stated public ideals, the sinking level of public discourse, the corruption of authority, the substitution of media entertainment for education and distortion for political argument, the descent of the American public language – once so fresh, vigorous, and expressive – into a collection of wisecracks and half-remembered platitudes – all this is explainable only in terms of what was once a nation, lost and seeking a new soul. The dissolution has not affected America alone. Britain, the nations of western Europe, even ancient Russia and the "nations" artificially erected by elites in Africa, Southeast Asia, and the Middle East, are in disarray. Japan's time is yet to come. We are none of us nations any longer, but regions, classes, networks, multinational firms, our high culture one of international experiences shared via movies, TV, fast travel. An international half-Americanized world is spreading, while paradoxically, but consistent with the levels on which the limited human creatures still must operate, local cultures, face-to-face relations, ethnic heritages, and history in the most personal and intimate sense are strengthening, too.

In some networks of regions and super-regional authorities, the world, if it does not explode, must gradually settle down. One thing is as certain as anything history teaches: The old structures of nations, their armies, their officials, their wars, their patriotism, bolstered by the mere reassertion of our grandparents' values within their traditional forms – these alone will never sustain or save us. Instead, Americans must return to engage in that painful search for freedom within the constraints of law, following, by much painful reassessment and re-education, ideals and values consistent with the social existence of our human race. The search must be peaceful, now that war is obsolete. But optimism, which is both our deepest and our shallowest trait, can tell us that the history may be happy, rich, productive, fulfilling – a social life out to the limits of the intricate physical, emotional, expressive, intellectual, acquisitive natures that God has given us. We can follow out with strength and dignity and joy, the space and time that remains to mankind on this planet, repairing where we can the social and ecological damage caused by our intolerances, our zeal, our greed and excessive appetites, and living vigorously with whatever we can salvage, until the end of time.

IV

One comes at last and, as of now, to the end – in time but not in momentum – of these episodes of the American regions' growth and decay. The links which the American economy made with the international one were strong enough already in 1929 to interrupt domestic prosperity. Then not the regions, but the nation, could to a degree shut itself off from foreign trade and financial flows while it reorganized its economic life and initiated restructuring and recovery. But that recovery had truly nationalized the domestic regional economies and was busy in the 1950s exporting large chunks of Americanization abroad – to Japan, to Europe, to parts of the non-industrial world. Not simply products, but tastes, demand patterns, styles of living, production equipment and techniques, styles in political life and economic control – all went abroad in the company of American foreign investment and the dominant dollar. When that cycle of economic expansion and cultural penetration crashed in 1968–74, in the moral and political confusion of the Nixon years, what was left?

America in the world today is a nation-state; it is a slogan probably still capable of rallying, shoving, or compelling its large population – a population the size of western Europe's – into war. Its central government has a military force of just less than overwhelming strength that it risks repeatedly in diplomatic and strategic maneuver. America is also a national economy, which in a world of free markets should mean nothing, but in a world of national mercantilisms is capable of much creative action and also of much mischief, much distortion, much destruction in a world where the possibility of interference and controls, and the awkwardness and risks of altering rates of currency conversion, overhang the atmosphere. Penetrating through the boundaries of the world's formal political and economic life, America is also a body of cultural characteristics developed out of experiences of rural settlement, urban immigration, industrial development in one after another of its regions and the rough homogenization of those local cultures. It is a style of behavior deriving in turn from some common hopes and values, from common ideals, even a common cynicism, from a sense of power and possibilities, alternating with a sense of hesitation, fear, doubt, and self-mistrust. It moves over a wide spectrum, from narrow religious and racial bigotry to curiosity, tolerance, openness, and the ready giving of friendship and affection. The American character, developed first in the economic experiences of the Midwest, is not confined to the native inhabitants of the United States. Americanization, the dream of the 1950s, showed that it had elsewhere some penetrative power wherever men were open to a new material culture and to the rhetoric and often the reality of tolerance and the liberal conception of life.

It seems to me, as I wrote earlier at the outset of these volumes, that human society may contain, locked in the physical and emotional machinery of its members, "all its elements, at all points and simultaneously *in posse* if not *in esse*." A national society, from the experiences of its survival, expansion, and internal interactions, develops in its members a certain characteristic emphasis, a certain clustered weighting of mutually

296

reinforcing and integrating characteristics, and with this character its members enter into the great arena of world affairs. The types meet and mingle and modify one another. New generations are born in new social environments. New syntheses of the elements, new institutions, new routinized and custom-created patterns of regulated behavior, develop to guide, constrain, and train, to alter and perpetuate.

Over the past 125 years, internal peace has been preserved and the means to what Americans call the abundant life left open in the United States by the maintenance, out of regional differences and rivalries, of a single sovereignty, and the diffusion within it of the powerful, if often superficial, values of an industrial culture, with its political accompaniment, its pragmatism, its sense for freedom and justice, its tolerance, and its eye on the main chance. It can only grow wiser and deeper by exposure to the variety of vitality and villainy of the social life in the world at large. This is true, one may suggest, even if, like the Midwest, it loses in the process many of its treasured virtues and advantages, even some of that proud nationality so painfully and uncertainly acquired. It is true even if the United States, with all the world's other nation-states, should, like the American southern Confederacy a century and a quarter ago, lose through trans-national arrangements of common institutions the option to enjoy unlimited national sovereignty. Only in the institutionalization of super-regional and super-national political forms lies the opportunity for what midwesterners would have called success in the human enterprise. Such forms, if they arise in world history before Armageddon, will in turn derive strength and reliability from our sense not merely of tolerance, but of a positive enjoyment of our common humanity.

15

European industrialization in an American mirror

I

An old-fashioned American – and almost everyone who has passed a certain age finds moments when he claims to be one – contained, as an Hegelian would suspect, an internal contradiction. He liked things big and done in a big way. But this was a nineteenth-century vice shared with the entire elite of Europe in that period, in politics, in business enterprise, even, according to one modern critic,[1] in literature. What else was the unification of Italy and Germany but a tidying up of the history of those peoples into national states, the sweeping away of ridiculous, fussy, "petty" principalities, of lesser and impotent local sovereignties? How else to explain the death-grip of the Hapsburg monarchy on southeastern Europe, the determined, ruthless power of the tsarist army and bureaucracy over the peoples of Eurasia, the imperialism, cultural and political, of a centralized French Republic, and of course, Britain:

> Wider still and wider
> Shall thy bounds be set,
> God who made thee mighty
> Make thee mightier yet!

sang the British hymn, as law, Christianity, morality, and free trade were carried by the British navy and regiments to the five continents and most of the intervening islands (except, significantly, the Japanese archipelago).

A contribution to the discussion at a conference on the Gerschenkron hypothesis in the light of recent research and thought, held at Bellagio, Italy, in October 1988, under the sponsorship of the Rockefeller Foundation, Gianni Toniolo (University of Venice) and Richard Sylla (New York University), organizers. I am much indebted to Professor Sylla for some frank and timely comments and criticisms. I doubt, however, that my corrections will have wholly satisfied him.

[1]George Steiner. I am in correspondence with Dr. Steiner in an effort to locate the reference.

European industrialization in an American mirror

In North America, between British Canada and Mexico (those outposts, respectively, of Scotland and Spain) the experiment of government
in a republican form, extending itself to the continental scale without
fragmentation and without collapse, like its Roman predecessor, into
absolutism, continued to be played out past one successive meridian after
another, westward to the Pacific. Its presidents, from Jefferson, Polk,
Lincoln to the Roosevelts, with the intervening Wilson and the succeeding Truman and Johnson, continued the vision and the thrust of its manifest destiny.

In American history, this intangible impulse appears indeed as the only
plausible answer to the question: Why did the North fight the Civil
War? The answer was Lincoln's: that a government of the people, by the
people, and for the people should not perish from the earth – and not
only not perish from the earth, but extend itself out over the earth. Old-
fashioned, nineteenth-century America came out of the twentieth century's two world wars with that dream still intact – a dream of making
the world safe, first, for a republic as against monarchy and aristocracy,
then for bourgeois democracy as against Fascist corporatism, Nazism,
and, on a world theater, Marxian socialism. It had a culture ensconced
behind the social machinery of a national state's three means of protecting and extending itself: (1) through enlightenment (called education
and communication), (2) through trade and trade policy, (3) through
diplomacy and force of arms. Europe's "long nineteenth century" of
expansion within and beyond national boundaries by all three means
began, according to one's perspective, in 1763, 1789, 1815, 1848, or
1870 – and ran to 1914. America's twentieth century began in 1940,
with the fact and date of its termination a matter, at the moment, of
partisan dispute into which the mere economic historian is perhaps un-
wise to enter.

But for an old-fashioned American, with mind, heart, culture, and
even costume established before 1940, there lies just here in all this
imperialism the contradiction. For alongside the admiration of large-
scale accomplishment – the spanning of a continent; the plowing of the
Plains to wheat; the assembly line that turns out a million cars; Texas,
New York, Chicago, California; everything that is the biggest and the
best, and best because it is biggest and biggest because it is best (a
simple re-statement of the law of natural selection) – the old-fashioned
American as a political animal revealed a deep mistrust of concentrated
power.

Perhaps it began with the Revolution, which was really not very revolutionary, except from the point of view of King George and a few thousand
of his officials and the Tory adulators of monarchy. The seventeenth century's established colonial churches, Episcopal and Congregationalist,

were already unraveling by 1750, and the whole power and prestige structure – the structure of deference to which John Adams was still wedded but from which Jefferson and Franklin, in their different ways, were half-emancipated – had fallen apart in the back country, that is, thirty miles beyond the coast. Only in the tidewater and plantation South did it maintain its hold, though it threw long shadows up into the southern hills and gave a coloration of residual deference or of outlandish, intensely individualistic or clannish localism to the social democracy of the upcountry. After the brilliant and violent outbreak of democracy from Jackson through Polk, when the expansion of the political system of the United States reached its continental limits, and once and for all (we used to be taught) with Lincoln's noble words and (we now say, also) his ruthless politics, democracy and capitalist economic organization based on personal, individual liberty – a legal freedom of thought and person and, even more, of thoughtless action within the social sanctions of the local community, together with governance, not by an executive, but by law-makers and judges – became established alongside private property, which, as its elder brother among American freedoms, still kept pride of place.

Democracy and "wealth" (called prosperity when used without pejorative connotation, and considered a "flow" rather than a stock) maintained their dialectic struggle through the decades 1870–1930, when the great American industrial region, the Northeast and the eastern Middle West, experienced modern industrial growth. The absolutely equal joint position of these two principles in the American public pantheon was confirmed in the presidential election of 1896, when the nation was made safe for the gold standard and the fundamental rights of capital were written in stone in the bland visage of William McKinley by the exercise of the ballot. The contradiction between property and democracy was sealed over by the concordat of "progressivism" in both political parties and across all the Wests – Middle, South, and Far. The arrangement included the charade of antitrust, the token federal regulatory commissions, the rather appreciable regulation and licensing of public utility monopolies at the state level, and sporadic intrusions of the law in matters of worker safety, health standards, weights and measures, and the like. Through the strong rising tides of prosperity from 1896 to 1929, in the boom of 1896–1903, the war, and the twenties between 1922 and 1928, the Emersonian observation of nearly a century earlier was applicable once again: "Things are in the saddle and ride mankind." For "things" to be in the saddle meant in the American ideological context, economic, and in this earlier period particularly industrial, growth.

That democracy, or at least a perception of the ultimate possibility of democracy, could make large-scale capitalistic organization work was shown by the behavior of the industrial labor force as it grew by leaps and bounds. A quick summary has room to mention only three features in the formation of an industrial culture of proletarians and petty bureaucrats: (1) the conversion of a generation of farm and small-town native youth to the jobs and life of urban and suburban cultures, an army of tens of thousands pouring in every year from the countryside; (2) the Americanization of twenty-five millions of European immigrants, both of the "old" immigration from Germany, Scandinavia, and the British Isles and, after 1880, of the "new" immigration from Italy and central Europe; (3) the taming of the labor movement by political bossism and the courts. In these respects and in many others, particularly by the action of rising wages and the provision of public education, liberal democracy strengthened the workings of capitalism. This is not surprising, except to those who see the history backwards from the present. Democracy and capitalism grew up hand in hand as prosperity diffused the evidences of material improvement – and the promises of still more – widely enough to strengthen their marriage, despite fears of monopoly, dehumanizing routines, bosses, and the capital's frequent ruthless use of its superior legal position. Despite, or perhaps because of, some growth in scale and discipline in plants and a surge of financial and organizational concentration in firms, the system worked through the 1920s to produce continuous rises in the production and productivity indexes in agriculture as well as manufacturing. A third essential element in the American ideology, pragmatic materialism, gives meaning to the phrase "the system worked."

The violent withdrawal of public confidence in the "conservative–liberal," or traditionally progressive, program in the election of 1932 struck at both its ideological bases in the interests of just such a pragmatism. Unrestricted control over labor, finance, and capital was withdrawn from the private sector and the skittishness about concentrations of public power in a central authority away from the local community suddenly evaporated in the sunshine of a president's winning smile. That the system and the ideology could support such legalized violence against its principles in the interest of getting fast results in a new and threatening situation had already been shown in Wilson's drastic war preparedness measures in 1916–18. The New Deal programs at first sought only immediate results in a dozen different directions which, though in fact closely inter-related, were dealt with by various and, to a degree, mutually contradictory laws. The third "leg" of the ideology, which was in effect to have no ideology at all except action directed by a striving for "prosperity," had survived the collapse of the other two.

The period over which the old-fashioned American ethos worked and was valid thus showed a way around what an Hegelian might have seen as its fatal contradiction. Liberty and prosperity could both be preserved by a convincing show of government, by the fostering of homogeneity of goals, even of character structures, in the population if done in an atmosphere of high economic opportunity and continued growth in jobs, output, and welfare. Like a bicycle, the two wheels of the American system, democracy and property, could keep the rider balanced and whizzing forward if he carried his weight right, had a smooth road, and pedaled like hell. When the road got rocky in the 1930s, the bicycle wobbled. And when it righted itself after 1948, it was, to change the sports metaphor slightly, a decidedly different ball game.

II

Most Americans know nothing of European history. There are indeed no historians of Europe, as such, in America or even in Europe.[2] Imagine such a one, all-seeing, all-wise, who knows the geography, the culture, the technology, the tastes, and the behavior of the people over long spans of time, one who, like Fernand Braudel, can speak of "the Mediterranean" as a unit or, in one breath, of the fishing and shipping cultures from the North Sea coasts, the British Isles, and the Atlantic coastline, as D. W. Meinig[3] has done for colonial North America, who at first glance into the interior sees not feudal fiefdoms, boundaries, and wars, but the great central European plain broken by the Rhine, as the Mississippi breaks the Midwest, and sees in the cities, not provincial and national capitals, but trading points, nodes of economic activity and social communication. Such a one (it would have to be an American to have so broad a continental perspective and so deep a detailed ignorance) would view nineteenth- and twentieth-century European industrial history rather differently from even the widest views of Europe-born historians.

Yet the economic histories of the two continents are not so different after all. In both, in the late eighteenth and early nineteenth centuries, several regions of intense mercantile activity entered into light industry – textiles, metalworking, and machine tools – located in relation to water power, the markets and commercial facilities of ports, and pre-existing supplies of some skilled rural and craft labor. The phenomenon first appeared along the west coast in England, then in the iron and coal lands of the Midlands, South Wales, and southern Scotland; on the continent it began to occur along the Seine, the Meuse, the Rhine and its tributaries, and in some of the ancient craft cities along the North Sea and Baltic coasts, in southern Germany and northern Italy, in Alsace and along the Rhone at Lyon. The northeastern United States is but another example, at the commercial cen-

[2]However, there is a notable one in Australia.
[3]D. W. Meinig, *The Shaping of America,* Vol. 1, *Atlantic America, 1492–1800* (New Haven: Yale University Press, 1986).

ters located on the Delaware and the Hudson (Philadelphia and New York), from Boston in a semi-circle forty miles to the west from Providence to southern New Hampshire and in the Connecticut Valley as far north as southern Vermont.

By mid-century, after accumulation of both real and financial capital, and with the experience of financing governments and wars (which in the United States meant the Civil War), banking and capital markets weighed in in time to help create the railroads and large-scale processes which a common industrial technology made available. On both continents, coal played its agglomerating and concentrating role from the 1840s on. After 1850, the huge steel plants burst from the ground, like giant mushrooms, in the valleys of the Rhine and the Ohio Rivers and their tributaries: the Ruhr, the Saar, the Moselle, the Allegheny and the Monongahela, the Mahoning and the north-emptying Meuse (Maas), Sambre, Scheldt, and Cuyahoga. Both along the Rhine, its tributaries and canals, and down the Great Lakes, the systems of water and rail transport moved ores, coal, coke, heavy equipment, and iron and steel products to and from remote sources of minerals and dense industrial districts – the fast-multiplying sites of machinery manufacture, the railroad shops and marshaling yards, and the coastal centers of shipping, banking, and the earlier light industrial manufacture. The growth and diffusion of the market for manufactures over wide areas, the proliferation and exchanges of a common technology, the mobility of international capital – all in all, the continuous spread of a modern, successful, bourgeois culture, like a sheet of water over western Europe and northeast and north central United States – drew one region, one state, one national unit, one local culture after another into the whirl. In the careful tracing of each nation's history by Alan Milward and Berek Saul,[4] nothing is more impressive than the record of smaller nations (Switzerland, Sweden, Belgium, Norway, Denmark, finally the Netherlands and, in Germany, Saxony and Würtemburg/Baden), areas vastly different in resources, access to transport, industrial history, and many details of agrarian culture. All, between 1850 and 1900, found something to do to produce national income growth rates of between 15 and 25 percent per decade.[5]

Even more astonishing from an Anglocentric economist's view are the

---

[4]Alan Milward and S. B. Saul, *The Development of the Economies of Continental Europe, 1850–1914* (Cambridge, Mass.: Harvard University Press, and London: G. Allen and Unwin, 1977), Chs. 3, 4, 5, 10.

[5]Simon Kuznets, *Modern Economic Growth: Rate, Structure, Spread* (New Haven: Yale University Press, 1965), 64–65, Table 2.5. See also my tabulation of these data in "Economic History Seen Through the National Income Accounts," *Zeitschrift für die Gesamte Staatswissenschaft*, Vol. 124, No.1 (1968), 148–158, esp. Table 2.

areas deep in central Europe that come to life, both the old mining centers of the sixteenth century and those that had experienced the eighteenth-century textile industrialization – Saxony, Silesia, Bohemia. The spilling of this over the Alps into the North Italian lands of the Renaissance completes the nineteenth century's series of "spurts" of modernization in western Europe. It is paralleled in a small way in the United States by the outcropping, and eventual in-migration from New England, of the major part of the textile manufacture in the southeastern Piedmont, the echo effect of the northern heavy industry growth at the Birmingham coal and ore deposits, and some modern urbanization in the rail terminal city of Atlanta. Then, beginning in the 1880s, what Schumpeter termed the Third Kondratieff, the burst of new technology in electricity and chemical processes, including in the latter the internal combustion engine, carried large-scale industry into the twentieth century.

The history, then, is that of the growth, like the tangled grasses, vines, bushes, and trees in a fertile river valley (in this case an ocean valley), of one huge, inter-communicating capitalist culture. In all the basic components of a growing economy, similar trends and tendencies manifest themselves. The characteristic Western demographic pattern begins to appear. Death rates fall toward a lower asymptote of fifteen to twenty per thousand; the falling urban middle-class birth rate infects the whole income distribution, above and below. Differences in the timing create local or national population bulges, to which for some areas migration provides an adjustment in local factor proportions over the whole two-continent space. Educational systems, state-controlled and financed, are erected, literacy increases, and new structures of scientific and technical training and discovery are superimposed on the ancient ecclesiastical centers of humanistic and theological learning. The scientific theories and knowledge underlying modern technology are elaborated along a common front from Moscow to Berkeley, California, and the specific arts of invention develop, colored by local cultures, individual mental sets, and economic opportunities. Ideas and inventions, wherever created, are readily picked up and carried to points of advantageous application.

This mass of innovation, of creativity, of industrial and agricultural production was mediated, as it were, by the human organizations through which individual men, alone and in associated groups, dominated, persuaded, or purchased the services and allegiances of others in what was in effect, if not in spirit, a cooperative social enterprise. But the forms of organization and their modes of operation and control required, and ordinarily exhibited, the finest of adjustment to techniques, materials, products, and market, on the one hand, and to the social characteristics of the local regional human environments, on the other. Until late into the nineteenth century, on both sides of the Atlantic an intensely competitive business atmosphere prevailed; entrepreneurs and rentiers followed Marx's "law of Moses and the prophets" – to accumulate and to exploit and expand. After 1880 at many points, private entrepreneurs banded together, to shelter themselves from one another's competition, in syndicates, cartels, and large financial combinations and structures. This was a universal tendency in Europe and the United States. In America, a "progressive" ethos produced the idea of "antitrust," enforcing competition in manufacturing and, where competition did not promise to work, the idea of state regulation and control. Perhaps the very fractionation of sovereignty, the strength of individual states as organizational units in America favored this. Many progressives, too, displayed a technocratic mentality, and revealed a bias toward professional government, a government by experts. In Europe the state in the period behaved somewhat differently. The consciousness of social subordination, remaining, no doubt, from the imprinting of a thousand years of feudalism and Catholic doctrine, had not died. The church and large sections of the peasantry were fundamentally and philosophically not liberal and not at all capitalistic in attitudes and values. European capitalism had not had its slate wiped as clean as in America of what had been written on the board hundreds of years before: a close sense of community, of social interdependence. Socialism was an important counterforce, and governments were pushed to develop worker welfare programs. Labor parties formed in a futile effort to bring to pass democratic socialism as the means to harness the expansive and exploitative power of capital.

The political response of continental national societies to this international subversion by liberal capitalism and socialism alike was the idealization of the nation. This gave Europe a collection of strong and varied cultures and an exciting body of literature and art. But in the end, the word "nation" served conservative politicians and later Fascist demagogues as ultimately "race" served the politicians of the American South: as a point around which to rally the conservative fears and hatreds of the "little people." The simultaneous growth of socialist and nationalist emotion after 1900 produced in the political crisis of 1914 the enlistment of the German, British, and French socialist parties under the flags of their respective empires. The enemy was not within but across the Rhine, and out of that mind-set, in the 1920s (which from 1923 to 1928 in Germany were a time of brilliant technological achievement), National Socialism was born. The progressivist, experimental, energetic New Deal in America in the 1930s was matched in Europe by the immersion of large-scale industry in the totalitarian state in central Europe and the breakdown into impotence of the governments of France and Britain.

In the end, an economic historian must bring "ideology" back on center stage. It is not a word that an old-fashioned American liberal can admire. It is a European word and has a nasty polemical ring. The role of the ideology of nationalism can indeed be most clearly seen by looking at European developments, not from the West looking east, but from the East looking west, i.e., by looking at Europe in a Russian mirror. The next to last book[6] of that remarkable emigré scholar, Alexander Gerschenkron, bears in fact this title, although it says more about Russian history and the mirror for Europe which Gerschenkron fashioned out of it than about Europe itself. His schema can be shown as follows, with the addition of a column on an aspect on which he is not very precise, i.e., ideology:

Country	Source of capital and management	Presumed political ideology
Britain	Small-scale "original accumulations," factor markets	"Bourgeois" democracy
Germany and mid-continent	Large credit banks, firms, and combines	Corporatism
Russia	Centralized state, mercantilism	Absolutism

Industrialization, he says, was achieved by each of these routes sequentially in Europe, a nation's particular history depending on the time, circumstances, posture, and especially its state of "relative backwardness" on the eve of its "great spurt."

Now this schema had a certain interest at the time and place at which it was advanced, i.e., the Harvard Department of Economics in the 1950s. It emphasized that a national production index could "spurt" under several different organizational forms and in a variety of cultural and historical contexts. It threw off a colored light from the complex, many-sectioned crystal of Europe's national histories, and it put in the shade the simpler models of development then in vogue and in use. At points, Gerschenkron's schema invites comparison in scope and "scientific" pretension with that of Schumpeter, his immediate predecessor and evident model in the role of great European scholar in the Harvard department. But Schumpeter's attitudes and sweep were essentially aristocratic and imperial; he took all economic thought, and the whole dynamic capitalist world, as his oyster. Gerschenkron's focus throughout was on the national economy, *its* power structure, *its* organization, *its* controls, *its* position as a mercantilist power relative to its rivals.

[6]Alexander Gerschenkron, *Europe in a Russian Mirror* (Cambridge: Cambridge University Press, 1970). The book also offers a backwards look into the body of Gerschenkron's thought and attitudes as they crystallized in the 1950s and 1960s in his concept of "relative backwardness" and its application to the cases of the various western European nations.

This is a richer view than one which considers all states or social structures to have been alike at all places and all times. It explains the specific patterns of institutional "substitution" that evolved in different states as the formation of modern industry took shape. But the emphasis is on the formal style and organization of leadership under which a country's "great spurt" occurred when its time had arrived. It is a notion that might have been evolved in the mind of a rather enlightened but essentially authoritarian-minded Russian bourgeois, one who had stared too long perhaps at the blinding mercantilistic achievements of Peter the Great.[7] It leaves no room to consider the profound questions of the relation within the capitalist culture as a whole between the growth of knowledge of techniques and resource supplies, on the one hand, and the expansion and focus of final demand, on the other, a relationship which sets the limits of opportunity for entrepreneurs, however organized, and determines for a given region a zone of time within which its D-Day can take place. Certainly in the growth of the various European industrial regions, these fundamental elements of production and trading opportunities – technological change, resource availabilities, population growth through natural increase and through net migration – weigh more heavily in setting the timing and extent of a "spurt" than does the "relative backwardness" of the various nation-states that defined the political map of the continent. The resounding "theses" of Gerschenkron tell the size and shape and weave of the stockings the family hangs out on Christmas eve but say nothing of when or why Santa Claus comes down the chimney. "Relative backwardness" is thus a feature of almost no value in explaining the economic rise of a whole inter-connected continental culture. It has no interest for American economic history, and this means that, taking a continental view, it has very little for Europe, either.[8]

[7]Ibid., Lecture 3, 62–96. Unlike the acceptance given to these ideas by Gerschenkron's students, who sat in his lectures and directly felt the force of his personality and his learning, my own attitude to his work and influence, based on his writings, is decidedly ambivalent. These views, which are not appropriate to be aired in this space, are elaborated in a separate essay, presented to the Social Science History Association at its meetings in Washington, D.C., in November 1989.
[8]This is obviously an overstatement. The division of an area into separate political sovereignties has both retardative and stimulating effects on its rate of economic growth. The retardative effects are those dwelt on in all the economics descended from Adam Smith's original insight about the division of labor and the extent of the market and Ricardo's model of the gains from trade and international specialization. Free product and factor flows, equalization of marginal costs and marginal revenues, free exchanges of information within a single state – all these features contribute to the formation of an efficiently functioning capitalistic economic machine. This is the positive side to political unification on a continen-

The political and cultural forms and relationships by which labor and enterprise are organized within the system of ideas and values by which men live, i.e., their ideologies, have, of course, when the chips are down, the greatest importance and interest for social life. They create not simply, or even principally, the economy, but the society which operates, with whatever results, in terms of human happiness as the technical wonders and miseries of modern industrialization unfold. The political and ideological accompaniments of Gerschenkron's three paths to a spurt of industry are by no means mere indifferent, value-free substitutes. He recognized this and wrote about it with passion in the case of the Soviet path. But nowhere in his writings did he dwell on the blank that is left under the heading of political economy in the second "big bank" form, i.e., the German form, centralized and planned without the overlordship or ownership of assets by the state. Yet the preservation of the social and cultural values of liberal, market capitalism under twentieth-century production conditions has been the agonizing task of twentieth-century political and social organization in America and Europe alike.

* * * * *

By "Europe in an American mirror," then, I have meant European history as seen by an old-fashioned American liberal, one who clings to the idea that freedom and plenty, rather than power and plenty, are indissolubly linked. From such a view, the history of the national states, their forms and their rivalries, is a distracting nightmare. The common progress and the common confusion and disaster on both sides of the pond is the imperfect product of liberal thought and attitudes, when

tal or a world scale. This analysis, however, neglects important features of the historical development of industry within the multinational world capitalism of the past two hundred years. In particular, it neglects, as Gerschenkron emphasized, the incentive effects of the nations' competitive mercantilisms and the value of a variety of separate local sources of creative innovation. These are indeed "powers of production" spoken of by Friedrich List in *The National System of Political Economy* (1841). They must develop within a specific environment before their more generalizable features can be extracted and disseminated throughout the world. Like the varieties of vegetation and wildlife, much is lost by cultural homogenization in the interests of a narrowly conceived engineering efficiency passing itself off as a set of prices and economic values.

The subject is too grand and complex to be treated in a footnote at the end of an already long volume. A very suggestive treatment of the economic significance of a customs union for the political unification of an area is offered by Hubert Kiesewetter for the German Zollverein in the national unification of the German states under the Prussian-led empire in 1870. Hubert Kiesewetter, "Economic Preconditions for Germany's Nation-Building in the Nineteenth Century," in H. Schulze, ed., *National-Building in Central Europe* (Leamington Spa/Hamburg/New York: Berg, 1987), 81–105.

pursued within the binding limits of national cultures. The important lesson of nineteenth-century history is the general growth of income and wealth over western Europe and North America, when markets opened, factors gained mobility, technology became continuously fertile, and enterprise ceaselessly active. The fumbling fingers of the national states, ancient and monarchical or newly formed, even under bourgeois domination, sometimes pushed development along within national boundaries but as often interfered out of local, particularistic, or military interests, and their efforts ended in disaster when the states themselves, like the early modern absolutist and bureaucratic empires to their east, became too centralized, too powerful, too far distanced from their base in liberal democracy. No doubt a truly common market would have been better. Even such a continent-wide arrangement, which America acquired in 1789, demands the encouragement, enforcement, and monitoring of a body of officials, themselves responsible to an electorate. The social effects of unbridled capitalism and the long-run social interest in the environment and the care and preservation of the mind and the arts against the rude force of unrestricted democracy still require organizational structures that command respect and power equivalent to those of the economy. But all this is what Europe between today and 1992 – and beyond – is trying to achieve. A new "new economic history," written in a United Europe or a United West or a United Great Power World, will focus on and reveal the structures and motions of life, both below the level of the nation and above it, far more than the national case histories of the 1950s and 1960s, whether examined alone or comparatively within Gerschenkron's curious model of relative backwardness.

But this is a dream not only for Europe but for America as it fumbles its way into the twenty-first century. Here it is a harder job since the simple goal of creating a homogeneous common market has long been attained. The "problem" has been rather how to create a common society which is not a steamroller, one which can pass over the ground efficiently and still leave some varied life. Part of the problem lies in the educational system, where today America seems sometimes simply to have given up. It is as one does with one's lawn sometimes: Weary of trimming and rolling and endlessly mowing, one sits on the front porch and watches the grass and shrubs revert to the tangled wilderness. More immediately it concerns the relation of the culture to a vast and potentially powerful federal state, lurching in convulsive spurts from one social problem to another, rushing to fires, indeed, but better equipped with TV cameras to capture the headlines than with hose and hook-and-ladder to put the fire out. It is not individual geographical entities that America must consolidate into an ordered union; it is individual interest groups, localities, classes, networks of associations, professions, age groups. The solution is not to abolish that state, but to make it responsible to social interests other than national defense and national aggression. America, as always, presents what a United Europe might become – the same possibilities, the same risks, and the same dangers. Which continent today, one may ask, has the happier prospects ahead?

* * * * *

The principal source of America's and Europe's economic and political disasters in the period between wars lay outside the boundaries of any one nation, in a wholly ungoverned world of national individualisms, in the variety of sovereignties and their uneven states of economic development and discordant governmental forms. There is now a chance for perhaps a half-dozen superpowers to form: America, Europe, Japan, China, possibly India, and whatever will lie within the boundaries of the Soviet Union. Africa, Latin America, and the Middle East will still presumably remain "trouble spots" in organizational chaos, still with the potential they showed in the nineteenth century for luring the "Great Powers" into conflict on their terrain. The great power blocs today in relation to one another really are powerless since no one can dominate the others without destroying itself. A form then of social order imposed in each of them is ultimately the model for peace, order, and amity among them all. American history shows a society forming within such a federal model, expanding for seventy years, then blowing apart, only to re-form as the frame for an industrializing expansion, again of vast dimensions, which ran another seventy years before a crisis. God forbid that anyone should add to economists' collection yet another cycle which would predict the dissolution of the unity forged originally by the New Deal and World War II, starting in the year 2000. But whether extended decades of hard times and ghastly internal political misery do come again to the industrialized West depends now not only on the behavior of its own national entities, either individually or as a corporate group, but also on the course of history of the other of today's and tomorrow's great powers, both individually and in the development of a world order resting on structures and purposes in common. Perhaps, with eternal American optimism and less than usual American egotism, we may feel that that is a cause not for despair, but for hope.

Annexes

Annex A

A look backward

Quantification and the counter-factual in American agricultural history, 1850–1910: a re-examination

All, all of a piece throughout:
Thy chase had a beast in view;
Thy wars brought nothing about
Thy lovers were all untrue.
Tis well an old age is out,
And time to begin a new.
– J. Dryden, Chorus from
the Secular Masque

INTRODUCTION

Between 1958 and 1962, an effort was begun at the University of North Carolina to employ quantification in the historical study of the principal branches of the American agricultural industry: (1) the plantation and small cotton farms of the South; (2) the mixed grain and livestock farms in the Northeast and North Central (Middle West) states; (3) the specialized wheat farms and cattle ranches of the Great Plains; (4) the specialized dairy and hay farming in the market areas of the coastal cities of the Northeast and around the Great Lakes. The decades 1840–1860 and 1900–10 were chosen as end points to catch these regional groups of specialized producers at significant points in their modern history. The

Prepared for the joint US–USSR Conference on Agrarian History, held at Talinn, Estonian S.S.R., June 6–10, 1987. Published in *Agricultural History*, Vol. 62, No. 3 (1988).

To the accumulated pile of acknowledgements for these studies, I should add one to the members of the Yale dissertation workshop in economic history. An earlier and much flawed version of this survey was presented there in February 1987. I am indebted to the members of the workshop, and particularly to David Weiman for both corrections and reassurance.

313

cotton regions were to be shown first, at the height of the slave labor system and then after the full evolution of the postbellum organization of free farms as share tenancies and share and wage labor plantations. For the grain and meat producers the dates captured the organization before and after the great expansion from the eastern edge of the Plains to the Rockies, and the evolution of the complex market system of open range with seasonal drives and shipment through the feeding and fattening areas to central slaughtering points, to be combined with animals from the older mixed-grain and livestock farms. The study of dairying was designed to cover the period of market growth through the rail deliveries in urban milksheds as the heavy industrial development in the North Atlantic seaboard and upper Middle West took place.

The data for this work were found in the three main sorts of sources mined by the "fathers" of American agrarian history, Malin, Shannon, Phillips, Gray, Gates, Webb, and Bidwell and Falconer: (1) the manuscript returns of the federal censuses, available for 1850–80; (2) the published compilations of the Census, the earlier statistics and reports made to the agricultural office in the U. S. Patent Bureau and after 1863 to the U.S. Commissioner (later Secretary) of Agriculture; (3) data yielded as part of "literary" evidence: plantation records, travelers' accounts, and farm diaries, published proceedings of agricultural societies, reports of state boards and commissioners of agriculture, and most especially, the collections of that peculiarly American journalistic enterprise, the farm journals and periodicals which appeared from the presses in a number of major cities adjoining the farming areas, the combined circulation of which in the 1880s must have totaled, on conservative estimate, at least several hundred thousand. Among the news of new developments in farming, endless letters from readers, moralistic sermons, poems about the farm home, accounts of the world's natural and man-made wonders, and other similarly entertaining, instructive, and self-revealing information, are contained occasional bits of concrete fact: acreages, yields, animal weights and diet, uses of labor time, effect of various practices and improvements.

The manuscript census materials for 1860 drawn in the UNC (Parker–Gallman) sample have since been greatly extended by the later researches of Swan, Foust, Fogel and Engerman, Wright, Sutch, Ransom, and others. Most recently, a sample has been drawn for the northern areas in 1860 by Bateman and Atack. A large body of data now exists to survey and compare the state of U.S. agriculture, North and South, as of 1860.

The other sources described above were utilized in a research effort designed to measure the changes in labor productivity in the various operations of crop production, livestock raising, and farm capital formation in the major producing areas. This work made a wide survey of the farm journals and government publications to derive sets of contemporaneous observations on man-hours in each specific operation sufficient to mark central tendencies in the different regions in the two terminal periods. Per-acre yields and, for animals, average weights, milk yields, and slaughter rates were compiled. Each commodity study, when completed, was designed thus to measure the impact of three factors in the productivity growth: (1) changes in the distribution of the output over regions of differing original natural character, i.e., westward movement and farmers' (Smithian) response to commercial opportunities; (2) changes in mechanical techniques in operations on the soil or in livestock handling over the period; and (3) changes in biochemical technology and knowledge affecting fertility of the soil, genetic features of seed and breeds, insect control, and the like. Data on production and yields were drawn largely from published Census and USDA sources, by county or state.

Studies on the following products then were planned:

(1) Farm-formed capital: land clearing, fencing, construction;
(2) Dairy products: raw milk, cream, butter, cheese, buttermilk;
(3) Field crops: cotton, corn, wheat, oats, hay;
(4) Power: numbers and utilization of draft animals – horses, mules and oxen, both on the farms and in cities;
(5) Meat: pork and beef, with the mix changing toward the latter following changing tastes and relative costs.

Production data were gathered on sheep and wool, tobacco, potatoes, poultry, and other minor crops, but the effort stopped far short of measuring labor inputs in this heterogeneous body of output.

Of these studies, those on capital formation, dairying (in terms of raw milk), and the grains were completed by the UNC group so far as the data allowed. A partial study on cotton (reprinted as Chapter 4, above) was issued much later. A list of these publications is appended below. Many data were collected for studies of livestock, but the work was held up by two seemingly insuperable obstacles: (1) the measurement of supplies of wild forage in animal diets in the earlier period (the so-called grass and acorn problem) and (2) the complexity of the systems of range and feedlot prevailing in the Middle West in the later period. Left unpublished also was a crowning effort to combine all the studies to show the complete time budget for farm labor in the United States as it changed between the earlier and later periods and to trace the influence of each of the three fundamental sources of productivity change in producing the composite result, i.e., the four- to ninefold expansions of output of the various products under conditions of constant or rising yields per acre and per animal accompanying a growth of the farm labor force from 3.8 million to 1850 to 9.1 million in 1900, – a rise of about 150 percent above its 1850 level.

A look backward

The paper presented here reviews what appear in retrospect to have been the most significant findings of this uncompleted effort with respect to the influence of the three major historical factors affecting labor productivity growth in these agricultural operations. I regret having to defer – probably forever – the completion of the livestock and cotton studies and any effort to add up the results on the individual crops into national totals. The aging of research work sometimes gives new perspective on what was done, but it cannot make new data grow where none grew before or convert what would be sheer guesswork into defensible estimates. An effort is made, however, to understand and take into account the criticism of – and improvement on – the study of the major grains contained in a paper of F. M. Fisher and P. Temin and to use that discussion as an opening to a wider investigation in the realms of a highly speculative counter-factual history of American development.

I

DATA AND METHOD

It would be idle to re-examine and criticize in detail the individual studies – either those accomplished or those stillborn – that constitute the literary remains of this ambitious project. In all cases the method of research and estimation was roughly identical. Contemporary sources from the middle and the end of the century were sifted to find specific statements about the man-hours used in specific farm tasks, given per acre or animal or per unit of final output, (L_1/A) or (L_2/O), and to complement these with statements about product yields per acre or per animal, (O/A).[1] Labor productivity in the crop was then expressed

---

[1] Labor input is expressed in the sources per acre or per animal (L_1/A) for most tasks, requiring then a yield or weight figure (O/A) to show productivity (O/L_1). For operations directly on the crops (cotton picking, corn husking and shelling, grain threshing, sometimes milking), the figure is given relative to the volume of output (L_2/O).

The estimates of per acre yields were derived by straight line backward projection from 1866–75 values by state, from USDA estimates. These are in fact much lower than the optimistic statements from various contemporary sources, especially for the West, and would seem hence to yield an upper bound to the actual productivity growth from 1840/60 to 1900/10. Recently, however, Atack and Bateman estimated the yields by a regression of crop outputs on total acreage for their large sample of farms from the manuscript census of 1860. They found that, on average, yields were even lower, so that our estimates of the productivity growth appear as much as 20 percent too low. See J. Atack and J. F. Bateman, *To Their Own Soil: Agriculture in the Antebellum North* (Ames: Iowa State University Press, 1987).

from these three sets of estimates in some variant of the following equation:

$$\frac{O}{L} = \frac{1}{\dfrac{L_1}{L} \times \dfrac{L_1/A}{O/A} + \dfrac{L_2}{L} \times \dfrac{L_2}{O}}$$

In the three completed sets of studies – land clearing, milk, and grain – the producing areas of the nation as of mid-century were divided into regions. For land clearing, the division was simple – between the forested and the non-forested areas. For dairying, the mid-century data were available only on a state basis, but here the distinction appeared between the Northeast, where commercial milk markets already existed, and rural areas, where small local sales prevailed or where the cow was simply a part of the family subsistence economy. For the grains, regions were defined on the basis of yields, following the usual sectional divisions. For each region, then, at mid-century and again at the end of century (up to 1910) the data required to estimate the equation were arrayed. Averages – more usually medians – were taken and their significance assessed by inspection of the range and clustering. In only a few cases were the data plentiful enough to allow or suggest the computation of standard statistical measures of dispersion. Yet in the three completed groups of studies, the eyeballing technique, done in an honest and orderly fashion, with some help from elementary statistics, produced plausible results. Since no substantive hypotheses were being tested, the temptation to skew the results one way or another was not present.

Combining the regional estimates of productivity in each period into a national average, where the regions – Northeast, South, and West (R_1, R_2, R_3) – were weighted by relative shares in acreage or animal herd, gave the basis for a national index of productivity change over the period. Extracted from the three completed studies, this measure was as shown in Table 1. It made apparent that this composite change was the arithmetic

Table 1. *Indices of labor productivity change in three groups of farm products, 1900*

Land clearing	Acres per man-day (1850s = 100)	340
Milk	Pounds per man-hour (1850s = 100)	83
Grains		
Corn	Bushels per man-year (1840/60 = 100)	365
Wheat	Bushels per man-year (1840/60 = 100)	417
Oats	Bushels per man-year (1840/60 = 100)	363

Sources: Primack (1962); Bateman (1969); Parker and Klein (1966).

result of changes, individually and in interactive combination, among the three variables – the regional weights or shares in national output (V), regional yields (O/A), and regional labor inputs per acre or in some operations directly per output unit (L/A, L/O). Having gone this far, we found the temptation irresistible to try to give a quantitative assessment of the relative importance of these three factors in producing the composite result. This game seemed the more important since, as stated above, each of the three factors could be related to a significant element in America's agrarian history, viz.:

Regional weights – westward movement and regional specialization
Yields per acre and animal – improvements in farm practices, genetic changes, fertilizers, pest control, etc.
Labor per acre or directly per output unit – improvements in tools, machinery, and power

The solution was suggested by a statistician, Leo Katz, of Michigan State University, on a model used in fertilizer experiments in Britain.[2] In fullest extension the model in the study on grains yielded a set of eight indices, combining the values of each of the three variables alternately at their Period 1 (1840/60) and Period 2 (1900/1910) levels.[3]

As Mançur Olson, the political theorist and economic historian, is said to have said and has himself clearly exemplified, "To a boy with a new hammer, the whole world looks like a nail." I should have appreciated the risks of assumptions implicit when a method – a rather primitive one at that – of statistical testing is transferred from controlled physical experiments and tests to the data of an historical record, where not only seeds, weather, and life processes were involved, but also the infinite variation derived from the behavior of the society of two-footed human animals. Most unreal was the assumption that the 1910 outputs could have been produced under the 1850 regional distributions among regions without sharply rising marginal costs in the 1850 regions. This problem and its implications for statistical studies of causation and influence in history are taken up in the next section. First, however, I wish to examine what the data of three completed sets of studies did seem to show, even where not put to the extreme torture of counterfactual quantification.

[2]See W. Parker and J. L. V. Klein, "Productivity Growth in Grain Production in the United States: 1840–60 and 1900–10," in *Output, Employment and Productivity in the United States After 1800*, National Bureau of Economic Research: Studies in Income and Wealth, No. 30 (1966), Appendix C. The reference is to F. Yates, *The Design and Analysis of Factorial Experiments*, Technical Communication 35 (Harpenden, England: Imperial Institute of Soil Science, 1937).
[3]See ibid., 529, and for an example, 532–533.

A look backward

The work altogether produced completed studies of three products, and in each, three factors responsible in combination for the result. Disregarding statistical refinements, a look simply at the average values computed from the data suggests a very curious observation. In each case there is a distinction between an active factor, where the difference between 1850 values and those of 1910 is pronounced, and two relatively passive factors whose values either remain stable and simply prevent serious declines in productivity despite the growing quantities of output and other changes that did take place. In each case, this active factor is a different one of the three. Thus:

	Factor		
	1	2	
	Regional	Farm	3
Products	shifts	practices	Machinery
1. Land clearing	Active	Passive	Passive
2. Milk	Passive	Active	Passive
3. Grains	Passive	Passive	Active

Land clearing provides the simplest, starkest case since the "crop" involved is simply cleared acreage and Factor 2 – yields, genetic improvement, and subtle changes in practices – is not involved. Here, as Table 2, drawn from Primack's study, shows, the difference between labor costs

Table 2. *Labor costs in land clearing, 1850s and 1900s*

	Man-days/acre		Range divided by median
	Median	Range	
1850s			
Forest	33.0[a]	+17.0,[a] − 7.0	+0.50, −0.21
Non-forested area	1.5	±.5	±0.33
1900s			
Forest	25.0[a]	+8.0, −10.0	+0.32, −0.40
Non-forested area	0.75	+0.25, −0.50	+0.33, −0.67

[a]Including stump-pulling at thirteen man-days in 1850s and five man-days with stump-pullers in 1910s.
Source: Primack (1962).

319

for clearing forested areas are of the order of twenty to thirty times the costs of the first plowing of the grasslands.[4]

In the mid-century, 80 percent of the nearly five million acres of land cleared annually lay in the forested areas, whereas in the 1900s, of a newly cleared acreage nearly 50 percent greater, 70 percent was non-forested. The whole operation was estimated to have used up 11.6 percent of the farm labor force in the 1850s, and thanks largely to the movement west, only 2.3 percent in the 1910s. Set against this, the modest changes in techniques in either of the two types of cover have a distinctly minor influence. However one weights the regions or computes the indices, labor saving in this operation comes principally from the movement into the open West.[5]

J. F. Bateman's studies of dairying also present some individual and rather surprising features. Over the whole period the index of productivity per labor hour declines. The two major influences allowing the expansion

[4] "Before 1850, American farms were cut from the forest, and the work of forming a farm took time. Five acres of forest clearing in a year in addition to current crops was about the limit for a farm family. Even farmers who specialized in clearing land for sale might count on two hundred acres or so of forest clearing as the labor of a lifetime. Like nearly everything else, they existed in Yankee and southern variants whose use, however, was not confined to either region. Clearing was done by controlled burning in most cases; the differences lay in the method of killing the trees and the time allowed after drying the fallen timber. With the so-called Yankee method, probably adopted from Swedish settlers along the Delaware, the trees were felled by the ax into piles for burning and allowed to dry on the ground over a period of months or years. A first firing would leave large limbs and trunks to be cut into manageable lengths, repiled, and burned again. The repiling for the second burning was often the occasion of a frontier coöperative activity, the 'log-rolling.' An alternative method, adopted from the Indians and favored in the South, replaced the labor of the arm and ax by the action of wind and time. Here the larger trees were killed by girdling – the removal of a wide circle of bark from completely around the trunk. If this was done early enough in the season, the land could be ready for cultivation beneath the dead trees in the spring. As limbs and trees rotted or were blown down, they could be collected a few at a time and burned. Girdling had a low immediate labor cost and permitted quick cultivation over a large acreage, but livestock and crops were damaged by falling branches in the phantom forests, and ultimately the wood had to be collected and burned." Martin L. Primack, "Land Clearing Under Nineteenth-Century Techniques: Some Preliminary Calculations," *Journal of Economic History*, Vol. 22 (December 1962), 484–485.

[5] This is not to say that in the absence of any technical change the move on to the grasslands would have gone ahead at the same rate. Grassland farming required not only the improved steel-breaking plow, but all the numerous adaptations, especially windmills and barbed wire, described in W. P. Webb's classic study, *The Great Plains* (Boston: Ginn, 1931). Except in the very laborious operation of stump removal, clearing techniques of forest cover remained almost unchanged until well into the twentieth century. Blasting powder to remove or break up stumps, introduced in the 1880s, was virtually the only improvement.

of output both relate to the greater value of milk due to the growth of the commercial demand from cities. Part of the growth came through a lengthening of the average milk year for a cow from 237 to 300 days, an adjustment which does not economize on milking labor or on feed input and is only possible – indeed, went on half-unperceived by farmers – because of the use of family and off-peak labor in the barn. A second way, upgrading of the herds to give yields closer to the best yields of mid-century, created a 20 percent rise in daily yields per cow, a saving of fixed labor costs in care, feeding, and, to a large degree, milking as well. Improved stock came through diffusion of standard breeds, but there was little or no advance in the best levels of yield. The American herd in 1910 was still far from a collection of highly bred specialized dairy cattle. Against such improvement as occurred, there came stricter sanitary requirements in feeding, barn care, and milking which actually raised labor costs of the milk as it left the farm. Dairying responded, then, neither to improved technology nor to westward movement as such, but rather to the widespread growth of markets which added value to the product, thus inducing more work, care, and attention in how dairying was conducted.

Studies of beef and pork, could they be completed, would almost certainly show a similar absence of striking technical change. Spatial rearrangement following the railroad and centralized stockyards was important, and improvements of breed and feed would leave a mark. But such improvements would have to be set against much higher costs which the shrinking of the woodland and open range necessitated. Among the field crops, too, the tentative study of cotton shows the predominant influence of geographical shifts over technical change. The only major improvement was the substitution of the horse- (or mule-) drawn cultivator for the hoe, a very great improvement indeed but a very simple change made perhaps in part as a response to the disappearance of slavery.

Only in the grains, and more in the cereal grasses than in corn, was mechanical technology dominant in saving labor. To show what was done here, it is simplest to expand the list of variables as follows:

L_1 = Pre-harvest labor (man-hours)
L_2 = Harvest labor (man-hours)
L_3 = Post-harvest labor (man-hours)
R_1 = Northeast
R_2 = South (wheat and oats)
R_{2a} = Middle East (corn)
R_{2b} = South (corn)
R_3 = West (i.e., west of the Ohio River and the Mississippi)
A = Area (acres planted)
O = Output (bushels of threshed grain)
$a = L_1/A$ $y = O/A$
$b = L_2/A$ $v = O/\Sigma O$

$$c = L_3/A \qquad w = A/\Sigma A$$
$$1 = \text{Period 1 (1840–60)}$$
$$2 = \text{Period 2 (1900–10)}$$

$$\sum_{R_1}^{R_3} \left(\frac{a+b}{y} + c \right) v = \text{national average labor input per bushel}$$

Using these variables, Table 3 shows the averaged data for the four main cost variables arrayed by region with the regional output weights. It is evident by inspection that in wheat and oats the sharp fall occurred in harvesting and threshing costs in all regions to about a quarter of their earlier level with the introduction of the mechanical reaper, thresher, and combines. The strong shift toward regional specialization (from a roughly equal distribution of the acreage among the three regions to an 87 percent concentration in the West in the second period) affected second period costs in the "passive" sense of accommodating the great increases in output, but unlike the situation in land clearing, costs were not so different among the regions as to produce a strong, direct effect on the observed indices. Labor-saving in corn was largely confined to pre-harvest operations with the substitution of the cultivator for the hoe, as in cotton. The development of direct feeding in the field or from the shock reduced harvesting costs in the West, (R_3), but it is not clear where the growth of silage in dairy districts shows up in the cases on which the statistics are based. Overall in corn, as in dairying, technical change appears relatively unimportant compared to many small changes in practice made in response to the greater value of the fodder as feed for commercial meat production. It is noteworthy, too, that in all the grains, per-acre yields do not rise significantly, although adaptation to new soils and climates in the corn and wheat belts is presumably of decisive importance in keeping yields steady under great expansions of acreage and output.[6]

The three groups of studies, fragmentary and incomplete as they are, thus point to the quite diverse influence of the three productivity elements in one line of production relative to another. But the three studies, taken together, have a deeper meaning for American agricultural history as a whole. By lucky coincidence, each illustrates a different fundamental aspect of agricultural development and, indeed, of modern economic history in the large. The pattern is simple, and its logic is compelling.[7] In the Western world as a whole, population growth even in the twelfth to thir-

[6]See discussion in Section II, below.

[7]I have developed these ideas in *Europe, America, and the Wider World*, Vol. 1, *Europe and the World Economy* (Cambridge: Cambridge University Press, 1984), Ch. 11. It should be noted that in the 1850s, ignorance of how to handle prairies, soils, and grasses did cause settlers to go around them to seek out the familiar conditions of forested areas.

Table 3. *Labor inputs, land yields, and weights, Periods 1 and 2*

	a 1	a 2	b 1	b 2	y 1	y 2	c 1	c 2	v 1	v 2	w 1	w 2
Wheat												
R_1	19.1	11.6	15.0	3.0	14.5	17.5	0.73	0.19	0.334	0.046	0.259	0.037
R_2	11.3	10.7	12.5	3.0	8.4	12.3	0.73	0.29	0.342	0.075	0.459	0.085
R_3	12.4	4.7	15.0	2.3	13.0	14.0	0.73	0.19	0.324	0.879	0.282	0.878
U.S.	13.6	5.5	13.9	2.4	11.3	14.0	0.73	0.20				
Oats												
R_1	14.3	9.3	12.8	3.4	28.5	39.7	0.40	0.23	0.422	0.087	0.316	0.077
R_2	8.8	9.5	11.0	4.5	13.9	17.0	0.40	0.24	0.332	0.044	0.506	0.068
R_3	8.8	3.9	12.8	2.6	29.3	26.5	0.40	0.10	0.246	0.869	0.178	0.855
U.S.	10.5	4.7	11.9	2.8	21.3	26.1	0.40	0.12				
Corn												
R_1	98.3	46.4	13.0	13.0	33.5	36.8			0.097	0.029	0.057	0.020
R_{2a}	52.0	26.7	10.1	10.1	21.8	24.4			0.344	0.099	0.310	0.106
R_{2b}	67.3	21.3	4.3	4.3	11.8	16.1			0.279	0.175	0.465	0.285
R_3	46.2	14.2	13.0	7.6	32.7	31.0			0.280	0.697	0.168	0.589
U.S.	60.8	18.2	8.1	7.0	19.6	26.2						

For definition of variables, see text.
Source: Parker and Klein (1966).

teenth centuries, then again in the late fourteenth and fifteenth, did not meet at once the diminishing returns that led in the models of Ricardo and Mill to a stationary state or the periodic recurrence of Malthusian crises. Beginning in 1750, presence of rich lands on the frontier created growing surpluses which even in the late eighteenth century became available for trade. The American frontier in particular was full of bonanzas (minerals, deep soils, the treeless grasslands), and these presented not an obstacle, but a huge productive opportunity accelerating the advance into the continent. Overlapping the influence of population growth and richer resources, the expansion of the market continued the movements. The dairy study shows the self-reinforcing opportunities for growth as the market put a value on the time of farm labor, diffused known practices, and increased the possibilities of regional specialization. The productivity gains discovered by Adam Smith in specialized industrial production appeared in specialized agricultural regions as well. And finally, as Smith also predicted, intense specialization in the grains under the strains induced by growing market opportunity drew on technical innovation, specifically mechanical invention, a spinoff from mechanical industry, to continue its thrust forward. When this eco-technic process got underway, agriculture was carried with industry into the high tech of the twentieth century – the age of Schumpeter. Since the close of the period of our studies, the recurrent twentieth-century technological revolutions – in farm power, mechanical improvements, insect control, soil chemistry, plant and animal biochemistry, and genetics – have enabled the American agricultural labor force to produce itself almost to extinction.

II

The conclusions just drawn are those which, twenty years later, I would take from the studies. But at the time they were published, much attention was focused on the statistical operations imposed on the regional averages for each variable in the effort to give a precise measure of its effect, alone and in combination with the others.

In this effort, the basic measure, combining the variables for each region, was calculated with alternative values of the variables on the Period 1 base. This was done most elaborately in the grains study. Here the productivity indices shown in Table 1 were produced from the basic equation, written with Period 2 values, divided by the same index with Period 1 values. Then six intermediate indices were constructed on the base of the Period 1 index = 100 by varying each variable alone and in conjunction with each of the others, as shown in Table 4.

Following the method of Yates in the agricultural experiments, the study then computed the percentage contribution of each variable, alone

Table 4. *Labor requirements (U.S. average and indices) as affected by inter-regional shifts, regional yields, and regional labor inputs per acre*

Index	Period for values of			Labor requirement $(L/O)^a$			Productivity $(i_1/i_n \times 100)$		
	v	y	abc	Wheat (1)	Oats (2)	Corn (3)	Wheat (4)	Oats (5)	Corn (6)
i_1	1	1	1	3.17	1.45	3.50	100	100	100
i_2	1	2	1	2.68	1.37	2.94	118.3	105.8	119.0
i_3	1	1	2	1.29	0.78	1.54	245.7	185.9	227.3
i_4	2	1	1	2.90	1.18	2.70	109.3	122.9	129.6
i_5	1	2	2	1.05	0.72	1.32	302.1	201.2	265.2
i_6	2	1	2	0.84	0.39	1.06	377.3	371.7	330.2
i_7	2	2	1	2.69	1.23	2.45	117.8	117.9	142.9
i_8	2	2	2	0.76	0.40	0.96	416.7	362.6	364.6

$$^a\sum \left(\frac{a+b}{y} + c \right) \ v$$

For definition of variables, see text.
Source: Parker and Klein (1966), Table 2.

and in interaction with each of the others, to the total productivity growth. Adding the indices in which each variable and pair of variables appears in Period 2 values and subtracting those where it appears in Period 1 values,[8] the separate influence of each variable and of each pair of variables was calculated. Reducing the whole array in percentage terms yields the following measures of relative influence:

	Wheat	Oats	Corn
v	0.170	0.287	0.207
abc	0.598	0.506	0.562
y	0.082	0.005	0.084
$v(abc)$	0.158	0.234	0.120
vy	−0.049	−0.026	−0.007
$(abc)y$	0.046	0.004	0.032
$v(abc)y$	−0.005	−0.010	−0.002

Source: Parker and Klein, "Productivity Growth in Grain Production" (see note 2).

This measure shows specifically the principal conclusion derived by inspection from the data, i.e., that the variable (abc) – technology in the

[8]This is a rough approximation to Yates's method. See Parker and Klein, op. cit., Appendix C, and reference to Yates, there cited.

field operations — accounts statistically for between 50 and 60 percent of the whole productivity growth, and that this effect is especially powerful when taken in conjunction with the shift of all these crops into the Midwest — $v(abc)$ in index (i_6). Further torture of the data separated the independent effect of the three mechanization variables.

(a) Improved plows, seed drills, and in corn, the cultivator
(b) Mechanization in reaping
(c) Mechanization in threshing

to show that (b) and (c) accounted for nearly all the change in wheat and oats and (a) alone in corn. These offer simply a more precise statement of the conclusions arrived at in Section I.

In retrospect, this work appears neat, tidy, and precise: publishable research. But when one reflects upon its meaning and implications, the ground beneath it begins to tremble. At several points it appeared even at the time particularly vulnerable. First, the measurements had been at fixed points along the regional cost curves without reference to the volumes of output as they changed between the periods. Second, I had ignored factor substitution, assuming in effect two alternative technologies, each with fixed coefficients, with only the possibility of a shift from one to the other. This violated two sacred allied assumptions of economics: diminishing returns and factor substitutability. Moreover, the mere statistical measure of an interaction effect between technical change and westward movement did not include a "feedback" effect from one variable to the other. The fact that the combine was introduced at a time when wheat was moving into lands particularly suited to its use gave the two shifts a particularly powerful effect in conjunction with each other. But it did not in a sense credit the combine with encouraging the movement into just those lands or take into account that the presence of such lands may have incited just such a technological development.

On both these points it may be argued that the indices which tried to measure the effect of westward movement of the crops in the absence of technological change (i_4 and i_7) were less seriously flawed than those which did the reverse. To give an imaginary historical meaning to the indices, sheer common-sense plausibility had to be taken into account. With or without new agricultural technology, the westward movement of agriculture would have taken place. Mankind had been making similar moves for ten thousand years. That it occurred at the speed it did, in the presence of commercialization and with the release of labor that allowed industrialization to proceed in mid-America, was due, then, to the technical environment, notably the railroad and farm machinery, improved plows, and some improved knowledge about the crops. And these technological advances, being part of a movement across the whole Atlantic economy, were essentially independent of the terrains and soils of the regions into which they moved. The high levels of the indices including technical change (i_3 and i_5) and absent western movement compared to the low levels of those on the reverse assumption (i_4 and i_7) seemed a valid reason for stressing the importance of technical change in the growth.

Fortunately (for the cause of truth), these conclusions did not go un-challenged. Without westward movement and regional specialization, the whole commercialized growth in output, even in the presence of technical change, could not have occurred under conditions of constant costs. Lands poorer in quality and harder to farm would have been drawn on in the older regions. Moreover, the counter-factual here seemed less plausi-ble than the contrary one. Cost curves in the western region might be imagined to be essentially flat in the prairies (especially if the railroad is taken as available) even under the older technology. But it is much harder to imagine that, had this huge output growth been confined to its mid-century regional distribution, cost curves would not have violently risen, even under the new technology.

This point was made in painfully exacting detail and completeness in an article by F. M. Fisher and P. Temin in the 1970 *Review of Economics and Statistics*. The problem was recast by them in the form of a classic problem in farmers' response to price. In doing this, they were able to make use of the USDA annual estimates of acreage (planted or har-vested), output, and farm price by states for the forty-seven years, 1867–1914. No doubt the recent availability of Nerlove's technique of estima-tion, using lagged output to capture farmers' adjustment over time, was a powerful incentive to the work. This permitted them to calculate some-thing which could be called long-run supply curves for these grains by state, testing a specification of farmers' behavior in their decisions about crop choice. The conclusions, made on the basis of the share of acreage planted to wheat relative to the price of wheat relative to other grains, formed a kind of lower limit to the rise in supply costs since the need to increase the supplies of all products simultaneously in the East would have pushed all prices up much further. They found that, even within the low levels of acreage in which production actually occurred east of the Mississippi, the long-run elasticity of supply was less than 2.0, meaning a tripling of price to extract a sixfold increase in output. This they called "a gross under-estimate of what costs would have been."

So ingenious an econometrical study clearly constituted a further move down the track of better-specified counter-factual history. To one who has not used the technique himself, lingering, atavistic doubts remain, partly from one's dim recollection of these matters from Marshall's text in graduate school days. The project appears to test farmers' response to price, but is that decision the most relevant one in understanding the

history? What about the decision to shift technologies or the decision to
move west or to leave farming altogether? Did these all depend on the
lagged prices of wheat? Perhaps a suspicious economist who is only semi-
neoclassical can be forgiven for suspecting that when those using these
techniques come on to the scene, they are in the end only testing farmers'
"rationality" for the nth time. If the farmers again pass that test, what is
left to help us explain all the environmental changes to which they are
making so rational a response? These, it is said, are all compounded in a
"shift" variable t – for time, which seems a shorthand for everything in
which a historian is interested. *Timeo Danaos et dona ferentes*. Still, one
must be grateful both for the correction and for the spirit in which it was
given. My study itself will have served a valuable social purpose if it
should lead two such careful scholars and exact thinkers a little way
down the slippery slope of freer imaginative exercises.

For what in this case is the real counter-factual? What would American history have been like without the West? A number of lines of
adjustment – four in demand, one in supply – suggest themselves. Those
affecting demand include:

(1) Reduced population growth, both through lower birth rates and curtailed
immigration.
(2) An altered diet, feeding to humans the vast quantities of corn fed to hogs.
(3) Conversion of part of the eastern cotton lands to other crops, as has occurred in soybeans since 1940. Given the strong position of U.S. cotton supplies
on world markets, this might have caused no loss in foreign exchange.
(4) Countless readjustments in foreign trade, allowing industrial exports to
make up for the loss of the exported farm "surpluses" no longer available to
weigh down farm prices.

Altogether these adjustments, especially that in diets, might not have
eaten seriously into the country's real income growth. Diets without the
West would have had less beef, pork, and wheat, more cornmeal and
potatoes. Are we prepared to say that would have been a "bad thing"?
And unless an animal protein diet is essential to a development of heavy
industry, industrialization would not need to have been much affected.
Chicago would have been much smaller (also possibly not a bad thing?),
but supplies of iron and steel could have been just as great, and the
industrial and urban development to its east below the Lakes, to Pittsburgh, and through central New York to the western shore of the Atlantic
could have been unchanged. Without western railroads, the iron and steel
industry might have found demand reduced, but a few less railroads and
a few less steel plants for the "robber barons" to profit from might have
made life (and the economic historian's job) much simpler and cleaner.
Perhaps the main effect of a truncated geography would not have been in
agriculture at all, but in the loss of the Texas–Oklahoma oil fields after

the automobile was invented. To contemplate the United States without Texas *or* California may indeed give one pause.

A final line of argument might be that without the Prairies and Plains, the direction of agricultural technology would somehow have altered. This possibility was contemplated in the paper on grains. As Fisher and Temin write, "Parker and Klein were aware of this problem (of supply elasticity) but they did not pursue it. They said instead that the pressure of increased demand might have led to technical change in the East in the absence of the ability to expand in the West. But having mentioned this possibility, they immediately discounted it."[9]

Yet how, pray, is history of technological change – hypothetical or real – to be written simply under the guidance of the economist's great "tool," elasticity and factor substitution in response to relative price? On the reef of hard facts from the supply side in technological history the frail barks of growth models splinter apart. Historians credulous enough to climb aboard have had to shed most of their baggage to keep afloat. Noah's Ark sheltered the trusting animals that boarded it and kept them alive during a hard time. But surely neither they nor Noah rejoiced when, on emerging, they found themselves on Mt. Ararat, in an air so rarified and at a height so lofty that they still could not make out the ground below. We are still waiting for the theorists to provide us, not an Ark to float us above the floods of facts, but a railroad – or even a canal – to push us through them.[10]

APPENDIX ON TOTAL FACTOR PRODUCTIVITY

John W. Kendrick's work on "total factor productivity"[11] was published just as the research described in this paper was coming to an end. It represents the most thorough and definitive effort to measure productiv-

[9]Franklin M. Fisher and Peter Temin, "Regional Specialization and the Supply of Wheat in the United States, 1867–1914," *The Review of Economics and Statistics,* Vol. 52 (May 1970): 134–149.

[10]Theoretical work at the Industriens Utredningsinstitut (IUI, Stockholm), under Gunnar Eliasson and others, has something evidently new, though complex and ultimately somewhat mysterious, to say on modeling innovation, following the paths of Schumpeter, Erik Dahmen, and Nelson and Winter. See R. H. Day and G. Eliasson, eds., *The Dynamics of Market Economies* (Amsterdam: North Holland, 1986), and various IUI working papers by Eliasson and others. It is still difficult to see how such models can be used by an historian to explain in concrete terms the emergence of, say, an electrical technology in the late nineteenth century, without a specification of the path of intellectual development for the underlying science and an understanding of the limits placed on engineering by the state of scientific development.

[11]John W. Kendrick, *Productivity Trends in the United States,* National Bureau of Economic Research (Princeton: Princeton University Press, 1961).

ity growth as output, in "real" price-deflated money terms relative to a weighted index of inputs of labor and capital. It is based on two inter-related concepts of modern economics as it stood in the 1950s to 1970s: (1) the concept of an aggregate supply curve, or production function $O = f(L,K)$, shifting through time and (2) a measurement of the changing physical volume of capital by deflating a series of estimated net stock (annual purchases less depreciation allowances) by a price index.

In a study of nineteenth-century agriculture, I felt that such measures concealed and confused more than they revealed. Had I had any clear and operational understanding of the concept of a production function out-side of the engineering limits of a single plant or plot of ground in which test conditions can be established and experiments can be performed, and of measuring "capital" as a cause and not a result of historical change, I could no doubt have strained credulity and conscience even further than I did, grubbed up the data somewhere, performed the necessary statistical operations, and throwing a bone to Kendrick's lion in the path, I could have tiptoed by.

My uneasiness about value measures, derived from the well-known paradoxes of long-run aggregation and measurement, was compounded in these studies by the many peculiarities of agriculture as an industry. Land, the farmer's principal asset, not only possesses an original and indestructible productive power, but also serves as a store of value; hence it serves as a retirement fund, a promise of future gains, and an assurance of social position and good character. Its value is affected by all these considerations. Moreover, as an input, only the annual depletion of land and the expense of restoring its fertility should be measured. The same is true of land improvements, many of which – ditching, fencing, barn-building, road construction – are very long-lived indeed. Furthermore, this whole body of farm capital was created and maintained largely by farmers' own labor. Use of a single value measure of capital added to the usual problems of appropriate depreciation rates and price weights the problem of valuation of farm labor, much of it done in off-hours and at idle seasons in the farm year. Would it not be enough for my study of the nineteenth century, then, to discover how the productivity of that labor, applied to the tasks of capital formation and maintenance, had changed over time? I would then be working with a mental picture of the industry as shown roughly in Figure 1.

In such a treatment, if I could have further developed it, "capital" would be both an output and an input in current production, a structure or medium, like skills or social organization, through which labor works and so an intermediate element in the process of long-run output growth.

I was led into looking at labor productivity also through the related question of welfare measurement. "Capital-saving inventions" can, to be

Figure 1. *Input and output flows in the nineteenth-century agricultural sector*

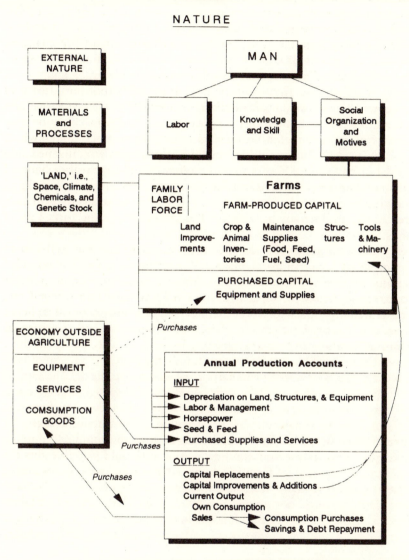

sure, increase a society's productive capacity, but the final measure of progress is still income per capita, not per machine or per resource unit. Within the limits of nineteenth-century agriculture, a rise in welfare meant an economizing of the efforts of the farm labor force, in its heavy tasks of farm formation, maintenance, and land renewal, as well as in the annual production of crops and livestock products. In this effort thoroughly to think through my research problem of explaining long-run change, I appear to have, temporarily and for heuristic purposes, moved back to a labor standard of value.

This rationalization of the main problem of long-run measurement was not quite perfect, as I now see. In agricultural history in this period, the problem of capital inputs is better put as the problem of the amounts of inputs produced by the non-farm sector, i.e., the transportation and manufacturing sectors, a contribution inherent in commercial agriculture and mechanical technology. These inputs have grown enormously since the end of the nineteenth century, as powered machinery and tractors have replaced the horse, and especially since 1940, when inputs of land and labor have actually shrunk and biological and chemical technology have come in force to the farm. In the nineteenth century, a growth of knowledge of agronomy and of animal breeding and husbandry contributed to the productivity growth, both in permitting expansion onto new lands and in maintaining yields steady on all lands under the pressure of tremendous output expansion. But even in nineteenth-century America the setting of the agricultural expansion in the midst of a rapidly developing industrial sector meant that the contribution of the non-farm sector occurred most markedly by way of the growth of mechanical technology. And in handling mechanization the problem remains: How much of the productivity growth was due to (1) increased "amounts" of "capital," (2) improved qualities of "capital," (3) falls in the price of capital goods, i.e., technological change in the farm machinery industry?

Nevertheless, a "labor" productivity index, while itself containing enormous problems of aggregation over labor hours of varying intensity and laborers of various degrees of strength and skill, tells a very large part of the story for the nineteenth-century farming. It measures the saving in human effort produced by the action of all the other "inputs" used by labor, both the purchased equipment and materials and the invisible inputs of labor quality, technical knowledge, specialization, and social organization. It is, then, in a sense a "total factor productivity" measure even though it does not permit a separate assessment of the "contribution" of its several tangible and intangible components.

BIBLIOGRAPHY OF COMPLETED STUDIES

Atack, Jeremy, and J. Fred Bateman. 1984. "Mid-Nineteenth-Century Crop Yields and Labor Productivity Growth in American Agriculture: A New Look at Parker and Klein." In Gavin Wright, ed., *Technique, Spirit and Form in the Making of the Modern Economies,* Essays in Honor of William N.

Parker. Research in Economic History, Supplement 3. Greenwich, Conn., and London: JAI Press, 215–242.

——. 1987. *To Their Own Soil: Agriculture in the Antebellum North*. Ames: Iowa State University Press.

Bateman, J. Fred. 1968. "Improvement in American Dairy Farming, 1850–1910: A Quantitative Analysis." *Journal of Economic History*, Vol. 28 (June): 255–273.

——. 1969. "Labor Inputs and Productivity in American Dairy Agriculture, 1850–1910." *Journal of Economic History*, Vol. 29 (June): 206–229.

Fisher, Franklin M., and Peter Temin. 1970. "Regional Specialization and the Supply of Wheat in the United States, 1867–1914." *The Review of Economics and Statistics*, Vol. 52 (May): 134–149.

Parker, William N. 1971. "Productivity Growth in American Grain Farming: An Analysis of its 19th-century Sources." In Robert Fogel and Stanley Engerman, eds., *The Reinterpretation of American Economic History*. New York: Harper & Row, 175–186.

——. 1972. "A Note on Regional Culture in the Corn Harvest." *Agricultural History*, Vol. 46, No. 1 (January): 181–189.

——. 1979. "Labor Productivity in Cotton Farming: The History of a Research." *Agricultural History*, Vol. 53, No. 1 (January). 228–244.

——, and S. DeCanio. 1982. "Two Hidden Sources of Productivity Growth in American Agriculture, 1850–1930." *Agricultural History*, Vol. 56, No. 4 (October): 648–662.

——, and Judith L. V. Klein. 1966. "Productivity Growth in Grain Production in the United States: 1840–60 and 1900–10." In *Output, Employment and Productivity in the United States After 1800*, National Bureau of Economic Research: Studies in Income and Wealth, Vol. 30.

Primack, Martin L. 1962. "Land Clearing Under Nineteenth-Century Techniques: Some Preliminary Calculations." *Journal of Economic History*, Vol. 22 (December): 484–497.

——. 1963. *Farm-formed Capital in American Agriculture, 1850–1910*. Ph.D. dissertation, University of North Carolina.

——. 1965. "Farm Construction as a Use of Farm Labor in the United States, 1850–1910." *Journal of Economic History*, Vol. 25 (March): 114–125.

——. 1969. "Farm Fencing in the Nineteenth Century." *Journal of Economic History*, Vol. 29 (June): 287–291.

Whartenby, Franklee. 1963. *Land and Labor Productivity in United States Cotton Production, 1800–1840*. Ph.D. dissertation, University of North Carolina, Department of Economics.

Annex B

A look forward

Understanding productivity: the ways of economics and of history

The effectiveness of an economy's behavior and organization is often described and evaluated by the terms *product* and *productivity*. These terms have been the more welcome to economists since they appear superficially but delightfully to yield themselves to scientific measurement – and not only to aggregative measurement, but also to partitioning and an attribution of the relative contributions of various elements to the whole, statically and over time. So they have, despite pious denials, appeared to be suggestive of causation, prediction, and operational significance. In the ambitious phases of their careers, even thoughtful economic historians have embraced these concepts. An earlier generation constructed the income and product series and discovered thence much new knowledge of features in the operation and growth of national economies. Now a second or third generation has pushed bushels of the fathers' painfully garnered historical statistics into the hungry furnaces of aggregate production functions and extracted therefrom light, heat, and ashes, assessed at various levels of significance.

Yet to many of the older and even of the intermediate generation, aging now and relieved of excessive pressures to publish (or even to be respectable), philosophical doubt creeps in. This paper reflects on the mysteries of productivity growth as revealed through the formulations and measurements of the identities of national income accounting. And so as not to end, like the bad witch at the party, on a wholly negative note, it ventures in Section II to present in very general terms an "historical sketch" of the

This paper was given as the A. C. Davidson Lecture to the Meeting of The Australian Economic History Society at the Australian Economic Congress, at Canberra, August 31, 1988. It is published in the *Australian Economic History Review,* March 1990 issue. A slightly different version also appears as a contribution to the tenth anniversary issue of the *Journal of Economic Behavior and Organization.* I am grateful to Richard Ruggles and the late Nancy Ruggles for suggesting the topic and for both the tone and the content of comments made at the meeting and by readers and editors of the published version.

productivity growth implicit in westward movement and the development of regional industrial cultures in the course of American history.

Any effort at social theory to underpin this history must borrow obviously by many circuitous routes from an older vision of socioeconomic change contained in American institutionalist economics, Parsonian sociology, functionalist anthropology, and Schumpeterian economics. It is incompatible with some, but I think not all, the currently more fashionable formulations, e.g., the "total history" of Braudel and the *Annalistes*, the "new ethnography" of Geertz, or Lévi-Strauss's structuralism, as best I can fathom the nature and thrust of that characteristically French enterprise. It does *not* – at least not yet – claim kinship with the more purely intellectual, philosophical, literary, or rhetorical formulations of Foucault and the "new historicism." It is hoped that the economist's study of productivity growth may be fused thus with the "stories" of traditional narrative history in the effort to allow sensible discourse on the subject to continue. A preliminary effort to show some of this "deep structure" is offered by computer graphics in Section III.

I. THE CLIOMETRICS OF PRODUCTIVITY (AND VICE VERSA)

François Quesnay, the first macroeconomist, it will be remembered, was a medical doctor, and he modeled the first sketch of the circular flow of income and product on Harvey's discovery of the circulation of the blood. It was the model of a real product passing through the social organism by a network of ducts into different chambers, or sectors, against a counter-flow of payments in exchange. Agriculture, through human effort, knowledge, and the gifts of a kindly nature, gave the portion which started the cycles of exchange. The share of its contribution above production costs was in a sense free, and that surplus constituted the society's net product. It could be seized or taxed to support the noble landowners, academics, a government, and other unproductive workers. To Quesnay's physiocratic model, English political economists brought an effort to define something called value and to find its source not in the land, the sun, and the rain, but in labor. The so-called neoclassical economists added scarcity and demand to the definition of value and imagined a self-regulating system in equilibrium, sustained by the equalization of pressures – marginal utilities on the demand side and marginal costs of supply. Joseph Schumpeter gave essentially the same picture in his circular flow, and now the system of general equilibrium, shorn of Schumpeter's dynamic concept of innovation and set into unchanging perpetual motion, is daily polished by mathematical economists until it shines like an antique car in the hands of a collector. A few daring spirits like Jeffrey Williamson get behind the wheel of this car and try to drive it over the pot-holed course we call history.

In this development of an idea, something must be attributed to the simultaneous development in the nineteenth-century business world of commercial accounting, an art not always highly regarded by economic theorists, but more akin to their efforts than they might imagine. Accounting grew out of trade in the fifteenth century, not out of production. In early manufacturing it did not easily handle, any more than the notion of a general equilibrium can handle, the idea of increase in value of a net product, or surplus. Double-entry bookkeeping was a Renaissance invention perhaps on the model of a goldsmith's scales, and in it the act of creating a credit is simultaneous with the creation of a debit. When applied in the later nineteenth century to the internal controls of the manufacturing plant, it required much ingenuity and numerous fictional conventions – book value, net worth, fixed capital, depreciation, imputed interest, etc. – to handle the accounting where no real or recorded exchange was involved.

The grand concept of accounts for an entire economy, as if it were a single firm composed of sectors, expressed finally in input–output accounting with an array of capital and consumer goods industries, grew up in Britain and the United States after 1935 out of the needs and pressures for national policies to regulate and stimulate the level of economic activity. Under Simon Kuznets's wise guidance, it accepted as its domain a national economy composed mostly of a collection of markets, governed by prices and exchange – the world of the circular flow. At the same time, it contained implicitly the concept of a net product, a final bill of output which could grow over time and had a presumed correlation with economic welfare. (One recalls Kuznets's concern over whether the government's output should be counted as a final or an intermediate good.) The repeated denials of any connection between real product per capita and welfare served only to confirm that the accountants' consciences kept troubling them.

The governing philosophy in all this work was and is a breathtaking pragmatism. Macroeconomists between 1936 and 1970 felt they had a job to do, not simply in tidying up economic models or overhauling the received theories, but out there – in the great world of economic policy and public affairs. For this they needed the macro concepts which Keynes offered, and they needed numbers which national income estimates could supply. Before long the game, as games do, got more sophisticated. The sophistication came in several directions.

First, when by 1950 the gross unemployment of the 1930s did not reappear, the Keynesians used their energies to produce even finer results. The coefficients derived from the income figures affected not only spending, but also tax policy, which, requiring enactments by the Parliament or the Congress, proved far too clumsy an instrument, with lags much too long, for such delicate work. Spending pressures arose and institutional changes affecting wage and price formation were little taken into account. The result – especially after the oil shocks of the 1970s – was inflation in the presence of rising unemployment. The accompanying intellectual crisis in economics destroyed the authority of Keynesian policies and left nothing but anarchy for a guide.

Simultaneous with these efforts to use national income numbers as a base for domestic fiscal policy, the UN's need to assess its members in proportion to their national incomes and the statistical needs of American programs for foreign development extended the market for such estimates. Comparative national accounts accompanied American policy efforts at economic development in the Third World. How far were the Asian, African and Latin American countries "behind"? It seemed important to have numbers – total and per capita – converted into U.S. dollars, to see where more dollars should be spent. The passion was felt not only for exact numbers, but for a single number, a statistic that wrapped the state of a country – any country – into one ball. For comparative purposes economies of all sorts and flavors had to be pressed into a square in a table labeled Real GNP per capita in 1954 dollars. The exercise gave even Kuznets pause at one point when an incredibly low figure in U.S. dollars for China would not have been enough even to sustain life in the United States. That old devil, the index number problem, had arisen in the choice of price weights for bundles of commodities, even where long-time series were not required. In the great international surveys of Kuznets and Reynolds, the estimation went beyond the GNP to an estimation of component sectors in an effort to derive empirical laws of development.

A breath of this enthusiasm for numbers blew into the sails of that sturdy bark, economic history. Two conferences of the National Bureau's Conference on Research in Income and Wealth, 1957 and 1964, were framed around the record for the North American nineteenth century, and Kuznets's SSRC Committee financed similar efforts for most of the European countries as far back as any numbers could be found or formulated. Noel Butlin's massive books for Australia were perhaps the most thorough and judicious of these explorations. The effort was crowned by Kuznets's synthesis,[1] where the empirical regularities so discovered are set forth. For policy purposes, Walt Rostow's *Stages of Growth* and Alexander

---

[1] Simon Kuznets, *Modern Economic Growth: Rate, Structure, Spread* (New Haven: Yale University Press, 1966); Lloyd G. Reynolds, *Economic Growth in the Third World: 1850–1980* (New Haven: Yale University Press, 1985). See also Reynolds, *Image and Reality in Economic Development* (New Haven: Yale University Press, 1977).

Gerschenkron's Relative Backwardness models were suggested by the statistics, though they failed to receive Kuznets's wholehearted endorsement.[2]

At this point the growth theorists entered the arena, moving on from Keynes's short – or medium – run. They declared this to be like the National Bureau's business cycle work, another case of measurement without theory. Their remedy was to create growth models, logical structures of yet more empty boxes, and to look to econometricians, whose skills and tools were growing sharper every year, to attack the output and input data, shaky as they were, and give both flesh and precision to an aggregate production function containing not only labor and capital, but resources, education, and technology. Alas! If only Harrod and Domar had never noticed that investment, which yields jobs in the short run, yields increased output in the long run, that it changes proportions along the same production function and interlaces in some obscure way with changing institutions, skills, and technology to shift functions over time. How many muddles, how much confusion and argument would have been avoided! But theorists are nothing if not sharp, and as we know, they sit in the saddle and ride economics. So they imposed on the profession, specifically on their econometrician-slaves, the cruel and unending task of detailing, measuring, giving statistical life to their systems of abstractions and moving them through the tangled intangibles of history. It has been a task like those imposed in the stories of classical mythology – a torture of Tantalus, a labor of Sisyphus, a web of Penelope.

At first the game must have seemed very easy. Imagine a production function aggregated over the whole economy and valid over long stretches of historical time. The labor force could be counted and changes in the capital stock could be measured in successive money values deflated by a price index. But then Abramovitz told economists what historians like Usher had tried to tell them for two generations.[3] The only difference is that Abramovitz did it with numbers that the profession had to believe. When the growth of labor and capital, measured as the accountants had always measured them, were set against the growth of output, an enormous gap appeared. Investment, then, and movements along the aggregate production function could not "explain" more than half the growth of labor productivity. But since in an input/output accounting system, and by

[2]Walt W. Rostow, *The Stages of Economic Growth* (Cambridge: Cambridge University Press, 1960); also Alexander Gerschenkron, "Economic Backwardness in Historical Perspective," in B. Hoselitz, ed., *The Progress of Underdeveloped Countries* (Chicago: University of Chicago Press), reprinted in *Economic Backwardness in Historical Perspective* (Cambridge, Mass.: Harvard University Press, 1962; paperback, New York and London, F. Praeger, 1965); also Gerschenkron, *Europe in a Russian Mirror* (Cambridge: Cambridge University Press, 1970).

[3]M. Abramovitz, "Resource and Output Trends in the United States since 1870," *American Economic Review*, Vol. 46 (May 1956): 5–23.

the deepest principle of economics, there is no free lunch, *something* measurable and costly must have created the rest. The two most likely suspects were those less commensurable variables in the growth equations: labor skills, improved capital equipment, and improved organization, including reduced transactions costs and economies of scale at all levels. Other potential candidates would be improved resource availability (important in the nineteenth century), higher motivations, and improving terms of trade, but the importance of these did not attract much attention. Solow's famous 1957 article showed the same thing, as also did the valuable and laborious efforts of John Kendrick. The *tour de force* of Evsey Domar, equally ingenious as theorist and critic, provided further clarification.[4] Such variables could, of course, be included in production functions of multi-dimensions or more simply by a shift variable called t, for time, i.e., for history. But that did not solve the problem of how to formulate a comprehensive capital concept for them, from which costed inputs could flow. Even for plain and simple capital – dirty old K – a terrible controversy broke out about its measurability over time. Equally serious was the problem of formulating a production function for knowledge, organization, labor skills. Despite the efforts of the Human Capitalists, the economic theorists of technology and the polemicists of neo-institutionalism, it has proved impossible to quantify the inputs from these in any way except in terms of their results. These concepts are hardly operational, and Solow's candid comment on his own article is the best judgment that could be passed:

... I would not try to justify what follows by calling on fancy theorems on aggregation and index numbers. Either this kind of aggregate economics appeals or it doesn't. Personally I belong to both schools. If it does, I think one can draw some crude but useful conclusions from the results.[5]

Here the whole matter might have rested, and economists gone happily about their short-run concerns. Why, a naive historian wonders, might the economists not have taken a page from Quesnay's book, and declared that the economy yielded indeed a "net product" derived not from nature, but from society as a whole?[6] That would have cracked neoclassical

---

[4]R. E. Solow, "Technical Change and the Aggregate Production Function," *Review of Economic Statistics*, Vol. 39 (August 1957): 312; J. Kendrick, *Productivity Trends in the United States* (Princeton: Princeton University Press, 1961); E. Domar, "On the Measurement of Technological Change," *Economic Journal*, Vol. 81 (December 1961): 702–729; Domar, "On Total Productivity and All That," *Journal of Political Economy*, Vol. 70 (December 1962): 597–609.

[5]Solow, "Technical Change," 312.

[6]Philip Mirowski has reminded me that the analogy to the physiocratic system is, of course, not perfect. That system did not really focus on growth, but only on the net product as the basis of the circular flow, which repaid each year the annual advances for its reproduction.

accounting in two, leaving its pieces to writhe dynamically on the ground. That would have meant a free lunch, but it would have "accounted for growth" by means of the actual, if non-quantifiable, record of human action, i.e., by real history. For what is productivity growth by means of clever technology, a deft touch in organization, the generation of men and women who enjoy organizing work? What is it but a huge free lunch not balanced by any real conventionally accountable costs or even any necessary resource re-allocations?

In the 1970s, world events – the competition among industrializing and de-industrializing nations on world markets – revived the effort and the concepts. *Productivity* then became the buzz word of the 1970s, and its measurement and analysis, removed now from the fastnesses of history, became matters of immediate policy concern. Pragmatism again gave a public to Kendrick's calculations and made interesting the death-defying partitionings of Ed Denison.[7] An important finding was made. Not only had the growth in quantities of capital and labor declined, but the residual itself had shrunk. This was what everyone had felt, but to confirm it with numbers made it truly believed, despite the authors' scrupulous disclaimers in view of the staggering assumptions on which the estimates were based. Indeed, I cannot suppress the feeling that the estimates are believed partly *because* of those self-exculpating footnotes, the analytical acumen displayed, the transparent honesty, the vigor of the self-flagellation. Only a saint, one feels, would put so much labor into something so risky, only someone incredibly tough-minded would put such figures to any use. It is in the spirit of the French general who cried, "My left flank is overrun, my right flank is crushed, my center is crumbling. I attack!"

These gross findings have had value just as Keynesian models had value for policy purposes for the 1960s, and Kuznets's and Reynolds's international comparisons for the time and purposes for which they were devised. Truth is relative to the problem to be solved and to its environment, and this is as true of numbers and estimates as it is of concepts and theories. In each case, the useful efforts have not been amiss. But the academicization of them, the theorists' urge to create complete, self-consistent, mathematically expressible systems, and many econometricians' childish insistence that no economist comes to the truth but through them – it is these urges in our art that are its undoing. We get in

[7]Edward F. Denison, *The Sources of Economic Growth in the United States and the Alternatives Before Us* (New York: Committee on Economic Development, 1962); Denison, *Why Growth Rates Differ: Postwar Experience in Nine Western Countries* (Washington: The Brookings Institution, 1967); Denison, *Trends in American Economic Growth, 1929–1982* (Washington: The Brookings Institution, 1983).

trouble in the fine tuning, and we get in trouble in the big orchestrations. Keynes, we should remember, told economists they ought to think of themselves as dentists.

It may be that my judgments here contain a passion and a severity born of naiveté and resentment at having been had. I am an economic historian, and I have the feeling that the blind and ferocious insistence of econometricians on pursuing the quantification of the production function is born of a desperation in them that there is no other path to knowledge. I consider most of them – those with good manners, good will, and common sense – my friends. But I know what many of them think of history: They think that it is either a dull, mindless chronicle of facts or that it is "poetry," nice to read but not to live by, in any case no path to scientific knowledge. And I have experienced and seen on the careers of students the devastating effects of their narrowness and bigotry, their "toughness" and all too ready scorn. Yet it is exactly this kind of problem, lying outside their grasp as economists – intimate questions of causation in the individual case and large, vaguely perceived phenomena of massive change in social organization and behavior, huge shiftings of the clouds – that first occasioned the rhetoric of history to be invented in order to permit human discourse.[8] When the students of society have denied themselves access both to poetic intuition and to the art of comfortable, plausible narration, they have indeed shut themselves in a barred and narrow cell which only a perception shrunken and distorted by such an environment would mislabel science.

In any case, beyond economics there is a larger and a deeper problem. The circulatory system is not the only system in the body. We may know all there is to know about it, but if we ask, Where does the blood come from? what governs the pulsations of the heart? how does the body walk or jump or crawl? what makes it think and sweat and scream in pain or in ecstasy? our answer is not found in the system of tubes and valves that delivers to all its parts an essential nutritive fluid. The study of the circulation runs beyond its mechanized limits when an inquiry to find out how the body of an economy gains weight must stretch and strain its concepts, redefine them, spin them out so as to encompass intangibles like education, technology, national defense, the pleasures of domestic life, applying the mercantile calculus to areas where merchants never trod. Then it becomes a science like Ptolemaic physics – and cannot find within itself a new Galileo.

[8]I am grateful to Don McCloskey, in a very short discussion after a session at the EHA meetings in San Francisco in September 1987 and in later correspondence, for sharpening my awareness of this point. My debt to the kind of thinking developed and articulated in McCloskey's recent writings should be apparent. See his contribution to a recent collection of opinions in W. Parker, ed., *Economic History and the Modern Economist* (Oxford: Basil Blackwell, 1986), 63–69.

Analogies of society to the human body are, of course, notably archaic and *déclassé* in social science. But without pushing matters too far, one can see in society bodies of systematic relationships akin to the economic bloodstream but acting on completely different impulses. The most obvious is the political system, which like the economy, has a clear objective apart from the activity itself. Politics has an objective function: the acquisition and maintenance of the power to influence and command men. This is not measurable as income is, except to a degree in a democratic system by votes, but games are played, rules are formulated, choices with consequences are enforced. A power element is present in other systems, in the economic notably, but also in social life, just as an economic motivation for tangible exchangeable gain can invade not only the polity, but the familial and social life, too. The economy is attached at its nerve ends to these other systems of politics, intellectual activity, familial and social life, all the systematic expressions of innumerable human urges and drives which themselves also feed and motivate and control behavior in economic life. When analysis of the economy on its own terms runs out of steam, faces insoluble problems of deflation and measurement, breaks against Kuznets's two self-imposed limits (the nation-state and the market economy as such) it is time to call, if not on God, then on the other social sciences and on that mysterious body of rhetoric and discourse called history.

II. PRODUCTIVITY HISTORY IN THE SPIRIT OF SCHUMPETER

Economic accounting, then, leads into economic history. It measures national and sectoral growth rates, input series (insofar as they are commensurable), and the size of the "residual" remaining "unexplained." But economic history has no neat, internally consistent, measured, self-corroborating explanatory models. Instead it displays endless case studies, narratives, and loose generalizations.

Joseph Schumpeter brought theory, statistics, and history into about as close touch with one another as they have ever been. Figure 1 pictures the system of Schumpeter's circular flow – the capitalist world market and the organizations that function within it. On the side are placed the five major sources of growth, both in output and in productivity, as Schumpeter's survey of the nineteenth century saw them: new resources, new populations, new production functions, new patterns of demand, and new organizational forms. In the generation of all of these opportunities the animating spirit is exactly the opposite of the close, calculating spirit by which capitalist firms keep the circular flow in its channels by the equation of marginal costs to marginal revenues. Weber pointed out these two sides of capitalist civilization: the spirit of rational calculation with

Figure 1. *A national economy in its operation within the culture*

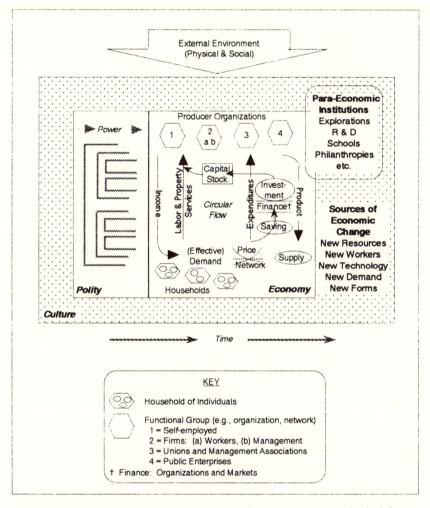

The schema may be adapted to other limits – world economy, region, individual firm, or household. For these purposes the income and product concept must be altered, and the designation of the organizations specified.

the development of routine procedures and the imaginative, creative, risk-taking spirit of innovation. If Figure 1 is thought of as moving to the right, through time, one can imagine the circular flow whirring like a tire lunging forward in a ditch, but sucking in novelty. In its circular flow, efficiency is maintained, while growth and innovation are swept out from the culture and incorporated into efficient and purposeful routines.

343

These origins of novelty lie, then, initially not within the economy, but are scattered through other systems of the culture.[9] They lie in its adventurous, intellectual, familial, political, sportive, or purely idiosyncratic activities. In newly settled regions in the nineteenth century, new resources were opened up first as the by-product of geographical and military expeditions. New population came as the result of the conjunction of birth and death rates, but in any specific region, also through the arrivals of immigrants, and restless internal migration. Very early in the history of each region in North America, a new population settled into farmsteads and family-organized agriculture. The transplantation of capitalist economic forms – property, contract, the use of money and credit, prices, and the promises of speculation – sharpened farming into a respectably rational economic activity, taking advantage of market opportunities as soon as they presented themselves. The movement of trappers, soldiers, surveyors, and farmers over the soil uncovered the minerals deposits. In transportation and manufacturing, new techniques were at first imported from England; then a native inventive tradition took shape, and its products merged with the international stream of new technology. In America after 1870, as westward movement completed its enlargement of the geographical span of the economy, the railroad moved across the continent in Schumpeter's second Kondratieff, and institutional innovation occurred again in the adaptation of the corporate form and the growth of large-scale organization, in trusts and combinations, and in public regulatory bodies. At some point, too, the development of new production functions began to occur under an organization more planned and less wasteful than the shops of the independent craftsmen. Science and technology got a toehold, not only as economic, but as intellectual activities, and moved ahead a little on their own lines. Finally in all this, the balance of savings and consumption was maintained – the one encouraged by endless organizational innovations in finance, and the other not only by the large capital needs of a continental economy, but by a popular, democratic, imitative taste – propelled and channeled by advertising – rushing out to spend as income rose. Throughout the whole experience up to 1930, the growth and productivity rises were sustained by a ferocious, all-pervasive spirit of work, optimism, and risk taking and by sheer, crude, materialistic energy.

Productivity rose by very simple ways in this nineteenth-century setting. Movement into new lands at higher yields and lower per-acre costs of cultivation could be accounted a productivity rise. A notable example in America was the move from forested areas to the treeless prairies and plains that cut the costs of a first clearing to one-fifteenth to one-twentieth

[9]This thumbnail history of productivity growth is derived from the earlier essays in Parts III and IV and Annex A of this volume.

of what they had been in the forested areas.[10] Growth of regional specialization permitted by market growth and transport improvement, and the closer adjustment of plantings to market demand, yielded a growth of output over material inputs. And finally the application of very simple principles of mechanical invention in farm machinery yielded even more, and more spectacular, cost savings. The case in manufacturing was somewhat more complex since the socialization of immigrant labor, the development of systems of organization and management, was required to accommodate the gains of the technology of larger scale. But the rapid growth of a secure, tariff-protected home market kept risks low and profits high. And in all this progress before 1930, the functioning of the institutions of education, research, and government in America, as in the other so-called Anglo-Saxon countries, can be called adequate, though not spectacular.

Formal education, designed in New England to train ministers and to give a believing population personal access to the Bible, was secularized and transformed into a fundamental social convenience. Skills necessary for minimal social communication across wide distances – reading, writing, and the universal language of arithmetic – were drilled into the young. The public and compulsory character of the system made the groups in the population grow up in contact with one another, but the teaching cadre showed no shyness in inculcating the virtues of a God-fearing capitalist ethic: hard work, ambitiousness, competition, sobriety, patriotism, and respect for law and for democratically established authority. Family, church, school, neighborhood, and community – all these instruments of socialization showed themselves in a wide variety of forms. But whatever their characteristics in the individual case, their structures combined to bring to maturity in successive generations a population competent to the tasks and participatory roles in adult society, yet retaining a freedom, indeed, an eagerness, to innovate, to improve.

The history of American government shows similarly a blind loyalty to forms and symbols – the Constitution and the Union, the system of courts and the law, the structures of states and municipalities, even the often archaic organization of local government – together with allegiances to one or the other of the two political parties, all floating uneasily on a frequently irreverent, even cynical attitude toward politicians and a restless, reforming, if not revolutionary, spirit. The agro-industrial civilization of the North, legitimized through the ideals of a written constitution, ruthlessly pushed its forms of property, state power, individual rights, and judicial domination through the institutional system, asserting them through superior military power over the South and later over restless farmers and

[10]Martin Primack, "Land Clearing Under the Nineteenth-Century Techniques," *Journal of Economic History* (December 1962), 484–495.

factory workers roundabout. Strength, peace, essential order and justice, a flexibility that had room for both corruption and reform, a substantial freedom to the owners of large property and the pleasant noises of public regulation for the comfort of the population at large – these were the blessings of liberty, insured to Americans, old and new, and to their posterity.

It is easy to see how, in the presence of abundant resources, a prosperous economy, exhibiting growth and many acts of productivity improvement, could be built, despite frequent tremors of instability, on such an ideological and institutional foundation. Then in the 1930s, as the transition had to be made in many resources from abundant reserves exploited under conditions of ample demand to an economy of restricted resources and potentially satiated demand, several weaknesses appeared. With the crash of 1929 and the ensuing unprecedentedly deep and long depression, a weak federal government was overhauled by the institutional innovations of the New Deal. Public confidence in capitalism was revived as a floor was built under the level of employment and incomes of many disadvantaged groups. At the same time, American technology was badly in need of an overhaul. In mechanical contrivances it had led the world, and in the generation and applications of electric power it had produced many household and industrial wonders, though by methods painfully empirical and roundabout. There was no shortage of engineers, trained after the 1880s at the institutes of technology – MIT, Rennselaer, Case – and one or another of the state universities and colleges – Cornell, Michigan, Ohio State, Illinois. But without penetration into the next level of natural secrets (the structure and behavior of the atom and the living cell, the generation and control of energy in all its forms), a technology based on nineteenth-century science seemed about to run out of ideas.

The erection of an institutional structure behind technological innovation, the intellectual traditions and techniques, the ready and steady financial support needed to encourage pure curiosity and pure theorizing, had not come easily to a business culture. Investment certainly came almost to a halt in the 1930s; it was as if Schumpeter's process of creative destruction had gone on a holiday.[11] And while a slow-down in invention can be attributed superficially to unprofitable economic conditions, there is at least room for the suspicion, particularly in so fundamental an activity in

[11] The idea of a slow-down in technical change is suggested in Michael Bernstein's striking recent book, *The Great Depression: Delayed Recovery and Economic Change in America, 1929–1939* (Cambridge and New York: Cambridge University Press, 1987), esp. Ch. 4, based on his 1982 Yale Ph.D. thesis. However, Bernstein emphasizes economic and structural reasons for the slow-down, rather than intellectual ones, and concludes that in any case "lack of technical change cannot . . . be taken as the primary cause of the depression's length." He is thus not to be held responsible for the rash conclusion about the imponderables of technical change as a process, advanced here.

which American practice had become an ingrained habit, that the causation ran the other way.

The New Deal saved the American institutional structure, and the new agencies of the federal government, passing through the fire of the Second World War, fused with the old Republican structures to support the prosperity of the 1950s and 1960s and to contain, barely, the social tensions that that prosperity created. Similarly, the events of the 1930s in Europe, and the not wholly fortuitous simultaneity of the mass migration of German scientists with the pressing needs and loose spending of a military budget, created American postwar science. In some industries – chemicals, drugs, agricultural machinery and materials, electronics – the fusion of science and technology captured the imagination of large private firms and monopolies, and the Schumpeterian Age was indeed upon us.

* * * * *

This then is the merest sketch of an historical narrative of American productivity growth to 1970, its natural, ideological, intellectual, and sociological origins. There is serious question whether the concept of productivity, resting as it does on the time-honored separations of costs and benefits, the sacred trinity of three productive factors, the statistical monstrosities of aggregation and attribution, has value even for short-run policy and analysis. If history and economics together could produce a larger framework, incorporating more of the thousand intangibles that affect the statistics, then the claims of a science, or at least a useful art, for economics would be justified. Perhaps plausible statements could even be made then about the prospects for the 1990s (making, of course, *ceteris paribus* assumptions about the behavior of the rest of the world). But without the understanding of the cultural underlay of the economy, an understanding that requires examination of what we were and how we got to where we are as a civilization, economic analysis is like a knife without a cutting board, or, to use the familiar Marshallian analogy, one blade of a pair of scissors, snipping vainly against the air. It is to keep the eye obsessively strained to exploring an equilibrium world through an econometric microscope when telescopes lie at hand, waiting to be employed to observe the mingled order and chaos that constitute the dynamics of the universe.

III. A FRAMEWORK FOR ANALYSIS*

Now I wish to suggest in diagrammatic form the first elements of a framework that might be used as a basis for a general "social science

*This section was prepared jointly with H. Salome of the Yale Council on West European Studies, to whom the working out of the diagrams and many clarifications and elaboration of the concepts, as well as some of the phrasing, are due.

347

Figure 2. *A social space: individuals in connection with organizations within a culture, showing intergenerational reproduction*

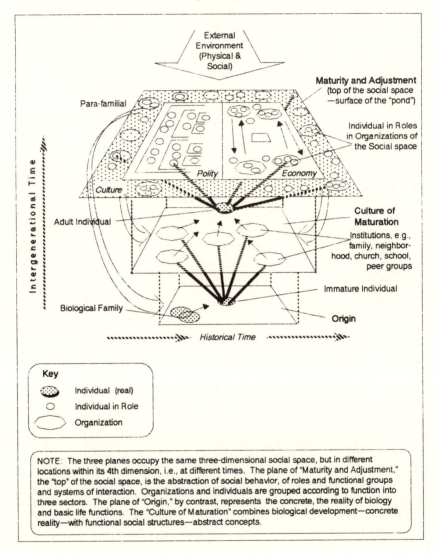

NOTE: The three planes occupy the same three-dimensional social space, but in different locations within its 4th dimension, i.e., at different times. The plane of "Maturity and Adjustment," the "top" of the social space, is the abstraction of social behavior, of roles and functional groups and systems of interaction. Organizations and individuals are grouped according to function into three sectors. The plane of "Origin," by contrast, represents the concrete, the reality of biology and basic life functions. The "Culture of Maturation" combines biological development—concrete reality—with functional social structures—abstract concepts.

history." The specific focus in Figure 1 in the previous section was on the history and present position of the American national economy. But since in any such approach the unit of analysis (and of synthesis) is itself a variable, that figure, as well as Figure 2, presented here, can be taken to represent other geographical units – world regions, nations, geographical

Figure 2a. *Makeup of the individual*

MAKEUP OF THE INDIVIDUAL

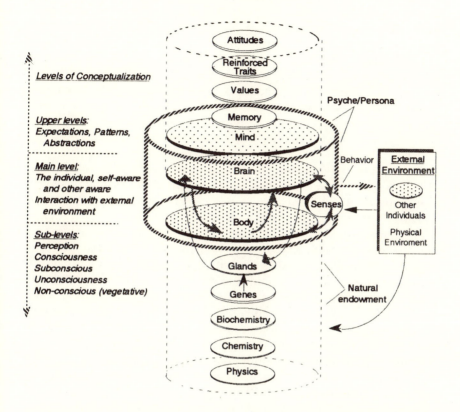

sub-regions, local cultures, or human groupings defined by sets of conditions dependent not on geographical contiguity, but on communications links or simply on similarities in external natural or social environments: empires, churches, industries, crafts, etc. The figures are intended as part of a set of templates, or "transparencies" for the presentation and study of the interactions among humans, their organizations, and the phenomena of the physical world over time.

Figure 2 is the fundamental "micro" diagram, building the persistence and modifications of a society and its culture up from the activities and reproduction of the biological individuals within its boundaries. At the lowest level, the individual is formed – a physical and chemical structure incorporating a physique, a brain, and certain predispositions, aptitudes, and sensitivities. In order to show the sort of individual organism which we have in mind at the center of the two bottom planes in Figure 2, Figure 2a is

attached, showing the individual at the confluence of genetic and environmental elements in his or her makeup and experience. Certain diseases may
be built into this structure, and also, it may be presumed, certain behavioral traits, mental qualities, passions, and sensitivities. Immediately from
birth these in turn are affected, channeled, modified, perhaps even
created – through the interaction with the physical surroundings by way
of the senses, and with the social surroundings by way of relations with
other individuals, themselves placed in a social context. During physical
maturation, the individual spends the time in one or another of the more or
less organized social contexts round about – the institutions of socialization and personality formation: family, immediate neighborhood, play
groups, school, church, etc. In modern society perhaps the most powerful
of these is the television screen and its succession of theatrical images of
reality or of the imagination. To each of these situations or postures the
child brings its person as developed to that point. From each it takes away
some learning which, stored in memory, modifies its personality as an
individual being, capable of social interaction.

These structures of body, energies, and experience are then brought
together in what is termed, with only very rough accuracy, the "mature"
individual, who then attaches himself or is attached by others to the
organizations and groups of adult society – to a new family, job, clubs, a
state, and the other more or less defined units of the social culture. When
he and she reproduce, a new individual is formed, and the cycle begins in
the presence of the social groups, modified, even drastically altered, by
what occurs through the passage of time.

Figure 1, presented in Section II above, then, is a "macro" diagram of
the society, its constituent organizations, as supported, perpetuated, and
energized by the massed individuals lying just beneath its surface. In
relation to Figure 2, Figure 1 showed the surface of the social space,
looking straight down on its two dimensions; it focused on one particular
sector of it, the economy, to afford a more detailed study. What is labeled
Culture in the diagrams may be likened to a viscous liquid given off by
the energies of the active individuals, colored by such values, beliefs,
ideas, ways of thought and feeling as they hold in common. The culture is
in another sense a medium of communication, made concrete and objective in characteristic material objects, language, visual images, signs of
the group. At points in it, a thickening occurs as individuals form habit-
ual relationships and interactions in social circles, and these become objectified and formalized in varying degrees in organizations – families,
clubs, parties, interest groups, business associates, and all the rest. These
float on the visible surface like the curds in a cheese vat, while suspended
beneath float the individuals of Figure 2, each of whom is attached to a
number of organizations in the different functional compartments of

social life. Within each organization or relationship, the individual brings to bear a whole personality, but the behavior is channeled and restricted by the expectations of others as to the role to be fulfilled. It is then an *abstracted* individual, whose function and motives as revealed by behavior on the surface can be analyzed in relation to the specific environment of the observed organization or "significant other."

The "culture," with all that word's original yeasty evocations, then, covers the surface of the diagrams. A complete picture would show the many overlapping, multi-form organizations, of varying definitions, rigidity, and density, to which individuals are attached. Cultural and social analysis then requires that these organizations, as well as the active, unorganized individuals, be grouped so as to show: (a) grouped similarities in internal culture, especially according to the individual motivations they appeal to and appear to satisfy, and (b) the functional substitutability and inter-dependence of organizations with one another. These groupings are often said to form systems or sets corresponding to specific social activities, a set of inter-related organizations appearing to satisfy for the society some one of the conditions of its existence and continuity through history. Figure 2 shows the reproduction of a society's individuals, physically and socially. So similarly the functioning of organizational systems may be observed to preserve, continue, readjust the society's economy, government, religion – all its systems of expression, creation, and protection – within three environments: (a) physical nature, (b) other societies roundabout, (c) the inner needs of the individuals themselves, as the society has helped to develop them – their expectations, sense of self-worth, and ideas of justice, their visions of a satisfying and fulfilling life.

Now most of the organizations appearing on the surface of the culture are linked principally to (c) above. Families, clubs, sports groups, organized amusements – even where professionalized for profit – all have the activity itself, the pleasure of self-expression or of social intercourse, as main purpose and function. Such groups could be shown on the Figures as floating in the marginal space labeled Culture. Almost certainly a close look would show that they serve some essential social functions. But at the center of the space, like the two halves of an open book, we have pulled together the organizations specialized to two functions and forming internal cultures where two human motivations are characteristic: the political system, by which inter-personal and inter-group relations are established and adjusted so that power and order are achieved, and the economy, whose product is the material goods and command over services, by which subsistence, wealth, and material welfare are attained. These, in our view, have a certain privileged position in social analysis by virtue of their better defined functions and their indispensability to society's continuity within its environment.

351

Government and its controls through political behavior and organization are indispensable to protect the society from external enemies and to monopolize and manage the means of force and violence by which, if unrestrained, the members of a population might engage in mutual slaughter. Together with a number of other social institutions, it has the task of maintaining and passing on the culture itself, i.e., the set of values, skills, internalized controls, and rules and practices by which the very desire to resort to violence is eliminated or held in check. All this, however, is a complex matter, requiring separate diagramming and treatment. We have shown in the politics block only a nested structure of hierarchies to symbolize the formal organization, channeling, and distribution of power in the state or other hierarchies. To this simple concept must be added the power over opinions and group decisions lodged in invisible networks of influence and communication and the phenomenon of leadership, or charisma, by which the structures may function.

The economy was shown in the detailed section of Figure 1 as a great single market within which firms, households, and financial institutions make their exchanges. Under the familiar conventions of national income accounting, the currents of income, expenditure, savings, investment – the Keynesian categories – move in the circular flow. It is this flow that theorists study so intensely, stating and restating the conditions of its stable maintenance. Under a completely stable circular flow, with stable organization, demand, and techniques, and with measured inputs and product, it is evident that no increases or diminution of the product stream, or any change in its relation to the inputs of labor and property services can take place. The total social productivity ratio equals 1. The achievement of general equilibrium theory is to set the economy like a top spinning across the surface of history and to elaborate the conditions under which it will exhibit perpetual motion.

The truly dynamic forces in the history are thrown, as it were, into the circular flow of Figure 1, like sugar into a cotton candy machine, by other organizations and processes in the culture. Material supplies grow with growing knowledge of resources; labor, with population growth and changes in popular attitudes toward the participation of the elements of the population in the labor force. The aggregate savings function depends much on income distribution, corporate organizations, and relative price changes, but the "propensities" of the groups and individuals are highly volatile. The generation of new technology demands a diagram of its own; the relation to the culture is intimate and complex, and the same may be said for that other technology, the re-arrangement of the organizational structure. Economists, wandering out from the simple designs and motives of the circular flow into these grounds are on very marshy soil. The propositions and contrived measurements of economics, which they throw down like plants to walk ahead on, do not support much weight.

These factor-increasing and implementing forces which lie behind both output expansion and productivity growth may be sucked into the circular flow directly by economic organizations. Economists indeed endeavor to insert economic rationality and rational expectations into the activities involved in their generation, as if babies, new ideas in science, the political schemes of industrial organization had no hidden supply or cost functions, but were turned out on demand when prices and markets made them profitable, like a new brand of toothpaste. Many of these innovations are domesticated into the economy by what Figure 1 showed as "para-economic," ostensibly "non-profit," organizations with room for the thirst for adventure, the glow of altruism, curiosity, and devotion to learning, though admittedly the tax advantage accruing to such organization of these activities is a formidable element in their attractiveness. That tax exemption is itself an acknowledgment of the extra-territorial position of these activities, with one foot outside the circular flow, and so outside the economist's universe of exact discourse.

In the end, we must conceive of the whole social space, operating in all its component organizations, moving through historical time, a vast system of interactions, feedbacks, and impulses.[12] One is reminded of the crowning invention of nineteenth-century agricultural mechanical technology, the reaper-binder, which cut the grain, collected it in sheaves, and bound the sheaves with twine, even tying the knot, before depositing them in piles in the field. The whole apparatus was pulled by a team of horses which had to keep moving to cause the machinery to turn. So, too, the machinery of the social space, even the spinning circular flow itself, comes to a halt when the dynamic processes of history fail to operate. This is why economists and other social scientists need to grope and grapple with historical social change, even if only by crude, impressionistic methods, telling unverifiable stories, but concerned with the movements on the surface of the social pond, and in its depths, as far down as

---

[12]This can be shown in Figure 2 by separating the "layers" of the social space — cultural, political, intellectual, economic — and imagining them to move out to the right across a span of history at different rates. Then "tensions," as envisaged by Alexander Gerschenkron in his famous essay, "Relative Backwardness in Historical Perspective," become apparent, if the social process is set against some spiritual, normative, or functionally equilibrated state. This reduces the historical movement specifically to individual behavior — repetitive or innovative — in a specific sphere of social action in response to other specific alterations in the micro-environment of the social "actors." The debt of these formulations to Parsonian sociology, as discussed at the Harvard Center for Entrepreneurial History, in 1950–55, is obvious. For that controversy, and Gerschenkron's role in it, see the numbers of *Explorations in Entrepreneurial History* for those years.

they can see. At the bottom, in the primeval ooze, lie the roots of individual behavior – the dark biology and unilluminated psyches, the ultimate nature of which we, no doubt, with merely rational perceptions alone, may never fully understand.

Index

abolitionism, 266
Abramovitz, M., 338
accounting mentality, 104, 242; *see also* national income accounting
Act of 1796, 129–30
Acts of General Incorporation, 273
Adams, Henry, 183
Adams, John, 300
Adams Act, 153
adult eduction, 146–7
advertising, 91, 93–4, 146, 344
Africa, 310
agrarian culture, 108, 165, 167, 288; communications network in, 178–9; end of, 180; and midwestern ethic, 245; of northern Europe, 125; and regional styles of capitalism, 89–94
agrarian democracy, 264
agrarian history: of South, 68; westward movement in, 162–5
agricultural arts: borrowed from Europe, 11, 15, 16, 17; of migrants to Midwest, 122
agricultural base, Midwest, 204, 206
agricultural colleges, 147, 150, 153, 225
agricultural expansion, 15–16, 28
Agricultural Experiment Stations, 18, 139, 147, 153–5
Agricultural Extension system, 248n48
agricultural history: quantification and counter-factual in, 313–33
Agricultural History, 44n2
agricultural implements, 148, 149; *see also* mechanization
agricultural production, 172–6, 304–5
agricultural production function, 71–2
agricultural products, transport of, 220
agricultural revolution, 104
agricultural societies, 146–7
agricultural techniques, 139–43
agriculture: capital for, in Midwest, 228; capitalistic, 167; change in, with motorized transport, 222; competitive organization of, 242–4, 253; diversified, 80 (*see also* regional specialization); econo-

mies of scale, 240; family labor in, 184f; and industrialization in New England, 190–1; innovation in, 138–9; luck as factor in success in, 25n31; mechanization of, 17, 33, 167, 171, 173, 174; monocrop, 80; New England, 203; organization of, 88; regional character and, 97–8; scientific, 149–55; small-scale, 44; westward movement of, 139–40, 141, 325–7; *see also* commercial agriculture; farm labor; farming; farms; science, agricultural
agriculture, southern, 42, 43, 70–5, 78, 79–80, 81, 82–6; colonialism issue in, 82–3; exploitation by northern capitalists, 82–3, 85–6; lack of financial capital in, 75–7, 78–80; mechanization, 86; new opportunities in, 86; plantation in, 33–40
agro-business civilization/culture, 114, 167–71, 176, 177, 215; Midwest, 219–20; of North, 345–6
Alabama, 34, 105
America Firsters, 292
American Agricultural Press, The (Demaree), 156
American character, 120, 206–7, 296
American civilization, 290–1; European heritage in, 3–30
American culture, 19, 29–30, 114, 296, 299
American dream, 27, 28, 29
American ethos, 301–2
American Fur Company, 129
American Revolution, 7–9, 103, 189, 204, 281, 283, 299–300; and nationhood of United States, 281, 283–5
American society, xiv, 29–30; ability to experiment and adapt, 16; English-derived, 20–1; ethnic homogeneity of, 20–1, 26; historical movements in, 21–4; national origins of, 20–1
American system, 131, 135, 302
American Tobacco Company, 93–4
Americanism, 294

355

Index

nial, 288; components of, 113–14; defining characteristic of, 3; and democracy, 300–2; European, xiii–xiv, 5–6, 10; evolution of, 103–4; finance of capital in, 229–30; institutional structure of, 17–18; multinational, 87–8, 308n8; nineteenth-century, 277; in North American colonies, 8–10; and Puritanism, 106–8; and religion, 108–13; as secular religion, 29–30; small-scale, 23, 24, 83–4; social effects of, 309; southern style, 87–100; technology of, borrowed from Europe, 12–13

capitalist culture, growth of, 304–5; individualism of, 177

capitalist ethic, 111n7

capitalists, northern, 81–6; rivalries among, 269

Caribbean planters, 8

Carnegie, Andrew, 237

Carolinas (the), 105, 262; proprietors, 34

cartels, 94, 97, 305

caste system (South), 69

Cather, Willa, 157

Catholic Church, 107, 108, 117, 247, 305

cattle, 15–16, 33, 172, 215

cattle ranches, 313–33

Central Europe, 26

central European immigrants, 216, 226

centralism, 23

centralization, 280

Chandler, A. D., 207

charcoal iron production, 217

Charleston, 105, 133

Chase, Salmon P., 239

chemicals industry, 221

chemistry, 150, 221

Cherokee Indians, 162

Chesapeake (the), 105

Chicago, 113, 134, 137, 218, 255, 290

Chicago Marine and Fire Insurance Company, 231n29

child labor, 202

China, 29, 310

Chinese immigrants, 84

church–state, 107, 109

cigarette industry, 94

Cincinnati, 113, 131, 137

cities, 5, 23, 24, 28, 114, 117; blacks' migration to northern, 41; central market, 137; move from farms to, 225

city-states, 23, 29; North American colonies as, 8, 9–10, 20

Civil War, 9, 20, 23, 68, 69, 86, 121, 133, 165, 167, 179, 267, 281, 299, 303, 310; economic interests in, 135–7; meaning of, 270, 271–3

civilization; see American civilization

class consciousness, 98, 247

class interest: in South, 94, 96, 99

class structure, 7, 8

class struggle, 269

Clay, Henry, 131, 136

Cleveland, 113, 137, 218, 255

cliometrics of productivity, 335–42

clockmakers, 196–8, 199, 202–3, 206

coal, 113, 206, 217, 218, 220, 271, 303

coal chemistry, 221

Cochran, Thomas C., 286

collectivism vs. individualism, 278–80

colonialism, hypothesis re, in southern economic development, 82–6

Colt, Samuel, 198, 199

Columbus, 220

commercial agriculture, 118, 121–2, 126, 141–2, 172–6, 267, 273, 326, 327; opportunities in, 167–8

commercial institutions, Midwest, 204

commercial revolution, 104

commercialism in North, 117; and settlement, 166

commodities, 239

commodity markets, 243, 244, 271

common law, 8, 284

common market, 309

Commons, John R., 27, 227n22

communication in rural neighborhoods, 178–9

communications technology, 271, 278

Communism, 100

community, national, 283

community interest, balance with private right, 19

community organization, 207

community spirit in Midwest character, 124, 125, 126

competition, 94, 145, 178–9, 305

Confederation, 281–3

Congregationalism, 107n4, 108, 299–300

Connecticut, 201, 202–3, 282, 284

Connecticut Valley, 193, 194–9, 303

Connecticut Western Reserve, 200

Connecticut Yankee in King Arthur's Court, A, 10

Connellsville seam, 218

conservatism, 285

Constitution (U.S.), 10, 12, 281, 283, 284; framework for nationhood in, 285; slaves in, 285; Thirteenth Amendment, 68; Fourteenth Amendment, 68

Constitutional Convention, 283

construction projects, financing of, 232–3

consumption, 39, 43, 142, 344

Continental Congresses, 281

contract, 5, 10; laws of, 17, 117, 169; right of, 88, 274; share/fixed rent, 73–4, 75, 79

control, systems of, 271

conversion experience, 106

convertibility, 236, 239

Coolidge, Calvin, 255, 285

Cooper, Carolyn, 199n14

Cooper, J. F., 269

copper discoveries, 128, 132, 196

Copperheads, 267

corn, 17, 148, 163–4

Corn Belt, 33

corporate organization, 207, 264–5

357

Index

Index

United Provinces of the Netherlands, 104
United States: ambivalence toward Europe, 10–11, 20; and resurgence of democracy in Europe, xiii–xiv; self-image, 292–3; status of, 296; as superpower, 310; in world, 297
U.S. Agricultural Society, 147, 150
U.S. Department of Agriculture, 53–4, 56, 147, 150; Office of Experiment Stations, 152, 153; publications of, 156–7
United States Steel Corporation, 85
university(ies), 18, 29
unskilled labor, 26, 93, 202
urban growth, 141
urban industrial population, Midwest, 227–8
urban-industrial society, 114; and American agriculture, 175–6; distinct from rural, 278
urbanization, 192, 220–1
Usher, A. P., 143, 338
Utah, 216

values, 295, 297; American, 143; business, 267–9, 280; of farm family, 178; hierarchy of, 24–5; in plantation as social system, 35; private, 279, 280; social organization and, in midwestern society, 249–50
Venice, 5
Vermont, 201, 283
vertical integration, 240n44
Vietnam, 254
village, 124–5; lacking in America, 178; Puritan, 107–8
Virginia, 6, 15, 105, 187, 262, 283; American Revolution in, 8, 284; government of, 282; land claims of, 281; plantations in, 34; settlement of, 129; tobacco trade in, 36, 76
Virginia Company of London, 33–4
Virginia Military District, 129
Virginians, 126
Von Halle, W. E. H., 35
von Thünen, 172

wage economy in South, 71–2
wage labor, 33, 90–1
wages, 26, 42, 275, 301; tariff and, 250, 251–2
Wagner Act, 254
Walker, Francis, 27
Walker, Francis A., 227n22
Waltham system, 242
war economy, 86
War of 1812, 200, 285
War of 1845–48, 285
Washington, George, 16, 281–2, 283; Farewell Address, 291
water power, 137, 217, 302
water transport, 303
Wayne, Michael, 97

wealth, 4, 105, 230, 265, 268; in agriculture, 176; democracy and, 300; as evidence of success, 179, 245–6; farmers' pursuit of, 178; growth of, 309; as indication of virtue, 25; as merchant families, 111; in Midwest culture, 91–2, 123, 124, 249–50; in New England, 203; opportunity for, 169–71
wealth distribution and social structure, 123–4
Webb, Walter P., 16
Weber, Max, 106, 111n7, 278, 342–3
Webster, Daniel, 136
Weiss, Thomas, 49–50
welfare, 136; measurement of, 330–2
welfare programs, 254
Wertenbaker, Thomas, 34
West (the), 109, 115, 117, 119, 141, 290
West Point, 12
West Virginia, 271
Western development, xi
Western Europe, capitalism in, 5–6, 88
Western Reserve, 122
westward movement, 113, 118, 119, 162–5, 287, 290, 299, 344; and agricultural innovation, 148–9; of agriculture, 139–40, 141, 325–7; effect on New England industrialization, 200–1; of farmers, 224; northern stream of, 189; productivity growth implicit in, 335, 342–7; railroad and, 216
wheat, 132, 133, 141, 172, 176
wheat farms, 33; quantification and counter-factual in historical study of, 313–33
Whigs, 131, 136
white Anglo-Saxon Protestant class (WASPs), 27–8, 29, 291, 294
whites, southern, 167, 180; see also poor whites
Whitin works, 203
Whitman, Walt, 98
Whitney, Eli, 17, 197, 198, 199, 203
William the Conqueror, 262–3
Williamson, Hugh, 12n15
Williamson, Jeffrey, 336
Wilson, James, 153
Wilson, Woodrow, 28–9, 291, 292, 293, 294, 299, 301
Wisconsin, 22, 90, 113, 161, 224, 281; immigrants to, 122, 123
Wisconsin Marine and Fire Insurance Company, 231n29
women, 224, 254; farm labor, 185; in labor force, 194, 202, 225; position in farm family, 142, 177–8
woodworking, 197
work, systematization of, 202
work ethic, 107
workers, discipline of, 241; and progressivism, 276; see also labor
Working, Holbrook, 53
world economy, 4–5, 24, 254, 293; plantation vs. small farms in, 37–40

371